Lecture Notes in Computer Sc

Edited by G. Goos, J. Hartmanis and J. van

Springer
Berlin
Heidelberg
New York
Barcelona
Budapest
Hong Kong
London
Milan
Paris
Santa Clara
Singapore
Tokyo

Eiji Okamoto George Davida
Masahiro Mambo (Eds.)

Information Security

First International Workshop, ISW'97
Tatsunokuchi, Ishikawa, Japan
September 17-19, 1997
Proceedings

 Springer

Series Editors

Gerhard Goos, Karlsruhe University, Germany
Juris Hartmanis, Cornell University, NY, USA
Jan van Leeuwen, Utrecht University, The Netherlands

Volume Editors

Eiji Okamoto
School of Information Science
Japan Advanced Institute of Science and Technology
1-1 Asahidai Tatsunokuchi Nomi Ishikawa, 923-1292 Japan
E-mail: okamoto@jaist.ac.jp

George Davida
Department of Electrical Engineering and Computer Science
University of Wisconsin-Milwaukee
3200 N. Cramer Street, Milwaukee, WI 53201, USA
E-mail: davida@cs.uwm.edu

Masahiro Mambo
Education Center for Information Processing, Tohoku University
Kawauchi Aoba Sendai, 980-8576, Japan
E-mail: mambo@tohoku.ac.jp

Cataloging-in-Publication data applied for

Die Deutsche Bibliothek - CIP-Einheitsaufnahme

Information security : first international workshop ; proceedings /
ISW '97, Tatsunokuchi, Ishikawa, Japan, September 17 - 19, 1997.
George Davida ... (ed.). - Berlin ; Heidelberg ; New York ; Barcelona
; Budapest ; Hong Kong ; London ; Milan ; Paris ; Santa Clara ;
Singapore ; Tokyo : Springer, 1998
   (Lecture notes in computer science ; Vol. 1396)
   ISBN 3-540-64382-6

CR Subject Classification (1991): E.3, G.2.1, D.4.6, K.6.5, F.2.1-2, C.2, J.1,
E.4

ISSN 0302-9743
ISBN 3-540-64382-6 Springer-Verlag Berlin Heidelberg New York

This work is subject to copyright. All rights are reserved, whether the whole or part of the material is
concerned, specifically the rights of translation, reprinting, re-use of illustrations, recitation, broadcasting,
reproduction on microfilms or in any other way, and storage in data banks. Duplication of this publication
or parts thereof is permitted only under the provisions of the German Copyright Law of September 9, 1965,
in its current version, and permission for use must always be obtained from Springer -Verlag. Violations are
liable for prosecution under the German Copyright Law.

© Springer-Verlag Berlin Heidelberg 1998
Printed in Germany

Typesetting: Camera-ready by author
SPIN 10636992   06/3142 – 5 4 3 2 1 0   Printed on acid-free paper

Preface

ISW'97, the 1997 Information Security Workshop, was held at the Ishikawa High-Tech Conference Center in JAIST, Japan Advanced Institute of Science and Technology, Ishikawa, Japan, September 17-19. The workshop was sponsored by JAIST, Ministry of Education, Science, Sports and Culture, Engineering Sciences Society of IEICE (The Institute of Electronics, Information and Communication Engineers), Telecommunications Advancement Foundation, and Ishikawa Prefecture. The workshop was organized in cooperation with Tokyo Chapter of IEEE Information Theory, and Society of Information Theory and Its Applications. We are grateful to all these organizations for their support of the workshop.

One of the goals of ISW'97 was to give young researchers into the field of information security an opportunity to present papers at an international conference. For that purpose, a number of stipends were available to those unable to obtain funding to attend the workshop.

The workshop program addressed a range of topics from theory, technique, applications, and experimental work on topics relevant to information security and cryptography. The program committee invited Dr. Mihir Bellare (University of California at San Diego), Dr. Yvo Desmedt (University of Wisconsin at Milwaukee), Dr. Bart Preneel (Katholieke Universiteit Leuven, Belgium) and Dr. Yuliang Zheng (Monash University, Australia). Dr. George Robert Blakley (Texas A&M University) opened the workshop with general code theory and Dr. René Peralta (University of Wisconsin at Milwaukee) had a special talk on fast software encryption. Their talks were stimulating and informative.

The program committee accepted 25 papers from 39 submissions covering cryptanalysis, public-key cryptosystem, signature, hardware/software implementation, key management, key sharing, security management, electronic commerce and quantum cryptology. The accepted papers came from many countries: Australia, Belgium, Brazil, China, India, Korea, Singapore, Taiwan, USA, United Kingdom, and Japan. We commend the members of the program committee for this excellent program.

Organizing an international workshop is a time-consuming task. We would like to thank the steering committee members, organizing committee members, JAIST section for academic exchanges, and JAIST students in Dr. Okamoto's Laboratory for helping with many local details. We also thank all session chairs, speakers and authors who submitted papers and all participants at ISW'97.

February 1998

Eiji Okamoto
George Davida
Masahiro Mambo

Information Security Workshop
(ISW'97)

Sponsored by
Japan Advanced Institute of Science and Technology
The Engineering Sciences Society of IEICE
The Ministry of Education, Science, Sports and Culture
The Telecommunications Advancement Foundation
Ishikawa Prefecture

In cooperation with
IEEE IT Society, Tokyo Chapter, and SITA

Steering Committee
Masayuki Kimura (**Co-chair**, JAIST, Japan)
Bob Blakley(**Co-chair**, Texas A&M, USA)
Masayasu Hata (Nagoya Inst. of Tech., Japan)
Hideki Imai (Univ. of Tokyo, Japan)
Yoshihiro Iwadare (Nagoya Univ., Japan)
Masao Kasahara (Kyoto Inst. of Tech., Japan)
Hatsukazu Tanaka (Kobe Univ., Japan)
Hideyoshi Tominaga (Waseda Univ., Japan)
Shigeo Tsujii (Chuo Univ., Japan)

Program Committee
George Davida (**Co-chair**, Univ. of Wisconsin, Milwaukee, USA)
Eiji Okamoto (**Co-chair**, JAIST, Japan)
Jinhui Chao (Chuo Univ., Japan)
Ivan Damgård (Århus Univ., Denmark)
Toru Fujiwara (Osaka Univ., Japan)
Akira Hayashi (Kanazawa Inst. of Tech., Japan)
Tzonelih Hwang (Cheng Kung Univ., Taiwan, R.O.C)
Toshiya Itoh (Tokyo Inst. of Tech., Japan)
Kunikatsu Kobayashi (Yamagata Univ., Japan)
Naohisa Komatsu (Waseda Univ., Japan)
Arjen Lenstra (Citibank, USA)
Tsutomu Matsumoto (Yokohama National Univ., Japan)
Shiho Moriai (TAO, Japan)
Yuko Murayama (Hiroshima City Univ., Japan)
Andrew Odlyzko (AT&T, USA)

René Peralta (Univ. of Wisconsin, Milwaukee, USA)
Philip Rogaway (Univ. of California, Davis, USA)
Ryuichi Sakai (Osaka Electro-Communication Univ., Japan)
Kouichi Sakurai (Kyushu Univ., Japan)
Hiroki Shizuya (Tohoku Univ., Japan)

Organizing Committee

Masahiro Mambo (**Chair**, Tohoku Univ., Japan)
Kunihiko Hiraishi (JAIST, Japan)
Mineo Kaneko (JAIST, Japan)
Yasushi Sengoku (Kanazawa Inst. of Tech., Japan)

Contents

Special Lecture

Key Management

Invited Lecture

Implementation(Hard/Soft)

Invited Lecture

Security Management

Signature/Authentication

Invited Lecture

Payment Scheme

Key Sharing

A General Theory of Codes, II:
Paradigms and Homomorphisms

G.R. Blakley and I. Borosh

Texas A&M University, College Station, TX 77843-3368, USA
e-mail: blakley@math.tamu.edu, borosh@math.tamu.edu

Abstract. When two competing paradigms bear on a single area of study, investigators have more choices at their disposal. This is not always an advantage.

This paper, like its predecessor, adopts a paradigm for codes. This paradigm ignores the purposes which might have given rise to a code, the size of the code, or the arithmetic used in implementing the code. It concentrates solely on the (set-theoretic) structure of that code.

Once adopted, this structure-oriented paradigm leads naturally to a theory of homomorphisms for the general theory of codes. Code homomorphisms satisfy the standard isomorphism theorems, respect certain important properties of codes, are compatible with products and quotients, and possess other desirable features. Thus, codes fit into general algebra alongside such familiar objects as groups, graphs and posets.

1   Introduction

Most codes information theorists write about are purposeful, finite, arithmetical, and function-oriented. Indeed, we can think of these properties as four dominant paradigms for codes in the current information-theoretic scene.

A human being designs a code for some conscious purpose (secrecy, error control, data compression, ...), and describes the code in a manner in which the purpose plays a fundamental role.

The code uses finite symbol sets, and algorithms which terminate quickly.

The code is far from amorphous. It uses well known finite arithmetics – groups, boolean algebras, even fields – to calculate its encode or decode processes, rather than relying on huge memory lookups.

And the code's basic processes, encode and decode, are functions. There is no ambiguity about the output corresponding to an input symbol.

The reader can no doubt think of exceptions to each of these statements. But they are rare, and in several cases seemingly archaic, the exceptions which probe the rule. In information theory these four properties thus amount to dominant paradigms.

Our predecessor paper [BLA98] flanks all four by treating the presence, or absence, of any one of these four attributes as irrelevant to whether an object of study is a code or how it behaves. The general theory of codes described therein is based solely on (set-theoretic) structure. So it applies as readily to the ostensibly purposeless genetic code as to the purposeful Golay code, as readily to analog scrambling as to digital encryption, as readily to the arithmeticless Library of Congress classification system as to the highly arithmetical DSS, as readily to a 19th century codebook replete with homophones, polyphones, and nulls as to the pair of functions which encode and decode a Caesar cipher message.

That predecessor paper [BLA98] gives much of the rationale for the general theory, as well as numerous examples, and a selection of basic results. It also introduces graphical conventions which make several aspects of the theory easy to visualize.

It points out that there are several types of "duality" inherent in the (set-theoretic) structure of a code and explores properties of "duals" and of "self-dual" objects. It explores the (set-theoretic) structural properties of codes related to homophones, polyphones and nulls, and sets the stage for a group-theoretic analysis of symmetries of codes. It shows how to represent all bipartite digraphs as codes, and how to represent codes as bipartite digraphs. And it gives numerous examples of codes – whether demonstrably purposeful or ostensibly purposeless, finite or infinite, arithmetical or not, function-based or not. Many of these examples are familiar, but not all are commonly called codes.

The sequel paper below makes use of a very few of the definitions and results of [BLA98]. It is largely devoted to the general algebra of a code, its products, quotients, homomorphisms and isomorphism.

We have attempted to make this follow-on to [BLA98] self contained, and so Chapters 3 and 4 below consist of a selection of notions and results from [BLA98] sufficient to support the subsequent developments.

Chapters 7, 8 and 9 below present the details of a formal treatment of the notion of homomorphism in very general terms within information theory. We will show that homomorphisms of codes do a lot of what we have come to expect of homomorphisms.

Many fundamental properties of codes should descend from any ancestral code A to every one of its homomorphic image descendant codes, D. Any (Cartesian) product $P \times Q$ of codes should have a homomorphism Φ which amounts to a projection of $P \times Q$ along a copy of P onto a copy of Q.

Every homomorphic image of a code P should arise out of an appropriately defined quotient in which P is the dividend, and conversely. Every code P should have the property that an iterated quotient of the special form $(P/\Gamma) / (\Delta/\Gamma)$ should be isomorphic to a simple quotient P/Δ, for any Γ and Δ which enable us to make sense of both expressions.

Predictably, construction of a general theory of codes involves both systematization of existing practices – many of which make no use of the word homomorphism – and discovery of new results concerning homomorphisms.

Such a general theory must affect the regnant paradigms of information theory, especially since they tend to come in pairs – a dominant paradigm, coupled with an alternate paradigm – often involving both confusion and conflict. In some cases such a theory will weigh in on one side. In others it will reconcile. But it can seldom stand entirely aloof.

We will therefore begin with a description of some ways a paradigm pair can evolve. Though not directly dependent on Catherine Meadows' [MEA98] approach, which treats how a single paradigm can evolve in isolation, our paradigm-pair approach is not entirely independent of it.

2 Paradigm Pairs

2A Five Evolutionary Paths

There are a variety of ways to deal with two variant, or even conflicting, approaches to a situation, *e.g.* choice, muddling through, Hegel synthesis, Bohr complementarity, synopsis.

For purposes of illustration, consider two monoglot populations who arrive simultaneously in empty territory – speakers of the Thesis language and speakers of the Antithesis language.

Events can force a *choice* of languages on the population, with the result that, after a century, most residents of the territory speak Antithesis and few speak Thesis.

Older Thesis speakers might *muddle through*, picking up a few necessary Antithesis phrases, but sticking to Thesis speech whenever possible, or learning a pidgin which amounts to a tiny parody of Antithesis. Similarly older Antithesis speakers. In this way, each tongue may persist indefinitely in half the population.

Children who speak Thesis may unwittingly and effortlessly – over the course of a single decade – join with equally young Antithesis speakers to produce a totally new (creole) language, call it *Synthesis*. Rooted in both Thesis and Antithesis, it is nevertheless a genuine language with a structure of its own, and may be attractive in recruiting speakers of both other languages. And it may well replace both tongues.

Alternatively both languages may persist indefinitely, each skillfully used by a majority of residents. It can happen that each tends to be spoken in some situations (*e.g.* among aristocrats and writers) but not in others (*e.g.* among merchants and prisoners). When this happens, we say that the two languages exhibit *complementarity*.

Or an attractive ideographic script may be devised and popularized in such a way that the separate monoglot populations go on in the old ways, but each feels that the script transcribes its tongue. The upshot is that *synopsis* can produce a polyglot monograph population – many tongues spoken (and understood), but only one script written (and understood) – a situation which can persist for ages.

This paper and its predecessor [BLA98] are an attempt at synopsis of current paradigms for codes, especially the purposeful/purposeless, finite/infinite, arithmetical/nonarithmetical, and function-oriented/non-function-oriented pairs.

The general theory of codes is intended as a long-term synopsis umbrella under which paradigm pairs, as well as the chemists, biologists, neuroscientists, computer scientists, cryptographers, information theorists, storekeepers, librarians, locksmiths and lexicographers who adhere to them, can for a long period of time shelter somewhat amicably – and in ever closer proximity – in purely structural investigations as the inevitable muddlings, choices, complementarities and syntheses continue among the four paradigm pairs aforementioned.

3   Definitions and Notations

This paper employs a few notations, terminologies and results from [BLA98]. To keep it self-contained, the next four sections state what is necessary from [BLA98].

3A   Partial Functions and Subdiagonal Relations

Let $\mathbb{T}$, $\mathbb{V}$ and $\mathbb{W}$ be sets. Suppose that $r \subseteq \mathbb{T} \times \mathbb{V}$, and that $q \subseteq \mathbb{V} \times \mathbb{W}$. Let

$$r^{nv} = \{\, (\, a\, ,\, b\,) \in \mathbb{V} \times \mathbb{T} : (\, b\, ,\, a\,) \in r \,\}$$

be the *converse* of the (binary) relation r from $\mathbb{T}$ to $\mathbb{V}$. The set $\mathrm{DOM}(\, r\,) \subseteq \mathbb{T}$ is the *domain* of the relation r. Similarly, the set $\mathrm{RAN}(\, r\,) \subseteq \mathbb{V}$ is the *range* of the relation r. The set

$$\mathbf{diag}(\, \mathbb{T}^2\,) = \{\, (\, t\, ,\, t\,) : t \in \mathbb{T} \,\}$$

is called the *diagonal* of the Cartesian square $\mathbb{T}^2 = \mathbb{T} \times \mathbb{T}$. The relation $\mathbf{diag}(\, \mathbb{T}^2\,)$ is obviously a (total) function, the identity function $i_{\mathbb{T}} : \mathbb{T} \rightarrow \mathbb{T}$. A relation r on $\mathbb{T}$ is called a *subdiagonal* relation on $\mathbb{T}$ if $r \subseteq \mathbf{diag}(\, \mathbb{T}^2\,)$. The relation

$$qr = q \circ r \subseteq \mathbb{T} \times \mathbb{W}$$

is the *composite relation*, q *following* r. The ordered pair (t, w) belongs to $q \circ r$ if and only if there exists $v \in \mathbb{V}$ such that (t, v) belongs to r and (v, w) belongs to q.

3B   Precodes and Codes

Throughout this paper, let $\mathbb{PA}$ (the *plaintext alphabet*) and $\mathbb{CO}$ (the *codetext alphabet*) be sets. In terms of them, e (the *encode relation* from $\mathbb{PA}$ to $\mathbb{CO}$) and d (the *decode relation* from $\mathbb{CO}$ to $\mathbb{PA}$), are assumed to be of the forms

$$e \subseteq \mathbb{PA} \times \mathbb{CO}, \qquad d \subseteq \mathbb{CO} \times \mathbb{PA}.$$

The four-entry list $\mathcal{P} = (\, \mathbb{PA}\, ,\, \mathbb{CO}\, ,\, e\, ,\, d\,)$ will be called a *precode* (from $\mathbb{PA}$ to $\mathbb{CO}$).

Definition 3B1. The precode $\mathcal{P}$ will be called a *code* (from $\mathbb{PA}$ to $\mathbb{CO}$) if the composite relation $d \circ e \subseteq \mathbb{PA}^2$ is a subdiagonal relation on $\mathbb{PA}$, *i.e.* is an identity partial function from $\mathbb{PA}$ to $\mathbb{PA}$.

To attain uniformity, and save space, we adhere to several notations and conventions throughout this paper. The two sets $\mathbb{PA}$, $\mathbb{CO}$, the three subsets $\mathbf{e}$, $\mathbf{d}^{nv}$, $\mathbf{c}$ of $\mathbb{PA} \times \mathbb{CO}$, and the four-entry list $\mathcal{P} = (\ \mathbb{PA}\ ,\ \mathbb{CO}\ ,\ \mathbf{e}\ ,\ \mathbf{d}\ )$ are always assumed to be as described in Definition 3B2 below.

Definition 3B2. Let

$$\mathbb{PA}(\ \mathcal{P}\ ) = \mathbb{PA}, \qquad\qquad \mathbb{CO}(\ \mathcal{P}\ ) = \mathbb{CO},$$

$$\mathbf{e}(\ \mathcal{P}\ ) = \mathbf{e}, \quad \mathbf{d}(\ \mathcal{P}\ ) = \mathbf{d}, \quad \mathbf{c}(\ \mathcal{P}\ ) = \mathbf{c} = \mathbf{e} \cap \mathbf{d}^{nv}$$

We will need more than one fully equipped precode below. So we will also make frequent use of three other precodes

$$\widehat{\mathcal{P}} = (\ \widehat{\mathbb{PA}}\ ,\ \widehat{\mathbb{CO}}\ ,\ \hat{\mathbf{e}}\ ,\ \hat{\mathbf{d}}\ ), \qquad\qquad \overline{\mathcal{P}} = (\ \overline{\mathbb{PA}}\ ,\ \overline{\mathbb{CO}}\ ,\ \overline{\mathbf{e}}\ ,\ \overline{\mathbf{d}}\ ),$$

$$\widetilde{\mathcal{P}} = (\ \widetilde{\mathbb{PA}}\ ,\ \widetilde{\mathbb{CO}}\ ,\ \tilde{\mathbf{e}}\ ,\ \tilde{\mathbf{d}}\ )$$

without repeated reintroductions below.

Proposition 3B3. $\mathcal{P}$ is a code if and only if

$$\mathbf{d} \circ \mathbf{e} = \mathbf{i}_{\mathrm{DOM}(\mathbf{c})} = \mathrm{diag}(\ \mathrm{DOM}(\ \mathbf{c}\ )^2\ ).$$

Suppose that $\mathcal{P}$ is a code. Then $\mathbf{d} \circ \mathbf{e}$ is an identity (partial) function on $\mathbb{PA}$, and $\mathbf{c}^{nv} \circ \mathbf{c} = \mathbf{d} \circ \mathbf{e}$, and $\mathbf{c}^{nv}$ is a (partial) function.

Definition 3B4. $\widehat{\mathcal{P}}$ is a *subprecode* of $\mathcal{P}$ (and $\mathcal{P}$ is a *superprecode* of $\widehat{\mathcal{P}}$) if

$$\widehat{\mathbb{PA}} \subseteq \mathbb{PA}, \qquad \widehat{\mathbb{CO}} \subseteq \mathbb{CO}, \qquad \hat{\mathbf{e}} \subseteq \mathbf{e}, \qquad \text{and } \hat{\mathbf{d}} \subseteq \mathbf{d}.$$

A subprecode which is a code is called a *subcode*. Similarly *supercode*.

Evidently, a subprecode $\widehat{\mathcal{P}}$ of a code $\mathcal{P}$ is a code, and is a subcode of $\mathcal{P}$.

Definition 3B5. The intersection, $\mathcal{P} = \overline{\mathcal{P}} \cap \widehat{\mathcal{P}}$, of $\overline{\mathcal{P}}$ and $\widehat{\mathcal{P}}$ is the precode

$$\begin{aligned} \mathcal{P} &= (\ \mathbb{PA}\ ,\ \mathbb{CO}\ ,\ \mathbf{e}\ ,\ \mathbf{d}\ ) \\ &= (\ \overline{\mathbb{PA}} \cap \widehat{\mathbb{PA}}\ ,\ \overline{\mathbb{CO}} \cap \widehat{\mathbb{CO}}\ ,\ \overline{\mathbf{e}} \cap \hat{\mathbf{e}}\ ,\ \overline{\mathbf{d}} \cap \hat{\mathbf{d}}\ ) \end{aligned}$$

Clearly, $\overline{\mathcal{P}} \cap \widehat{\mathcal{P}}$ is a code if either $\overline{\mathcal{P}}$ or $\widehat{\mathcal{P}}$ is a code.

4 Notions Akin to Duality

4A Companions. Self-Companion Codes

Definition 4A1. The *companion* of $\mathcal{P}$ is

$$\mathcal{P}^{pn} = (\ \mathbb{PA}^{pn}\ ,\ \mathbb{CO}^{pn}\ ,\ \mathbf{e}^{pn}\ ,\ \mathbf{d}^{pn}\ )$$
$$= (\ \mathbb{PA}\ ,\ \mathbb{CO}\ ,\ \mathbf{d}^{nv}\ ,\ \mathbf{e}^{nv}\ ).$$

Suppose that $\mathcal{P}^{pn} = \mathcal{P}$, *i.e.* that $\mathbf{d} = \mathbf{e}^{nv}$. Then $\mathcal{P}$ is said to be a *self-companion* precode. The *companion of a code,* and a *self-companion code,* are defined in the obvious fashion.

A precode $\mathcal{P}$ is a code from $\mathbb{PA}$ to $\mathbb{CO}$ if and only if its companion $\mathcal{P}^{pn}$ is a code from $\mathbb{PA}$ to $\mathbb{CO}$. $\mathcal{P}$ is a self-companion code if and only if $\mathbf{d}$ is a partial function and $\mathbf{e} = \mathbf{d}^{nv}$. A self-companion code has a one-to-many encode relation and a many-to-one decode relation.

Definition 4A2. The *self-companion kernel* (the *nub*) $\mathcal{N}$ of $\mathcal{P}$ is the precode from $\mathbb{PA}$ to $\mathbb{CO}$ defined by setting

$$\mathcal{N} = \mathcal{NUB} = \mathcal{NUB}(\ \mathcal{P}\ ) = (\ \mathbb{PA}\ ,\ \mathbb{CO}\ ,\ \mathbf{c}\ ,\ \mathbf{c}^{nv}\ ).$$

4B Opposites. Self-Opposite Codes

Definition 4B1. The *opposite* $\mathcal{P}^{op}$ of $\mathcal{P}$ is the precode from $\mathbb{CO}$ to $\mathbb{PA}$ defined by setting

$$\mathcal{P}^{op} = (\ \mathbb{PA}^{op}\ ,\ \mathbb{CO}^{op}\ ,\ \mathbf{e}^{op}\ ,\ \mathbf{d}^{op}\ )$$
$$= (\ \mathbb{CO}\ ,\ \mathbb{PA}\ ,\ \mathbf{d}\ ,\ \mathbf{e}\ ).$$

Suppose that $\mathcal{P}^{op} = \mathcal{P}$, *i.e.* that $\mathbb{PA} = \mathbb{CO}$ and $\mathbf{e} = \mathbf{d}$. Then $\mathcal{P}$ is said to be *self-opposite*. The *opposite of a code,* and a *self-opposite code,* are defined in the obvious fashion.

We have now seen all the parts of [BLA98] which are necessary for our study of homomorphisms. However, that paper goes on to discuss various structural features of codes, including homophony, polyphony and nulls. It provides numerous examples, drawn from biology, locksmithing, calculus, lexicography, cryptology, error control and elsewhere. It presents various graphical representations of codes.

5 Homomorphisms

The rest of this paper is devoted to the definition of the notions of product, quotient, and homomorphism among precodes (and therefore among codes). Our policy will be to reduce consideration of a property of a precode to consideration of the corresponding property for two related relations wherever possible below.

This means that we will often treat a precode (or code) as little more than a pair of related relations. So we shall discuss relation homomorphisms first.

The treatment below is along the lines of Mal'cev's approach [MAL73] to algebraic systems, typically equipped with both operations and relations. Those involving only operations are called *algebras*, and those involving only relations are called *models*. In this terminology, codes are models.

Mal'cev's formulation is in terms of a single carrier, whereas this paper rests on two, *viz*. $\mathbb{PA}$ and $\mathbb{CO}$. So we will not make direct use of [MAL73]. But our debts to that work are obvious. In particular, the distinction between homomorphism and strong homomorphism is also found in a general context in [MAL73].

6   Preliminaries on Relations

6A   A Notational Convention

It is a useful terse explicit convention to be able to say that $(\ \mathbb{G}\ ,\ \mathbb{H}\ ,\ \mathbf{r}\ )$ *is a relation* when we mean that $\mathbf{r}$ is a (binary) relation from $\mathbb{G}$ to $\mathbb{H}$. We will often employ it below. A relation $(\ \widehat{\mathbb{G}}\ ,\ \widehat{\mathbb{H}}\ ,\ \mathbf{m}\ )$ is called a *subrelation* of $(\ \mathbb{G}\ ,\ \mathbb{H}\ ,\ \mathbf{r}\ )$ if

$$\widehat{\mathbb{G}} \subseteq \mathbb{G}, \qquad \widehat{\mathbb{H}} \subseteq \mathbb{H}, \quad \text{and} \qquad \mathbf{m} \subseteq \mathbf{r}.$$

As usual, the power set of $\mathbb{A}$ is written

$$2 \uparrow \mathbb{A} = \{\ \mathbb{B} : \mathbb{B} \subseteq \mathbb{A}\ \}$$

Let $(\ \mathbb{G}\ ,\ \mathbb{H}\ ,\ \mathbf{r}\ )$ be a relation. It is an abuse of notation and language to employ the symbol $\mathbf{r}$ again to denote a set-valued function of sets and write both

$$\mathbf{r} : 2 \uparrow \mathbb{G} \ \rightarrow\ 2 \uparrow \mathbb{H}$$

and

$$\mathbf{r}(\ \mathbb{A}\ ) = \{\ \eta \in \mathbb{H} : \text{There exists } \alpha \in \mathbb{A} \text{ such that } (\alpha, \eta) \in \mathbf{r}\ \}.$$

But it is commonly done, and we will frequently and harmlessly employ it below, since no confusion can arise. Thus the relation such that

$$\mathbf{r} = \{\ (1,1)\ ,\ (1,2)\ ,\ (2,2)\ \},$$

gives rise to the function such that

$$\begin{aligned}
\mathbf{r}(\ \emptyset\ ) &= \emptyset \\
\mathbf{r}(\ \{\ 1\ \}\ ) &= \{\ 1,\ 2\ \} \\
\mathbf{r}(\ \{\ 2\ \}\ ) &= \{\ 2\ \} \\
\mathbf{r}(\ \{\ 1\ ,\ 2\ \}\ ) &= \{\ 1,\ 2\ \}.
\end{aligned}$$

6B Images, Ancestors and Descendants

Throughout this section we will assume that

$$(\, \mathbb{G} \, , \, \mathbb{H} \, , \, \mathbf{r} \,), \qquad (\, \widehat{\mathbb{G}} \, , \, \widehat{\mathbb{H}} \, , \, \mathbf{m} \,) \, ,$$
$$(\, \mathbb{G} \, , \, \widehat{\mathbb{G}} \, , \, \mathbf{g} \,), \qquad (\, \mathbb{H} \, , \, \widehat{\mathbb{H}} \, , \, \mathbf{h} \,)$$

are relations. Clearly, then,

$$(\, \mathbb{G} \, , \, \mathbb{G} \, , \, \mathbf{r}^{nv} \circ \mathbf{r} \,), \qquad (\, \mathbb{H} \, , \, \mathbb{H} \, , \, \mathbf{r} \circ \mathbf{r}^{\,nv} \,)$$

are symmetric relations.

Proposition 6B1. $\mathbf{r} \circ \mathbf{r}^{nv} \subseteq i_{\mathbb{H}} \Leftrightarrow$ $\mathbf{r}$ *is a partial function from* $\mathbb{G}$ *to* $\mathbb{H}$.

$\mathbf{r}^{nv} \circ \mathbf{r} \supseteq i_{\mathbb{G}} \Leftrightarrow$ $\mathrm{DOM}(\, \mathbf{r} \,) = \mathbb{G}$.
$\mathbf{r} \circ \mathbf{r}^{nv} \supseteq i_{\mathbb{H}} \Leftrightarrow$ $\mathrm{RAN}(\, \mathbf{r} \,) = \mathbb{H}$.

Proposition 6B2. $\mathbf{r}$ *is an injection* $\Leftrightarrow \mathbf{r} \circ \mathbf{r}^{nv} \subseteq i_{\mathbb{H}}$ *and* $\mathbf{r}^{nv} \circ \mathbf{r} = i_{\mathbb{G}}$.

$\mathbf{r}$ *is a surjection* $\Leftrightarrow \mathbf{r} \circ \mathbf{r}^{nv} = i_{\mathbb{H}}$ *and* $\mathbf{r}^{nv} \circ \mathbf{r} \supseteq i_{\mathbb{G}}$.
$\mathbf{r}$ *is a bijection* $\Leftrightarrow \mathbf{r} \circ \mathbf{r}^{nv} = i_{\mathbb{H}}$ *and* $\mathbf{r}^{nv} \circ \mathbf{r} = i_{\mathbb{G}}$.

The following proposition can be found in [MAL73].

Proposition 6B3. *Suppose that* $(\, \mathbb{G} \, , \, \mathbb{G} \, , \, \mathbf{s} \,)$ *and* $(\, \mathbb{G} \, , \, \mathbb{G} \, , \, \mathbf{u} \,)$ *are equivalence relations. Then*

$(\, \mathbb{G} \, , \, \mathbb{G} \, , \, \mathbf{s} \cap \mathbf{u} \,)$ *is an equivalence relation.*
$(\, \mathbb{G} \, , \, \mathbb{G} \, , \, \mathbf{s} \circ \mathbf{u} \,)$ *is an equivalence relation* $\Leftrightarrow \mathbf{s} \circ \mathbf{u} = \mathbf{u} \circ \mathbf{s}$.
$(\, \mathbb{G} \, , \, \mathbb{G} \, , \, \mathbf{s} \cup \mathbf{u} \,)$ *is an equivalence relation* $\Leftrightarrow \mathbf{s} \cup \mathbf{u} = \mathbf{s} \circ \mathbf{u}$.

Even though none of the relations described above is as yet assumed to be a function, we will present a diagram as a mnemonic and a heuristic.

Diagram 6B4.

$$
\begin{array}{ccc}
\mathbb{G} & \xrightarrow{\;\mathbf{r}\;} & \mathbb{H} \\
\mathbf{g} \downarrow & & \downarrow \mathbf{h} \\
\widehat{\mathbb{G}} & \xrightarrow[\mathbf{m}]{} & \widehat{\mathbb{H}}
\end{array}
$$

The *ancestor/descendant* terminology of functions extends naturally to relations.

Definition 6B5. Suppose that $(\gamma, \hat{\gamma}) \in \mathbf{g}$. Then we say that γ is a **g-ancestor** of $\hat{\gamma}$, and that $\hat{\gamma}$ is a **g-descendant** of γ. Suppose that $(\gamma, \hat{\gamma}) \in \mathbf{g}$, and that $(\eta, \hat{\eta}) \in \mathbf{h}$. Then we say that the pair (γ, η) is a $(\, \mathbf{g} \, , \, \mathbf{h} \,)$-**ancestor** of the pair $(\hat{\gamma}, \hat{\eta})$, and that the pair $(\hat{\gamma}, \hat{\eta})$ is a $(\, \mathbf{g} \, , \, \mathbf{h} \,)$-**descendant** of the pair (γ, η).

Proposition 6B6. $m \subseteq h \circ r \circ g^{nv}$ *if and only if*

every pair in m *has an ancestor pair in* r.

$r \subseteq h^{nv} \circ m \circ g$ *if and only if*
every pair in r *has a descendant pair in* m.

$m \supseteq h \circ r \circ g^{nv}$ *if and only if*
all descendants of pairs in r *are pairs in* m.

$r \supseteq h^{nv} \circ m \circ g$ *if and only if*
all ancestors of pairs in m *are pairs in* r.

In particular, suppose that the relations $(G , \widehat{G} , g)$ and $(H , \widehat{H} , h)$ are actually (total) functions

$$g : G \to \widehat{G}, \qquad\qquad h : H \longrightarrow \widehat{H},$$

Then $r \subseteq h^{nv} \circ m \circ g$ if and only if $m \supseteq h \circ r \circ g^{nv}$. Recall that every pair belonging to r has exactly one descendant pair belonging to m.

6C   Quotients and Canonical Maps

Definition 6C1. If (G , G , s) is an equivalence relation, then the *quotient*, G modulo s, is the set

$$G / s = \{ s(\{\gamma\}) : \gamma \in G \} \subseteq 2 \uparrow G$$

i.e. the (set-theoretic) *partition* of G induced by the equivalence relation s. Its *cells* are its members. Each member is a (necessarily nonvoid) set of the form $s(\{\gamma\})$.

Any total function $g : G \to \widehat{G}$ effects a partition

$$\Psi[g] = \{ g^{nv}(\{\hat{\gamma}\}) : \hat{\gamma} \in \text{RAN}(g) \}.$$

And it is obvious that $s = g^{nv} \circ g$ is the equivalence relation s such that $G / s = \Psi[g]$.

Definition 6C2. The *canonical map* [GOD68, p. 80] f_s *determined by* the equivalence relation (G , G , s) is the function

$$f_s : G \to G / s$$

such that
$$f_s = \{ (\gamma , s(\{\gamma\})) : \gamma \in G \}.$$

Evidently

Lemma 6C3.

$$f_s{}^{nv} \circ f_s = s$$
$$f_s \circ f_s{}^{nv} = \textbf{diag} ([G / s]^2) = i_{G/s}$$

Lemma 6C4. *Suppose that* $(\,G\,,\,G\,,\,s\,)$ *and* $(\,G\,,\,G\,,\,u\,)$ *are equivalence relations. The partition* $G\,/\,s$ *is a refinement of the partition* $G\,/\,u$ *if and only if* $s \subseteq u$. *If* $s \subseteq u$, *then*

$$u \circ s = s \circ u = u.$$

Definition 6C5. Suppose that $(\,G\,,\,H\,,\,r\,)$ is a relation, and that $(\,G\,,\,G\,,\,s\,)$ and $(\,H\,,\,H\,,\,t\,)$ are equivalence relations. Then we define a quotient relation.

$$(\,\overline{G}\,,\,\overline{H}\,,\,k\,) = (\,G\,,\,H\,,\,r\,)\,/\,(\,s\,,\,t\,)$$

by stipulating that $\overline{G} = G\,/\,s$, that $\overline{H} = H\,/\,t$, and that

$$
\begin{aligned}
r\,/\,(\,s\,,\,t\,) &= k \\
&= f_t \circ r \circ f_s{}^{nv} \\
&= \{\ (\ s(\{\gamma\})\ ,\ t(\{\eta\})\ )\ :\ (\,\gamma,\,\eta\,)\in r\ \}.
\end{aligned}
$$

In other words, an s cell of G is related to a t cell of H under $k = r\,/\,(\,s\,,\,t\,)$ if these cells contain elements which are related under r.

Throughout the rest of this section, we will let $(\,G\,,\,G\,,\,s\,)$ and $(\,G\,,\,G\,,\,u\,)$ be equivalence relations such that $s \subseteq u$. In accord with common usage, we will write

$$
\begin{aligned}
(\,\overline{G}\,,\,\overline{G}\,,\,\bar{u}\,) &= (\,G\,,\,G\,,\,u\,)\,/\,(\,s\,,\,s\,) \\
u\,/\,s &= \bar{u}.
\end{aligned}
$$

Thus

$$(\,G\,,\,G\,,\,u\,)\,/\,(\,s\,,\,s\,) = (\,G/s\,,\,G/s\,,\,u/s\,).$$

Theorem 6C6. *The relation* $(\,G/s\,,\,G/s\,,\,u/s\,)$ *is an equivalence relation.*

Proof. By Lemma 6C3,

$$u/s = f_s \circ u \circ f_s{}^{nv} \supseteq f_s \circ i_G \circ f_s{}^{nv} = f_s \circ f_s{}^{nv} = i_{G/s}.$$

Hence u/s is reflexive. To verify that u/s is symmetric, note that

$$(\,f_s \circ u \circ f_s{}^{nv}\,)^{nv} = (\,f_s{}^{nv}\,)^{nv} \circ u^{nv} \circ f_s{}^{nv} = f_s \circ u \circ f_s{}^{nv}.$$

The verification of transitivity uses Lemmas 6C3 and 6C4. In fact

$$
\begin{aligned}
(\,f_s \circ u \circ f_s{}^{nv}\,)^2 &= f_s \circ u \circ f_s{}^{nv} \circ f_s \circ u \circ f_s{}^{nv} \\
&= f_s \circ u \circ s \circ u \circ f_s{}^{nv} \\
&= f_s \circ u \circ u \circ u \circ f_s{}^{nv} \\
&= f_s \circ u \circ u \circ f_s{}^{nv} \\
&= f_s \circ u \circ f_s{}^{nv}. \qquad \square
\end{aligned}
$$

See Appendix 6C6 in Chapter 11 below for a fairly paradigmatic pictorial representation of the sets $(\mathbb{G} / s) / (u / s)$, $\mathbb{G} / s$, $\mathbb{G} / u$. This illustration is also a pictorial introduction to the canonical map $f_{u/s}$ described in set-theoretic terms immediately below.

Lemma 6C7. *The function* $f_{u/s} : \mathbb{G}/s \to (\mathbb{G}/s) / (u/s)$ *has the property that*

$$f_{u/s} (\; s(\{\gamma\}) \;) = [\, f_s \circ u \circ f_s^{nv} \,] (\; \{ \; s(\{\gamma\}) \; \} \;)$$
$$= \{ \, s(\{\lambda\}) : (\lambda , \gamma) \in u \, \}$$

for every $\gamma \in \mathbb{G}$. *This formulation is well defined, i.e. does not depend on the representatives* γ *or* λ *of the cells in question.*

7 Homomorphisms of Relations

7A Definitions

Definition 7A1. A *relation homomorphism* from one relation $(\mathbb{G} , \mathbb{H} , r)$ to another relation $(\widehat{\mathbb{G}} , \widehat{\mathbb{H}} , m)$ is a pair (g , h) of (total) functions

$$g : \mathbb{G} \to \widehat{\mathbb{G}}, \qquad\qquad h : \mathbb{H} \to \widehat{\mathbb{H}}$$

such that $m \supseteq h \circ r \circ g^{nv}$. The relation homomorphism (g , h) is called a *relation epimorphism* if g and h are surjections.

Definition 7A2. A relation homomorphism (g , h) from a relation $(\mathbb{G} , \mathbb{H} , r)$ to a relation $(\widehat{\mathbb{G}} , \widehat{\mathbb{H}} , m)$ is a *strong relation homomorphism* from $(\mathbb{G} , \mathbb{H} , r)$ to $(\widehat{\mathbb{G}} , \widehat{\mathbb{H}} , m)$ if $m \subseteq h \circ r \circ g^{nv}$.

Example 7A3. *Not every relation homomorphism is strong.* Suppose that g and h are functions, and that $r = \emptyset \neq m$. Then the pair (g , h) is a relation homomorphism, but not a strong relation homomorphism.

Definition 7A4. Suppose that $g : \mathbb{G} \to \widehat{\mathbb{G}}$ and $h : \mathbb{H} \to \widehat{\mathbb{H}}$ are functions. Suppose that the function pair (g , h) is a relation homomorphism from $(\mathbb{G} , \mathbb{H} , r)$ to $(\widehat{\mathbb{G}} , \widehat{\mathbb{H}} , m)$, and that the function pair (g^{nv} , h^{nv}) is a relation homomorphism from the relation $(\widehat{\mathbb{G}} , \widehat{\mathbb{H}} , m)$ to the relation $(\mathbb{G} , \mathbb{H} , r)$. Then we say that (g , h) is a *relation isomorphism* from $(\mathbb{G} , \mathbb{H} , r)$ to $(\widehat{\mathbb{G}} , \widehat{\mathbb{H}} , m)$.

Proposition 7A5. *Suppose that the function pair* (g , h) *is a relation isomorphism from* $(\mathbb{G} , \mathbb{H} , r)$ *to* $(\widehat{\mathbb{G}} , \widehat{\mathbb{H}} , m)$. *Then* g *and* h *are bijections. Moreover,* (g , h) *and* (g^{nv} , h^{nv}) *are strong relation homomorphisms.*

Not every relation homomorphism (g , h) for which g and h are bijections is a relation isomorphism. A strong relation homomorphism (g , h) for which g and h are bijections is a relation isomorphism.

In view of the foregoing, there is no need to define a *strong relation isomorphism* in terms of strong relation homomorphisms. Such a definition of strong relation isomorphism would only coincide with relation isomorphism.

Definition 7A6. Let (g , h) be a relation homomorphism from

(G , H , r) to ($\widehat{G}$, $\widehat{H}$, m). Then the equivalence relation pair

$$(s , t) = (g^{nv} \circ g , h^{nv} \circ h)$$

is called the *kernel* of the homomorphism (g , h).

It follows from Definitions 6C5, 7A2 and 7A6 that

Theorem 7A7. *Let* (G , H , r) *be a relation. Let*

$$(G , G , s) \qquad and \qquad (H , H , t)$$

be equivalence relations. Let

$$(\overline{G} , \overline{H} , k) = (G , H , r) / (s , t).$$

Then the canonical map pair (f_s , f_t) *from the relation* (G , H , r) *to the relation* ($\overline{G}$, $\overline{H}$, k) *is a strong homomorphism with kernel* (s , t).

7B Isomorphism Theorems for Relations

This section is devoted to relation theoretic analogs of the three well known [PAL66, pp. 115, 118, 119] isomorphism theorems of group theory. It is in the spirit of [MAL73, pp. 45-49]. It prefigures the corresponding three theorems for precodes in Section 9B below.

Theorem 7B1. *Let* (g , h) *be a relation homomorphism from*

(G , H , r) *to* ($\widehat{G}$, $\widehat{H}$, m). *Let*

$$(s , t) = (g^{nv} \circ g , h^{nv} \circ h)$$

be its kernel. Let

$$(\overline{G} , \overline{H} , k) = (G , H , r) / (s , t).$$

Let (f_s , f_t) *be the canonical map pair from* (G , H , r) *onto* ($\overline{G}$, $\overline{H}$, k). *Then :*

1) *The natural map pair* $n = (g \circ f_s^{nv} , h \circ f_t^{nv})$
   is a relation homomorphism from
   ($\overline{G}$, $\overline{H}$, k) *to* ($\widehat{G}$, $\widehat{H}$, m) ;
2) *If* (g , h) *is a strong relation epimorphism, then*
   $n = (g \circ f_s^{nv} , h \circ f_t^{nv})$ *is a relation isomorphism*
   from ($\overline{G}$, $\overline{H}$, k) *to* ($\widehat{G}$, $\widehat{H}$, m).

Proof. First we show that $g \circ f_s^{nv}$ is a function from $\overline{G}$ to $\widehat{G}$, and that $h \circ f_t^{nv}$ is a function from $\overline{H}$ to $\widehat{H}$. Note that $s = g^{nv} \circ g = f_s^{nv} \circ f_s$. Now

$$
\begin{aligned}
(g \circ f_s^{nv}) \circ (g \circ f_s^{nv})^{nv} &= g \circ (f_s^{nv} \circ f_s) \circ g^{nv} \\
&= g \circ (g^{nv} \circ g) \circ g^{nv} \\
&= (g \circ g^{nv}) \circ (g \circ g^{nv}) \\
&\subseteq i_{\widehat{G}} \circ i_{\widehat{G}} \\
&= i_{\widehat{G}}.
\end{aligned}
$$

Also, the domain of $g \circ f_s^{nv}$ is obviously $\overline{G}$, and the domain of $h \circ f_t^{nv}$ is obviously $\overline{H}$. The same argument shows that $(g \circ f_s^{nv})^{nv} = f_s \circ g^{nv}$ is also a function. So $g \circ f_s^{nv}$ is a bijection from $\overline{G}$ to some subset of $\widehat{G}$. In fact $g \circ f_s^{nv}$ and $h \circ f_t^{nv}$ are bijections from $\overline{G}$ to $\widehat{G}$ and $\overline{H}$ to $\widehat{H}$ respectively if and only if the maps g and h are onto. Since (f_s, f_t) is a strong relation homomorphism, it follows that

$$
\begin{aligned}
k &= f_t \circ r \circ f_s^{nv}, \\
&\subseteq f_t \circ (h^{nv} \circ m \circ g) \circ f_s^{nv} \\
&= (h \circ f_t^{nv})^{nv} \circ m \circ (g \circ f_s^{nv}).
\end{aligned}
$$

Consequently $(g \circ f_s^{nv}, h \circ f_t^{nv})$ is a relation homomorphism from $(\overline{G}, \overline{H}, k)$ to $(\widehat{G}, \widehat{H}, m)$. If (g, h) is a strong relation homomorphism from (G, H, r) onto $(\widehat{G}, \widehat{H}, m)$ then, as we have already shown, $g \circ f_s^{nv}$ and $h \circ f_t^{nv}$ are bijections. Moreover

$$
\begin{aligned}
m &\subseteq h \circ r \circ g^{nv} \\
&\subseteq h \circ f_t^{nv} \circ k \circ f_s \circ g^{nv} \\
&= (h \circ h^{nv}) \circ k \circ (f_s \circ g^{nv}).
\end{aligned}
$$

This demonstrates that

$$
((g \circ f_s^{nv})^{nv}, (h \circ f_t^{nv})^{nv}) = (f_s \circ g^{nv}, f_t \circ h^{nv})
$$

is also a relation homomorphism. Therefore $(g \circ f_s^{nv}, h \circ f_t^{nv})$ is a relation epimorphism from $(\overline{G}, \overline{H}, k)$ to $(\widehat{G}, \widehat{H}, m)$. $\square$

The proof of Theorem 7B1 is illustrated by the diagram in Appendix 7B1 in Chapter 11 below. The following two theorems correspond to the first and second isomorphism theorems of general algebra textbooks, and [MAL73] in particular.

Theorem 7B2. *Let* $(\widehat{G}, \widehat{H}, m)$ *be a subrelation of a relation* (G, H, r). *Let* (G, G, s) *and* (H, H, t) *be equivalence relations. Let*

$$
\begin{aligned}
\widetilde{G} &= s(\widehat{G}), \\
\widetilde{H} &= t(\widehat{H}) \\
j &= r \cap [\widetilde{G} \times \widetilde{H}] \\
x &= s \cap \widehat{G}^2, \\
y &= t \cap \widehat{H}^2.
\end{aligned}
$$

Then the natural map pair $n = (g, h)$ *from* $(\widehat{G}, \widehat{H}, m) / (x, y)$ *to* $(\widetilde{G}, \widetilde{H}, j) / (s, t)$ *is a relation homomorphism. Moreover its entries,* g *and* h, *are bijections. Finally,* $n = (g, h)$ *is a relation isomorphism if and only if*

$$j \subseteq t \circ m \circ s.$$

Comment. The natural map pair $n = (g, h)$ is defined by setting

$$g = \{ (x(\{\gamma\}), s(\{\gamma\})) : \gamma \in \widehat{G} \}$$
$$h = \{ (y(\{\eta\}), t(\{\eta\})) : \eta \in \widehat{H} \}.$$

Clearly, then g and h are functions

$$g : \widehat{G} / x \to s(\widehat{G}) / s \subseteq G / s \subseteq 2 \uparrow G$$
$$h : \widehat{H} / y \to t(\widehat{H}) / t \subseteq H / t \subseteq 2 \uparrow H.$$

Evidently g^{nv} is defined by setting

$$g^{nv} = \{ (s(\{\gamma\}), s(\{\gamma\}) \cap \widehat{G}) : \gamma \in s(\widehat{G}) \}$$

and is obviously a function $g^{nv} : s(\widehat{G}) / s \to \widehat{G} / x$. Similarly h^{nv}.

   The proof of Theorem 7B2 is illustrated by the diagram in Appendix 7B2 in Chapter 11 below. In this diagram, $i_{\widehat{G}}$ is the identity imbedding of $\widehat{G}$ into G, and similarly $i_{\widehat{H}}$. Note that $s(\widehat{G}) / s$ is $[f_s \circ i_{\widehat{G}}](\widehat{G})$, and that $t(\widehat{H}) / t$ is $[f_t \circ i_{\widehat{H}}](\widehat{H})$. The natural map pair $n = (g, h)$ can thus be obtained as

$$g = f_s \circ i_{\widehat{G}} \circ f_x^{\ nv}$$
$$h = f_t \circ i_{\widehat{H}} \circ f_y^{\ nv}.$$

Theorem 7B3. *Let* (G, H, r) *be a relation. Let*

$$(G, G, s), \qquad (G, G, u),$$
$$(H, H, t), \qquad (H, H, v)$$

be equivalence relations such that $s \subseteq u$ *and* $t \subseteq v$. *Then*

$$(G/s, G/s, u/s), \text{ and} \qquad (H/t, H/t, v/t)$$

are equivalence relations. And there is a natural map pair

$$n = (g, h)$$

from

$$(\widetilde{G}, \widetilde{H}, j) = [(G, H, r) / (s, t)] / (u / s, v / t)$$

to

$$(\hat{\mathbb{G}} , \hat{\mathbb{H}} , \mathbf{m}) = (\mathbb{G} , \mathbb{H} , \mathbf{r}) / (\mathbf{u} , \mathbf{v}).$$

Moreover, $\mathbf{n}$ *is a relation isomorphism.*

The proof is illustrated by the diagram in Appendix 7B3 in Chapter 11 below. From this it is clear that the natural map pair $\mathbf{n}$ is given by

$$\mathbf{g} = \mathbf{f_u} \circ \mathbf{f_s}^{nv} \circ (\mathbf{f_{u/s}})^{nv}$$
$$\mathbf{h} = \mathbf{f_v} \circ \mathbf{f_t}^{nv} \circ (\mathbf{f_{v/t}})^{nv}$$
$$\mathbf{n} = (\mathbf{f} , \mathbf{g}).$$

Comment. In elementary set-theoretic notation, the relation isomorphism statement in Theorem 7B3 amounts to three assertions. The first two are that the bijection

$$\mathbf{g} : (\mathbb{G} / \mathbf{s}) / (\mathbf{u} / \mathbf{s}) \rightarrow \mathbb{G} / \mathbf{u}$$

is the (well-defined) set of ordered pairs

$$\mathbf{g} = \{ \ (\ \{ \mathbf{s}(\{ \lambda \}) : (\lambda , \gamma) \in \mathbf{u} \} , \mathbf{u}(\{ \gamma \}) \ ) : \gamma \in \mathbb{G} \ \}$$
$$\subseteq \ [2 \uparrow (2 \uparrow \mathbb{G})] \times (2 \uparrow \mathbb{G}),$$

and analogously the bijection $\mathbf{h}$. The third assertion is that the one-to-one correspondence between the set

$$\mathbf{j} \subseteq [(\mathbb{G} / \mathbf{s}) / (\mathbf{u} / \mathbf{s})] \times [(\mathbb{G} / \mathbf{t}) / (\mathbf{v} / \mathbf{t})]$$
$$\subseteq [2 \uparrow (2 \uparrow \mathbb{G})] \times [2 \uparrow (2 \uparrow \mathbb{H})]$$

and the set

$$\mathbf{k} \subseteq (\mathbb{G} / \mathbf{s}) \times (\mathbb{H} / \mathbf{t})$$
$$\subseteq (2 \uparrow \mathbb{G}) \times (2 \uparrow \mathbb{H})$$

amounts to the (true) statement that, for every pair (γ , η) belonging to $\mathbb{G} \times \mathbb{H}$, we know that the pair

$$(\ \{ \mathbf{s}(\{ \lambda \}) : (\lambda , \gamma) \in \mathbf{u} \} , \{ \mathbf{t}(\{ \chi \}) : (\chi , \eta) \in \mathbf{v} \} \ )$$

belongs to $\mathbf{j}$ if and only if the pair

$$(\ \mathbf{u}(\{ \gamma \}) , \mathbf{v}(\{ \eta \}) \ )$$

belongs to $\mathbf{m}$.

8   Homomorphisms of Codes and Precodes

8A   Homomorphisms of Precodes

Definition 8A1. Let $g : \mathbb{PA} \to \widehat{\mathbb{PA}}$ and $h : \mathbb{CO} \to \widehat{\mathbb{CO}}$ be functions. Then (g, h) is a *precode homomorphism* from $\mathcal{P}$ to $\widehat{\mathcal{P}}$ if both of the following conditions hold.

1) (g, h) is a relation homomorphism
   from $(\mathbb{PA}, \mathbb{CO}, e)$ to $(\widehat{\mathbb{PA}}, \widehat{\mathbb{CO}}, \hat{e})$, and
2) (h, g) is a relation homomorphism
   from $(\mathbb{CO}, \mathbb{PA}, d)$ to $(\widehat{\mathbb{CO}}, \widehat{\mathbb{PA}}, \hat{d})$.

A *precode epimorphism* is a precode homomorphism (g, h) such that g and h are surjections.

Proposition 8A2. *Definition 8A1 above is equivalent to requiring that:*

3)
$$\hat{e} \supseteq h \circ e \circ g^{nv};$$

4)
$$\hat{d} \supseteq g \circ d \circ h^{nv}.$$

Definition 8A3. Let g and h be as in Definition 8A1 above. Suppose that (g, h) is a precode homomorphism from $\mathcal{P}$ to $\widehat{\mathcal{P}}$, and that:

5)
$$\hat{e} \subseteq h \circ e \circ g^{nv}$$

6)
$$\hat{d} \subseteq g \circ d \circ h^{nv}.$$

Then (g, h) is a *strong precode homomorphism* from $\mathcal{P}$ to $\widehat{\mathcal{P}}$.

Strong precode epimorphism is defined the obvious way.

Definition 8A4. A precode homomorphism (g, h) from $\mathcal{P}$ to $\widehat{\mathcal{P}}$ is called a *precode isomorphism* if (g^{nv}, h^{nv}) is a precode homomorphism from $\widehat{\mathcal{P}}$ to $\mathcal{P}$.

This amounts to saying that (g, h) is a relation isomorphism from $(\mathbb{PA}, \mathbb{CO}, e)$ to $(\widehat{\mathbb{PA}}, \widehat{\mathbb{CO}}, \hat{e})$ and that (h, g) is a relation isomorphism from $(\mathbb{CO}, \mathbb{PA}, d)$ to $(\widehat{\mathbb{CO}}, \widehat{\mathbb{PA}}, \hat{d})$. And this, in turn, is equivalent to the stipulation that $(g(\pi), h(\kappa)) \in \hat{e}$ if and only if $(\pi, \kappa) \in e$, and similarly for $\hat{d}$ and d.

As in Proposition 7A5 above, we easily see that the natural definition of *strong precode isomorphism* coincides with the definition of precode isomorphism.

The precode homomorphic image of a precode is, of course, a precode. However, the precode homomorphic image of a code (even under a strong precode homomorphism) is not necessarily a code.

Example 8A5. *The image of a code is not always a code.* Let

$$\mathbb{PA} = \{\, 1\, ,\, 2\,\}, \qquad \mathbb{CO} = \{\, 3\, ,\, 4\,\},$$
$$\mathbf{e} = \{\,(1,3)\,\}, \qquad \mathbf{d} = \{\,(4,2)\,\}.$$

In this case $\mathbf{d} \circ \mathbf{e} = \emptyset$, whence $\mathcal{P}$ is a code. Let

$$\widehat{\mathbb{PA}} = \{\, 5\, ,\, 6\,\}, \qquad \widehat{\mathbb{CO}} = \{\, 7\,\},$$
$$\hat{\mathbf{e}} = \{\,(5,7)\,\}, \qquad \hat{\mathbf{d}} = \{\,(7,6)\,\}.$$

Then $\hat{\mathbf{d}} \circ \hat{\mathbf{e}} = \{\,(5,6)\,\} \not\subseteq \mathbf{diag}(\mathbb{PA}^2)$. Hence $\widehat{\mathcal{P}}$ is not a code. Let

$$\{\,(1,5)\, ,\, (2,6)\,\} = \mathbf{g} : \mathbb{PA} \to \widehat{\mathbb{PA}}$$
$$\{\,(3,7)\, ,\, (4,7)\,\} = \mathbf{h} : \mathbb{CO} \to \widehat{\mathbb{CO}}.$$

Then

$$\hat{\mathbf{e}} = \mathbf{h} \circ \mathbf{e} \circ \mathbf{g}^{nv} = \{\,(5,7)\,\},$$
$$\hat{\mathbf{d}} = \mathbf{g} \circ \mathbf{d} \circ \mathbf{h}^{nv} = \{\,(7,6)\,\}.$$

Consequently $(\, \mathbf{g}\, ,\, \mathbf{h}\,)$ is a strong precode homomorphism from $\mathcal{P}$ to $\widehat{\mathcal{P}}$.

It is, however, possible to give a sufficient condition that the precode homomorphic image of a code be a code.

Theorem 8A6. *Let $\mathcal{P}$ be a code. Let $\widehat{\mathcal{P}}$ be a precode. Let the pair $(\, \mathbf{g}\, ,\, \mathbf{h}\,)$ be a precode epimorphism from $\mathcal{P}$ to $\widehat{\mathcal{P}}$ with the two additional properties that*

$$\mathbf{e} \supseteq \mathbf{h}^{nv} \circ \hat{\mathbf{e}} \circ \mathbf{g}, \qquad \mathbf{d} \supseteq \mathbf{g}^{nv} \circ \hat{\mathbf{d}} \circ \mathbf{h}.$$

Then $\widehat{\mathcal{P}}$ is a code.

Remark. The first inclusion above says that every $(\, \mathbf{g}\, ,\, \mathbf{h}\,)$ ancestor of every pair $(\, \hat{\pi}\, ,\, \hat{\kappa}\,)$ belonging to $\hat{\mathbf{e}}$ belongs to $\mathbf{e}$. The second says that every $(\, \mathbf{h}\, ,\, \mathbf{g}\,)$ ancestor of every pair $(\, \hat{\kappa}\, ,\, \hat{\pi}\,)$ belonging to $\hat{\mathbf{d}}$ belongs to $\mathbf{d}$.

Proof. $\mathbf{h}$ is a surjection. Consequently $\mathbf{h} \circ \mathbf{h}^{nv} = \mathbf{i}_{\mathbb{CO}}$. Therefore

$$\mathbf{i}_{\mathbb{PA}} \supseteq \mathbf{d} \circ \mathbf{e}$$
$$\supseteq \mathbf{g}^{nv} \circ \hat{\mathbf{d}} \circ \mathbf{h} \circ \mathbf{h}^{nv} \circ \hat{\mathbf{e}} \circ \mathbf{g}$$
$$\supseteq \mathbf{g}^{nv} \circ \hat{\mathbf{d}} \circ \mathbf{i}_{\widehat{\mathbb{CO}}} \circ \hat{\mathbf{e}} \circ \mathbf{g}$$
$$\supseteq \mathbf{g}^{nv} \circ \hat{\mathbf{d}} \circ \hat{\mathbf{e}} \circ \mathbf{g}.$$

So it follows that

$$\mathbf{g} \circ \mathbf{g}^{nv} \circ \hat{\mathbf{d}} \circ \hat{\mathbf{e}} \circ \mathbf{g} \circ \mathbf{g}^{nv} \subseteq \mathbf{g} \circ \mathbf{i}_{\mathbb{PA}} \circ \mathbf{g}^{nv} = \mathbf{g} \circ \mathbf{g}^{nv}.$$

However $\mathbf{g}$ is a surjection. It follows that $\mathbf{g} \circ \mathbf{g}^{nv} = \mathbf{i}_{\widehat{\mathbb{PA}}}$. But then $\hat{\mathbf{d}} \circ \hat{\mathbf{e}} \subseteq \mathbf{i}_{\widehat{\mathbb{PA}}}$. We are now able to conclude that $\widehat{\mathcal{P}}$ is a code. $\square$

8B Companions and Opposites

Theorem 8B1. *Let* (g, h) *be a precode homomorphism from* $\mathcal{P}$ *to* $\widehat{\mathcal{P}}$. *Then* (g, h) *is a precode homomorphism from* $\mathcal{P}^{pn}$ *to* $(\widehat{\mathcal{P}})^{pn}$.

Proof. By $(\widehat{\mathcal{P}})^{pn}$ we mean

$$\widehat{\mathcal{P}}^{pn} = (\widehat{PA}, \widehat{CO}, \hat{d}^{nv}, \hat{e}^{nv}).$$

Clearly

$$
\begin{aligned}
e^{pn} &= d^{nv} \\
&\subseteq (g^{nv} \circ \hat{d} \circ h)^{nv} \\
&= h^{nv} \circ \hat{d}^{nv} \circ g \\
&= h^{nv} \circ \hat{e}^{pn} \circ g.
\end{aligned}
$$

Similarly $d^{pn} = e^{nv} \subseteq g^{nv} \circ \hat{d}^{pn} \circ h$. $\quad\square$

Proposition 8B2. *Let* (g, h) *be a precode homomorphism from* $\mathcal{P}$ *to* $\widehat{\mathcal{P}}$. *Then* (g, h) *is a precode homomorphism from* $\mathcal{NUB}(\mathcal{P})$ *to* $\mathcal{NUB}(\widehat{\mathcal{P}})$.

Proof.

$$
\begin{aligned}
\hat{c} &= \hat{e} \cap \hat{d}^{nv} \\
&\supseteq (h \circ e \circ g^{nv}) \cap (g \circ d \circ h^{nv})^{nv} \\
&= (h \circ e \circ g^{nv}) \cap (h \circ d^{nv} \circ g^{nv}) \\
&\supseteq h \circ [(e \circ g^{nv}) \cap (d^{nv} \circ g^{nv})] \\
&\supseteq h \circ (e \cap d^{nv}) \circ g^{nv} \\
&= h \circ c \circ g^{nv}
\end{aligned}
$$

Also $\hat{c}^{nv} \supseteq (h \circ c \circ g^{nv})^{nv} = g \circ c^{nv} \circ h^{nv}$. $\quad\square$

Example 8B3. *Precode homomorphism does not always preserve the self-companion property.* Let

$$PA = \widehat{PA} = CO = \widehat{CO} = \{0\},$$

$$d = e = \hat{d} = \emptyset, \qquad\qquad g = h = \hat{e} = \{(0,0)\}.$$

Clearly $\mathcal{P}$ and $\widehat{\mathcal{P}}$ are codes, since $d \circ e = \hat{d} = \emptyset$. Also

$$e = \emptyset \subseteq h^{nv} \circ \hat{e} \circ g, \qquad\qquad d = \emptyset \subseteq g^{nv} \circ \hat{d} \circ h.$$

Consequently (g, h) is a precode homomorphism from $\mathcal{P}$ to $\widehat{\mathcal{P}}$. Also $d = \emptyset = e^{nv}$. Therefore $\mathcal{P}$ is self-companion. But $\hat{d} = \emptyset \neq \{(0,0)\} = \hat{e}^{nv}$. So $\widehat{\mathcal{P}}$ is not self-companion.

Theorem 8B4. *Let* $\mathcal{P}$ *be a self-companion precode, and let* $(\mathbf{g}, \mathbf{h})$ *be a strong precode homomorphism from* $\mathcal{P}$ *to* $\hat{\mathcal{P}}$*. Then* $\hat{\mathcal{P}}$ *is self-companion.*

Proof.

$$\hat{e} = \mathbf{h} \circ e \circ \mathbf{g}^{nv}$$
$$\hat{d} = \mathbf{g} \circ d \circ \mathbf{h}^{nv}$$
$$\hat{d}^{nv} = \mathbf{h} \circ d^{nv} \circ \mathbf{g}^{nv} = \mathbf{h} \circ e \circ \mathbf{g}^{nv} = \hat{e}. \qquad \square$$

Proposition 8B5. *Let* $(\mathbf{g}, \mathbf{h})$ *be a precode homomorphism from* $\mathcal{P}$ *to* $\hat{\mathcal{P}}$*. Then* $(\mathbf{h}, \mathbf{g})$ *is a precode homomorphism from* $\mathcal{P}^{op}$ *to* $\hat{\mathcal{P}}^{op}$*.*

Proof. We need to prove either that both

$$e^{op} \subseteq \mathbf{g}^{nv} \circ \hat{e}^{op} \circ \mathbf{h} \quad \text{and} \quad d^{op} \subseteq \mathbf{h}^{nv} \circ \hat{d}^{op} \circ \mathbf{g},$$

or, equivalently, that both

$$d \subseteq \mathbf{g}^{nv} \circ \hat{d} \circ \mathbf{h} \quad \text{and} \quad e \subseteq \mathbf{h}^{nv} \circ \hat{e} \circ \mathbf{g}.$$

But the latter two statements are true, since $(\mathbf{g}, \mathbf{h})$ is a precode homomorphism. $\square$

Example 9A7 below applies to self-opposite codes. It amounts to a stronger caveat than Example 8B3 in such a context.

8C Quotients of Precodes

Definition 8C1. Let $(\mathbb{PA}, \mathbb{PA}, \mathbf{s})$ and $(\mathbb{CO}, \mathbb{CO}, \mathbf{t})$ be equivalence relations. Then we write

$$\overline{\mathcal{P}} = \mathcal{P} / (\mathbf{s}, \mathbf{t}) = (\overline{\mathbb{PA}}, \overline{\mathbb{CO}}, \bar{e}, \bar{d}),$$

where

$$(\overline{\mathbb{PA}}, \overline{\mathbb{CO}}, \bar{e}) = (\mathbb{PA}, \mathbb{CO}, e) / (\mathbf{s}, \mathbf{t}),$$
$$(\overline{\mathbb{CO}}, \overline{\mathbb{PA}}, \bar{d}) = (\mathbb{CO}, \mathbb{PA}, d) / (\mathbf{t}, \mathbf{s}).$$

And we say that $\overline{\mathcal{P}}$ is the *quotient precode* of $\mathcal{P}$ by the pair $(\mathbf{s}, \mathbf{t})$.

Example 8C2. *The quotient of a code by a pair of equivalence relations is not always a code.* Let

$$\mathbb{PA} = \{1, 2\}, \qquad \mathbb{CO} = \{3, 4\},$$
$$e = \{(1,3)\}, \qquad d = \{(4,2)\},$$

$$s = \mathbf{diag}(\mathbb{PA}^2) = \{(1,1), (2,2)\},$$
$$t = \mathbb{CO}^2.$$

It follows that

$$\overline{\mathbb{PA}} = \{s(\{1\}), s(\{2\})\} = \{\{1\}, \{2\}\}$$
$$\overline{\mathbb{CO}} = \{t(\{3\}), t(\{4\})\} = \{\{3,4\}\}$$
$$\bar{e} = \{(\{1\}, \{3,4\})\}$$
$$\bar{d} = \{(\{3,4\}, \{2\})\}$$
$$d \circ e = \emptyset \subseteq \mathbf{diag}(\mathbb{PA}^2)$$
$$\bar{d} \circ \bar{e} = \{(\{1\}, \{2\})\} \not\subseteq \mathbf{diag}(\overline{\mathbb{PA}}^2)$$

Consequently $\mathcal{P}$ is a code. But $\overline{\mathcal{P}} = \mathcal{P}/(s, t)$ is not a code.

Theorem 8C3. *The pair* (f_s, f_t) *is a strong precode epimorphism from* $\mathcal{P}$ *to* $\overline{\mathcal{P}}$, *where*

$$f_s : \mathbb{PA} \rightarrow \mathbb{PA}/s$$

is the canonical map, and

$$f_t : \mathbb{CO} \rightarrow \mathbb{CO}/t$$

is the canonical map.

Before proving Proposition 8C5 below, which gives a necessary and sufficient condition for a quotient to be a code, we need a technical lemma.

Lemma 8C4. *Suppose that* $(\mathbb{PA}, \mathbb{PA}, s)$ *and* $(\mathbb{CO}, \mathbb{CO}, t)$ *are equivalence relations Let*

$$\overline{\mathcal{P}} = \mathcal{P}/(s, t).$$

Let f_s *be the canonical map*

$$f_s : \mathbb{PA} \rightarrow \overline{\mathbb{PA}},$$

and let f_t *be the canonical map*

$$f_t : \mathbb{CO} \rightarrow \overline{\mathbb{CO}}.$$

Then

$$\bar{d} \circ \bar{e} = f_s \circ (d \circ t \circ e) \circ f_s^{nv}.$$

Proof. We can factor s as $s = f_s^{nv} \circ f_s$ and t as $t = h^{nv} \circ f_t$. Since (f_s, f_t) is a strong precode homomorphism, it follows that

$$\bar{d} \circ \bar{e} = (f_s \circ d \circ f_t^{nv}) \circ (f_t \circ e \circ f_s^{nv})$$

$$= (\mathbf{f_s} \circ \mathbf{d}) \circ (\mathbf{f_t}^{nv} \circ \mathbf{f_t}) \circ (\mathbf{e} \circ \mathbf{f_s}^{nv})$$
$$= (\mathbf{f_s} \circ \mathbf{d}) \circ \mathbf{t} \circ (\mathbf{e} \circ \mathbf{f_s}^{nv})$$
$$= \mathbf{f_s} \circ (\mathbf{d} \circ \mathbf{t} \circ \mathbf{e}) \circ \mathbf{f_s}^{nv} \qquad \square$$

Proposition 8C5. $\mathcal{P} / (\mathbf{s} , \mathbf{t})$ *is a code if and only if*

$$\mathbf{s} \supseteq \mathbf{d} \circ \mathbf{t} \circ \mathbf{e}.$$

Proof. If $\mathbf{s} \supseteq \mathbf{d} \circ \mathbf{t} \circ \mathbf{e}$, then it follows from Lemma 8C4 that

$$\bar{\mathbf{d}} \circ \bar{\mathbf{e}} \subseteq \mathbf{f_s} \circ \mathbf{s} \circ \mathbf{f_s}^{nv}$$
$$= (\mathbf{f_s} \circ \mathbf{f_s}^{nv}) \circ (\mathbf{f_s} \circ \mathbf{f_s}^{nv})$$
$$= \mathbf{i}_{\overline{\mathrm{PA}}} \circ \mathbf{i}_{\overline{\mathrm{PA}}}$$
$$= \mathbf{i}_{\overline{\mathrm{PA}}}$$

since $\mathbf{f_s}$ is a precode epimorphism. Therefore $\overline{\mathcal{P}}$ is a code. On the other hand, suppose that $\overline{\mathcal{P}}$ is a code. Then it follows from Lemma 8C4 that

$$\mathbf{i}_{\overline{\mathrm{PA}}} \supseteq \bar{\mathbf{d}} \circ \bar{\mathbf{e}} = \mathbf{f_s} \circ (\mathbf{d} \circ \mathbf{t} \circ \mathbf{e}) \circ \mathbf{f_s}^{nv}.$$

Therefore

$$\mathbf{f_s}^{nv} \circ \mathbf{i}_{\overline{\mathrm{PA}}} \circ \mathbf{f_s} \supseteq (\mathbf{f_s}^{nv} \circ \mathbf{f_s}) \circ (\mathbf{d} \circ \mathbf{t} \circ \mathbf{e}) \circ (\mathbf{f_s}^{nv} \circ \mathbf{f_s})$$
$$\mathbf{f_s}^{nv} \circ \mathbf{f_s} \supseteq (\mathbf{f_s}^{nv} \circ \mathbf{f_s}) \circ (\mathbf{d} \circ \mathbf{t} \circ \mathbf{e}) \circ (\mathbf{f_s}^{nv} \circ \mathbf{f_s})$$
$$\mathbf{s} \supseteq \mathbf{s} \circ (\mathbf{d} \circ \mathbf{t} \circ \mathbf{e}) \circ \mathbf{s}$$
$$\mathbf{s} \supseteq \mathbf{i}_{\mathrm{PA}} \circ (\mathbf{d} \circ \mathbf{t} \circ \mathbf{e}) \circ \mathbf{i}_{\mathrm{PA}}$$
$$= \mathbf{d} \circ \mathbf{t} \circ \mathbf{e} \qquad \square$$

We note that Proposition 8C5 does not assume that $\mathcal{P}$ is a code.

9 Isomorphism of Precodes

9A Definitions and Basic Results

Proposition 9A1. *Precode isomorphism is an equivalence relation on precodes from* $\mathbb{PA}$ *to* $\mathbb{CO}$.

Theorem 9A2. *Let* $\mathcal{P}$ *be a precode. There is a precode* $\widehat{\mathcal{P}}$ *which is precode isomorphic to* $\mathcal{P}$, *and has the property that*

$$\widehat{\mathbb{PA}} \cap \widehat{\mathbb{CO}} = \emptyset.$$

Proof. We use the standard trick which replaces sets by disjoint sets. Let

$$\widehat{PA} = PA \times \{0\}, \qquad \widehat{CO} = CO \times \{1\},$$
$$\hat{e} = \{((\pi, 0), (\kappa, 1)) : (\pi, \kappa) \in e\},$$
$$\hat{d} = \{((\kappa, 1), (\pi, 0)) : (\kappa, \pi) \in d\}. \square$$

Definition 9A3. A precode $\mathcal{P}$ is *separated* if $PA \cap CO = \emptyset$. If $\widehat{\mathcal{P}}$ is a separated precode which is precode isomorphic to $\mathcal{P}$, then $\widehat{\mathcal{P}}$ is called a *separation* of $\mathcal{P}$.

So Theorem 9A2 says that every precode has a separation.

Definition 9A4. An *intrinsic* property of a precode is a property preserved by precode isomorphism.

Clearly the notions – introduced in [BLA98] – of one-way precode, one-way code, self-companion precode, self-companion code, janiform precode, and janiform code are intrinsic. On the other hand, self-opposite is not an intrinsic notion.

Example 9A5. *Precode isomorphism does not always preserve the self-opposite property.* Let

$$PA = CO = \{1, 2\},$$
$$\widehat{PA} = \{3, 4\}, \qquad \widehat{CO} = \{5, 6\},$$

$$e = d = \{(1,2), (2,1)\}, \qquad \hat{d}^{nv} = \hat{e} = \{(3,5), (4,6)\},$$
$$g = \{(1,3), (2,4)\}, \qquad h = \{(1,6), (2,5)\}.$$

Then (g, h) is clearly a precode isomorphism from the code $\mathcal{P}$ to the code $\widehat{\mathcal{P}}$. And $\mathcal{P}$ is self-opposite, but $\widehat{\mathcal{P}}$ is not.

9B Isomorphism Theorems for Precodes

Theorem 9B1. Let (g, h) be a precode homomorphism from $\mathcal{P}$ to $\widehat{\mathcal{P}}$. Let $(s, t) = (g^{nv} \circ g, h^{nv} \circ h)$ be its kernel. Let $\overline{\mathcal{P}} = \mathcal{P}/(s, t)$. Then the following three statements hold.

1) If $\widehat{\mathcal{P}}$ is a code, then $\overline{\mathcal{P}}$ is also a code.
2) The natural map pair $n = (g \circ f_s, h \circ f_t)$ is a precode homomorphism from $\overline{\mathcal{P}}$ to $\widehat{\mathcal{P}}$.

3) *If* (**g** , **h**) *is a strong precode epimorphism, then* **n** *is a precode isomorphism from* $\overline{\mathcal{P}}$ *to* $\widehat{\mathcal{P}}$.

Proof. The only thing necessary to show is Part 1) above. To this end, note that

$$
\begin{aligned}
\mathbf{d} \circ \mathbf{t} \circ \mathbf{e} &= \mathbf{d} \circ \mathbf{h}^{nv} \circ \mathbf{h} \circ \mathbf{e} \\
&\subseteq (\mathbf{g}^{nv} \circ \hat{\mathbf{d}} \circ \mathbf{h}) \circ \mathbf{h}^{nv} \circ \mathbf{h} \circ (\mathbf{h}^{nv} \circ \hat{\mathbf{e}} \circ \mathbf{g}) \\
&= \mathbf{g}^{nv} \circ \hat{\mathbf{d}} \circ (\mathbf{h} \circ \mathbf{h}^{nv}) \circ (\mathbf{h} \circ \mathbf{h}^{nv}) \circ \hat{\mathbf{e}} \circ \mathbf{g} \\
&\subseteq \mathbf{g}^{nv} \circ \hat{\mathbf{d}} \circ \mathbf{i}_{\widehat{\mathrm{CO}}} \circ \mathbf{i}_{\widehat{\mathrm{CO}}} \circ \hat{\mathbf{e}} \circ \mathbf{g} \\
&= \mathbf{g}^{nv} \circ \hat{\mathbf{d}} \circ \hat{\mathbf{e}} \circ \mathbf{g} \\
&\subseteq \mathbf{g}^{nv} \circ \mathbf{g} \\
&= \mathbf{s}.
\end{aligned}
$$

So, according to Proposition 8C5, $\overline{\mathcal{P}}$ is a code.   □

Analogously to Theorems 7B2 and 7B3 above, the next two theorems about precode homomorphisms amount to what general algebra textbooks would call the first and second isomorphism theorems for precodes. And they follow directly from Theorems 7B2 and 7B3.

Theorem 9B2. *Let* $\widehat{\mathcal{P}}$ *be a subprecode of a precode* $\mathcal{P}$. *Let*

(PA , PA , **s**)   *and*   (CO , CO , **t**)   *be equivalence relations. Let* $\mathbf{x} = \mathbf{s} \cap \widehat{\mathrm{PA}}^{2}$, *and* $\mathbf{y} = \mathbf{t} \cap \mathrm{CO}^{2}$. *Then*

($\widehat{\mathrm{PA}}$, $\widehat{\mathrm{PA}}$, **x**) *and*   ($\widehat{\mathrm{CO}}$, $\widehat{\mathrm{CO}}$, **y**)

are equivalence relations. Define a new precode $\mathcal{Q}$ *equal to*

($\mathbf{s}(\widehat{\mathrm{PA}})$, $\mathbf{t}(\widehat{\mathrm{CO}})$, $\mathbf{e} \cap [\, \mathbf{s}(\widehat{\mathrm{PA}}) \times \mathbf{t}(\widehat{\mathrm{CO}}) \,]$, $\mathbf{d} \cap [\, \mathbf{t}(\widehat{\mathrm{CO}}) \times \mathbf{s}(\widehat{\mathrm{PA}}) \,]$)

Then there is a natural map pair, **n** $=$ (**g** , **h**) *from* $\widehat{\mathcal{P}} / (\mathbf{x} , \mathbf{y})$ *to* $\mathcal{Q} / (\mathbf{s} , \mathbf{t})$. *Here* **g** , **h** *are bijections, and* (**g** , **h**) *is a precode homomorphism. Moreover,* (**g** , **h**) *is a precode isomorphism if and only if*

$$\mathbf{e} \cap [\, \mathbf{s}(\widehat{\mathrm{PA}}) \times \mathbf{t}(\widehat{\mathrm{CO}}) \,] \subseteq \mathbf{t} \circ \hat{\mathbf{e}} \circ \mathbf{s}$$

and

$$\mathbf{d} \cap [\, \mathbf{t}(\widehat{\mathrm{CO}}) \times \mathbf{s}(\widehat{\mathrm{PA}}) \,] \subseteq \mathbf{s} \circ \hat{\mathbf{d}} \circ \mathbf{t}.$$

Theorem 9B3. *Let* $\mathcal{P}$ *be a code. Let*

(PA , PA , **s**),   (PA , PA , **u**) ,
(CO , CO , **t**),   (CO , CO , **v**)

be equivalence relations such that $\mathbf{s} \subseteq \mathbf{u}$, and $\mathbf{t} \subseteq \mathbf{v}$. Then there is a natural map pair $\mathbf{n} = (\mathbf{g}, \mathbf{h})$ from

$$[\mathcal{P} / (\mathbf{s}, \mathbf{t})] / (\mathbf{u} / \mathbf{s}, \mathbf{t} / \mathbf{v})$$

to

$$\mathcal{P} / (\mathbf{u}, \mathbf{v}),$$

and $\mathbf{n} = (\mathbf{g}, \mathbf{h})$ is a precode isomorphism.

9C Products of Precodes

Definition 9C1. The (*Cartesian*) product $\mathcal{P} = \overline{\mathcal{P}} \times \widehat{\mathcal{P}}$ of the precodes $\overline{\mathcal{P}}$ and $\widehat{\mathcal{P}}$ is the precode

$$\begin{aligned}
\mathcal{P} &= (\mathbb{PA}, \mathbb{CO}, \mathbf{e}, \mathbf{d}) \\
&= (\overline{\mathbb{PA}} \times \widehat{\mathbb{PA}}, \overline{\mathbb{CO}} \times \widehat{\mathbb{CO}}, \mathbf{e}, \mathbf{d})
\end{aligned}$$

from $\mathbb{PA} = \overline{\mathbb{PA}} \times \widehat{\mathbb{PA}}$ to $\mathbb{CO} = \overline{\mathbb{CO}} \times \widehat{\mathbb{CO}}$ defined by setting

$$\begin{aligned}
\mathbf{e} = \{\, (\,(\bar{\pi}, \hat{\pi})\,, (\bar{\kappa}, \hat{\kappa})\,) \in (\overline{\mathbb{PA}} \times \widehat{\mathbb{PA}}) \times (\overline{\mathbb{CO}} \times \widehat{\mathbb{CO}}) : \\
(\bar{\pi}, \bar{\kappa}) \in \bar{\mathbf{e}} \text{ and } (\hat{\pi}, \hat{\kappa}) \in \hat{\mathbf{e}}\,\},
\end{aligned}$$

$$\begin{aligned}
\mathbf{d} = \{\, (\,(\bar{\kappa}, \hat{\kappa})\,, (\bar{\pi}, \hat{\pi})\,) \in (\overline{\mathbb{CO}} \times \widehat{\mathbb{CO}}) \times (\overline{\mathbb{PA}} \times \widehat{\mathbb{PA}}) : \\
(\bar{\kappa}, \bar{\pi}) \in \bar{\mathbf{d}} \text{ and } (\hat{\kappa}, \hat{\pi}) \in \hat{\mathbf{d}}\,\}.
\end{aligned}$$

Proposition 9C2. *The (Cartesian) product of two codes is a code.*

Theorem 9C3. *Let* $\mathcal{P} = \overline{\mathcal{P}} \times \widehat{\mathcal{P}}$. *Let* $(\mathbf{g}, \mathbf{h}) : \mathcal{P} \to \overline{\mathcal{P}}$ *be defined by setting*

$$\begin{aligned}
\mathbf{g}(\,(\bar{\pi}, \hat{\pi})\,) &= \bar{\pi} \text{ for every } (\bar{\pi}, \hat{\pi}) \in \overline{\mathbb{PA}} \times \widehat{\mathbb{PA}}, \\
\mathbf{h}(\,(\bar{\kappa}, \hat{\kappa})\,) &= \bar{\kappa} \text{ for every } (\bar{\kappa}, \hat{\kappa}) \in \overline{\mathbb{CO}} \times \widehat{\mathbb{CO}}.
\end{aligned}$$

In other words $(\mathbf{g}, \mathbf{h})$ *is a projection of* $\mathcal{P}$ *onto* $\overline{\mathcal{P}}$. *Under these hypotheses it follows that:*

1) $(\mathbf{g}, \mathbf{h})$ *is a precode homomorphism from* $\mathcal{P}$ *to* $\overline{\mathcal{P}}$;
2) *If* $\hat{\mathbf{e}} \neq \emptyset$ *and* $\hat{\mathbf{d}} \neq \emptyset$, *then* $(\mathbf{g}, \mathbf{h})$ *is a strong precode homomorphism.*

Proof. To prove 1), it suffices to prove that

$$\mathbf{e} \subseteq \mathbf{h}^{nv} \circ \bar{\mathbf{e}} \circ \mathbf{g}, \quad \text{and} \quad \mathbf{d} \subseteq \mathbf{g}^{nv} \circ \bar{\mathbf{d}} \circ \mathbf{h}.$$

We will prove only the first inclusion. The other is similar. Let

$$(\,(\bar{\pi}, \hat{\pi})\,, (\bar{\kappa}, \hat{\kappa})\,) \in \mathbf{e}.$$

Then
$$(\bar{\pi} , \bar{\kappa}) \in \bar{e}.$$

Since
$$((\bar{\pi} , \hat{\pi}) , \bar{\pi}) \in \mathbf{g}, \text{ and} \qquad (\bar{\kappa} , (\bar{\kappa} , \hat{\kappa})) \in \mathbf{h}^{nv},$$

we then find that
$$((\bar{\pi} , \hat{\pi}) , (\bar{\kappa} , \hat{\kappa})) \in \mathbf{h}^{nv} \circ \mathbf{e} \circ \mathbf{g}.$$

To prove 2), we also need to show that
$$\bar{e} \subseteq \mathbf{h} \circ \mathbf{e} \circ \mathbf{g}^{nv}, \text{ and} \qquad \bar{d} \subseteq \mathbf{g}^{nv} \circ \mathbf{d} \circ \mathbf{h}.$$

Since $\hat{e}$ is not empty, choose some
$$(\hat{\pi} , \hat{\kappa}) \in \hat{e}.$$

If
$$(\bar{\pi} , \bar{\kappa}) \in \bar{e}$$

then
$$((\bar{\pi} , \hat{\pi}) , (\bar{\kappa} , \hat{\kappa})) \in \mathbf{e},$$

whence $(\bar{\pi} , \bar{\kappa}) \in \mathbf{h} \circ \mathbf{e} \circ \mathbf{g}^{nv}.$ □

Remark: If
$$\hat{e} = \emptyset \text{ and } \bar{e} \neq \emptyset,$$

or if
$$\hat{d} = \emptyset \text{ and } \bar{d} \neq \emptyset,$$

then the precode homomorphism is not strong.

A precode homomorphic image of a product precode determined in a natural way by a "kernel" corresponding to one of its factors amounts to the other factor, except in the degenerate cases noted immediately above.

Theorems 9B1 and 9C3 have the following

Corollary 9C4. *Let*

$$(\overline{PA} \times \widehat{PA} , \overline{PA} \times \widehat{PA} , s) ,$$
$$(\overline{CO} \times \widehat{CO} , \overline{CO} \times \widehat{CO} , t)$$

be the relations defined by stipulating that the ordered pair of pairs

$$((\bar{\psi} , \hat{\psi}) , (\bar{\pi} , \hat{\pi}))$$

belongs to **s** if $\bar{\psi} = \bar{\pi}$. And similarly **t**. Then these two relations are equivalence relations. It follows that $[\,\overline{\mathcal{P}} \times \widehat{\mathcal{P}}\,]\,/\,(\,s\,,\,t\,)$ is precode isomorphic to $\overline{\mathcal{P}}$ unless $\hat{e} = \emptyset$ or $\hat{d} = \emptyset$.

Clearly, the pair $(\,s\,,\,t\,)$ constitutes the kernel of the projection precode homomorphism pair $(\,g\,,\,h\,)$ in Theorem 9C3.

10 Discussion

Precode homomorphisms of codes obviously do a great deal of what mathematicians expect of them. We intend to show, at some length, elsewhere that both the designers and the attackers of cryptosystems, as well as the designers of error control codes, frequently employ products, quotients and precode homomorphisms without calling them by these names. Conscious use of the general properties of such structures may enhance such efforts.

It is hard to avoid wondering whether the related notions of quotients and precode homomorphisms of codes lead still farther on, and whether there is some sort of Jordan/Hölder/Schreier theory for some sort of solvable codes.

Bob Blakley brought Catherine Meadows' paper [MEA98] to our attention. Lidong Chen's extremely early insight into how homomorphism must behave toward companionship and opposition decisively influenced Section 8B above. Hao Zheng provided the graphics in Chapter 11 below. We are grateful to them.

11 Visual Appendices

As in [BLA98], we have tried to provide mathematical graphics in the spirit of [TUF83; TUF90; TUF96]. They are intended to lay bare the structural ideas behind Theorems 6C6, 7B1, 7B2 and 7B3, and therefore also 9B1, 9B2 and 9B3.

The infinite set $\mathbb{G}$ is a polygonal patch which contains infinitely many members. Every member is a point.

A coarse finite partition $\mathbb{G}/\mathbf{u}$ of the infinite set $\mathbb{G}$. The partition $\mathbb{G}/\mathbf{u}$ corresponds to the equivalence relation $(\mathbb{G}, \mathbb{G}, \mathbf{u})$, and consists of 5 infinite cells (vertical stripes) whose union is $\mathbb{G}$.

A fine finite partition $\mathbb{G}/\mathbf{s}$ of $\mathbb{G}$. The partition $\mathbb{G}/\mathbf{s}$ corresponds to the equivalence relation $(\mathbb{G}, \mathbb{G}, \mathbf{s})$, and consists of 14 infinite cells (rectangular patches) whose union is $\mathbb{G}$. Every one of the 14 cells of $\mathbb{G}/\mathbf{s}$ is an infinite subset of one of the 5 cells of $\mathbb{G}/\mathbf{u}$.

A coarse finite partition $(\mathbb{G}/\mathbf{s}) \,/\, (\mathbf{u}/\mathbf{s})$ of the finite 14–member set $\mathbb{G}/\mathbf{s}$. The partition $(\mathbb{G}/\mathbf{s}) \,/\, (\mathbf{u}/\mathbf{s})$ corresponds to the equivalence relation $(\mathbb{G}/\mathbf{s}, \mathbb{G}/\mathbf{s}, \mathbf{u}/\mathbf{s})$, and consists of 5 finite cells (vertical stripes). No cell of $(\mathbb{G}/\mathbf{s}) \,/\, (\mathbf{u}/\mathbf{s})$ contains more than 4 members, and every one of its members is a cell belonging to $\mathbb{G}/\mathbf{s}$.

Appendix 6C6. The relationship between the 5–cell partition $\mathbb{G}/\mathbf{u}$ of the infinite set $\mathbb{G}$ and the 5–cell partition $(\mathbb{G}/\mathbf{s}) \,/\, (\mathbf{u}/\mathbf{s})$ of the finite set $\mathbb{G}/\mathbf{s}$ is obvious. There is a natural bijection between the cells of $\mathbb{G}/\mathbf{u}$ and the cells of $(\mathbb{G}/\mathbf{s}) \,/\, (\mathbf{u}/\mathbf{s})$.

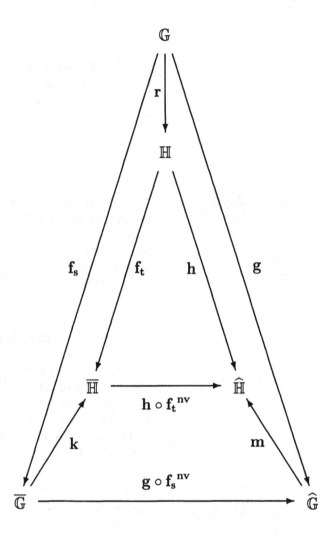

Appendix 7B1. The prismatic diagram which illuminates Theorem 7B1 and its proof.

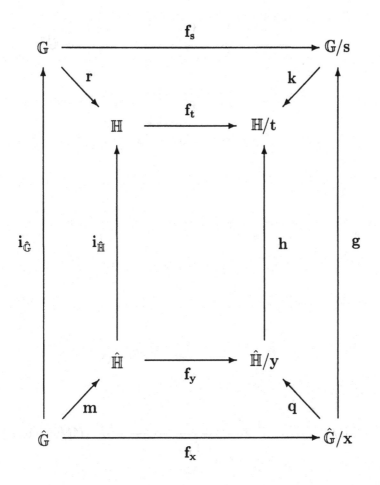

Appendix 7B2. The cubic diagram which illuminates Theorem 7B2 and its proof.

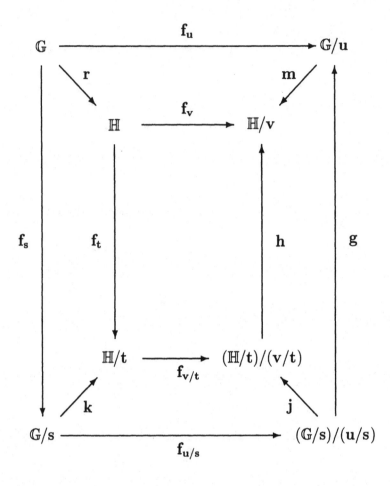

Appendix 7B3. The cubic diagram which illuminates Theorem 7B3 and its proof.

References

[BLA89] G.R. Blakley and Catherine Meadows, *Information theory without the finiteness assumption, III: Data compression and codes whose rates exceed unity*, in H.J. Beker and E.C. Piper (Editors), *Cryptography and Coding*, Proceedings of the IMA Conference on Cryptography and Coding at the Royal Agricultural College, Cirencester, December, 1986, Clarendon Press, Oxford (1989), pp. 67-93.

[BLA95] G.R. Blakley, *Management of secret information: An abstract theory of codes, some implications for PKCs and secret sharing, and homomorphisms of relations and codes*, in *Proceedings, JAIST International Forum on Multimedia and Information Security*, Japan Advanced Institute of Science and Technology, Tatsunokuchi, Ishikawa, Japan, 1-2 November (1995), pp. 55-83.

[BLA96] G.R. Blakley and I. Borosh, *Codes*, in *Pragocrypt, '96, Part 1, Proceedings of the First International Conference on the Theory and Applications of Cryptography, Pragocrypt '96*, CTU Publishing House, Zikova 4, Prague 6, Czech Republic (1996), pp. 253-271.

[BLA98] G.R. Blakley and I. Borosh, *A general theory of codes, I: Basic concepts*, in *Contributions to General Algebra, 10*, Proceedings of the Klagenfurt Conference on General Algebra, May 29-June 1, 1997, (1998) in press.

[GOD68] R. Godement, *Algebra*, Hermann, Paris, and Houghton Mifflin, New York (1968).

[GRA68] G. Grätzer, *Universal Algebra*, Van Nostrand, Princeton, New Jersey (1968).

[KAH67] D. Kahn, *The Codebreakers*, Macmillan, New York (1967).

[KOL56] A.N. Kolmogorov, *On the Shannon Theory of Information in the Case of Continuous Signals*, IEEE Transactions on Information Theory, vol. IT-2 (1956), pp. 102-108, Reprinted as pages 238-244 in D. Slepian (Editor) *Key Papers in the Development of Information Theory*, IEEE Press, New York (1974).

[MAL73] A.I. Mal'cev, *Algebraic Systems*, Springer-Verlag, New York (1973).

[MEA98] Catherine Meadows, *Three paradigms in computer security*, Proceedings of the 1997 New Security Paradigms Workshop, ACM (1998), in press.

[PAL66] H. Paley and P.M. Weichsel, *A First Course in Abstract Algebra*, Holt, Rinehart and Winston, New York (1966).

[TUF83] E.N. Tufte, *The Visual Display of Quantitative Information*, Graphics Press, Cheshire, Connecticut (1983).

[TUF90] E.N. Tufte, *Envisioning Information, Graphics Press*, Cheshire, Connecticut (1990).

[TUF96] E.N. Tufte, *Visual Explanations: Images and Quantities, Evidence and Narrative*, Graphics Press, Cheshire Connecticut (1996).

Improving the Higher Order Differential Attack and Cryptanalysis of the $\mathcal{KN}$ Cipher

Takeshi Shimoyama*, Shiho Moriai*, Toshinobu Kaneko*[†]

{shimo,shiho,toshi}@yokohama.tao.or.jp

* Telecommunications Advancement Organization of Japan
1-1-32 Shin'urashima-cho, Kanagawa-ku, Yokohama, 221 Japan
[†] Science University of Tokyo
2641 Yamazaki, Noda-shi, Chiba, 278 Japan

Abstract. Since the proposal of differential cryptanalysis and linear cryptanalysis in 1991 and 1993, respectively, the resistance to these cryptanalyses have been studied for many cryptosystems. Moreover, some block ciphers with provable security against differential and linear cryptanalysis have been proposed. One of them is the $\mathcal{KN}$ cipher proposed by Knudsen and Nyberg. The $\mathcal{KN}$ cipher is a prototype cipher with provable security against ordinary differential cryptanalysis, and has been proved to be secure against linear cryptanalysis, too. Recently a new method of attacking block ciphers, the higher order differential attack, was proposed, and Jakobsen and Knudsen showed that the $\mathcal{KN}$ cipher can be attacked by this method in FSE4. In this paper, we improve this attack to reduce both of the required chosen plaintexts and running time, and apply it to the cryptanalysis of the $\mathcal{KN}$ cipher. We show that, for the attacking of the $\mathcal{KN}$ cipher with 6 rounds, the number of required chosen plaintexts can be reduced by half and running time reduced from 2^{41} to 2^{14}, and that all round keys can be derived in only 0.02 seconds on a Sun Ultra 1 (UltraSPARC 170MHz).

1 Introduction

In [NK95] Knudsen and Nyberg demonstrated how to construct a cipher which is provably secure against differential cryptanalysis[BS91]. The shown cipher was a Feistel cipher using a cubing function $\mathcal{X}^3$ in $GF(2^{33})$ in the round function. In [JK97] Jakobsen and Knudsen called it the $\mathcal{KN}$ cipher, and in this paper we follow it. The $\mathcal{KN}$ cipher is defined to be used with at least 6 rounds and since $\mathcal{X}^3$ is differentially 2-uniform, it has been proved that this yields a provably secure cipher against differential cryptanalysis. Moreover, the $\mathcal{KN}$ cipher has been proved to be secure against linear cryptanalysis[M93] in [N94].

However, a block cipher with provable security against differential and linear cryptanalysis does not guarantee its security against other attacks. In [JK97] Jakobsen and Knudsen showed that the $\mathcal{KN}$ cipher can be broken by a new method of attack, i.e. the higher order differential attack, with much less complexity than differential and linear attacks. The differential (or linear) attack of the $\mathcal{KN}$ cipher with 6 rounds requires more than 2^{60} pairs of chosen (or known) plaintexts and ciphertexts. On the other hand, the higher order differential attack needs only 2^9 pairs (or only 2^5 pairs, which requires more complexity) of chosen plaintexts and ciphertexts.

Based on the notion of higher order derivatives introduced by Lai[L94], Knudsen proposed a higher order differential attack in [K95]. It is a chosen plaintext attack and useful for attacking ciphers with low degree. For the $\mathcal{KN}$ cipher, since the degree of the round function is 2, the degrees of the $\mathcal{KN}$ cipher with 3, 4, and 5 rounds are 8, 16, and 32, respectively. Jakobsen and Knudsen's strategy for attacking the $\mathcal{KN}$ cipher in [JK97] is as follows.

(1) Using the proposition that if a polynomial has degree m, the $(m+1)$-th order differential of it is 0, set up the equations with respect to the keys.
(2) Check whether the equations hold for every possible key exhaustively to find the right key.

On the other hand, our strategy described in this paper is as follows.

(1') Using the proposition that if a polynomial has degree m, the m-th order differential of it is constant, set up the equations with respect to the keys.
(2') Solve the equations algebraically.

Compared with (1), the required number of chosen plaintexts and ciphertexts in (1') is reduced to half. Moreover, since the equations in step (1') can be proven to be linear equations, we also reduce the required complexity in step (2').

By the procedure above, we can determine the last-round key of the $\mathcal{KN}$ cipher with n rounds. Once the last-round key is found, it is easy to determine the remaining keys: compute the output after $(n-1)$-th round using the last-round key, and the $(n-1)$-th round key is also found similarly. Repeat this procedure until the 1-st round key is determined.

We made computer experiments to actually break the $\mathcal{KN}$ cipher. We show that, for the attacking of the $\mathcal{KN}$ cipher with 6 rounds, the number of required chosen plaintexts can be reduced by half and running time reduced from 2^{41} to 2^{14}. We succeed in deriving all round keys of the $\mathcal{KN}$ cipher with 6 rounds with 2^8 chosen plaintexts and ciphertexts in only 0.02 seconds on a Sun Ultra 1 (UltraSPARC 170MHz). On the same computer the $\mathcal{KN}$ cipher with 7 rounds was broken with 2^{16} chosen plaintexts and ciphertexts in only 6.07 seconds.

This paper is organized as follows. In Section 2 we give some definitions used in this paper, and Section 3 specifies the algorithm of the $\mathcal{KN}$ cipher. In Section 4 we present the general theory of the higher order differential attack. The higher order differential attack of the $\mathcal{KN}$ cipher by Jakobsen et al.[JK97] is described in Section 5.1, and our attack is given in Section 5.2 including our improvements and the required number of texts and computation complexity. In Section 6 we present the details of our computer experiments, and conclude in Section 7.

2   Preliminary

In this section, we introduce the notations used in this paper.

Definition 1 *Let $GF(2)^n$ be the n-dimensional vector space over $GF(2)$. We denote addition on $GF(2)^n$ by $+$. For $a, b \in GF(2)^n$, the inner product of a and b is denoted by $a \cdot b$. We define $V^{(m)}[a_m, ..., a_1]$ as the m-dimensional subspace of $GF(2)^n$ which is the set of all 2^m possible linear combinations of $a_m, ..., a_1$, where each a_i is in $GF(2)^n$ and linearly independent. We often use $V^{(m)}$ for $V^{(m)}[a_m, ..., a_1]$ when $[a_m, ..., a_1]$ is understood.*

Definition 2 *Let $GF(2)[X]$ be the polynomial ring of $X = \{x_{n-1}, ..., x_0\}$ over $GF(2)$. Let B be the ideal of $GF(2)[X]$ generated by $x_{n-1}^2 + x_{n-1}, ..., x_0^2 + x_0 \in GF(2)[X]$. We define $R[X]$ as the quotient ring of $GF(2)[X]$ modulo B, i.e. $GF(2)[X]/B$. We call $R[X]$ the boolean polynomial ring of X, and call each element of it a boolean polynomial. Since element f in $R[X]$ is regarded as function $f: GF(2)^n \to GF(2)$, it is also called a boolean polynomial function or a boolean function.*

Definition 3 *Let X and K be sets of variables. We define $R[X, K]$ as a boolean polynomial ring of $X \cup K$, i.e. $R[X \cup K]$. For a element $f(X, K) \in R[X, K]$, we define $\deg_X(f)$ as the degree of a multi-variable boolean polynomial f of X whose coefficients are in $R[K]$. We often use $\deg(f)$ as a short term for $\deg_X(f)$.*

Definition 4 *We call a vector of n tuple of boolean functions $\{f_{n-1}, ..., f_0\}$, for example $f = (f_{n-1}, ..., f_0)$, a vector boolean function. Each element of a vector boolean function is called a coordinate boolean function.*

3 The $\mathcal{KN}$ cipher

The $\mathcal{KN}$ cipher proposed by Knudsen and Nyberg[NK95] is a prototype cipher which is provably secure against ordinary differential cryptanalysis. The $\mathcal{KN}$ cipher is also provably secure against linear cryptanalysis[N94]: at least 2^{60} pairs of chosen (or known) plaintext and ciphertext are required for attacking the $\mathcal{KN}$ cipher by differential (or linear) cryptanalysis.

The $\mathcal{KN}$ cipher is a Feistel cipher with at least 6 rounds and block size 64 bits. The round function F is as follows (see Figure 1): for i-th round input $x \in GF(2)^{32}$ and i-th round key $k^{(i)} \in GF(2)^{33}$,

$$F(x, k^{(i)}) = d(g(e(x) + k^{(i)})),$$

where $e : GF(2)^{32} \to GF(2)^{33}$ is a function which extends its argument by concatenation with an affine combination of the input bits, $g : GF(2)^{33} \to GF(2)^{33}$ is the vector function to which a cubing function $\mathcal{X}^3$ in the finite field $GF(2^{33})$ is projected using a basis in $GF(2^{33})$, and $d : GF(2)^{33} \to GF(2)^{32}$ discards one bit from its argument.

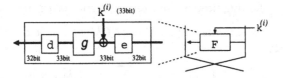

Fig. 1. Round function F of the $\mathcal{KN}$ cipher.

Let $X = \{x_{31}, ..., x_0\}$ be the set of the i-th round input bits, $X' = \{x'_{32}, ..., x'_0\}$ be the set of input bits of g, and $K^{(i)} = \{k^{(i)}_{32}, ..., k^{(i)}_0\}$ be the set of i-th round key bits. For every coordinate boolean function g_i of $g = (g_{32}, ..., g_0)$, which is an element of $R[X']$, it is shown that $\deg_{X'}(g_i) = 2$. From this, it follows that for every coordinate boolean function f_i of $F = (f_{31}, ..., f_0)$, which is an element of $R[X, K^{(i)}]$, it is shown that $\deg_X(f_i) = 2$ [NK95].

4 The higher order differential attack

In [L94], a basic notion of the higher order differential of boolean function was proposed. The higher order differential attack was proposed in [K95] and applied to the $\mathcal{KN}$ cipher in [JK97]. For an iterated block cipher with block size n bits and key size s bits, we denote an output by $y = (y_{n-1}, ..., y_0) \in GF(2)^n$, an input by $x = (x_{n-1}, ..., x_0) \in GF(2)^n$, and a key by $k = (k_{s-1}, ..., k_0) \in GF(2)^s$. The output y is represented by a vector boolean function

$$y = F(x, k) = (f_{n-1}(x, k), ..., f_0(x, k)) \in R[X, K]^n,$$

where $X = \{x_{n-1}, ..., x_0\}$, $K = \{k_{s-1}, ..., k_0\}$. One of coordinate boolean functions $f(x, k)$ of $F(x, k)$ is a boolean function $f[k](x)$ on X when k is fixed. In general $f[k](x)$ is represented as follows,

$$f[k](x) = \sum c_{i_{n-1}, ..., i_0}(k) \cdot x_{n-1}^{i_{n-1}} \cdots x_0^{i_0}$$

Definition 5 *We define $\Delta^{(i)}_{(a_i, ..., a_1)} f[k](x)$ as the i-th order differential of $f[k](x)$ with respect to X as follows,*

$$\Delta^{(1)}_{(a)} f[k](x) = f[k](x) + f[k](x + a)$$

$$\Delta^{(i)}_{(a_i, ..., a_1)} f[k](x) = \Delta^{(1)}_{(a_i)}(\Delta^{(i-1)}_{(a_{i-1}, ..., a_1)} f[k](x))$$

where $a \in GF(2)^n$ and $\{a_i, ..., a_1\} \subset GF(2)^n$. In this paper, since we consider only the higher order differential with respect to X, we omit "with respect to X."

Definition 6 *We define the higher order differential of vector boolean function $F = (f_{n-1}, ..., f_0)$ as follows,*

$$\Delta^{(i)}_{(a_i, ..., a_1)} F = (\Delta^{(i)}_{(a_i, ..., a_1)} f_{n-1}, ..., \Delta^{(i)}_{(a_i, ..., a_1)} f_0).$$

We know the following propositions on the higher order differential[L94].

Proposition 1 *The i-th order differential of $f[k](x)$ can be calculated using the following property.*

$$\Delta^{(i)}_{(a_i,...,a_1)} f[k](x) = \sum_{a \in V^{(i)}[a_i,...,a_1]} f[k](x+a).$$

Proposition 2 *Let $\{a_{d+1},...,a_1\}$ be a subset of $GF(2)^n$. If $\deg_X(f[k](x)) = d$, then we have the following,*

$$\Delta^{(d)}_{(a_d,...,a_1)} f[k](x) \in R[K], \quad \Delta^{(d+1)}_{(a_{d+1},...,a_1)} f[k](x) = 0.$$

5 Attacks on the $\mathcal{KN}$ cipher

5.1 The attack by Jakobsen & Knudsen

By using the notion of higher order differential, Jakobsen and Knudsen showed that the $\mathcal{KN}$ cipher could be solved theoretically[JK97]. They pointed out that the higher order differential attack is effective in attacking the $\mathcal{KN}$ cipher because the degree of the round function F is low. In this section, we explain their approach for attacking the $\mathcal{KN}$ cipher with 6 rounds.

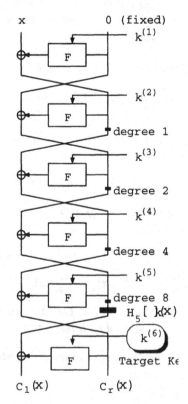

Figure 2. The $\mathcal{KN}$ cipher with 6 rounds.

First, we define some notations. (See Figure 2.) Suppose that the right hand half of the input is kept constant 0 vector in $GF(2)^{32}$. Let $C_l(x)$ and $C_r(x)$ be boolean functions of left hand half of the input x corresponding to the left and right hand halves of ciphertext. Let $H_5[k](x)$ is the right hand half of output of the 5-th round, where $k = (k^{(1)}, k^{(2)}, k^{(3)}, k^{(4)})$. (See also Definition 7 in Section 5.2.) $H_5[k](x)$ is a vector boolean polynomial function. According to Proposition 2 and the fact that $\deg_X H_5[k](x) = 8$, we have the following equation for any key vector k and any subset $\{a_9, ..., a_1\}$ of $GF(2)^{32}$:

$$\Delta_{(a_9,...,a_1)}^{(9)} H_5[k](x) = 0.$$

Also we get the following equation using Proposition 1.

$$\sum_{a \in V[a_9,...,a_1]} H_5[0](a) = 0.$$

Finally, we get the equation for recovering the key $k^{(6)}$ of the 6-th round.

$$\sum_{a \in V[a_9,...,a_1]} F[k^{(6)}](C_r(a)) + \sum_{a \in V[a_9,...,a_1]} C_l(a) = 0. \tag{1}$$

For setting up equation (1), we need 2^9 chosen plaintexts. Then, for every possible value $k^{(6)}$ of the 6-th round, we check whether the equation (1) holds, and if it does, we can found the correct key with high probability. In Table 1, we show the number of required chosen plaintexts and running times for this approach for attacking the $\mathcal{KN}$ cipher. We note that the running time represents the number of computations of round function F.

#rounds	#chosen plaintexts	running time
6	2^9	2^{41}
7	2^{17}	2^{49}

Table 1. Higher order differential attack of the $\mathcal{KN}$ cipher by Jakobsen and Knudsen.

5.2 Our attack of the $\mathcal{KN}$ cipher

The purpose of this section is to improve Jakobsen and Knudsen's approach for attacking the $\mathcal{KN}$ cipher using higher order differential. In this section, we use the same notations and definitions given in Section 5.1. Let $X, K^{(i)}$ be variable sets $\{x_{31}, ..., x_0\}$, $\{k_{32}^{(i)}, ..., k_0^{(i)}\}$ (i is an non-negative integer), respectively. We show the following propositions on the round function F of the $\mathcal{KN}$ cipher $F[k](x) = d(g(e(x) + k))$.

Definition 7 Let $F[k](x)$ be the round function of the $\mathcal{KN}$ cipher. We define the sequence of H_i, which is the vector boolean polynomial function of the right hand half of the values after i-th rounds, as follows.

$$
\begin{aligned}
H_1(x) &= 0 \\
H_2[k^{(1)}](x) &= x + F[k^{(1)}](0) \\
H_i[k^{(1)}, ..., k^{(i-1)}](x) &= F[k^{(i-1)}](H_{i-1}) + H_{i-2}, \quad (i \geq 3)
\end{aligned}
$$

where $x = (x_{31}, ..., x_0) \in GF(2)^{32}$, $k^{(i)} = (k_{32}^{(i)}, ..., k_0^{(i)}) \in GF(2)^{33}$.

Proposition 3 *Let $\{a_{2^m-2}, ..., a_1\} \subset GF(2)^{32}$ be a set of linearly independent 2^{m-2} elements over $GF(2)$. If $m \leq 8$ then*

$$\Delta_{(a_{2^m-2}, ..., a_1)}^{(2^{m-2})} H_m[k^{(1)}, ..., k^{(m-1)}](x) = const. \in GF(2)^{32}.$$

In other words, the value of the left hand side above is constant for any x, $k^{(1)}, ..., k^{(m-1)}$.

Proof: Let h be a coordinate boolean function of H_m. By using induction for m, we get $\deg_X(h) \leq 2^{m-2}$. Moreover, if m is less than or equal to 8, we get $\deg_{X, K^{(1)}, ..., K^{(m-1)}}(h) \leq 2^{m-2}$. Therefore all coefficients of the terms of degree 2^{m-2} of h with respect to the variable set X are elements in $GF(2)$. □

Proposition 4 *For a coordinate boolean function $f_i[k](x)$ ($i \in \{0, ..., 31\}$) of the round function $F[k](x)$ of the $\mathcal{KN}$ cipher, we have*

$$\deg_K(\Delta_a^{(1)} f_i[k](x)) \leq 1$$

for any non-zero element a in $GF(2)^{32}$.

Proof: Because $\deg_{X,K}(f_i[k](x)) = \deg_X(f_i[k](x)) = 2$, all the terms of degree 2 of f_i with respect to K are constant terms with respect to X. Therefore, first order differential of f_i with respect to X does not have the terms with degree 2 with respect to K. □

Now we consider attacking the $\mathcal{KN}$ cipher with 6 rounds. According to Proposition 3, we get

$$\Delta_{(a_8, ..., a_1)}^{(8)} H_5[k^{(1)}, ..., k^{(4)}](x) = \Delta_{(a_8, ..., a_1)}^{(8)} H_5[0, ..., 0](x),$$

where $\{a_8, ..., a_1\} \subset GF(2)^{32}$ is a linearly independent set over $GF(2)$. From Proposition 1 and the definitions of $C_l(x)$ and $C_r(x)$, we have the equation as follows,

$$\sum_{a \in V[a_8, ..., a_1]} F[k^{(6)}](C_r(a)) + \sum_{a \in V[a_8, ..., a_1]} C_l(a) = \sum_{a \in V[a_8, ..., a_1]} H_5[0, ..., 0](a). \quad (a)$$

Moreover,

$$\sum_{a \in V[a_8, ..., a_1]} F[k^{(6)}](C_r(a)) = \sum_{a \in V[a_8, ..., a_1] \setminus \{0\}} \left\{ F[k^{(6)}](C_r(a)) + F[k^{(6)}](C_r(0)) \right\}$$

$$= \sum_{a \in V[a_8, ..., a_1] \setminus \{0\}} \Delta_{C_r(a)+C_r(0)}^{(1)} F[k^{(6)}](C_r(a)).$$

$$(b)$$

According to Proposition 4, the formula of the right hand side of equation (b) is linear with respect to the variable set $K^{(6)}$. Finally, we get the attacking linear equation for $k^{(6)}$ as follows.

$$\sum_{a \in V[a_8,...,a_1] \setminus \{0\}} \Delta_{C_r(a)+C_r(0)}^{(1)} F[k^{(6)}](C_r(a)) + \sum_{a \in V[a_8,...,a_1]} C_l(a)$$
$$= \sum_{a \in V[a_8,...,a_1]} H_5[0,...,0](a) \qquad (c)$$

We can recover $k^{(6)}$ by solving linear equation (c). By replacing the exhaustive key search in Jakobsen and Knudsen's approach with solving the linear equation, we can succeed in reducing the complexity for recovering the key. We note that, we just made use of the fact that round function F is a quadratic multi-variable boolean function in applying our attack. Therefore, it follows that all Feistel ciphers of less than 9 rounds with such round functions are breakable.

In Jakobsen and Knudsen's approach, most of the running time for attacking the $\mathcal{KN}$ cipher is spent in an exhaustive search of the key. In our approach, however, the most time-consuming part is setting up linear equation (c). Now, we discuss the complexity for attacking the $\mathcal{KN}$ cipher by our approach.

In order to set up equation (c), we have to compute the following for each element a in $V[a_8,...,a_1]$: (1) cipher texts $C_l(a)$ and $C_r(a)$, (2) $H_5[0,...,0](a)$ and (3) $\Delta_{C_r(a)+C_r(0)}^{(1)} F[k^{(6)}](C_r(a))$ $(a \neq 0)$. Each part needs 6, 4 and 34 times of the computation of function F, respectively. (See Section 6.2.) In total, the running time for the computation of equation (c) is about $2^8 \cdot (6+4+34) \leq 2^{14}$ times of the computation of round function F. In Table 2, we show the ratio of each part of the running time for finding the 6-th round key. We note that the running time for solving the linear equation is estimated from the CPU time in Table 4.

	running time ($\times 2^8$)	ratio (%)
(1)	6	13.4
(2)	4	9.0
(3)	34	76.0
solving the equation	(0.7)	1.6

Table 2. Ratio of each part of the running time for finding the 6-th round key.

In Table 3, we show the number of chosen plaintexts, running times and CPU times in our experiments on a Sun Ultra 1 (UltraSPARC 170MHz) for recovering all the round keys of the $\mathcal{KN}$ cipher with 6, 7 and 8 rounds. We note that the required CPU time for breaking the $\mathcal{KN}$ cipher with 8 rounds is estimated from those of 6 and 7 rounds. In Section 6, we will present the details of our computer experiments.

#rounds	#chosen plaintexts	running time	CPU time
6	2^8	2^{14}	0.02 seconds
7	2^{16}	2^{22}	6.07 seconds
8	2^{32}	2^{38}	110 hours

Table 3. Higher order differential attack of the $\mathcal{KN}$ cipher using our approach.

6 Experimental Considerations

6.1 Implementation of the round function F

For implementation of the $\mathcal{KN}$ cipher, the most important part is how to implement the operation $\mathcal{X}^3$ in $GF(2^{33})$ efficiently. Although computation using a pre-calculated lookup table is very fast in general, the size of the $\mathcal{X}^3$ function in $GF(2^{33})$ is too big to allow use of a lookup table. In our implementation, we compute $\mathcal{X}^3$ in $GF(2^{33})$ by using the successive extension method. That is, we represent elements of $GF(2^{33})$ as polynomials of degree 2 with coefficients in $GF(2^{11})$, and calculations in $GF(2^{11})$ are carried out using a lookup table. The lookup table is a list of log-exp pairs (x, a^x) (a is a primitive element of $GF(2^{11})$) whose size is 27K bytes[MS97].

In our implementation of round function F, we define function e as zero-extension to the most significant bit, that is,

$$e : (x_{31}, ..., x_0) \in GF(2)^{32} \mapsto (0, x_{31}, ..., x_0) \in GF(2)^{33},$$

and function d as elimination of the most significant bit, that is,

$$d : (x_{32}, x_{31}, ..., x_0) \in GF(2)^{33} \mapsto (x_{31}, ..., x_0) \in GF(2)^{32}.$$

The resistance of the $\mathcal{KN}$ cipher defined as above to differential cryptanalysis and linear cryptanalysis is the same as that of the original[NK95].

6.2 Computation of the linear attacking equation

In this section, we explain the details of the computation of the left hand side of equation (c) in Section 5.2, which is most time-consuming. (See Table 2.) For any two different elements a, b in $GF(2)^{32}$, $\Delta_a F[k](b)$ is an affine map on the vector $k = (k_{32}, ..., k_0)$ over $GF(2)$. There exists a 32×33 matrix M and a 32-dimensional vector N such that

$$\Delta_a F[k](b) = M \cdot k + N.$$

Then, we can find M and N using the following equations,

$$N = \Delta_a F[0](b), \quad M_i = \Delta_a F[e_i](b) + N,$$

where M_i is the i-th column of M, $e_i = (0, ..., \overset{i}{1}, ..., 0)$ is a unit vector of $GF(2)^{33}$. In this way, in order to find M and N, we need to calculate the round function F 34 times.

6.3 CPU time of each part

In Table 4, we show the timing data of $\mathcal{X}^3$ in $GF(2^{33})$, round function F, the $\mathcal{KN}$ cipher with 6 and 7 rounds, solving a linear equation in our implementation on a Sun Ultra 1 (UltraSPARC 170MHz) with gcc version 2.6.3.

	CPU time
$\mathcal{X}^3$ over $GF(2^{33})$	1.13 micro seconds
round function F	1.51 micro seconds
the $\mathcal{KN}$ cipher with 6 rounds	11.78 micro seconds
the $\mathcal{KN}$ cipher with 7 rounds	13.81 micro seconds
solving a linear equation	266.40 micro seconds

Table 4. CPU time of each part in our implementation.

6.4 Algorithm for finding all the round keys

In this section, we describe the algorithm for finding all the round keys. We can determine the 6-th round key $k^{(6)}$ by solving the attacking linear equation shown in Section 5.2. Here we denote the linear equation by

$$M^{(6)} \cdot k^{(6)} + N^{(6)} = 0. \tag{d}$$

Equation (d) has $2^{33-\mathrm{rank}M}$ solutions. Using each solution, we can compute the output after the 5-th round from the ciphertexts, and set up the following equation with respect to the 5-th round key $k^{(5)}$ similarly.

$$M^{(5)} \cdot k^{(5)} + N^{(5)} = 0 \tag{e}$$

The required complexity is 2^{10} computation times round function F, which is much smaller than that for deriving equation (d). The needed number of chosen plaintexts and ciphertexts is 2^4 for deriving equation (e). If we reuse 2^4 out of 2^8 chosen plaintexts and ciphertexts which were required for deriving equation (d), we can derive 2^4 different equations (e). Using these equations, we can reduce the number of candidates of $k^{(5)}$. In our experiment, when we set up equation (e) using a wrong $k^{(6)}$, we can get no candidates of $k^{(5)}$. On the other hand, when we use the correct $k^{(6)}$, only one candidate of $k^{(5)}$ survives. Similarly, the remaining round keys can be determined.

7 Concluding remarks

We improved the higher order differential attack described in [JK97]. We applied the improved attack to the $\mathcal{KN}$ cipher, which was proposed as a block cipher with provable security against differential and linear attacks, and confirmed that the $\mathcal{KN}$ cipher is easy to break both theoretically and experimentally. We succeeded in deriving all round keys of the $\mathcal{KN}$ cipher with 6 rounds with 2^8 chosen plaintexts and ciphertexts in only 0.02 seconds, and the $\mathcal{KN}$ cipher with 7 rounds with 2^{16} chosen plaintexts and ciphertexts in only 6.07 seconds on a Sun Ultra 1 (UltraSPARC 170MHz). The required running time for breaking the $\mathcal{KN}$ cipher with 8 rounds was estimated about 110 hours using 2^{32} chosen plaintexts and ciphertexts.

In this paper we just made use of the fact that round function F is a quadratic multi-variable boolean function in applying our higher order differential attack. Therefore, it follows that all Feistel ciphers of less than 9 rounds with such round functions are breakable by this attack.

It is expected that further improvements are possible in the required number of texts and complexity for attacking the $\mathcal{KN}$ cipher. We are tackling this from the viewpoints of both theory and implementation.

We described only the higher order differential attack of the $\mathcal{KN}$ cipher in this paper, but we think some attacks using the higher order differential are applicable to other block ciphers. Our ongoing works include applying it to some real-world ciphers.

References

[BS91] E.Biham and A.Shamir, "Differential Cryptanalysis of DES-like Cryptosystems, " Journal of Cryptology, Volume 4, Number 1, pp.3–72, Springer Verlag, 1991.

[JK97] T.Jakobsen and L.R.Knudsen, "The Interpolation Attack on Block Ciphers," Fast Software Encryption – Fourth International Workshop, Lecture Note in Computer Science 1267, pp.28–40, Springer Verlag, 1997.

[K95] L.R.Knudsen, "Truncated and Higher Order Differentials," Fast Software Encryption – Second International Workshop, Lecture Note in Computer Science 1008, pp.196–211, Springer Verlag, 1995.

[L94] X.Lai, "Higher Order Derivatives and Differential Cryptanalysis," Communications and Cryptography, pp.227–233, Kluwer Academic Publishers, 1994.

[NK95] K.Nyberg and L.R.Knudsen, "Provable Security Against a Differential Attack," Journal of Cryptology, Volume 8, Number 1, pp.27–37, Springer Verlag, 1995.

[N94] K.Nyberg, "Linear Approximations of Block Ciphers," Advances in Cryptology – EUROCRYPT'94, Lecture Note in Computer Science 950, pp.439–444, Springer Verlag, 1995.

[M93] M.Matsui, "Linear Cryptanalysis Method for DES Cipher," Advances in Cryptology – EUROCRYPT'93, Lecture Notes in Computer Science 765, pp.386–397, Springer-Verlag, 1994.

[MS97] S.Moriai and T.Shimoyama, "Performance and Security of Block Ciphers Using Operations in $GF(2^n)$," Proceedings of SAC'97, pp.117–130, 1997.

An Optimised Linear Attack on Pseudorandom Generators Using a Non-linear Combiner

Hidema TANAKA   Tomoya OHISHI   Toshinobu KANEKO

Department Electronically Engineering,Scince University of Tokyo

2641 Yamazaki Noda Chiba 278 Japan

Phone:0471-24-1501(3754) Fax:0471-25-8651

E-mail:{tanaka,ooisi,kaneko}@kaneko01.ee.noda.sut.ac.jp

Abstract. We propose an optimised linear attack on pseudorandom generators using a nonlinear combiner. The generators consist of a number of Linear Feedback Shift Registers (LFSR) and a non linear function $f(\cdot)$. We derive an attacking equation (AEQ) using a linear approximation of $f(\cdot)$ and the generator polynomials of LFSRs. In the AEQ we focus on the initial value of one LFSR in the generator by eliminating the initial values of the other LFSRs using the elimination polynomial. The performance of the attack depends on the number of terms in the polynomial. We propose an optimised algorithm for an efficient elimination polynomial. Using this attack we can determine the initial value of the LFSR from the tapped bits whose number is much smaller than the period of the pseudorandom generator.

1 Introduction

Many pseudorandom generators, which are consisted of Linear Feedback Shift Registers (LFSRs) are proposed - Geffe generator, Pless generator, Multiplexer generator and so on [11]. These generators are used as the key stream generator in stream cipher, and evaluated by the linear complexity, the mutual information, the statistical distribution and so on.

Many attacking methods are also proposed. Correlation attack is the general method, which calculates the probability that the generator's output value coincides with the output value of one LFSR in the generator. BAA attack, which is proposed by Rueppel [8], calculates the Walsh transform for the non linear function of the generator to derive a best linear approximation. The method by Golić [2], is the generalization for attacking to the combiners with memory. His method transforms such generator to the one which can be attacked by the general method(e.g. Fast correlation attack). Differential attack [1] is the method which transforms the generator to the Natural Sequence Generator. Linear Syndrome Attack [15] regards an output sequence of the generator as an EX-OR sum of an output sequence of the LFSR and a noise sequence which is generated by the non linear function of the generator. By the majority logic decoding algorithm, the attack eliminates the noise sequence to recover the true output sequence of the LFSR. Linear Consistency Test [16] uses the deterministic equation which holds for the true initial value of LFSR. We attack pseudorandom generators which are consisted of a number of LFSRs and a non linear function $f(\cdot)$. A linear attack is the attacking method in which Matsui's linear cryptanalysis [5] is applied to the non linear function $f(\cdot)$ of the pseudorandom generator [12]. The linear attack derives the attacking equation(AEQ) from a linear approximate function $F(\cdot)$ of $f(\cdot)$. AEQ is the equation which makes focus on the output sequence of one LFSR, by eliminating the initial values of the other LFSR in a function $F(\cdot)$. We call the polynomial, which is used in this procedure, as the elimination polynomial. The performance of AEQ depends on the weight and the degree of the elimination polynomial. We optimize the AEQ by the algorithm which derives the optimal elimination polynomial. The algorithm bases on the knowledge of the generator polynomials of LFSR. By regarding AEQ as the binary symmetric channel, we estimate the number of tapped bits for a successful attack, by its channel capacity. The results of computer simulation show that the estimated number is enough for a successful attack and that the number of tapped bits is much smaller than the period of the pseudorandom generator.

2 Pseudorandom generators using a non linear combiner

A pseudorandom generator using a non linear combiner is shown in Figure 1. It is composed of n LFSRs:LFSR#1,LFSR#2,...,LFSR#n and a nonlinear combining function $f(\cdot)$. The generator outputs the random sequence by inputting sequences of each LFSR to the non linear function $f(\cdot)$. If the pseudorandom generator is used as the key stream generator in the stream cipher, it is necessary to hold the following conditions [11].
- Long periodicity
- Linear complexity
- Statistical property
- Non linearity
- Correlation immunity
Let $X(t)$ be the n outputs of constituent LFSR.

$$X(t) = (x_1(t), x_2(t), \ldots, x_n(t)) \tag{1}$$

where $x_i(t)$ be the output sequence of LFSR#i.

These outputs $X(t)$ are combined by the non linear function $f(\cdot)$ to generate a random sequence $R(t)$.

$$R(t) = f(X(t)) \tag{2}$$

Each LFSR#i is a L_i-stage M sequence generator whose generator polynomial is

$$G_i(x) = 1 \oplus g_{i1}x \oplus g_{i2}x^2 \oplus \cdots \oplus x^{L_i} \tag{3}$$

where $g_{ij} \in GF(2)$, $\oplus$ is EX-OR sum.

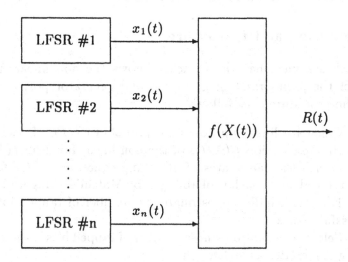

Fig. 1. A pseudorandom generator using a non linear combiner with n LFSRs

A sequence $x_i(t)$ is generated by the recurrence relation.

$$x_i(t) = g_{i1}x(t-1) \oplus g_{i2}x(t-2) \oplus \ldots \oplus x(t-L_i) \tag{4}$$

In the delay operator D formula,

$$G_i(D)x_i(D) = 0. \tag{5}$$

Each sequence $x_i(t)$ is determined by its initial value INI_i.

$$INI\_i = (x(L_i - 1), x(L_i - 2), \ldots, x(0)) \qquad (6)$$

To maximize its period, the number of stages L_is are selected to be relatively prime.

$$G.C.D(L_1, L_2, \ldots, L_n) = 1 \qquad (7)$$

The period N of the pseudorandom generator is

$$N = \prod_{i=1}^{n} (2^{L_i} - 1). \qquad (8)$$

3 Outline of the Linear Attack

3.1 Condition and Procedure

This attack assumes that the attacker knows the non linear function $f(X(t))$ of the pseudorandom generator and generator polynomials of LFSR. The procedure is as follows

Phase-1 Calculate linear approximate probabilities P_L of each linear approximate function $F(X(t))$ of the non linear function $f(X(t))$.

Phase-2 Derive the candidates of attacking equation (AEQ) for each $F(X(t))$. Calculate each probability S by Matsui's Piling up Lemma.

Phase-3 For each candidate, estimate the number of tapped bits for a successful attack.

Phase-4 Select the equation whose number of tapped bits is the smallest among candidates as AEQ.

Phase-5 Estimate the initial value of LFSR by using AEQ from the tapped sequence.

3.2 Linear approximate probability

To make the expression simpler, we omit the variable t in this section, for example $f(X)$ represents $f(X(t))$. Let $F(X)$ be the linear approximate function of $f(x)$.

$$F(X) = c_0 \oplus c_1 x_1 \oplus c_2 x_2 \oplus \cdots \oplus c_n x_n \qquad (9)$$

where $X = (x_1, x_2, \ldots, x_n)$ and $c_n, x_i \in GF(2)$.

The linear approximate probability P_L is as follows.

$$P_L = \text{Prob}\{f(X) = F(X)\} \tag{10}$$

3.3 Probability S

Let $\stackrel{P}{=}$ be the equal sign which denotes that the equation holds with probability P. for example, a linear approximate function $F(X(t))$ which holds probability P_L is as follows.

$$R(t) = f(X(t)) \stackrel{P_L}{=} F(X(t)) \tag{11}$$

Let LFSR#j be a LFSR which has non-zero coefficient c_j in a linear approximate function $F(X(t))$. We analyze the initial state variables of LFSR#j from the tapped sequence. Let J be the index set i of LFSR#i($i \neq j$) which has non-zero coefficient in a linear approximate function $F(X(t))$. Let $G_J(x)$ be the product of generator polynomials.

$$G_J(x) = \underset{i \in J}{LCM}\{G_i(x)\} \tag{12}$$

Let $E(x)$ be a polynomial which is divisible by $G_J(x)$.

$$G_J(x)|E(x) \tag{13}$$

The terms except $x_j(t)$ can be eliminated by using recurrence relation $E(D)$, where D is the delay operator. We denote $E(D)R(t)$ as the coefficient of D^t in $E(D)R(D)$. Then the candidate of AEQ is derived as follows.

$$E(D)R(t) \stackrel{S}{=} E(D)F(X(t)) = E(D)x_j(t) \tag{14}$$

And we calculate the probability S of each candidate of AEQ by using Matsui's piling up lemma [4], which is used in the linear cryptanalysis of DES by Matsui. Since AEQ is derived from the system of M linear approximated functions, where M is the number of terms in $E(x)$, probability S is as follows.

$$S = 2^{M-1}(P_L - \frac{1}{2})^M + \frac{1}{2} \tag{15}$$

3.4 Tapped bits for a successful attack

Morii [6] conjectured that the immunity against the correlation attack is estimated by the mutual information of the linear approximate functions. We extend his discussion and conjecture that the immunity against the linear attack is estimated by the channel capacity of AEQ. If we regard the right hand side of eq.(14) as the input, and regard the left hand side as the output of a communication channel, then AEQ is the binary symmetric channel with following channel matrix.

$$T = \begin{bmatrix} S & 1-S \\ 1-S & S \end{bmatrix} \tag{16}$$

The channel capacity C of the channel T is as follows.

$$C = 1 - H(S) \tag{17}$$

where $H(\cdot)$ is the entropy function as follows.

$$H(P) = P \log_2 \frac{1}{P} + (1-P) \log_2 \frac{1}{1-P} \tag{18}$$

The number of the unknown variables in AEQ is the number of stages L_j of LFSR#j. To determine the L_js unknown variables, we need $\frac{L_j}{C}$ tapped bits by the channel capacity analysis. AEQ at time t is the EX-OR sum of the previous $deg\{E(x)\}$ outputs. Thus the number of tapped bits T for a successful attack is estimated by information theoretical analysis, as follows.

$$T = \frac{L_j}{C} + deg\{E(x)\} \tag{19}$$

3.5   Attacking algorithm

The attacker analyzes the initial value of LFSR#j by using AEQ from the tapped bits. The attacking algorithm is as follows.

Stage-1 Calculate the left hand side of AEQ from the tapped bits.

Stage-2 Calculate the right hand side of AEQ from the bits generated by each assumed initial value of LFSR#j.

Stage-3 Count the probability with which AEQ holds for each assumed initial value of LFSR#j.

For the true initial value, AEQ will hold with probability S. For any false initial values, it will hold with probability $\frac{1}{2}$. Thus we can determine the true initial value INI_j from sufficient length of the tapped sequence.

4   Optimize the effectiveness of the attack

The probability S converges to $\frac{1}{2}$ exponentially with the increase of the number of terms M in $E(x)$. In the case of $S \approx \frac{1}{2}$, the number of tapped bits T becomes infinity, and the attack will be infeasible. To avoid this difficulty, we considere the optimal elimination polynomial.

The elimination polynomial is the polynomial which derives the candidate of AEQ. In [12], $G_J(x)$ (eq.(12)) is the elimination polynomial. In this paper, we use the optimal elimination polynomial which minimize the number of tapped bits T.

4.1 Optimal elimination polynomial

Let $E_{[j,m]}(x)$ be a set of code word polynomials generated by $G_J(x)$, whose weight is m.

$$E_{[j,m]}(x) = \{E(X)|(G_J(x)|E(x)), wt\{E(x)\} = m\} \qquad (20)$$

In $E_{[j,m]}(x)$, let the minimum degree polynomial be $e_{[j,m]}(x)$.
Let N_J be the period of $G_J(x)$, then the following elimination polynomial exists.

$$e_{[j,2]}(x) = x^{N_J} + 1 \qquad (21)$$

Let T_i be the number of tapped bits for a successful attack by AEQ derived by $e_{[j,i]}(x)$. (If there is no polynomial in $E_{[j,m]}(x)$ then we consider $T_i = \infty$.) Let T_{opt} be the minimum value in $\{T_2, T_3, \ldots, T_\infty\}$. Then the optimal elimination polynomial $E_j(x)$ for LFSR#j as follows.

$$E_j(x) = e_{[j,opt]}(x) \qquad (22)$$

The following discussion shows that we need not search around over $T_2, T_3, \ldots, T_\infty$. Let $\tilde{T}_{opt}(k)$ is the locally minimum among the set $\{T_2, T_3, \ldots, T_k\}$. T_{k+1} is expressed as follows.

$$T_{k+1} = \frac{L_j}{C_{k+1}} + deg\{e_{[j,k+1]}(x)\}, \qquad (23)$$

where C_{k+1} is the channel capacity of AEQ derived from any polynomial in $E_{[j,k+1]}(x)$.

$$S_{k+1} = 2^k (P_L - \frac{1}{2})^{k+1} + \frac{1}{2} \qquad (24)$$

$$C_{k+1} = 1 - H(S_{k+1}) \qquad (25)$$

If $\tilde{T}_{opt}(k) < T_{k+1}$ then the degree of elimination polynomial $e_{[j,k+1]}(x)$ must be

$$B(k+1) > deg\{e_{[j,k+1]}(x)\}, \qquad (26)$$

where $B(k+1)$ is as follows.

$$B(k+1) = \tilde{T}_{opt}(k) - \frac{L_j}{C_{k+1}} \qquad (27)$$

If $B(k+1) < 0$, then there are no $e_{[j,k+1]}(x)$ which holds eq.(26). In this case, we need not search for $e_{[j,k+1]}(x)$. Since $\tilde{T}_{opt}(k)$ is monotone decreasing on k, and the second term $\frac{L_j}{C_{k+1}}$ in eq.(25) is monotone increasing, we can conclude that the $B(k+1)$ is monotone decreasing. Thus, if once $B(k+1) < 0$ we need not search for $e_{[j,m]}(x), m \geq k+1$. This algorithm searching for the optimal elimination polynomial is as follows.

Step-1 $E'_j(x) = e_{[j,2]}(x)$. Calculate T_k for $k = 2$. Estimate the minimum weight w of the cyclic codes generated by $G_J(x)$. Then $k = w - 1$.

Step-2 Calculate $B(k+1)$ from eq.(27). If $B(k+1) < 0$, then go to Step-5.

Step-3 Search the elimination polynomial $e_{[j,k+1]}(x)$ with $deg\{e_{[j,k+1]}(x)\} < B(k+1)$.

Step-4 If $e_{[j,k+1]}(x)$ exists, then $E'_j(x) = e_{[j,k+1]}(x)$. Calculate T_{k+1}. Go to Step-2 with $k = k+1$.

Step-5 The optimal elimination polynomial $E_j(x)$ is as follows.

$$E_j(x) = E'_j(x) \qquad (28)$$

We may use the algorithm [4] to estimate the minimum weight.

4.2 Optimal attacking equation

If a linear approximate function has K variables, there are K different index sets J. So there are K different optimal elimination polynomials for each $G_J(x)$. The candidate of AEQ is derived by the optimal elimination polynomial $E_j(x)$ whose number of tapped bits is the minimum among them.

By above procedure, the candidates of AEQ are derived from each linear approximate function. Among the candidates, the optimal AEQ is the one whose number of tapped bits is the minimum. The attacker uses the optimal AEQ in the algorithm of the section 3.5.

5 Example attack

For example, we attacked the summation generator with 3LFSRs [3],[11] (3SUM), with 4LFSRs(4SUM),and the revised dynamic pseudorandom generator [9](DRG-R). We assume that these summation generators have one bit memory. DRG [6] has the linear complexity and the mutual information which are much better than other pseudorandom generators in the same size. DRG-R is DRG, which is revised to be infeasible by the linear attack [12]. The constituent LFSRs and periods of these pseudorandom generators are shown in Table.1.

We abbreviate polynomials as follows.

$$x^m + x^n + 1 \quad \rightarrow \quad [m, n, 0] \tag{29}$$

The non linear function in nSUM ($n = 3, 4$) is as follows.

$$f_{nSUM}(X(t)) = \sum_{i=1}^{n} x_i(t) + Carry(t) \mod 2$$
$$Carry(t) = \left[\frac{\sum_{i=1}^{n} x_i(t-1) + Carry(t-1)}{2} \right] \mod 2 \tag{30}$$

	3SUM	4SUM
LFSR#1	[0,9,10,12,13]	[0,1,3]
LFSR#2	[0,9,11]	[0,2,5]
LFSR#3	[0,14,17]	[0,1,7]
LFSR#4		[0,2,11]
Period N	more than 2.2×10^{12}	more than 5.6×10^{7}

	DRG-R
LFSR#1	[0,2,3,5,6,8,9,10,11]
LFSR#2	[0,1,2,3,6,7,8,11,12]
LFSR#3	[0,1,2,7,8,10,12,13,14,15,17,22,23,25,27,28,29]
LFSR#4	[0,1,2,3,4,5,6,7,8,9,11,12,13]
LFSR#5	[0,1,2,5,6,8,9,11,12,14,15,16,17]
Period N	2.56×10^{23}

Table 1. Constituent LFSRs and period of each pseudorandom generator

In the summation generator, Carry(t) makes non linear property of $f_{nSUM}(X(t))$.

The non linear function in DRG-R is as follows.

$$f_{DRG-R}(X(t)) = x_1(t)x_2(t)x_3(t) \oplus x_1(t)x_2(t)$$
$$\oplus x_1(t)x_3(t) \oplus x_2(t)x_3(t)$$
$$\oplus x_2(t) \oplus x_4(t) \oplus x_5(t)$$
$$\oplus 1 \tag{31}$$

We attacked these pseudorandom generators by the procedure described in Sections 3 and 4.

The linear approximate functions $F(X(t))$ which derive the optimal AEQ, their linear approximate probability P_L, and the optimal elimination polynomial $E_j(x)$ for each pseudorandom generator are as follows.

[3SUM]

$$F(X(t)) = x_2(t) \oplus x_3(t)$$
$$P_L = 0.625$$
$$E_{opt}(x) = E_3(x) = [2047, 0] \tag{32}$$

[4SUM]

$$F(X(t)) = x_1(t) \oplus x_2(t) \oplus x_3(t) \oplus x_4(t)$$
$$P_L = 0.625$$
$$E_{opt}(x) = E_4(x) = [332, 291, 0] \tag{33}$$

	3SUM	4SUM	DRG-R
Probability S	0.5313	0.5078	0.5313
Channel capacity C	2.9×10^{-3}	1.8×10^{-4}	2.9×10^{-3}
Period N	2.2×10^{12}	5.6×10^{7}	2.56×10^{23}
The number of tapped bits T	8,100[bit]	6.6×10^4[bit]	14,024[bit]

Table 2. Performance of the AEQs of each pseudorandom generator.

Initial value	Probability		
	3SUM	4SUM	DRG-R
TRUE	0.5093	0.5052	0.5419
False-1	0.4974	0.5010	0.4981
False-2	0.4956	0.5007	0.5098
False-3	0.5061	0.4987	0.4969

Table 3. Results of the computer simulation

[DRG-R]

$$F(X(t)) = x_4(t) \oplus x_5(t) \oplus 1$$
$$P_L = 0.625$$
$$E_{opt}(x) = E_5(x) = [8191, 0] \tag{34}$$

Probability S, channel capacity C and the number of tapped bits for successful attacks T of these AEQs are shown in Table.2. Table.3 shows the probabilities calculated from the results of the computer simulation. Due to the limitation space, a part of simulated results is shown. Because the attacked LFSR has the number of initial value as well as a period of the LFSR. "TRUE"column shows the result for the true initial state and "False-i"columns show the example results for the false states. Each probability is the ratio with which AEQ holds. We used Fujitsu S-4/20 for the computer simulation. Table.4 shows that cputimes for the AEQ derivation phase and the attacking phase. "AEQ derivation phase"column shows the cputimes, which take to derive the optimal AEQ. "Attacking Phase"column shows the cputimes, which take the determination of the initial state value.

6 Conclusion

In this paper, we propose a new linear attack on the pseudorandom generators using a non linear combiner. The result of attack in the section.5

cputime	3SUM	4SUM	DRG-R
AEQ derivation phase	<1[s]	42[s]	<1[s]
Attacking phase	28[min]	7[min]	28[min]

Table 4. Cputime for the AEQ derivation phase and the Attacking phase

shows that each pseudorandom generator can be attacked by the tapped bits whose number is smaller than its period. we confirm that the number of tapped bits for a successful attack can be estimated by the channel capacity of AEQ.

This linear attack can be combined with Golić's method [2] to make the wide applicable attacking algorithm. This is an open problem.

References

1. Ding : "The Differential Cryptanalysis and Design of Natural Stream Ciphers", LNCS vol.809, pp.101-115, Springer-Verlag, Berlin, 1991

2. Golić : "Linear Cryptanalysis of Stream Ciphers", LNCS vol.1008, pp.154-169, Springer-Verlag, Berlin, 1995

3. Matsuzaki, Ohmori, Tatebayashi : "A Study on Stream Ciphers suitable for Conditional Access to Digital Broadcasting System", ISEC95-6

4. Mohri,Morii : "A Probabilistic Algorithm for Minimum Distance of Cyclic Codes",SITA96

5. Matsui : "Linear Cryptanalysis of DES Cipher (I)", SCIS93-3C

6. Moriyasu, Morii, Kasahara : "Nonlinear Pseudo-Random Sequence Generator with Dynamic Structure and Its Properties", ISEC93-7

7. Ruppel : "Correlation Immunity and the Summation Generator", LNCS vol.218, Springer Verlag

8. Rueppel : "Design and Analysis of Stream Ciphers", Springer Verlag

9. Shiraishi, Morii : "Some notes on the Non-linear Combiner Generator and that against a Linear Attack", ISEC96-3

10. Siegenthaler : "Decrypting a Class of Ciphers using Ciphertext only", IEEE C-34, pp.81-85, Jan.1985

11. Schneiner : "APPLIED CRYPTOGRAPHY", WILEY

12. Tanaka, Kaneko : "A Linear Attack to the Random Generator by Non Linear Combiner", The Transaction of the Institute of Electronics, Information and Communication Engineers, vol.J79, A, No.8, pp.1360-1368, 1996

13. Tanaka, Kaneko : "A Linear Attack to the Random Generator by Non Linear Combiner", ISITA96

14. Tanaka, Kaneko : "A Study on a Quadratic Approximation Attack to the Reformed Dynamic Random Generator", ISEC96-44

15. Zeng, Huang : "On the Linear Syndrome Method in Cryptanalysis", LNCS vol.403, pp.469-478, Springer-Verlag, Berlin, 1988

16. Zeng, Yang, Rao : "On the linear consistency test in cryptanalysis and its applications", LNCS vol.435, pp.164-174, Springer-Verlag, Berlin, 1989

Cryptanalysis of Message Authentication Codes

B. Preneel*

Katholieke Universiteit Leuven
Department Electrical Engineering-ESAT/COSIC
K. Mercierlaan 94, B-3001 Heverlee, Belgium
bart.preneel@esat.kuleuven.ac.be

Abstract. This paper gives a survey of attacks on Message Authentication Codes (MACs). First it defines the required security properties. Next it describes generic forgery and key recovery attacks on MACs. Subsequently an overview is presented of most MAC constructions and on attacks on these algorithms. The MACs described include CBC-MAC and its variants, the MAC algorithms derived from cryptographic hash functions, and the ISO banking standard Message Authenticator Algorithm, also known as MAA.

1 Introduction

Digital signatures, introduced in 1976 by W. Diffie and M. Hellman [15], allow to establish in an irrefutable way the origin and content of digital information. They are gaining widespread attention for applications such as electronic commerce, which requires a worldwide public key infrastructure. Almost all practical digital signature schemes (such as RSA [44]) depend on the (believed) hardness of a number theoretic problem. The technical problem of designing digital signature schemes and implementing them is well understood, but for some applications they require still too much storage and computation.

Therefore many applications still use conventional Message Authentication Code (MAC) algorithms to provide data integrity and data origin authentication. MACs provide weaker guarantees than signatures, as they can only be used in a symmetric setting, where the parties trust each other. In technical terms, they do not provide non-repudiation of origin. Moreover, MACs rely on shared symmetric keys, the management of which is more costly and harder to scale than that of asymmetric key pairs. Banks have been using MACs since the late seventies [14] for message authentication. Recent applications in which MACs have been introduced include electronic purses (such as Proton and Mondex) and credit/debit applications (e.g., the EMV specifications). MACs are also being deployed for securing the Internet (e.g., IP security [3, 27]). For all these applications MACs are preferred over digital signatures because they are two to three orders of magnitude faster, and MAC results are 4...16 bytes long

---

* F.W.O. postdoctoral researcher, sponsored by the National Fund for Scientific Research – Flanders (Belgium).

compared to 40...128 bytes for signatures. On present day machines, software implementations of MACs can achieve speeds from 10...100 Mbit/s and more, and MACs require very little resources on inexpensive 8-bit smart cards and on the currently deployed Point of Sale (POS) terminals.

In order to use a MAC, sender and receiver need to share a secret key K (a random bit-string of k bits – typical values for k are 56...128). In order to protect a message, the sender computes the MAC corresponding the message, which is bit-string of m bits, and appends this string to the message (typical values for m are 32...64). The MAC is a complex function of every bit of the message and the key. On receipt of the message, the receiver recomputes the MAC and verifies that it corresponds to the transmitted MAC value (see also Fig. 1).

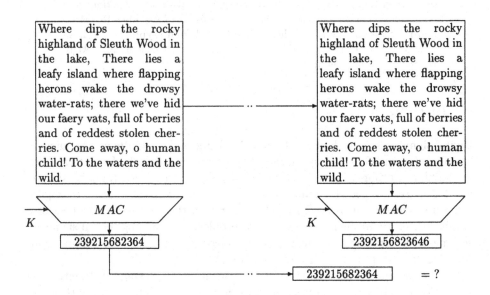

Fig. 1. Using a Message Authentication Code for data integrity.

2 Security of MAC algorithms

An opponent who tries to deceive the receiver, does not know the secret key. It will be assumed that he knows the format of the messages, and the description of the MAC algorithm. His goal is to try to inject a fraudulent message and append a MAC value which will be accepted by the receiver. He can choose one of two attack strategies:

forgery attack: this attack consists of predicting the value of $\text{MAC}_K(x)$ for a message x without initial knowledge of K. If the adversary can do this for a single message, he is said to be capable of *existential forgery*. If the adversary is able to determine the MAC for a message of his choice, he is said to be capable of *selective forgery*. Ideally, existential forgery is computationally infeasible; a less demanding requirement is that only selective forgery is so. Practical attacks often require that a forgery is *verifiable*, i.e., that the forged MAC is known to be correct on beforehand with probability near 1.

key recovery attack: this attack consists of finding the key K itself from a number of message/MAC pairs. Such an attack is more powerful than forgery, since it allows for arbitrary selective forgeries. Ideally, any attack allowing key recovery requires about 2^k operations (here k denotes the bit-length of K). Verification of such an attack requires k/m text-MAC pairs.

In addition, one requires that computing $MAC_K(x)$ is easy, given $MAC()$, K, and an input x.

The attacks above can be further classified according to the type of control an adversary has over the device computing the MAC value. In a *chosen-text attack*, an adversary may request and receive MACs corresponding to a number of messages of his choice, before completing his (forgery or key recovery) attack. For forgery, the forged MAC must be on a message different than any for which a MAC was previously obtained. In an *adaptive* chosen-text attack, requests may depend on the outcome of previous requests.

Note that in certain environments, such as in wholesale banking applications, a chosen message attack is not a very realistic assumption: if an opponent can choose a single text and obtain the corresponding MAC, he can already make a substantial profit. However, it is better to be on the safe side, and to require resistance against chosen text attacks.

One can now write down a formal definition of security for a MAC, by stating that, after a number of chosen/known texts, a forgery with a certain probability requires a certain amount of time. See for example [8] (note that this definition does not distinguishes between chosen and known texts).

In the following, different attacks on MACs are considered: brute force key search, guessing of the MAC, a generic forgery attack, and attacks based on cryptanalytical weaknesses.

2.1 Brute force key search

A brute force key search needs a few known message-MAC pairs (about k/m, which is between 1 and 4 for most MAC algorithms). It is reasonable to assume that such a small number of message-MAC pairs is available. The opponent tries all the possible keys and checks whether they correspond to the given message-MAC pairs. Note that unlike for confidentiality protection, the opponent can only make use of the key if it is recovered within its active lifetime (which can be reasonably short). On the other hand, a single success during the lifetime of the system might be sufficient. This depends on a cost/benefit analysis, i.e., how much one loses as a consequence of a forgery.

The only way to preclude a key search is to choose a sufficiently large key. Currently finding a 56-bit key during a period of 1 year will require an investment of 50 000$, and it can be done in a few months by using idle cycles on the Internet, as was demonstrated in the Spring of 1997. Moreover, one also has to take into account what is known as 'Moore's Law': the computing power for a given cost is multiplied by four every 3 years. This implies that if a system is deployed with an intended lifetime of 15 years, an extra security margin of about 10 bits is recommended. The important conclusion is that keys over 90 bits are sufficient for 15 years or more. More details on key lengths (but for confidentiality protection) can be found in the reports of M. Wiener [48] and of Blaze et al. [9].

2.2 Guessing of the MAC

A second very simple 'attack' is to choose an arbitrary fraudulent message, and to append a randomly chosen MAC value. Ideally, the probability that this MAC value is correct is equal to $1/2^m$, where m is the number of bits of the MAC value. This value should be multiplied with the expected profit corresponding to a fraudulent message, which results in the expected value of one trial. Repeated trials can increase this expected value, but note that in a good implementation, repeated MAC verification errors will result in a security alarm (the forgery is not verifiable). For most applications $m = 32 \ldots 64$ is sufficient to make this attack uneconomical.

2.3 Generic forgery attack

This attack exploits the fact most MAC algorithms consist of the iteration of a simple compression function. The MAC input x is padded to a multiple of the block size, and is then divided into t blocks denoted x_1 through x_t. The MAC involves a *compression function* f and an n-bit $(n \geq m)$ *chaining variable* H_i between stage $i-1$ and stage i:

$$H_0 = IV$$
$$H_i = f(H_{i-1}, x_i), \qquad 1 \leq i \leq t$$
$$\mathrm{MAC}_K(x) = g(H_t).$$

Here g denotes the *output transformation*. The secret key may be employed in the IV, in f, and/or in g.

For an input pair (x, x') with $\mathrm{MAC}_K(x) = g(H_t)$ and $\mathrm{MAC}_K(x') = g(H'_t)$, a collision is said to occur if $\mathrm{MAC}_K(x) = \mathrm{MAC}_K(x')$. This collision is called an *internal* collision if $H_t = H'_t$, and an *external* collision if $H_t \neq H'_t$ but $g(H_t) = g(H'_t)$.

In [37], B. Preneel and P.C. van Oorschot describe a general forgery attack that applies to all iterated MACs. Its feasibility depends on the bitsizes n of the chaining variable and m of the MAC result, the nature of the output transformation g, and the number s of common trailing blocks of the known texts ($s \geq 0$). The basic attack requires several known texts, but only a single chosen text.

However, under certain conditions restrictions are imposed on the known texts; for example, if the message length is an input to the output transformation, all messages must have equal length. The attack starts with the following simple observation (e.g., [26, 37]):

Lemma 1. *An internal collision for an iterated MAC allows a verifiable MAC forgery, through a chosen-text attack requiring a single chosen text.* ∎

This follows since for an internal collision (x, x'), $\text{MAC}_K(x \parallel y) = \text{MAC}_K(x' \parallel y)$ for any single block y; thus a requested MAC on the chosen text $x \parallel y$ provides a forged MAC (the same) for $x' \parallel y$ (here $\parallel$ denotes concatenation). Note this assumes that the MAC algorithm is deterministic. Also, the forged message is of a special form, which may limit the practical impact of the attack.

The main question is to determine how one can find such an an internal collision for a given MAC algorithm. The answer is given by Proposition 2 [37, 40].

Proposition 2. *Let* $\text{MAC}()$ *be an iterated MAC with n-bit chaining variable, m-bit result, a compression function f which behaves like a random function (for fixed x_i), and output transformation g. An internal collision for MAC can be found using u known text-MAC pairs, where each text has the same substring of $s \geq 0$ trailing blocks, and v chosen texts. The expected values for u and v are: $u = \sqrt{2/(s+1)} \cdot 2^{n/2}$; $v = 0$ if g is a permutation or $s + 1 \geq 2^{n-m+6}$, and otherwise*

$$v \approx 2 \left(\frac{2^{n-m}}{s+1} \cdot \left(1 - \frac{1}{e}\right) + \left\lfloor \frac{n - m - \log_2(s+1)}{m-1} \right\rfloor + 1 \right). \tag{1}$$

∎

A simple way to preclude this attack is to append a sequence number at the *beginning* of every message and to make the MAC algorithm stateful. This means that the value of the sequence number is stored to ensure that each sequence number is used only once within the lifetime of the key. While this is not always practical, it has the additional advantage that it prevents replay attacks [14].

2.4 Weaknesses of the algorithm

The above attacks assume that no shortcuts exist to break the MAC algorithm (either for forgery or for key recovery). Since most existing MAC algorithms are not provably secure, it is recommended to use only well established algorithms which have been subjected to an independent evaluation. Even if this has been performed, a regular review of the algorithm based on progress in cryptanalysis is recommended.

3 Practical MAC algorithms

Compared to the number of block ciphers and hash functions, there relatively few MAC algorithms have been proposed. The main reason is that MACs have been derived from other primitives (initially from block ciphers and currently from hash functions), which reduces the need for dedicated proposals. This section reviews the known constructions.

3.1 Based on block ciphers

The most popular MAC algorithm is certainly CBC-MAC; it has been adopted by many standardization committees including ANSI and ISO/IEC [1, 2, 22, 23]. It is widely used with DES [17] as the underlying block cipher. CBC-MAC is an iterated MAC, with the following compression function:

$$H_i = E_K(H_{i-1} \oplus x_i), \quad 1 \le i \le t.$$

Here $E_K(x)$ denotes the encryption of x using the k-bit key K with an n-bit block cipher E and $H_0 = 0$. The MAC is then computed as $\mathrm{MAC}_K(x) = g(H_t)$, where g is the output transformation. The mapping g is required to preclude the following simple forgery: given $\mathrm{MAC}(x)$, $\mathrm{MAC}(x\|y)$, and $\mathrm{MAC}(x')$, one knows that $\mathrm{MAC}(x'\|y') = \mathrm{MAC}(x\|y)$ if $y' = y \oplus \mathrm{MAC}(x) \oplus \mathrm{MAC}(x')$.

One approach is for g to select the leftmost m bits. However, L. Knudsen has shown that the simple attack can be extended to this case [28]; it requires then approximately $2^{(n-m)/2}$ chosen texts and 2 known texts.

A widely used and better alternative is to replace the processing of the last block by a two-key triple encryption (with keys $K_1 = K$ and K_2); this is commonly known as the ANSI retail MAC, since it first appeared in [2]:

$$g(H_t) = E_{K_1}(D_{K_2}(H_t)) = E_{K_1}(D_{K_2}(E_{K_1}(x_t \oplus H_{t-1}))).$$

Here D denotes decryption. This mapping requires little overhead, and has the additional advantage that it precludes an exhaustive search against the 56-bit DES key.

A second alternative is the use of a derived key K' (as opposed to a second independent key):

$$g(H_t) = E_{K'}(H_t) = E_{K'}(E_K(x_t \oplus H_{t-1})).$$

This solution was proposed by the RIPE Consortium in [41] and has been included in IS 9797 [23].

All these variants are vulnerable to the forgery attack described in Sect. 2.3, which requires a single chosen message and about $2^{n/2}$ known messages (for DES this corresponds to 2^{32} known messages). For $m < n$, an additional 2^{m-n} chosen messages are required, which makes the attack less realistic.

For the ANSI retail MAC, one does not only obtain a forgery, but one can also recover the key in time $3 \cdot 2^k$ encryptions, compared to 2^{2k} encryptions for exhaustive search [39]. If DES is used, this implies that key recovery may become feasible. Another key recovery attack needs only a single known text, but requires about 2^k MAC verifications. Moreover, it reduces the effective MAC size from m to $\min(m, k)$.

In the light of these recent attacks, ISO/IEC SC27 has recently started the process to revise IS 9797 [23]

Bellare et al. provide in [8] a proof of security for CBC-MAC, i.e., they establish a lower bound to break the system under certain assumptions on the block cipher. It almost matches the upper bound of the attack of Sect. 2.3.

An alternative to CBC-MAC is RIPE-MAC, which adds a feedforward [41]:

$$H_i = E_K(H_{i-1} \oplus x_i) \oplus x_i, \ 1 \le i \le t.$$

It has the advantage that the round function is harder to invert (even for someone who knows the secret key). An output transformation is needed as well.

XOR-MAC is another scheme based on a block cipher [7]. It is a randomized algorithm and its security can again be reduced to that of the block cipher. It has the advantage that it is parallellizable and that small modifications to the message (and to the MAC) can be made at very low cost. The use of random bits clearly helps to improve security, but it has a cost in practical implementations. Also, the performance is typically 25 to 50% slower than CBC-MAC.

Note that cryptanalysis of the underlying block cipher can often be extended to an attack on CBC-MAC, even if $m < n$, which implies that an attacker obtains less information than in conventional cryptanalysis on the ECB mode (see [32, 35] for the case of DES).

3.2 Based on cryptographic hash functions

The availability of fast dedicated hash functions (such as MD4 [42] and MD5 [43]) has resulted in several proposals for MAC algorithms based on these functions. As it became clear that these hash functions are weaker than intended, they are currently being replaced by RIPEMD-160 [16] and by SHA-1 [18].

The first proposed constructions were the secret prefix and secret suffix methods which can be described as follows: $\text{MAC}_K(x) = h(K\|x)$, $\text{MAC}_K(x) = h(x\|K)$. However, the first one allows for extension attacks, and the second one opens the possibility of off-line attacks (see [37] for a more detailed discussion).

The next proposal the secret envelope method, which can be described as $\text{MAC}_K(x) = h(K_1\|x\|K_2)$ (for example Internet RFC 1828 [31]). For this method, Bellare et al. provide a security proof based on the assumption that the compression function of the hash function is pseudo-random [5]. While this is an interesting result, it should be pointed out that the compression function of most hash functions has not been evaluated with respect to this property. Also, it was shown in [38] that $2^{n/2}$ known texts does not only allow a forgery (cf. Sect. 2.3), but also a key recovery attack.

MDx-MAC extends the envelope method by also introducing secret key material into every iteration [37]. This makes the pseudo-randomness assumption more plausible. Moreover, it precludes the key recovery attack by extending the keys to complete blocks.

HMAC is yet another variant, which uses a nested construction (also with padded keys):

$$\text{MAC}_K(x) = h(K_2\|h(x\|K_1)).$$

HMAC will be used for providing message authentication in the Internet Protocol [3, 27]. The security of HMAC is guaranteed if the hash function is collision resistant for a secret value H_0, and if the compression function itself is a secure MAC for 1 block (with the secret key in the H_i input and the message in the x_i input) [6]. While these assumptions are weaker, we believe that the the latter one still requires further validation for existing hash functions.

3.3 Dedicated MACs

The most important dedicated MAC algorithm is certainly the Message Authenticator Algorithm (MAA). MAA was designed by D. Davies [12, 13] and became an ISO banking standard in 1987. Recently several weaknesses of MAA have been exposed in [36, 38]. The forgery attack of Sec. 2.3 can be optimized; it requires only 2^{24} messages of 1 Kbyte; a corresponding key recovery attack needs 2^{32} chosen texts consisting of a single message block. The number of off-line multiplications for this attack varies between 2^{44} for one key in 1000 to about 2^{51} for one key in 50. This should be compared to about $3 \cdot 2^{65}$ multiplications for an exhaustive key search. Finally, several classes of weak keys of MAA have been identified.

The DSA algorithm (Decimal Shift and Add, not to be confused with the Digital Signature Algorithm) was designed in 1980 by Sievi of the 'German Zentralstelle für das Chiffrierwesen,' and it is used as a message authenticator for banking applications in Germany [14]. Weaknesses of this algorithm have been identified in [20, 33]. The scheme by F. Cohen [10] and its improvement by Y. Huang and F. Cohen [21] proved susceptible to an adaptive chosen message attack [34]. Attacks were also developed [33] on the weaker versions of this algorithm that are implemented in the ASP integrity toolkit [11]. Recently a new proposal was made by Bakhtiari et al. [4]; further research is required to assess its security. Several MAC algorithms exist that have not been published, such as the S.W.I.F.T. authenticator and Dataseal [30].

4 Concluding remarks

In the design and selection of algorithms for future applications, one should take into account that the additional computation required for a strong MAC algorithm with a large key is quite modest. It is suggested to use a minimum key length of at least 90 bits, but if the application permits it, a 128-bit key is recommended.

A second observation is that provably secure schemes (in the information theoretic sense) are becoming very attractive: recently major improvements have been found both in terms of speed of computation and the key size [19, 24, 25, 29, 45]. These constructions, which follow the model of Simmons [46] (who called them authentication codes or A-codes) and Wegman-Carter [47] require a one-time use of the key. They can be reduced to a potentially efficient computationally secure scheme by generating the keys using a cryptographically strong pseudo-random string generator. For the same security level against forgery attacks, the MAC will be about twice as long. Both elements indicate that this approach will mainly be suited for high speed applications with long messages.

References

1. ANSI X9.9 (revised), *"Financial Institution Message Authentication (Wholesale),"* American Bankers Association, April 7, 1986.
2. ANSI X9.19 *"Financial Institution Retail Message Authentication,"* American Bankers Association, August 13, 1986.
3. R. Atkinson, "Security architecture for the Internet Protocol," Internet Request for Comments 1825, August 1995.
4. S. Bakhtiari, R. Safavi-Naini, J. Pieprzyk, "Keyed hash functions," *Cryptography: Policy and Algorithms, LNCS 1029*, E. Dawson and J. Golić, Eds., Springer-Verlag, 1996, pp. 201–214.
5. M. Bellare, R. Canetti, H. Krawczyk, "Pseudorandom functions revisited: The cascade construction and its concrete security," *Proc. 37th Annual Symposium on the Foundations of Computer Science, IEEE*, 1996, pp. 514–523.
   Full version via http://www-cse.ucsd.edu/users/mihir.
6. M. Bellare, R. Canetti, H. Krawczyk, "Keying hash functions for message authentication," *Advances in Cryptology, Proceedings Crypto'96, LNCS 1109*, N. Koblitz, Ed., Springer-Verlag, 1996, pp. 1–15.
   Full version: http:// www.research.ibm.com/security/.
7. M. Bellare, R. Guérin, P. Rogaway, "XOR MACs: new methods for message authentication using block ciphers," *Advances in Cryptology, Proceedings Crypto'95, LNCS 963*, D. Coppersmith, Ed., Springer-Verlag, 1995, pp. 15–28.
8. M. Bellare, J. Kilian, P. Rogaway, "The security of cipher block chaining," *Advances in Cryptology, Proceedings Crypto'94, LNCS 839*, Y. Desmedt, Ed., Springer-Verlag, 1994, pp. 341–358.
9. M. Blaze, W. Diffie, R.L. Rivest, B. Schneier, T. Shimomura, E. Thompson, M. Wiener, "Minimal key lengths for symmetric ciphers to provide adequate commercial security. A Report by an Ad Hoc Group of Cryptographers and Computer Scientists," January 1996.
10. F. Cohen, "A cryptographic checksum for integrity protection," *Computers & Security*, Vol. 6, No. 5, 1987, pp. 505–510.
11. F. Cohen, *"The ASP integrity toolkit. Version 3.5,"* ASP Press, Pittsburgh (PA), 1991.
12. D. Davies, "A message authenticator algorithm suitable for a mainframe computer," *Advances in Cryptology, Proceedings Crypto'84, LNCS 196*, G.R. Blakley and D. Chaum, Eds., Springer-Verlag, 1985, pp. 393–400.
13. D. Davies, D.O. Clayden, "The message authenticator algorithm (MAA) and its implementation," *NPL Report DITC 109/88*, Feb. 1988.
14. D. Davies, W. Price, *Security for Computer Networks*, 2nd ed., Wiley, 1989.
15. W. Diffie, M.E. Hellman, "New directions in cryptography," *IEEE Trans. on Information Theory*, Vol. IT–22, No. 6, 1976, pp. 644–654.
16. H. Dobbertin, A. Bosselaers, B. Preneel, "RIPEMD-160: a strengthened version of RIPEMD," *Fast Software Encryption, LNCS 1039*, D. Gollmann, Ed., Springer-Verlag, 1996, pp. 71–82.

17. FIPS 46, *Data encryption standard,* NBS, U.S. Department of Commerce, Washington D.C., Jan. 1977.

18. FIPS 180-1, *Secure hash standard,* NIST, US Department of Commerce, Washington D.C., April 1995.

19. S. Halevi, H. Krawczyk, "MMH: Software message authentication in the Gbit/second rates," *Fast Software Encryption, LNCS 1267,* E. Biham, Ed., Springer-Verlag, 1997, pp. 172–189.

20. F. Heider, D. Kraus, M. Welschenbach, "Some preliminary remarks on the Decimal Shift and Add algorithm (DSA)," *Abstracts Eurocrypt'86, May 20–22, 1986, Linköping, Sweden,* p. 1.2. (Full paper available from the authors.)

21. Y.J. Huang, F. Cohen, "Some weak points of one fast cryptographic checksum algorithm and its improvement," *Computers & Security,* Vol. 7, No. 5, 1988, pp. 503–505.

22. ISO 8731:1987, *Banking – approved algorithms for message authentication, Part 1, DEA, Part 2, Message Authentication Algorithm (MAA).*

23. ISO/IEC 9797:1994, *Information technology - Data cryptographic techniques - Data integrity mechanisms using a cryptographic check function employing a block cipher algorithm.*

24. T. Johansson, "Bucket hashing with a small key size," *Advances in Cryptology, Proceedings Eurocrypt'97, LNCS 1233,* W. Fumy, Ed., Springer-Verlag, 1997, pp. 149–162.

25. T. Johansson, G. Kabatianskii, B. Smeets, "On the relation between A-codes and codes correcting independent errors," *Advances in Cryptology, Proceedings Eurocrypt'93, LNCS 765,* T. Helleseth, Ed., Springer-Verlag, 1994, pp. 1–11.

26. B. Kaliski, M. Robshaw, "Message authentication with MD5," *CryptoBytes (RSA Laboratories Technical Newsletter),* Vol. 1, No. 1, Spring 1995, pp. 5–8.

27. S. Kent, "Security architecture for the Internet Protocol," Internet Draft, July 1997.

28. L. Knudsen, "Chosen-text attack on CBC-MAC," *Electronics Letters,* Vol. 33, No. 1, 1997, pp. 48–49.

29. H. Krawczyk, "New hash functions for message authentication," *Advances in Cryptology, Proceedings Eurocrypt'95, LNCS 921,* L.C. Guillou and J.-J. Quisquater, Eds., Springer-Verlag, 1995, pp. 301–310.

30. C. Lindén, H. Block, "Sealing electronic money in Sweden," *Computers & Security,* Vol. 1, No. 3, 1982, p. 226–230.

31. P. Metzger, W. Simpson, "IP Authentication using Keyed MD5", Internet Request for Comments 1828, August 1995.

32. K. Ohta, M. Matsui, "Differential attack on message authentication codes," *Advances in Cryptology, Proceedings Crypto'93, LNCS 773,* D. Stinson, Ed., Springer-Verlag, 1994, pp. 200–211.

33. B. Preneel, "Analysis and design of cryptographic hash functions," *Doctoral Dissertation,* Katholieke Universiteit Leuven, 1993.

34. B. Preneel, A. Bosselaers, R. Govaerts, J. Vandewalle, "Cryptanalysis of a fast cryptographic checksum algorithm," *Computers & Security,* Vol. 9, No. 3, 1990, pp. 257–262.

35. B. Preneel, M. Nuttin, V. Rijmen, J. Buelens, "Cryptanalysis of the CFB mode of the DES with a reduced number of rounds," *Advances in Cryptology, Proceedings Crypto'93, LNCS 773,* D. Stinson, Ed., Springer-Verlag, 1994, pp. 212–223.

36. B. Preneel, V. Rijmen, P.C. van Oorschot, "A security analysis of the Message Authenticator Algorithm (MAA)," *European Transactions on Telecommunications*, Vol. 8, No. 5, 1997, pp. 455–470.

37. B. Preneel, P.C. van Oorschot, "MDx-MAC and building fast MACs from hash functions," *Advances in Cryptology, Proceedings Crypto'95, LNCS 963*, D. Coppersmith, Ed., Springer-Verlag, 1995, pp. 1–14.

38. B. Preneel, P.C. van Oorschot, "On the security of two MAC algorithms," *Advances in Cryptology, Proceedings Eurocrypt'96, LNCS 1070*, U. Maurer, Ed., Springer-Verlag, 1996, pp. 19–32.

39. B. Preneel, P.C. van Oorschot, "A key recovery attack on the ANSI X9.19 retail MAC," *Electronics Letters*, Vol. 32, No. 17, 1996, pp. 1568–1569.

40. B. Preneel, P.C. van Oorschot, "On the security of iterated Message Authentication Codes," submitted.

41. RIPE, *"Integrity Primitives for Secure Information Systems. Final Report of RACE Integrity Primitives Evaluation (RIPE-RACE 1040),"* LNCS 1007, A. Bosselaers and B. Preneel, Eds., Springer-Verlag, 1995.

42. R.L. Rivest, "The MD4 message digest algorithm," *Advances in Cryptology, Proceedings Crypto'90, LNCS 537*, S. Vanstone, Ed., Springer-Verlag, 1991, pp. 303–311.

43. R.L. Rivest, "The MD5 message-digest algorithm," Request for Comments 1321, Internet Activities Board, Internet Privacy Task Force, April 1992.

44. R.L. Rivest, A. Shamir, L. Adleman, "A method for obtaining digital signatures and public-key cryptosystems," *Communications of the ACM*, Vol. 21, No. 2, 1978, pp. 120–126.

45. P. Rogaway, "Bucket hashing and its application to fast message authentication," *Advances in Cryptology, Proceedings Crypto'95, LNCS 963*, D. Coppersmith, Ed., Springer-Verlag, 1995, pp. 29–42.

46. G.J. Simmons, "A survey of information authentication," in *"Contemporary Cryptology: The Science of Information Integrity,"* G.J. Simmons, Ed., IEEE Press, 1991, pp. 381–419.

47. M.N. Wegman, J.L. Carter, "New hash functions and their use in authentication and set equality," *Journal of Computer and System Sciences*, Vol. 22, No. 3, 1981, pp. 265–279.

48. M.J. Wiener, "Efficient DES key search," *Technical Report TR-244*, School of Computer Science, Carleton University, Ottawa, Canada, May 1994. Presented at the rump session of Crypto'93.

The Least Witness of a Composite Number

R. Balasubramanian* and S. V. Nagaraj**

The Institute of Mathematical Sciences, Madras 600 113, India

Abstract. We consider the problem of finding the least witness of a composite number. If n is a composite number then a number w for which n is not a strong pseudo-prime to the base w is called a *witness* for n. Let $w(n)$ be the least witness for a composite n. Bach [7] assuming the Generalized Riemann Hypothesis (GRH) showed that $w(n) < 2 \log^2 n$. In this paper we are interested in obtaining upper bounds for $w(n)$ without assuming the GRH.

Burthe [15] showed that $w(n) = O_\epsilon(n^{1/(8\sqrt{e})+\epsilon})$ for all composite numbers n which are not a product of three distinct prime factors. For the three prime factor case he was able to show that $w(n) = O_\epsilon(n^{1/(6\sqrt{e})+\epsilon})$. We improve his result to show $w(n) = O_\epsilon(n^{1/(8\sqrt{e})+\epsilon})$ for all composite numbers n except Carmichael numbers $n = pqr$ for which $\nu_2(p-1) = \nu_2(q-1) = \nu_2(r-1)$. For the special Carmichaels we use an argument due to Heath-Brown to get $w(n) = O_\epsilon(n^{1/(6.568\sqrt{e})+\epsilon})$.

We conjecture $w(n) = O_\epsilon(n^{1/(8\sqrt{e})+\epsilon})$ for every composite number n and look at open problems. It appears to be very difficult to settle our conjecture.

1 Introduction

The problem of quickly determining the prime or composite nature of a number n is a very important problem in algorithmic number theory and cryptography and has been the subject of much research [1, 2, 4, 7, 10, 29]. A fast $O((\log n)^{4+o(1)})$ time deterministic algorithm for this problem is known under the assumption of the as yet unresolved Generalized Riemann Hypothesis (GRH) [7, 26]. However the best known deterministic algorithm for this problem without the assumption of any unproved hypothesis [4] runs in sub-exponential time having a time complexity of $O((\log n)^{O(\log \log \log n)})$. It has also been proved that there is a probabilistic algorithm [1] that for prime n leads to a primality proof (proof that the number is actually a prime) in $O((\log n)^k)$ expected time for some $k \geq 1$.

A first approach to test if a given positive integer n is a prime, is to choose an integer a such that $1 < a < n$ and $\gcd(a, n) = 1$ and n passes the Fermat test i.e. $a^{n-1} \equiv 1 \bmod n$. If $a^{n-1} \not\equiv 1 \bmod n$ then n is not a prime. A composite number

---

* Email: balu@imsc.ernet.in
** Research done while at The Institute of Mathematical Sciences. Current Affiliation: IBM Tokyo Research Laboratory, 1623-14, Shimotsuruma, Yamato-shi, Kanagawa-ken 242, Japan. Email: nagaraj@trl.ibm.co.jp, svn@imsc.ernet.in

n which passes the Fermat test for a given base a is called a Fermat pseudo-prime to the base a. There are certain composite numbers n called as Carmichael numbers [23] for which $a^{n-1} \equiv 1 \bmod n$ for every a for which $\gcd(a, n) = 1$. It has been proved recently [5] that there are infinitely many Carmichael numbers. Hence a different approach is required.

A further improvement to the Fermat test is known [23] which uses the Legendre-Jacobi symbol (see [23]). If p is an odd prime and $\gcd(a, p) = 1$ then $a^{(p-1)/2} \equiv (\frac{a}{p}) \bmod p$. This test recognizes composite numbers not recognized as composite by the Fermat test.

A composite number n is called an Euler pseudo-prime to the base a if $\gcd(a, n) = 1$ and $a^{(n-1)/2} \equiv (\frac{a}{n}) \bmod n$. It is known [23] that no odd composite number can be a Euler pseudo-prime for all the possible bases a for which $\gcd(a, n) = 1$.

An improvement on the Euler pseudo-prime test is the strong pseudo-prime test also called as the Miller-Rabin test [29]. Let n be a positive odd number for which $n - 1 = 2^s t$ where t is odd. If $1 \le a \le n - 1$ then n is defined to be a strong pseudo-prime to the base a if:

> either $a^t \equiv 1 \bmod n$ or $a^{2^i t} \equiv -1 \bmod n$ for some $i \in \{0, 1, \ldots, s - 1\}$.

Note 1. Many of the problems we consider have polynomial time algorithms for solving them if the Generalised Riemann Hypothesis (GRH) is true. However, we are interested in algorithms for these problems, which do not assume the GRH.

Definition 2 (Witness). Let n be a composite number. We define an integer a for which $1 < a < n$ to be a "witness" to the compositeness of n if either $\gcd(a, n) > 1$ or n is not a strong pseudo-prime to the base a.

From our definition of "witness" it follows that we can test if a given integer a produces a certificate of compositeness of a given composite number n, in polynomial time. This property is very helpful in practice, when we want to quickly convince anyone (or ourselves), that a particular number is in fact composite.

For a composite number n it is desirable to give a good upper bound on the least witness $w(n)$ to the compositeness of n. It is known that $w(n) < 2\log^2 n$ under the assumption of the GRH [7]. From this it is easy to show that the average of $w(n)$ taken over odd composite numbers $\le x$ is asymptotic to 2 as $x \to \infty$ [15]. Burthe [15] showed that this is true even without the GRH assumption.

The last result has an interesting algorithmic interpretation:

Theorem 3. *There is a deterministic algorithm which finds a certificate of compositeness of a given composite number n, whose average running time is polynomial (asymptotically), without the assumption of any unproved hypothesis (such as the Generalized Riemann Hypothesis).*

We are not aware of any such result prior to Burthe's [15]. The average running time of the basic version of the fastest deterministic primality testing algorithm [4] is not polynomial as there are essentially no good cases for that algorithm, they are all the same case. There are versions of that algorithm [12] which use partial factorizations of $n^2 - 1$ etc., but few n's will have a factored portion big enough to influence the average running time.

The analogue of the above theorem for primes involves finding certificates of primality. There is an open problem here:

Open Problem 4. *Give a deterministic algorithm, which does not assume any unproved hypothesis, which finds certificates of primality for prime numbers, whose average running time is polynomial.*

In order to solve this open question one would at least have to show that a positive proportion of the primes can be recognized in deterministic polynomial time. The best result in this direction is that of S. Konyagin and C. Pomerance [24] who showed that $> x^{1-\epsilon}$ primes up to x can be recognized in deterministic polynomial time for any $\epsilon > 0$. We thank Carl Pomerance for the above observation.

The study of $w(n)$ is closely related [15] to $G(n)$, the smallest positive integer G such that the subgroup generated by the integers b for which $1 \leq b \leq G$ and $\gcd(b, n) = 1$ is $(Z/nZ)^*$. For odd composite numbers n it is known [15] that $w(n) \leq G(n)$. Bach [7] showed that the GRH implies $G(n) \leq 3\log^2 n$.

Number-theoretic estimates obtained without assuming the GRH are generally very weak when compared to those obtained using it. This observation also applies to estimates for $G(n)$.

Bach and Huelsbergen [8] offer heuristic arguments and numerical data supporting the idea that $G(n) \leq (\log 2)^{-1} \log n \log \log n$ asymptotically. They remark that by the Polya-Vinogradov inequality [18], for odd composite n, $G(n) = O(\sqrt{n} \log n \log \log n)$ hence $w(n) = O(\sqrt{n} \log n \log \log n)$. For a composite n we can show trivially that $w(n) < \sqrt{n}$ by observing that such a n has a non-trivial divisor less than $\sqrt{n}$.

Burthe [15] showed that $G(n) = O_\epsilon(n^{3/(8\sqrt{e})+\epsilon})$ for all $n \in Z^+$ and if n is cube-free, then one can replace 3/8 with 1/4.

Lenstra [25] obtained the following theorems, of independent interest. They give an algorithm useful for finding witnesses of numbers that are not square-free.

Theorem 5 (Lenstra). *Let n be a composite number, $n \neq 4$, and assume that $a^{n-1} \equiv 1 \bmod n$ for every prime number $a < (\log n)^2$. Then n is the product of distinct prime numbers.*

Theorem 6 (Lenstra). *Let p be an odd prime. Then we have $a^{p-1} \not\equiv 1 \bmod p^2$ for some prime number $a < 4(\log p)^2$.*

Burthe [15] obtained the following variation of the above results of Lenstra, by a different technique.

Theorem 7 (Burthe). *If n is an odd composite number that is not square-free then $w(n) < \log^2 n$.*

Lenstra's result has an interesting algorithmic consequence:

Theorem 8. *There is a deterministic algorithm that finds a certificate of compositeness of a number n that is not square-free, in polynomial time.*

Theorem 9. *There is a $O((\log n)^{4+o(1)}/\log\log n)$ time deterministic algorithm, for producing a certificate of compositeness of a number n that is not square-free.*

If we are able to improve on the exponent of $\log n$ in Lenstra's theorem then we improve on the above theorem but this appears to be very difficult [20]. We get an open problem here:

Open Problem 10. *Obtain a $o((\log^4 n)/\log\log n)$ time deterministic algorithm for finding a certificate of compositeness of a number n that is not square-free.*

Granville [21] showed that we can assume $a < (\log p)^2$ in Lenstra's theorem 6. Hence we get $w(n) < (1/4)\log^2 n$ in theorem 7.

We note that the algorithm referred to in theorem 8 may produce a certificate of compositeness of a composite n that is square-free. Hence it is not useful for distinguishing between square-free composites and integers that are not square-free. However we get an interesting result:

Theorem 11. *If there is a polynomial time algorithm for producing a certificate of compositeness of a square-free composite number n then we can transform that algorithm to a polynomial time algorithm for establishing the primality of any positive integer n.*

It is interesting to note that while there is a deterministic polynomial time algorithm for producing certificates of compositeness of numbers that are not square-free, there is no known deterministic polynomial time algorithm (see [3]) for testing if a number is square-free.

By using the results of Lenstra and Burthe we get $w(n) = O_\epsilon(n^{1/(4\sqrt{e})+\epsilon})$ for every odd composite number n.

By a careful consideration of the number of prime factors of n Burthe [15] obtained:

Theorem 12 (Burthe). *If n is an odd composite number and is not the product of three distinct primes then $w(n) = O_\epsilon(n^{1/(8\sqrt{e})+\epsilon})$ for every $\epsilon > 0$.*

Theorem 13 (Burthe). *If n is an odd composite number with exactly three prime factors then for every $\epsilon > 0$, $w(n) = O_\epsilon(n^{1/(6\sqrt{e})+\epsilon})$.*

Thus Burthe was able to show that for every odd composite number n, $w(n) = O_\epsilon(n^{1/(6\sqrt{e})+\epsilon})$.

2 Improving Burthe's Theorem

An interesting problem is to improve 1/6 to 1/8 in Burthe's theorem for odd composite numbers with three prime factors. Burthe [15] requires the following results for his theorem 13:

Lemma 14 (Burthe). *If n is odd and p and q are primes dividing n with $\nu_2(p-1) < \nu_2(q-1)$ and if $\left(\frac{a}{q}\right) = -1$ for $a \in Z^+$ then a is a witness for n. Furthermore if $\nu_2(p-1) = \nu_2(q-1)$ and $\left(\frac{b}{pq}\right) = -1$ for $b \in Z^+$ then b is witness for n.*

Lemma 15 (Burthe). *For every $\epsilon > 0$ there is some number C_ϵ with the following property: if p and q are primes that divide an odd number n and $\nu_2(p-1) < \nu_2(q-1)$ then $w(n) < C_\epsilon q^{1/(4\sqrt{e})+\epsilon}$.*

Theorem 16 (Burthe). *Let χ be a character mod n. For non-principal characters χ, define $B(\chi)$ to be the least positive integer a such that $\chi(a) \neq 1$ and $\chi(a) \neq 0$. Then for every $\epsilon > 0$, we have $B(\chi) = O_\epsilon(n^{3/(8\sqrt{e})+\epsilon})$. If in addition n is cube-free then for all $\epsilon > 0$, $B(\chi) = O_\epsilon(n^{1/(4\sqrt{e})+\epsilon})$.*

Burthe [15] in his proof of theorem 13 showed that we need to consider only the case $\nu_2(p-1) = \nu_2(q-1)$. By using the above results it is easy to strengthen this to $\nu_2(p-1) = \nu_2(q-1) = \nu_2(r-1)$. We prove for non-Carmichael numbers $n = pqr$ the least witness $w(n) = O_\epsilon(n^{1/(8\sqrt{e}+\epsilon)})$. Hence we have to solve our problem just for Carmichael numbers $n = pqr$ for which $\nu_2(p-1) = \nu_2(q-1) = \nu_2(r-1)$. This particular result also follows by a direct application of following lemmas in Adleman and Leighton's paper (see [2]).

Lemma 17 (Adleman-Leighton). *For any $\epsilon > 0$, there is a constant C such that, for every pair of primes p and q with $q \mid (p-1)$, there is a qth non-residue of p less than $Cp^{1/(4\sqrt{e})+\epsilon}$.*

Lemma 18 (Adleman-Leighton). *If $p \mid n$ and $p' \mid n$ for two primes p and p', $\nu_q(p-1) > \nu_q(p'-1) \geq 0$ for some prime q, a is a qth non-residue of p, and $\lambda(n) \mid (n-1)s$ for some s, then either a or $(a^{(n-1)s/q^k} \bmod n) - 1$ has a nontrivial greatest common divisor with n for some $1 \leq k \leq \nu_q((n-1)s)$.*

These two lemmas also tell us more, namely that if $n = pqr$ is a Carmichael number then there exists a prime Q such that the condition $\nu_Q(p-1) = \nu_Q(q-1) = \nu_Q(r-1)$ fails to hold and there will be an a satisfying $a = O_\epsilon(n^{1/(8\sqrt{e})+\epsilon})$ which will produce a certificate to the compositeness of n (by producing a nontrivial gcd as guaranteed by the lemma just stated). But it is not clear how we can quickly find such a Q.

Lemma 19. *If $n = pqr$ where $p < q < r$ are odd primes and n is not a Carmichael number then $w(n) = O_\epsilon(n^{1/(8\sqrt{e}+\epsilon)})$.*

Proof. Assume that n satisfies the given conditions but is not a Carmichael number. If $pq <= \sqrt{n}$ then $w(n) = O_\epsilon((n^{1/(8\sqrt{e})+\epsilon})$ by using $w(n) < O_\epsilon((pq)^{1/(4\sqrt{e})+\epsilon})$. Hence we assume $pq > \sqrt{n}$. Then $r < \sqrt{n}$ gives $p < q < r < \sqrt{n}$. By Burthe [15], we have for a prime P, $G(P) = O_\epsilon(P^{1/(4\sqrt{e})+\epsilon})$. This implies that the set of numbers $\{1,\ldots,l\}$ where $l = O_\epsilon(P^{1/(4\sqrt{e})+\epsilon})$ generate $(Z/PZ)^*$. The number n must satisfy $a^{n-1} \equiv 1 \bmod n$ for every $a = O_\epsilon(n^{1/(8\sqrt{e}+\epsilon)})$ otherwise we are done.

Say $P = p$. Since the numbers $1,\ldots,l$ generate G, and since $a^{n-1} \equiv 1 \bmod n$ for all a in $\{1\ldots l\}$, therefore $a^{n-1} \equiv 1 \bmod P$ for a in G. But G is cyclic, so $g^{n-1} \equiv 1 \bmod P$ for g a primitive root of P. Hence $|G| = P - 1$ divides $n - 1$. Similarly, setting $P = q$, $P = r$ and using the fact that n is square-free we get n is a Carmichael number. This contradiction concludes our proof. $\square$

Note that in the above proof we only require the weaker assumption that n is a pseudo-prime for the bases under consideration.

We also make use of the following lemma:

Lemma 20. *Assume $n = pqr$ where $p < q < r$ are odd primes. If n is a Carmichael number for which $\nu_2(p-1) = \nu_2(q-1) = \nu_2(r-1)$ then if n is a strong pseudo-prime to the base a then $(a/p) = (a/q) = (a/r)$.*

3 The Least Witness For the Special Carmichaels

Except for the case when the given composite number n is a Carmichael number with three prime factors with $\nu_2(p-1) = \nu_2(q-1) = \nu_2(r-1)$, we have succeeded in showing that the least witness $w(n)$ for a composite number n satisfies $w(n) = O_\epsilon(n^{1/(8\sqrt{e})+\epsilon})$. These exceptional numbers are in fact, among the worst case numbers for the strong pseudo-prime test [19]. The other numbers are 9, 25, 49 and numbers of the form $(m+1)(2m+1)$ and $(m+1)(3m+1)$. While these numbers can be recognized in deterministic polynomial time we have an open problem for the special Carmichaels.

Open Problem 21. *Give a deterministic polynomial time algorithm for producing a certificate of compositeness of a Carmichael number of the form $n = pqr$ where $p < q < r$ are odd primes, for which $\nu_2(p-1) = \nu_2(q-1) = \nu_2(r-1)$.*

In fact the problem is open for any Carmichael number.

3.1 An Improved Estimate of $w(n)$ for the Special Carmichaels

For the special Carmichaels we improve Burthe's estimate $w(n) = O_\epsilon(n^{1/(6\sqrt{e})+\epsilon})$ by using an argument due to Heath-Brown [22] to show $w(n) = O_\epsilon(n^{1/(6.568\sqrt{e})+\epsilon})$.

Theorem 22. *If $n = pqr$ is a Carmichael number for which $\nu_2(p-1) = \nu_2(q-1) = \nu_2(r-1)$ then $w(n) = O_\epsilon(n^{1/(6.568\sqrt{e})+\epsilon})$.*

Proof. Let $n = pqr$ be a Carmichael number for which $\nu_2(p-1) = \nu_2(q-1) = \nu_2(r-1)$.

Let $p < q < r$, and suppose that $(m/p) = (m/q) = (m/r)$ for $m < M$. Then $(m/pq) = (m/qr) = (m/pr) = 1$ for $m < M$, except when p or q or r divides m.

Method (i): we may apply the standard technique of Vinogradov for the least quadratic non-residue of the character $(*/pq)$. Let $K > M$ and sum (k/pq) for $k < K$, with $K = (pq)^{1/4+o(1)}$. By Burgess' bound (see [14] or p. 263 of [30]) this is $o(K)$. On the other hand we get a contribution $+1$ except when k has a prime factor at least M (or if p or q divides k). The sum is therefore at least $K - K/p - K/q - 2K \sum_{M \leq s < K} 1/s$, where s runs over primes. Hence

$$o(K) \geq K \left(1 - 2\log(\frac{\log K}{\log M}) - o(1)\right)$$

since p must tend to infinity as n does. Thus

$$M < (pq)^{1/4\sqrt{e}+o(1)}.$$

Method (ii): This time we consider $\sum_{k \leq K}(k/pq) + (k/pr) + (k/qr)$ for $K = (qr)^{1/4+o(1)}$, so that Burgess's bound shows the sum to be $o(K)$. This time we get a contribution of $+3$ unless k has a prime factor $s \geq M$ (or k is divisible by p, q, or r). However, for any k, the summand is at least -1 (this is the key point in the argument; the summand can never be -2 or -3). It follows that

$$o(K) \geq K \left(3 - 4/p - 4/q - 4/r - 4 \sum_{M \leq s < K} 1/s\right)$$

and hence that

$$o(K) \geq K \left(3 - 4\log(\frac{\log K}{\log M}) - o(1)\right)$$

We deduce that

$$M < (qr)^{1/4e^{3/4}+o(1)}.$$

Conclusion: It remains to use the two bounds as efficiently as possible, and this depends on what information one has as to the relative sizes of p, q and r. We have $r < pq$, and $q = O(p^2)$ (as well as $p < q < r$, of course) but there may be other constraints. Setting $p = n^a$, $q = n^b$, $r = n^c$ and $M = n^x$, one has $0 \leq a \leq b \leq c$, $a + b + c = 1$, $c < a + b$, $b \leq 2a + o(1)$ and we have to find the maximum of

$$x = min(\frac{(a+b)}{4\sqrt{e}}, \frac{(b+c)}{4e^{3/4}}) + o(1)$$

subject to these constraints. This is a linear programming problem.

We solved this linear programming problem using Mathematica to get $x \approx 1/(6.568\sqrt{e})$.

This establishes that $w(n) = O_\epsilon(n^{1/(6.568\sqrt{e})+\epsilon})$. □

4 Discussion

Finally we are led to the following conjecture:

Conjecture 23. *For every composite number n we have $w(n) = O_\epsilon(n^{1/(8\sqrt{e})+\epsilon})$.*

Our conjecture is based on Lemma 20. Obviously, our conjecture is true if the GRH holds due to Bach's result for $w(n)$ [7].

Several people including D. R. Heath-Brown, A. Hildebrand, Iwaniec, H. W. Lenstra, A. M. Odlyzko and C. Pomerance have remarked that it is not going to be easy to prove the conjecture though it is likely to be true.

It is easy to see that if our conjecture is true then we get an improvement over the primality test of Adleman and Leighton [2]. The new primality test will have a running time of $O_\epsilon(n^{1/(8\sqrt{e})+\epsilon})$.

No deterministic polynomial time algorithm is known for recognizing whether a number is a Carmichael number. However it is easy to show that these numbers can actually be factored in random polynomial time [10]. Finally, we note that the number of special Carmichaels up to x is actually $O(x^{5/14+o(1)})$ since it is known [9] that the number of Carmichael numbers up to a given number x, with exactly three prime factors is $O(x^{5/14+o(1)})$.

R. Pinch [28] has provided us with several interesting numerical examples and asked whether our bounds can be made explicit. R. Peralta has suggested exploring the connections of this paper to [27].

5 Acknowledgments

We thank Dr. Ronald Burthe and Prof. Leighton for providing their articles. We thank Prof. Heath-Brown for allowing us to use his argument. We thank Profs. A. Hildebrand, H. Iwaniec, N. Koblitz, H. W. Lenstra, A. M. Odlyzko, R. Peralta, C. Pomerance and I. Shparlinski for their helpful comments. We thank Prof. Richard Pinch for his comments and for providing several numerical results. We acknowledge use of the software package Mathematica. The second author thanks Prof. Eiji Okamoto, JAIST and ISW 97 for their financial support which made the presentation of this paper possible.

References

1. L. Adleman and M. Huang, Primality testing and two dimensional Abelian varieties over finite fields, *Lec. Notes in Math* **1512**, Springer-Verlag (1994).
2. L. Adleman and F. T. Leighton, An $O(n^{1/10.89})$ primality testing algorithm, *Math. Comp.* **36** (1981) 261–266.
3. L. Adleman and K. S. McCurley, Open problems in number-theoretic complexity-II, in: L. M. Adleman and M. D. Huang (eds.), Algorithmic Number Theory, *LNCS* 877, Springer-Verlag, Berlin (1994), 291–322.
4. L. Adleman, C. Pomerance and R. Rumely, On distinguishing prime numbers from composite numbers, *Ann. of Math.* **117** (1983) 173–206.
5. W. R. Alford, A. Granville and C. Pomerance, There are infinitely many Carmichael numbers, *Ann. of Math.* **140** (1994) 1–20.

6. W. R. Alford, A. Granville and C. Pomerance, On the difficulty of finding reliable witnesses, in: L. M. Adleman and M. D. Huang (eds.), Algorithmic Number Theory, *LNCS* 877, Springer-Verlag, Berlin (1994), 1–16.

7. E. Bach, Analytic methods in the analysis and design of number-theoretic algorithms, MIT Press, Cambridge, Mass. (1985).

8. E. Bach and L. Huelsbergen, Statistical evidence for small generating sets, *Math. Comp* **61** (1993), 69–82.

9. R. Balasubramanian and S. V. Nagaraj, Density of Carmichael numbers with three prime factors, *Math. Comp.* **66** (1997), 1705–1708.

10. P. Beauchemin, G. Brassard, C. Crepeau, C. Goutier and C. Pomerance, The generation of random numbers that are probably prime, J. Cryptology **1** (1988) 53–64.

11. D. Bleichenbacher, Efficiency and security of crypto-systems based on number theory, Ph.D Thesis, Swiss Federal Institute of Technology, Diss. ETH No. 11404, Zurich 1996.

12. W. Bosma and M. P. van der Hulst, Primality testing with cyclotomy, Ph.D Thesis, Faculteit Wiskunde en Informatica, Univ. of Amsterdam (1990).

13. D. A. Burgess, On character sums and primitive roots, *Proc. London Math. Soc.* **12** (1962) 179–192.

14. D. A. Burgess, On character sums and L-series II, *Proc. London Math. Soc.* **13** (1963) 524–536.

15. R. J. Burthe, The average witness is 2, Ph.D Thesis, University of Georgia (1995).

16. R. J. Burthe Jr., Uper bounds for least witnesses and generating sets, *Acta Arith.* **80** (1997) 311–326.

17. R. J. Burthe Jr., The average witness is 2, *Acta Arith.* **80** (1997) 327–341.

18. H. Davenport, *Multiplicative Number Theory*, 2nd Ed., (Springer Verlag, New York, 1980).

19. I. Damgaard, P. Landrock and C. Pomerance, Average case error estimates for the strong probable prime test, *Math. Comp* **61** (1993) 177–194.

20. A. Granville, Some conjectures related to Fermat's last theorem, in: Proc. of the First Conference of the CNTA, Alberta, April 1988, pp. 177–192, (Walter de Gruyter, Berlin 1990).

21. A. Granville, On pairs of co-prime integers with no large prime factors, *Expo. Math.* **9** (1991), 335–350.

22. D. R. Heath-Brown, Personal Communication, April 1997.

23. N. Koblitz, *A Course in Number Theory and Cryptography* Graduate texts in Mathematics, (Springer Verlag, New York 1987).

24. S. Konyagin and C. Pomerance, On primes recognisable in deterministic polynomial time, in: R. L. Graham and J. Nesetril (eds.), Mathematics of Paul Erdos, Springer-Verlag, Berlin (1997).

25. H. W. Lenstra, Jr., Miller's primality test, *Info. Proc. Lett.* **8** (1979) 86–88.

26. G. L. Miller, Riemann hypothesis and tests for primality, *J. Comput. System Sci.* **13** (1976), 300–317.

27. R. Peralta and V. Shoup, Primality testing with fewer random bits, *Comp. Compl.* **3** (1993), 355–367.

28. R. Pinch, Personal Communication, April 1997.

29. M. O. Rabin, Probabilistic algorithm for testing primality, *J. Number Theory* **12** (1980) , 128–138.

30. G. Tenenbaum, *Introduction to analytic and probabilistic number theory*, Cambridge Studies in Advanced Mathematics No. 46, (Cambridge University Press, 1995)

Fast Algorithm for Finding a Small Root of a Quadratic Modular Equation

Hidenori Kuwakado[1] and Hatsukazu Tanaka[1]

Kobe University,
1-1 Rokkodai Nada Kobe 657, Japan
E-mail: {kuwakado, tanaka}@eedept.kobe-u.ac.jp

Abstract. The security of some cryptosystems is based on the difficulty of solving a quadratic modular equation. This paper shows a new algorithm for finding the small root of the quadratic modular equation. While previous algorithms for finding the small root of the modular equation are based on the LLL algorithm, the new algorithm is based on the continued fraction. Using the new algorithm, we can find the root less than $n^{1/4}$, where n is the modulus. The new algorithm is more efficient than previous algorithms even if the modulus is large.

1 Introduction

If the factorization of the modulus is unknown, then it seems computationally difficult to solve the modular equation. The security of some public-key cryptosystems is based on its difficulty. Recently, Coppersmith proposed an algorithm for solving the modular equation (the Coppersmith algorithm) [2]. The size of the root that the Coppersmith algorithm can find is much smaller than that of the modulus.

In this paper, we focus on quadratic modular equations because the security of the Rabin scheme [5] and the reciprocal scheme [3] is based on the difficulty of solving the quadratic modular equation. We propose a new algorithm for computing the root of the quadratic modular equation. Although the size of the root found with our algorithm is smaller than that of the root found with the Coppersmith algorithm, our algorithm is more efficient than the Coppersmith algorithm. Differing from the Coppersmith algorithm, our algorithm is based on the continued fraction. Even if the modulus is large, our algorithm can be efficiently computed the small root.

It is known that solving the quadratic modular equation is one of the random self-reducible problems; if a non-negligible fraction of the instances can be solved efficiently, the entire instances can be done as well. Hence, the Coppersmith algorithm and our algorithm are effective for restricted instances. However, we can make use of these algorithms in the cryptanalysis as discussed in Sect. 4.

2 Proposed Algorithms

2.1 Notation

For any positive rational number r, the continued fraction expansion of r is defined as follows.

$$r = c_0 + \cfrac{1}{c_1 + \cfrac{1}{c_2 + \cdots \\ + \cfrac{1}{c_{m-1} + \cfrac{1}{c_m}}}},$$

where $c_i \in Z$ $(0 \le i \le m)$, $c_0 \ge 0$, $c_i > 0$ $(1 \le i \le m-1)$ and $c_m \ge 2$. Using the Euclid algorithm, we can compute c_i efficiently. The continued fraction expansion of r is denoted by $\langle c_0, c_1, \cdots, c_m \rangle$. We call m the length of the continued fraction expansion of r.

2.2 Extended continue fraction algorithm

Let α/β and γ/δ be positive irreducible fractions satisfying

$$\frac{\alpha}{\beta} = \frac{\gamma}{\delta}(1 - \varepsilon),$$

where ε is a non-zero rational number. Suppose that α/β is known, and γ/δ and ε are unknown. If ε is the small positive rational number, then γ/δ can be found with the continued fraction [8].

We extend the algorithm due to [8]; the extended continued fraction algorithm (ECFA) can compute γ/δ regardless of the sign of ε. In this algorithm, m is the length of the continued fraction expansion of α/β.

ECFA:
Input α, β.
Output γ, δ.
Step 1 Set $i \leftarrow 0$.
Step 2 If $i > m$, then the ECFA fails; otherwise compute c_i of the continued fraction expansion of α/β.
Step 3 For $j = 0, 1$, execute the following steps.
    Step 3-1 Compute the rational number $\gamma'/\delta' = \langle c_0, \cdots, c_{i-1}, c_i + j \rangle$.
    Step 3-2 If γ'/δ' is equal to γ/δ, then return γ' and δ' and halt.
Step 4 Set $i \leftarrow i + 1$ and go to Step 2. □

In Step 3-2, there must exist the checking method that determines whether γ'/δ' is correct without knowing γ/δ.

If $|\varepsilon|$ is not small enough, i.e., α/β is not a good approximation to γ/δ, then the ECFA can not find γ/β. The sufficient condition such that the ECFA succeeds is

$$|\varepsilon| < \frac{2}{3\gamma\delta}. \tag{1}$$

This inequality can be obtained from the property of the continued fraction [8].

2.3 Algorithms for solving the quadratic modular equation

Let n be a large composite number of unknown factorization. We consider the following quadratic modular equation.

$$x^2 + a_1 x + a_0 \equiv 0 \pmod{n}, \quad a_i \in Z_n^*, \tag{2}$$

where a_i $(i = 0, 1)$ and n are given. Suppose that Eq. (2) has the root x_0 satisfying

$$0 < x_0 < \frac{1}{3} n^{1/4}. \tag{3}$$

Since we have $a_i \approx n$, the value of the left side of Eq. (2) is larger than n. Hence, the simple real root-based method is not applicable.

We propose an efficient algorithm for finding x_0, which is based on the ECFA. First, we reduce the coefficient of x^2, i.e, 1, and the constant term a_0 simultaneously. Namely, we attempt to find the following b_0 and b_2.

$$b_2 a_0 \equiv -b_0 \pmod{n}, \quad 1 \le b_0 \le 2n^{3/4}, \quad 1 \le b_2 \le 18n^{1/4}. \tag{4}$$

The modular equation above can be transformed to the following equation.

$$\frac{a_0}{n} = \frac{k}{b_2}\left(1 - \frac{b_0}{kn}\right), \tag{5}$$

where k is an unknown integer. The input of the ECFA is a_0 and n, and the output is k and b_2. The checking method in Step 3-2 of the ECFA is to examine whether Eq. (4) holds. Note that Eq. (1) does not hold because of Eqs. (4)(5). However, we can obtain k and b_2 with high probability as shown in Subsect. 2.4. We notice that Eq. (1) is the sufficient condition.

Multiplying both sides of Eq. (2) by b_2, we have

$$b_2 x^2 + b_1 x - b_0 \equiv 0 \pmod{n}, \tag{6}$$

where $b_1 = b_2 a_1 \bmod n$. Accordingly, solving Eq. (2) is reduced to solving Eq. (6). Eq. (6) can be transformed to

$$\frac{b_1}{n} = \frac{\ell}{x_0}\left(1 - \frac{b_2 x_0^2 - b_0}{\ell n}\right),$$

where ℓ is an unknown integer. Since ℓ is not always relatively prime to x_0, the greatest common divisor of ℓ and x_0 is denoted by g. Since we have

$$\frac{|b_2 x_0^2 - b_0|}{\ell n} < \frac{2}{3\ell x_0} \le \frac{2}{3(\ell/g)(x_0/g)},$$

the ECFA can always find the irreducible fraction of ℓ/x_0. However, we wish to obtain ℓ/x_0, not the irreducible fraction of it. The ECFA can not be directly applied to finding x_0. We show the modified ECFA (MECFA) for finding x_0, which includes the computation for finding g. In this algorithm, m' is the length of the continued fraction expansion of b_1/n.

MECFA:

Input b_0, b_1, b_2, n.

Output x_0

Step 1 Set $i \leftarrow 0$.

Step 2 If $i > m'$, then the MECFA fails; otherwise compute c_i of the continued fraction expansion of b_1/n.

Step 3 For $j = 0, 1$, execute the following steps.

    Step 3-1 Compute the rational number $\ell'/x' = \langle c_0, \cdots, c_{i-1}, c_i + j \rangle$.

    Step 3-2 If $b_2 x'^2 + b_1 x' - b_0 \equiv 0 \pmod{n}$ holds, then return x' and halt.

    Step 3-3 Check if the following quadratic equation has a positive integer root.

$$b_2 x'^2 g^2 + (b_1 x' - \ell' n)g - b_0 = 0 \tag{7}$$

    Step 3-4 If Eq. (7) has the positive integer root g, then return gx' and halt.

Step 4 Set $i \leftarrow i + 1$ and go to Step 2.   □

Remark: If the exhaustive search on a few unknown high order bits of x_0 is carried out, Eq. (3) can be improved as $0 < x_0 < n^{1/4}$.

2.4 Performance

We examine the probability such that the ECFA finds b_0 and b_2 satisfying Eq. (4). The result of our numerical experiment is shown in Table 1. From Table 1, the probability of the discovery is high even if the modulus is large.

Table 1. Probability of the discovery

# of bits of n	probability [%]
1024	97.9
2048	98.8
4096	98.5

When a_0, a_1 and n in Eq. (2) are given, the average running time for computing the root x_0 is shown in Table 2. The computation in the ECFA and the MECFA requires $O(\log_2 n)$ arithmetic operations. Hence, we can efficiently compute the root x_0 even if n is large.

3 Comparison

The algorithms for solving the modular equation have been studied in [7][2]. These algorithms are based on the LLL algorithm [4].

$$x^e + a_{e-1} x^{e-1} + \cdots + a_0 \equiv 0 \pmod{n} \tag{8}$$

Table 2. Running time

# of bits of n	time [sec][†]
1024	3.2
2048	38.8
4096	765.2

[†] CPU: Pentium 166 [MHz]

The root of Eq. (8) is denoted by x_0. The range of the root found with the algorithm [7] is $0 < x_0 < n^{2/e(e+1)}$. On the other hand, in the Coppersmith algorithm [2], that is $0 < x_0 < n^{1/e}$. Hence, we focus on the Coppersmith algorithm.

In Table 3, we show the relationship between the number of bits of n and the dimension of the LLL algorithm used in the Coppersmith algorithm when the degree is 2.

Table 3. Dimension for the size of the modulus ($e = 2$)

# of bits of n	dim. of the LLL
1024	514
2048	1026

Comparing the Coppersmith algorithm with our algorithm, the advantage of the Coppersmith algorithm is as follows; the upper bound of the root is relatively high, and it can be applied to the modular equation with arbitrary degree. However, in the Coppersmith algorithm, the larger the modulus is, the larger the dimension of the LLL algorithm is. Namely, if the modulus is large, the Coppersmith algorithm is not so efficient. From Table 2, the speed of our algorithm is reasonable even if the modulus is large.

4 Applications

Our algorithm can be applied to the cryptanalysis of the Rabin scheme [5] and the reciprocal scheme [3]. The security of these schemes is based on the difficulty of solving the quadratic modular equation. Here, we focus on the reciprocal scheme. For the plaintext M ($\in Z_n^*$), the encryption function of the reciprocal scheme is defined as

$$C = M + \frac{w}{M} \bmod n,$$

where w and n are public keys, and C is the ciphertext. Hence, breaking the reciprocal scheme is reduced to solving the following the modular equation.

$$M^2 + (n - C)M + w \equiv 0 \pmod{n} \tag{9}$$

Consider that a plaintext M is sent to four receivers via the reciprocal scheme. The following system of modular equations is obtained.

$$\begin{cases} M^2 + (n_1 - C_1)M + w_1 \equiv 0 \pmod{n_1}, \\ M^2 + (n_2 - C_2)M + w_2 \equiv 0 \pmod{n_2}, \\ M^2 + (n_3 - C_3)M + w_3 \equiv 0 \pmod{n_3}, \\ M^2 + (n_4 - C_4)M + w_4 \equiv 0 \pmod{n_4}. \end{cases}$$

By using the Chinese remainder theorem, the four modular equations above can be combined to one modular equation;

$$M^2 + a_1 M + a_0 \equiv 0 \pmod{\prod_{i=1}^{4} n_i}, \tag{10}$$

where a_1 and a_0 are computed from $n_i - C_i$ and w_i $(1 \le i \le 4)$, respectively. Since $0 < M < (\prod_{i=1}^{4} n_i)^{1/4}$, Eq. (10) can be solved by using our algorithm. When n_i is 1024 [bits], i.e., $\prod_{i=1}^{4} n_i$ is 4096 [bits], the average running time for solving Eq. (10) is 765.2 [sec] (Table 2). On the other hand, using the Coppersmith algorithm, M can be computed from only two ciphertexts. However, the LLL algorithm with 1026 dimensions must be carried out.

5 Conclusion

We have proposed the algorithm for computing the small root of the quadratic modular equation. While previous algorithms are based on the LLL algorithm, our algorithm is based on the continued fraction. Since the computation of the continued fraction is more efficient than that of the LLL algorithm, our algorithm is more efficient than the previous algorithms. The size of the root that our algorithm can find is smaller than that of the root that previous algorithms can find. As the result of applying our algorithm to the cryptanalysis of the reciprocal scheme, the reciprocal scheme is not suitable for the broadcast communication.

References

1. Cohen, H.: A Course in Computational Algebraic Number Theory. Graduate Texts in Mathematics Springer-Verlag **138** (1993)
2. Coppersmith, D.: Finding a small root of a univariate modular equation. Lecture Notes in Computer Science Advances in Cryptology - EUROCRYPT'96 **1070** (1996) 155–165
3. Kurosawa, K., Ito, T., and Takeuchi, M.: A public key cryptosystem using a reciprocal with the same intractability as factoring a large number. IEICE Transactions **J70-A** 11 (1987) 1632–1636

4. Lenstra, A. K., Lenstra, H. W., and Lovász, L.: Factoring polynomials with rational coefficients. Mathematische Annalen **261** (1982) 515–534
5. Rabin, M. O.: Digital signatures and public-key functions as intractable as factorization. MIT Laboratory for Computer Science **MIT/LCS/TR-212** (1979)
6. Rivest, R. L., Shamir, A., and Adleman, L.: A method for obtaining digital signatures and public-key cryptosystems. Communications of the ACM **21** (1978) 120–126
7. Vallée, B., Girault, M., and Toffin, P.: How to guess ℓ-th roots modulo n by reducing lattice bases. Lecture Note in Computer Science **357** (1988) 427–442
8. Wiener, M. J.: Cryptanalysis of short RSA secret exponents. IEEE Transaction on Information Theory **36** 3 (1990) 553–558

Modified Finite Automata Public Key Cryptosystem

Feng Bao[1], Robert H. Deng[1], Xiang Gao[2], Yoshihide Igarashi[3]

[1] Institute of Systems Science, National University of Singapore, Singapore 119597
Email: {baofeng, deng}@iss.nus.sg
[2] Millstar Electronic Publishing Group, Langhorne, PA 19047, U.S.A
Email: hwxg@philly.infi.net
[3] Department of Computer Science, Gunma University, Kiryu 376, Japan
Email: igarashi@comp.cs.gunma-u.ac.jp

Abstract. Finite Automata Public Key Cryptosystem (FAPKC) appeared about 10 years ago in Chinese literature. FAPKC possesses many advantageous features: it is a stream-cipher capable of high-speed operation and it has a relatively small key size. Recently, FAPKC was broken in a way that the decryption automata can be derived directly from the encryption automaton [2]. However, the break is due to an oversight of the FAPKC designers. It does not reveal any weakness in its fundamental design principle. In this paper, we describe a modified FAPKC which retains all the desirable features of the original version. However, in order to resist a similar attack as that of [2], we require that the underlying automata used in the modified FAPKC satisfy certain conditions. We describe the attack and show how the automata satisfying these conditions can be constructed easily. We also show that the modified FAPKC is secure against several other known attacks.

1 Introduction

1.1 The History of FAPKC

Finite Automata Public Key Cryptosystem (FAPKC) is a public key cryptosystem based on the invertibility theory of finite automata. It was first proposed by Tao and Chen in the mid 1980's [15], [16]. FAPKC can be easily turned into digital signature systems.

FAPKC possesses the following distinguished features: 1) it is the only public key stream cipher in the open literature; 2) it is capable of high speed encryption/decryption operation since the underlying operations are "+" and "·" over a small sized finite field; 3) it has a relatively small key size (larger than RSA's but smaller than some others', such as McEilice's); 4) it is very easy to implement (only addition of vectors and multiplication of matrices with vectors).

The principle of FAPKC is similar to that of other public key systems, i.e., to disguise an easily computable class into a seemly difficult class. Roughly speaking, construction of FAPKC is based on the following: 1) it is difficult to generate the inverse automaton of a general non-linear automaton; 2) it is easy to generate an inverse automaton of a non-linear automaton in a special class; 3) by composing with a linear automaton, the non-linear automaton in the special class can be disguised as a general non-linear automaton. Since it is easy to construct an inverse automaton of any linear automaton, we can obtain the inverse automata of both the linear automaton and the non-linear automaton, and therefore form the decryption trapdoor.

Many papers on FAPKC and its relevant topics were published in China and few of them appeared in international journals or conferences. Two cryptography books mentioned FAPKC. One is Salamaa's "Public Key Cryptography"(in Section 5.3, [12]). The other one is Schneier's "Applied Cryptography"(in Section 19.10, [13]). A brief summary on the attack to FAPKC can be found in a recent paper [11].

FAPKC was broken in [2] in a way that the decryption automata can be directly derived from the encryption automaton. However, we believe that the success of this attack is due to an oversight of the FAPKC designers. It reveals no fundamental weakness in the theory of FAPKC. In this paper we modify the original FAPKC and demonstrate that the modified version resists the attack in [2]. We also show that the modified FAPKC is secure against several other attacks.

We understand that any cryptosystem needs to stand the test of time in order to have a reasonable confidence in its security. From this viewpoint, the security analyses of the modified FAPKC is still in its infancy. However, we think it is a worthwhile effort for the versatility of public key cryptography–FAPKC is based on a theory other than number theory. It is certainly not a desirable situation if all the public key systems are based on the same one or two theories.

1.2 The Contribution of This Paper

One obstacle for international readers to understand FAPKC is that mamy of the papers and related references are not easily accessible, either because they were published in China or because most of them were written in Chinese. We will try to make this paper self-contained so that the reader can understand FAPKC by just starting from here.

The modification to FAPKC mainly concentrates on the special class of non-linear automata whose inverse automata are easy to find. That class in the original FAPKC was not well chosen which led to the break of the system. In the modified FAPKC, we use a different class of non-linear automata, which we believe leads to a much more secure system than the original one. We show why the original FAPKC is insecure and compare it with the modified version.

We demonstrate an attack similar to that of [2] which works against some of the instances of the modified FAPKC. We call these instances "weak keys". Fortunately, weak keys can be clearly specified and therefore be avoided in the key generation process. Hence, this attack does not constitute a real threat to the security of the modified FAPKC.

There are *two critical points* in understanding FAPKC. The first is about linear *weakly invertible finite automaton (WIFA)* and the second is about the *composition of WIFAs.* We begin with the description of linear WIFA in the next section.

2 Linear WIFA

Both WIFA and IFA(*invertible finite automaton*) were intensively studied in the theory of invertible finite automata [14]. IFA is not used in FAPKC, so we only consider WIFA in our paper. The formal definition of WIFA can be found from [1, 2].

A WIFA *with delay r* is a FA (finite automaton) with input $x(i)$ and output $y(i)$ such that the input string $x(0), x(1), \cdots, x(n-r)$ can be uniquely determined from the output string $y(0), y(1), \cdots, y(n)$ and the initial state s_0. Consider the class of linear input-memory WIFA given by

$$y(i) = A_0 x(i) + A_1 x(i-1) + A_2 x(i-2) + \cdots + A_r x(i-r) \tag{1}$$

where $A_0, A_1, A_2, \cdots, A_r$ are 8×8 matrices over finite field $GF(2) = \{0, 1\}$, the input $x(i)$ and the output $y(i)$ at time i are 8-dimensional vectors over $GF(2)$, respectively. Corresponding to the input string $x(0)x(1) \cdots x(n)$ and the output string $y(0)y(1) \cdots y(n)$, we denote the initial state as $< x(-1), x(-2), \cdots, x(-r) >$. We regard (1) as a linear FA which is depicted in Figure 1(a). A WIFA with delay r is shown in Figure 1(b). (Note: the "$GF(2)$" and "8"(dimension) in FA

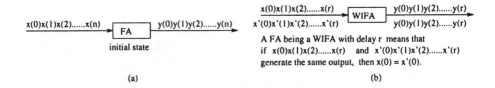

(a)

(b)

Fig. 1. (a) A FA; (b) A FA being a WIFA with delay r.

(1) can be generalized to $GF(q)$ and l, respectively. All the following discussions are valid for any $GF(q)$, l and r. In practical FAPKC, the parameters are $GF(2)$, $l = 8$ and $r = 20$ to 30.)

The properties of FA (1) are completely determined by the *linear coefficients* $A_0, A_1, A_2, \cdots, A_r$.

Claim 1 FA (1) is a WIFA with delay 0 if and only if A_0 is non-singular (full rank).

The proof is obvious. Given the initial state $x(-1), x(-2), \cdots, x(-r)$ and the output string, $y(0), y(1), \cdots, y(n)$, the input string $x(0), x(1), \cdots, x(n)$ is determined uniquely since the inverse of A_0 exists.

Claim 2 There exists a fast algorithm to determine whether FA (1) is a WIFA with delay r or not. Furthermore, if FA (1) is a WIFA with delay r, the algorithm can be used to generate the inverse of (1). (The definition of the inverse of a WIFA can be found in [2])

Now we illustrate the algorithm by the example of $r = 3$. Generalization to the case of any value r is straightforward. Because of (1), we have

$$
\begin{pmatrix} y(i) \\ y(i+1) \\ y(i+2) \\ y(i+3) \end{pmatrix} = \begin{pmatrix} A_0 & (0) & (0) & (0) \\ A_1 & A_0 & (0) & (0) \\ A_2 & A_1 & A_0 & (0) \\ A_3 & A_2 & A_1 & A_0 \end{pmatrix} \begin{pmatrix} x(i) \\ x(i+1) \\ x(i+2) \\ x(i+3) \end{pmatrix} + \begin{pmatrix} A_1 & A_2 & A_3 \\ A_2 & A_3 & (0) \\ A_3 & (0) & (0) \\ (0) & (0) & (0) \end{pmatrix} \begin{pmatrix} x(i-1) \\ x(i-2) \\ x(i-3) \end{pmatrix}
$$
(2)

where (0) denotes the 8×8 zero matrix over $GF(2)$. We can find a 32×32 matrix **P** such that

$$
\mathbf{P} \begin{pmatrix} A_0 & (0) & (0) & (0) \\ A_1 & A_0 & (0) & (0) \\ A_2 & A_1 & A_0 & (0) \\ A_3 & A_2 & A_1 & A_0 \end{pmatrix} = \begin{pmatrix} A_{0,0} & (0) & (0) & (0) \\ A_{1,1} & A_{1,0} & (0) & (0) \\ A_{2,2} & A_{2,1} & A_{2,0} & (0) \\ A_{3,3} & A_{3,2} & A_{3,1} & A_{3,0} \end{pmatrix}
$$
(3)

where the $A_{i,j}$s satisfy:

for any vectors $x_1, x_2, x_3, \exists$ vector x_0 such that $A_{3,0}x_0 = A_{3,1}x_1 + A_{3,2}x_2 + A_{3,3}x_3$;

for any vectors $x_1, x_2, \exists$ vector x_0 such that $A_{2,0}x_0 = A_{2,1}x_1 + A_{2,2}x_2$;

for any vectors $x_1, \exists$ vector x_0 such that $A_{1,0}x_0 = A_{1,1}x_1$.

The algorithm in Claim 2 is actually the one used to find matrix **P**. In order to keep the paper concise, we skip the description of the algorithm, which can be found in [2].

Observation 1. The FA in the above example is a WIFA with delay $r = 3$ if and only if $A_{0,0}$ is non-singular. If the FA is a WIFA with delay $r = 3$, we can easily construct its inverse automaton (note that this observation can be generalized to any r).

Proof. 1) Let θ denote the zero vector. Suppose that $A_{0,0}$ is singular. Then $\exists$ $x(0) \neq \theta, x(1), x(2)$ and $x(3)$ such that

$$
\begin{pmatrix} A_0 & (0) & (0) & (0) \\ A_1 & A_0 & (0) & (0) \\ A_2 & A_1 & A_0 & (0) \\ A_3 & A_2 & A_1 & A_0 \end{pmatrix} \begin{pmatrix} x(0) \\ x(1) \\ x(2) \\ x(3) \end{pmatrix} = \mathbf{P}^{-1} \begin{pmatrix} A_{0,0} & (0) & (0) & (0) \\ A_{1,1} & A_{1,0} & (0) & (0) \\ A_{2,2} & A_{2,1} & A_{2,0} & (0) \\ A_{3,3} & A_{3,2} & A_{3,1} & A_{3,0} \end{pmatrix} \begin{pmatrix} x(0) \\ x(1) \\ x(2) \\ x(3) \end{pmatrix} = \begin{pmatrix} \theta \\ \theta \\ \theta \\ \theta \end{pmatrix}
$$

That is, from the initial state $< \theta, \theta, \theta >$, the input strings $\theta\theta\theta\theta$ and $x(0)x(1)x(2)x(3)$ (note that $x(0) \neq \theta$) produce the same output string. Therefore, the FA is not a WIFA with delay 3.

2) Now assume that $A_{0,0}$ is non-singular. The FA is a WIFA with delay 3 since for any initial state $< x(-1), x(-2), x(-3) >$, input $x(0)$ is uniquely determined by the output $y(0), y(1), y(2), y(3)$. This will become apparent from the way of

constructing its inverse FA, which we demonstrate now. Multiply matrix $\mathbf{P}$ to both sides of (2):

$$\mathbf{P}\begin{pmatrix} y(i) \\ y(i+1) \\ y(i+2) \\ y(i+3) \end{pmatrix} = \begin{pmatrix} A_{0,0} & (0) & (0) & (0) \\ A_{1,1} & A_{1,0} & (0) & (0) \\ A_{2,2} & A_{2,1} & A_{2,0} & (0) \\ A_{3,3} & A_{3,2} & A_{3,1} & A_{3,0} \end{pmatrix} \begin{pmatrix} x(i) \\ x(i+1) \\ x(i+2) \\ x(i+3) \end{pmatrix} + \mathbf{P}\begin{pmatrix} A_1 & A_2 & A_3 \\ A_2 & A_3 & (0) \\ A_3 & (0) & (0) \\ (0) & (0) & (0) \end{pmatrix} \begin{pmatrix} x(i-1) \\ x(i-2) \\ x(i-3) \end{pmatrix}$$

Denote $\mathbf{P} = \begin{pmatrix} P_{0,0} & P_{0,1} & P_{0,2} & P_{0,3} \\ P_{1,0} & P_{1,1} & P_{1,2} & P_{1,3} \\ P_{2,0} & P_{2,1} & P_{2,2} & P_{2,3} \\ P_{3,0} & P_{3,1} & P_{3,2} & P_{3,3} \end{pmatrix}$ and $\mathbf{P}\begin{pmatrix} A_1 & A_2 & A_3 \\ A_2 & A_3 & (0) \\ A_3 & (0) & (0) \\ (0) & (0) & (0) \end{pmatrix} = \begin{pmatrix} Q_{0,1} & Q_{0,2} & Q_{0,3} \\ Q_{1,1} & Q_{1,2} & Q_{1,3} \\ Q_{2,1} & Q_{2,2} & Q_{2,3} \\ Q_{3,1} & Q_{3,2} & Q_{3,3} \end{pmatrix}$,

where $P_{i,j}, Q_{i,j}$ are 8×8 matrices. Since $A_{0,0}$ is non-singular, $A_{0,0}^{-1}$ exists. Denote $P_j = A_{0,0}^{-1} P_{0,j}$ for $j = 0, 1, 2, 3$ and $Q_j = A_{0,0}^{-1} Q_{0,j}$ for $j = 1, 2, 3$. We have

$$x(i) = P_0 y(i) + P_1 y(i+1) + P_2 y(i+2) + P_3 y(i+3) + Q_1 x(i-1) + Q_2 x(i-2) + Q_3 x(i-3) \tag{4}$$

Using (4) we can recover $x(0)x(1)\cdots x(n-3)$ from $x(-1)x(-2)x(-3)$ and $y(0)y(1)\cdots y(n)$. Hence, we can regard it as the expression formula for the inverse FA. Figure 2 shows the block diagrams of the linear WIFA and it inverse for general r.

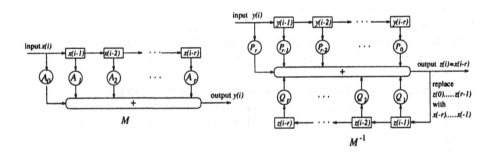

Fig. 2. A linear WIFA M and its linear weak inverse, both with delay r.

The linear FA we considered so far has only input-memory. All the results in this section can also be applied to linear FA with output-memory, i.e., the linear FA given by

$$y(i) = A_0 x(i) + A_1 x(i-1) + \cdots + A_r x(i-r) + B_1 y(i-1) + \cdots + B_r y(i-r)$$

For such a FA, we only need to consider the input-memory part $A_0 x(i) + A_1 x(i-1) + \cdots + A_r x(i-r)$ since it is this part which decides whether this FA is weakly invertible or not.

3 The Modified FAPKC

3.1 A Class of Non-Linear WIFA

The non-linear WIFA used in FAPKC can be generally expressed as

$$y(i) = \sum_{j=0}^{r} A_j x(i-j) + \sum_{j=1}^{r} B_j x(i-j) \cdot x(i-j-1) \tag{5}$$

where $\sum_{j=0}^{r} A_j x(i-j)$ is the linear part and $\sum_{j=1}^{r} B_j x(i-j) \cdot x(i-j-1)$ is the nonlinear part. The nonlinear operation "." can be taken as any nonlinear operation from two vectors to one vector. In a practical FAPKC, $(u_1, u_2, \cdots, u_8)^T \cdot (v_1, v_2, \cdots, v_8)^T$ is defined to be $(u_1 v_1, u_2 v_2, \cdots, u_8 v_8)^T$, where $u_i v_i$ is the multiplication of u_i and v_i, the elements of a finite field.

For some of the FAs defined by (5), it is easy to determine whether they are WIFAs, and if they are, it is easy to find their inverses. For example, it is easy to determine whether the following FA is a WIFA with delay 3 or not.

$$y(i) = A_0 x(i) + A_1 x(i-1) + \cdots + A_6 x(i-6) + B_4 x(i-4) \cdot x(i-5) + B_5 x(i-5) \cdot x(i-6)$$

This is because no non-linear terms contain $x(i), x(i-1), x(i-2)$ and $x(i-3)$ (we explain this later). However, so far no fast algorithm exists for determining whether this FA is a WIFA with delay 6.

Not much study has been done for nonlinear WIFA. One way to determine whether a given general nonlinear FA is a WIFA and to construct its inverse was given in [5]. But this method has a complexity of $O(|State|^2)$, where $|State|$ denotes the number of states of the FA. For the FA (5), $|State| = 2^{8(r+1)}$. Hence, this method is computationally infeasible. FAPKC is based on the following assumption.

Assumption 1. For reasonable large r and t, it is difficult to determine whether a given FA

$$y(i) = \sum_{j=0}^{r+t} A_j x(i-j) + \sum_{j=1}^{t} B_j x(i-r-j) \cdot x(i-r-j-1) \tag{6}$$

is a WIFA with delay $r+t$ and it is difficult to find its inverse FA with delay $r+t$.

However, it is easy to determine whether (6) is a WIFA with delay r and if yes, it is easy to find its inverse. This is stated in the following proposition [2].

Proposition 1. Let M_f and M_{f+g} be two FAs given by

$M_f :$ $\qquad\qquad y(i) = f\left(x(i), x(i-1), x(i-2), \cdots, x(i-r-t)\right),$

$M_{f+g} :$ $\qquad y(i) = f\left(x(i), \cdots, x(i-r-t)\right) + g(x(i-r-1), \cdots, x(i-r-t))$

respectively, where f and g can be any functions. Then, M_{f+g} is a WIFA with delay r if and only if M_f is a WIFA with delay r. Furthermore, if M_f is a WIFA with delay r and M_f^{-1} is its inverse, then we can construct the inverse of M_{f+g}, denoted by M_{f+g}^{-1}, from M_f^{-1}.

Let $s = < x(-1), x(-2), \cdots, x(-r-t) >$ be an initial state of M_f and M_{f+g}, and let s^{-1} be the match state of s for M_f^{-1}. By replacing the first r outputs of M_f^{-1} with $x(-r), x(1-r), \cdots, x(-1)$, we can construct the inverse of M_{f+g} as shown in Figure 3.

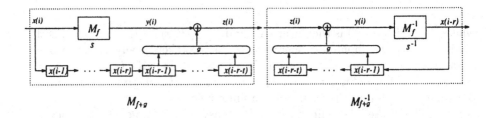

$$M_{f+g} \qquad\qquad\qquad M_{f+g}^{-1}$$

Fig. 3. M_{f+g} and its inverse M_{f+g}^{-1}, both with delay r.

From Proposition 1 and Section 2, we can construct a WIFA with delay r expressed by (6) and construct its inverse.

3.2 Composition of WIFAs and FAPKC

In this subsection, we show how to disguise a class of nonlinear WIFAs, whose inverses can be easily constructed, into a class of nonlinear WIFAs whose inverses seem difficult to find. As mentioned at the end of Section 1, this is the second critical point of FAPKC.

Consider two WIFAs, one linear, denoted by M_l, and one nonlinear, denoted by M_n. For simplicity, we continue to use small instances to illustrate the general principle. Let both M_l and M_n be WIFAs with delay 3:

M_l: $z(i) = A_0 y(i) + A_1 y(i-1) + A_2 y(i-2) + A_3 y(i-3)$

M_n: $y(i) = B_0 x(i) + B_1 x(i-1) + B_2 x(i-2) + B_3 x(i-3) +$
$\bar{B}_1 x(i-4) \cdot x(i-5) + \bar{B}_2 x(i-5) \cdot x(i-6) + \bar{B}_3 x(i-6) \cdot x(i-7)$

If we compose M_n and M_l by substituting the second formula into the first formula, we get a new FA, denoted by $M_n \circ M_l$. Note that $M_n \circ M_l$ is different from $M_n \cdot M_l$. However, for any state in $M_n \cdot M_l$ there exists an equivalent state in $M_n \circ M_l$. The new FA $M_n \circ M_l$ can be expressed by

$$z(i) = C_0 x(i) + \cdots + C_6 x(i-6) + \bar{C}_1 x(i-4) \cdot x(i-5) + \cdots + \bar{C}_6 x(i-9) \cdot x(i-10) \quad (7)$$

where $C_0 = A_0 B_0$, $C_1 = A_0 B_1 + A_1 B_0$, $C_2 = A_0 B_2 + A_1 B_1 + A_2 B_2$, $\cdots$, and $\bar{C}_1 = A_0 \bar{B}_1$, $\bar{C}_2 = A_0 \bar{B}_2 + A_1 \bar{B}_1$, $\bar{C}_3 = A_0 \bar{B}_3 + A_1 \bar{B}_2 + A_2 \bar{B}_1$, $\cdots$.

The relationship among the above coefficient matrices can be expressed in terms of matrix polynomials as follows. Let x be a formal variant. Let $\mathbf{A}(x) =$

$A_0 + A_1x + A_2x^2 + A_3x^3$, $\mathbf{B}(x) = B_0 + B_1x + B_2x^2 + B_3x^3$, $\bar{\mathbf{B}}(x) = \bar{B}_1x + \bar{B}_2x^2 + \bar{B}_3x^3$, $\mathbf{C}(x) = C_0 + C_1x + \cdots + C_6x^6$ and $\bar{\mathbf{C}}(x) = \bar{C}_1x + \cdots + \bar{C}_6x^6$. Then we have $\mathbf{C}(x) = \mathbf{A}(x)\mathbf{B}(x)$ and $\bar{\mathbf{C}}(x) = \mathbf{A}(x)\bar{\mathbf{B}}(x)$.

We can now illustrate the basic procedures in constructing the modified FAPKC with the case of $r = 3$ as an example. We first generate two WIFAs M_l and M_n, both with delay 3. Next, we find their inverses M_l^{-1} and M_n^{-1}. Finally, we compose M_l and M_n into $M_n \circ M_l$ as given by (7). Then we can do encryption with $M_n \circ M_l$ and do decryption with M_l^{-1} and M_n^{-1}. Hence, M_l and M_n (or equivalently M_l^{-1} and M_n^{-1}) plays the role of private key while $M_n \circ M_l$ plays the role of public key.

Security of the modified FAPKC is based on the following two assumptions.
Assumption 2. It is difficult to separate $M_n \circ M_l$ into M_n and M_l.

More precisely, for any given $M = M_n \circ M_l$, it is difficult to find any M_n' and M_l' such that $M_n' \circ M_l'$ is equivalent to M. This is because the separation of M is not unique. For example, for any non-singular matrix A, $M_n' = AM_n$ and $M_l' = M_lA^{-1}$ also constitute a separation. Here AM_n is the FA obtained by multiply A from left to every coefficient matrices (those A_js), while M_lA^{-1} is the FA obtained by multiply A^{-1} from right to every coefficient matrices (those B_js and $\bar{B}_j$s). That is, the trapdoor of FAPKC is not unique. But this does not affect the security of FAPKC since the trapdoors are sparse enough.

Assumption 2 can be expressed from matrix polynomial viewpoint. That is, for any $\mathbf{C}(x)(= \mathbf{A}(x)\mathbf{B}(x))$ and $\bar{\mathbf{C}}(x)(= \mathbf{A}(x)\bar{\mathbf{B}}(x))$, it is difficult to find $\mathbf{A}'(x), \mathbf{B}'(x)$, and $\bar{\mathbf{B}}'(x)$ such that $\mathbf{C}(x) = \mathbf{A}'(x)\mathbf{B}'(x)$ and $\bar{\mathbf{C}}(x) = \mathbf{A}'(x)\bar{\mathbf{B}}'(x)$. Because of Proposition 1, this assumption can be reduced to: it is difficult to find $\mathbf{A}'(x), \mathbf{B}'(x)$, and $\bar{\mathbf{B}}'(x)$ such that $\mathbf{C}(x) = \mathbf{A}'(x)\mathbf{B}'(x)$ and $\bar{\mathbf{C}}(x) \equiv \mathbf{A}'(x)\bar{\mathbf{B}}'(x) \bmod x^{r+1}$ (for the example of formula (7), it should be $\bmod x^4$ instead of $\bmod x^{r+}$).
Assumption 3. It is difficult to find the inverse of $M_n \circ M_l$.

It should be noted that Assumption 3 is different from Assumption 1. In Assumption 1, (6) is a general FA, where A_js and B_js have no constraints. In other words, (6) may not be a composition of two WIFAs. But $M_n \circ M_l$ is a composition of two WIFAs; hence, it is a special class of (6). We think Assumption 1 quite positively although we have not yet proven it. We have no idea about the validity of Assumption 3, though it seems correct so far. The security of the modified FAPKC hinges on Assumption 3. If the modified FAPKC were broken later, the breakthrough is most likely from here.

3.3 Description of the System

We use 8-dimensional vectors and 8×8 matrices over $GF(2)$ and $r = 20$ to 30.
Private Key: Generate matrices $A_0, A_1, \cdots, A_r$ and $B_0, B_1, \cdots, B_r$ such that both $y(i) = A_0x(i) + A_1x(i-1) + \cdots + A_rx(i-r)$ and $y(i) = B_0x(i) + B_1x(i-1) + \cdots + B_rx(i-r)$ are WIFAs with delay r. Furthermore, we can control the increasing ranks during the process of generating these matrices.) Arbitrarily choose matrices $\bar{B}_1, \cdots, \bar{B}_r$. We regard $A_0, A_1, \cdots, A_r$ and $B_0, B_1, \cdots, B_r$ and $\bar{B}_1, \cdots, \bar{B}_r$ as the private key.

Public Key: Let x be a formal variant. Set $\mathbf{A}(x) = \sum_{j=0}^{r} A_j x^j$, $\mathbf{B}(x) = \sum_{j=0}^{r} B_j x^j$ and $\bar{\mathbf{B}}(x) = \sum_{j=1}^{r} \bar{B}_j x^j$. Calculate $\mathbf{C}(x) = \mathbf{A}(x)\mathbf{B}(x) = \sum_{j=0}^{2r} C_j x^j$ and $\bar{\mathbf{C}}(x) = \mathbf{A}(x)\bar{\mathbf{B}}(x) = \sum_{j=1}^{2r} \bar{C}_j x^j$. We regard $C_0, \cdots, C_{2r}$ and $\bar{C}_1, \cdots, \bar{C}_{2r}$ as the public key.

Encryption: The encryption automaton is set to be

$$z(i) = \sum_{j=0}^{2r} C_j x(i-j) + \sum_{j=1}^{2r} \bar{C}_j x(i-r-j) \cdot x(i-r-j-1) \tag{8}$$

Let the plaintext be $x_0 x_1 \cdots x_n$, where each x_k is a vector. Arbitrarily choose $2r$ vectors $x_{n+1}, \cdots, x_{n+2r}$, and input $x_0 x_1 \cdots x_{n+2r}$ to (8) with initial state $< \theta, \theta, \cdots, \theta >$ (totally $3r + 1$ θs), where θ denotes the zero vector. The output $z_0 z_1 \cdots z_{n+2r}$ is the ciphertext.

Decryption: Let M_l and M_n be two WIFAs defined by

$$M_l : z(i) = \sum_{j=0}^{r} A_j y(i-j) \quad M_n : y(i) = \sum_{j=0}^{r} B_j x(i-j) + \sum_{j=1}^{r} \bar{B}_j x(i-r-j) \cdot x(i-r-j-1)$$

From Section 2 and Proposition 1, we can construct the inverse automata of M_l and M_n, denoted by M_l^{-1} and M_n^{-1}, respectively. Let $\theta_{s_l} = < \theta, \theta, \cdots, \theta >$ (totally r θs) be the zero state of M_l, and $\theta_{s_n} = < \theta, \theta, \cdots, \theta >$ (totally $2r+1$ θs) be the zero state of M_n. Denote the match state of θ_{s_l} by $\theta_{s_l}^{-1}$ (a state of M_l^{-1}), and the match state of θ_{s_n} by $\theta_{s_n}^{-1}$ (a state of M_n^{-1}). We first input $z_0 z_1 \cdots z_{n+2r}$ to M_l^{-1} with initial state $\theta_{s_l}^{-1}$. Denote the output by $y_{-r} \cdots y_{-1} y_0 \cdots y_{n+r}$, where $y_{-r} \cdots y_{-1}$ is the delay prefix. We discard this delay prefix, and then input $y_0 \cdots y_{n+r}$ to M_n^{-1} with initial state $\theta_{s_n}^{-1}$. The output must be $x_{-r} \cdots x_{-1} x_0 \cdots x_n$.

Explanation: The encryption is processed by $M_n \circ M_l$, while the decryption is processed actually by the inverse of $M_n \cdot M_l$. We need to illustrate that this does not cause any problem. We can regard $< \theta_{s_n}, \theta_{s_l} >$ as a state of $M_n \cdot M_l$. It is not difficult to verify that the state of $M_n \circ M_l$, $< \theta, \theta, \cdots, \theta >$ (totally $3r + 1$ θs) is equivalent to $< \theta_{s_n}, \theta_{s_l} >$.

4 Analyses of the Modified FAPKC

4.1 Comparison with the Original FAPKC

The major difference between the modified FAPKC and the original FAPKC is in selection of the non-linear WIFA M_n. In the original FAPKC, M_n was taken to be a WIFA with delay 0, in the form of

$$y(i) = x(i) + B_1 x(i-1) + \cdots + B_r x(i-r) + \bar{B}_1 x(i-1) \cdot x(i-2) + \cdots + \bar{B}_r x(i-r) \cdot x(i-r-1) \tag{9}$$

Hence, the encryption automaton in the original FAPKC is a WIFA with delay r, while the encryption automaton in the modified FAPKC is a WIFA with delay $2r$. This difference leads to different problems, which we need to solve in order to separate $M_n \circ M_l$ in the two versions of FAPKC. In other words, the Assumption 2 for the modified FAPKC is different from the corresponding assumption for the original FAPKC. But the latter has been proven to be fasle. That is, for the original FAPKC, the encryption automaton $M_n \circ M_l$ can be easily separated [2].

4.2 A New Attack and the Counter Measure

In this subsection, we present an attack to the modified FAPKC, which is similar to the attack given in [2]. For some instances, i.e., for certain coefficients A_js, B_js and $\bar{B}_j$s, the new attack can succeed. We call these A_js, B_js and $\bar{B}_j$s weak keys if the attack works against them. But for other instances, the attack does not work at all. Fortunately, we are able to avoid those weak keys in the key generation process; therefore, to resist the attack.

Let $\mathbf{A}(x) = \sum_{j=0}^{r} A_j x^j$, $\mathbf{B}(x) = \sum_{j=0}^{r} B_j x^j$, $\bar{\mathbf{B}}(x) = \sum_{j=1}^{r} \bar{B}_j x^j$, $\mathbf{C}(x) = \mathbf{A}(x)\mathbf{B}(x) = \sum_{j=0}^{2r} C_j x^j$ and $\bar{\mathbf{C}}(x) = \mathbf{A}(x)\bar{\mathbf{B}}(x) = \sum_{j=1}^{2r} \bar{C}_j x^j$, the same as defined in Section 3.3.

Description of the Attack The encryption automaton is $M_n \circ M_l$ where M_n is a nonlinear WIFA with delay r and M_l is a linear WIFA with delay r. In this attack, we try to find a non-linear WIFA with delay 0, M_n', and a linear WIFA with delay $2r$, M_l', such that we can derive the inverse of $M_n \circ M_l$ from the inverse of $M_n' \circ M_l'$. We set M_l' to be $z(i) = \sum_{j=0}^{2r} C_j y(i-j)$, and M_n' to be $y(i) = x(i) + \sum_{j=1}^{r} X_j x(i-j) \cdot x(i-j-1)$, where X_js are regarded as variant matrices to be solved later. Now we compare $M_n \circ M_l$ with $M_n' \circ M_l'$:

$$M_n \circ M_l : z(i) = \sum_{j=0}^{2r} C_j x(i-j) + \sum_{j=1}^{2r} \bar{C}_j x(i-r-j) \cdot x(i-r-j-1)$$

$$M_n' \circ M_l' : z(i) = \sum_{j=0}^{2r} C_j x(i-j) + \sum_{j=1}^{2r} D_j x(i-r-j) \cdot x(i-r-j-1)$$

where the D_js are the matrices obtained by combining C_js and X_js.

From Proposition 1, we can ignore $D_{r+1}, D_{r+2}, \cdots, D_{2r}$. Suppose we can find suitable X_js such that $D_1 = \bar{C}_1, D_2 = \bar{C}_2, \cdots, D_r = \bar{C}_r$, then, by Proposition 1, we can easily derive an inverse of $M_n \circ M_l$ from the inverse of $M_n' \circ M_l'$ (note that we are considering WIFAs with delay $2r$). The latter is easy to get since we know M_n' and M_l'.

Therefore, we need to find $X_1, X_2, \cdots, X_r$ such that

$$\begin{pmatrix} \bar{C}_1 \\ \bar{C}_2 \\ \vdots \\ \bar{C}_r \end{pmatrix} = \begin{pmatrix} D_1 \\ D_2 \\ \vdots \\ D_r \end{pmatrix} = \begin{pmatrix} C_0 & (0) & \cdots & (0) \\ C_1 & C_0 & \cdots & (0) \\ \vdots & \vdots & \ddots & \vdots \\ C_{r-1} & C_{r-2} & \cdots & C_0 \end{pmatrix} \begin{pmatrix} X_1 \\ X_2 \\ \vdots \\ X_r \end{pmatrix} \qquad (10)$$

Since we also have

$$
\begin{pmatrix} \bar{C}_1 \\ \bar{C}_2 \\ \vdots \\ \bar{C}_r \end{pmatrix} = \begin{pmatrix} A_0 & (0) & \cdots & (0) \\ A_1 & A_0 & \cdots & (0) \\ \vdots & \vdots & \ddots & \vdots \\ A_{r-1} & A_{r-2} & \cdots & A_0 \end{pmatrix} \begin{pmatrix} \bar{B}_1 \\ \bar{B}_2 \\ \vdots \\ \bar{B}_r \end{pmatrix}
$$

and

$$
\begin{pmatrix} C_0 & (0) & \cdots & (0) \\ C_1 & C_0 & \cdots & (0) \\ \vdots & \vdots & \ddots & \vdots \\ C_{r-1} & C_{r-2} & \cdots & C_0 \end{pmatrix} = \begin{pmatrix} A_0 & (0) & \cdots & (0) \\ A_1 & A_0 & \cdots & (0) \\ \vdots & \vdots & \ddots & \vdots \\ A_{r-1} & A_{r-2} & \cdots & A_0 \end{pmatrix} \begin{pmatrix} B_0 & (0) & \cdots & (0) \\ B_1 & B_0 & \cdots & (0) \\ \vdots & \vdots & \ddots & \vdots \\ B_{r-1} & B_{r-2} & \cdots & B_0 \end{pmatrix},
$$

we can write (10) as (11)

$$
\begin{pmatrix} A_0 & (0) & \cdots & (0) \\ A_1 & A_0 & \cdots & (0) \\ \vdots & \vdots & \ddots & \vdots \\ A_{r-1} & A_{r-2} & \cdots & A_0 \end{pmatrix} \left[\begin{pmatrix} \bar{B}_1 \\ \bar{B}_2 \\ \vdots \\ \bar{B}_r \end{pmatrix} + \begin{pmatrix} B_0 & (0) & \cdots & (0) \\ B_1 & B_0 & \cdots & (0) \\ \vdots & \vdots & \ddots & \vdots \\ B_{r-1} & B_{r-2} & \cdots & B_0 \end{pmatrix} \begin{pmatrix} X_1 \\ X_2 \\ \vdots \\ X_r \end{pmatrix} \right] = \begin{pmatrix} (0) \\ (0) \\ \vdots \\ (0) \end{pmatrix}
$$

$$(11)$$

If (11) has solution for $X_1, X_2, \cdots, X_r$, the attack is successful.

Counter Measure To avoid the attack, we need to generate the A_js, B_js and $\bar{B}_j$s in such a way that

    1) equation (11) has no solution, and

    2) A_js, B_js are coefficients of two linear WIFAs, respectively, both with delay r.

The problem is how to generate the above coefficient matrices such that both 1) and 2) hold. We denote

$$
\mathbf{MatrixA} = \begin{pmatrix} A_0 & (0) & \cdots & (0) \\ A_1 & A_0 & \cdots & (0) \\ \vdots & \vdots & \ddots & \vdots \\ A_{r-1} & A_{r-2} & \cdots & A_0 \end{pmatrix}, \quad \mathbf{MatrixB} = \begin{pmatrix} B_0 & (0) & \cdots & (0) \\ B_1 & B_0 & \cdots & (0) \\ \vdots & \vdots & \ddots & \vdots \\ B_{r-1} & B_{r-2} & \cdots & B_0 \end{pmatrix}
$$

Let $Range(\mathbf{MatrixB})$ denote the range space of $\mathbf{MatrixB}$ and $Null(\mathbf{MatrixA})$ denote the null space of $\mathbf{MatrixA}$. Then (11) has no solution means that $Null(\mathbf{MatrixA})$ has no intersection with $\{Range(\mathbf{MatrixB}) + (\bar{B}_1, \bar{B}_2, \cdots, \bar{B}_r)^T\}$, i.e.,

$$
\{Range(\mathbf{MatrixB}) + (\bar{B}_1, \bar{B}_2, \cdots, \bar{B}_r)^T\} \bigcap Null(\mathbf{MatrixA}) = \phi \qquad (12)
$$

Two points make the generation of required A_js, B_js and $\bar{B}_j$s very easy. The first point is that $\bar{B}_j$s can be arbitrarily chosen. The second point is from the following observation.

Observation 2. For any $A_0, A_1, A_2, \cdots, A_r$, either $y(i) = A_0 x(i) + A_1 x(i-1) + \cdots + A_r x(i-r)$ is a WIFA with delay r or we can change it to a WIFA with delay r by changing only A_r.

It is not difficult to verify this observation by carefully studying the reverse procedure of the algorithm for determining WIFA.

Hence, we can first arbitrarily generate B_js and $\bar{B}_j$s. Then we choose A_js such that (12) holds. If A_js are not coefficients of a linear WIFA with delay r, either we can adjust A_r or we can reselect $\bar{B}_j$s. Therefore, we have plenty space to maneuver in generating the required matrices.

4.3 Other Analyses

The analyses given in this section have been applied to the original FAPKC. As the original FAPKC, the modified FAPKC stands secure in these analyses.

Find Plaintext from Ciphertext Although FAPKC is stream cipher-like in its implementation, it can be treated as a block cipher in the following sense during decryption:

For any initial state $< x(-1), \cdots, x(-3r-1) >$ and $z(0), \cdots, z(2r)$, find any $x(0), \cdots, x(2r)$ such that the automaton (8) outputs $z(0), \cdots, z(2r)$ when taking $x(0), \cdots, x(2r)$ as input with initial state $< x(-1), \cdots, x(-3r-1) >$.

Of course the values $x(0), \cdots, x(2r)$ satisfying above condition are not unique, but $x(0)$ is uniquely fixed due to the nature of WIFA with delay $2r$. Among many sets of $x(0), \cdots, x(2r)$, if we find any of them, we find the true $x(0)$. If we can achieve above statement, we can find the plaintext $x(0), \cdots, x(n)$ recursively from the initial state $< x(-1), \cdots, x(-3r-1) >$ and the ciphertext $z(0), \cdots, z(n+2r)$. That is, find $x(0)$ from $< x(-1), \cdots, x(-3r-1) >$ and $z(0), \cdots, z(2r)$, then find $x(1)$ from $< x(0), \cdots, x(-3r) >$ and $z(1), \cdots, z(2r+1)$, and so on.

If we just consider (8) for time 0, i.e., $z(0) = \sum_{j=0}^{2r} C_j x(-j) + \sum_{j=1}^{2r} \bar{C}_j x(-r-j) \cdot x(-r-j-1)$, we can easily fix $x(0)$ to a set of vectors that is smaller than the set of all possible vectors. Specifically, $x(0)$ is confined to $C_0 x(0) = z(0) + \sum_{j=1}^{2r} C_j x(-j) + \sum_{j=1}^{2r} \bar{C}_j x(-r-j) \cdot x(-r-j-1)$. But we cannot determine the exact value of $x(0)$ from the above equation. Then by considering $z(1) = \sum_{j=0}^{2r} C_j x(-j) + \sum_{j=1}^{2r} \bar{C}_j x(-r-j) \cdot x(-r-j-1)$, we can further shrink the set of vectors $x(0)$ might be in. If we continue this procedure to $2r$, we can fix $x(0)$. However, the complexity of the above process increases exponentially in r. (Actually, this complexity is closely related to the increasing ranks. For detail, see [1]) On the other hand, before we fix $x(0)$, we cannot proceed to find $x(1)$ since any error in $x(0)$ may result in a different $x(1)$.

From the above description, we can see that it is difficult to find the exact value of $x(0)$, but it is easy to confine $x(0)$ to a set smaller than the set of all possible values. This is an undesirable situation for short plaintext. However, we can avoid this situation by adding a $2r$-vector long prefix (random pad) to the plaintext. This is because we cannot confine $x(2r)$ to any smaller set unless $x(0)$ is fixed. For details of the analyses, the reader is directed to [1].

Solving Quadratic Equation Group Another way to find $x(0)$ is to solve quadratic equation group $z(i) = \sum_{j=0}^{2r} C_j x(i - j) + \sum_{j=1}^{2r} \bar{C}_j x(i - r - j) \cdot x(i - r - j - 1)$, for $i = 0, 1, ..., 2r$. Although there are many solutions on $x(0), x(1), \cdots, x(2r)$, the value of $x(0)$ is uniquely determined. But finding any solution of $x(0), x(1), \cdots, x(2r)$ is difficult since solving quadratic equation group is NP-hard. Note that the number of possible solutions is affected by the increasing ranks.

Guessing the Inverse Automata Since we know that the encryption automaton must be composed of a linear WIFA M_l and a non-linear WIFA M_n, the forms of their inverses, M_l^{-1} and M_n^{-1}, are fixed. We can guess M_l^{-1} and M_n^{-1}, i.e., guess those coefficient matrices of M_l^{-1} and M_n^{-1}. Then from some plaintext/ciphertext pairs, set up equations for unknown coefficient matrices and solve them. Again here we meet the quadratic equation group. Hence, the method does not work.

Guessing Intermediate Values Recall that the decryption procedure is

$$z(0)z(1) \cdots z(n+2r) \longrightarrow y(-r) \cdots y(-1)y(0) \cdots y(n+r) \longrightarrow x(-2r) \cdots x(0) \cdots x(n)$$

where the step from $z(0)z(1) \cdots z(n + 2r)$ to $y(-r) \cdots y(-1)y(0) \cdots y(n + r)$ is implemented by M_l^{-1} as expressed in (4), i.e., $y(i) = \sum_{j=0}^{r} P_j z(i + r - j) + \sum_{j=1}^{r} Q_j y(i - j)$. In this attack, we take these P_js, Q_js, $y(i)$s and M_n (i.e., B_js and $\bar{B}_j$s) as unknown variants. For known plaintext/ciphertext pair $x(i)$s and $z(i)$s, we can establish the following equation group:

$$\sum_{j=0}^{r} B_j x(i-j) + \sum_{j=1}^{r} \bar{B}_j x(i-r-j) \cdot x(i-r-j-1) = y(i) = \sum_{j=0}^{r} P_j z(i+r-j) + \sum_{j=1}^{r} Q_j y(i-j)$$

Although the terms of B_js, $\bar{B}_j$s, and P_js are linear, the terms of Q_js and $y(i)$s are quadratic. Hence, once more we face the problem of solving quadratic equation group.

5   Concluding Remarks

In this paper we presented a modified FAPKC which is secure against the type of attacks which broke the original FAPKC. We also showed that the modified FAPKC resists several other known attacks. However, no assertion should be given to the security of the modified FAPKC until much more studies have been done.

Unlike RSA and some other PKCs, FAPKC is based on the algebra of matrix instead of number theory. This characteristic brings both advantage and disadvantage to FAPKC. The advantage is that it results in high speed operations while the disadvantage is that it makes its security analysis more complex.

Many problems remain to be studied further in the area of FAPCK and two of them are particularly important. The first problem relates to Assumption

2. Here issues such as the standard forms of M_n and M_l for separation, and separation studied from matrix polynomial viewpoint. Although [7] studied factorization of matrix polynomials, it only considered the case of $A_0 = I$. The second problem relates to Assumption 3, i.e., to establish the validity conditions of the assumption.

References

1. F. Bao, Y. Igarashi, "A randomized algorithm to finite automata public key cryptosystem", in Proc. of ISAAC'94, LNCS 834, Springer-Verlag, 1994, pp. 678-686.
2. F. Bao, Y. Igarashi, "Break Finite Automata Public Key Cryptosystem", in the Proc. of ICALP'95, LNCS 944, Springer-Verlag, 1995, pp. 147-158.
3. F. Bao, Y. Igarashi, X. Yu, "Some results on decomposition of WIFA", IEICE Trans. on Information and Systems, Vol. E79-D, No. 1, pp. 1-7.
4. S. Even, "Generalized automata and their information losslessness", in Switching Circuit Theory and Logic Design, 1962, pp. 144-147.
5. S. Even, "On information lossless automata of finite order", IEEE Trans. on Electric Computer, Vol. 14, No. 4, 1965, pp. 561-569.
6. X. Gao, F. Bao, "Decomposition of binary invertible finite automata", Chinese J. of Computers, Vol. 17, No. 5, 1994, pp.330-337. (in Chinese)
7. I. Gohberg, P. Lancaster, L. Rodman, Matrix Polynomials, Academic Press, New York.
8. D. A. Huffman, "Canonical forms for information-lossless finite-state logic machines", IRE Trans. on Circuit Theory, Vol. CT-6, Special Supplements, May, 1959, pp. 41-59.
9. J. Li, X. Gao, "Realization of finite automata public key cryptosystem and digital signature", in Proc. of the Second National Conference on Cryptography, CRYPTO-CHINA'92, pp. 110-115. (in Chinese)
10. J. L. Massey, M. K. Sain, "Inverse of linear sequential circuits", IEEE Trans. on Computers, Vol. 17, No. 4, 1968, pp. 330-337.
11. V. Niemi, "Cryptology: Language-theoretic aspects", Handbook of Formal Languages", Vol. 2, Ed. G. Rozenberg and A. Salomaa, Springer-Verlag, Berlin, 99. 507-524, 1997.
12. A. Salomaa, Public-Key Cryptography, EATCS Monographs on Theoretical Computer Science, Vol. 23, Springer-Verlag, 1990.
13. B. Schneier, "Applied Cryptography", second edition, 1996.
14. R. Tao, Invertibility of Finite Automata, Science Press, 1979, Beijing. (in Chinese)
15. R. Tao, S. Chen, "Finite automata public key cryptosystem and digital signature", Computer Acta, Vol. 8, No. 6, 1985, pp. 401-409. (in Chinese)
16. R. Tao, S. Chen, "Two varieties of finite automata public key cryptosystem and digital signature", J. of Computer Science and Technology, Vol. 1, No. 1, pp. 9-18.
17. R. Tao, "Invertibility of linear finite automata over a ring", in Proc. of ICALP'88, LNCS 317, Springer-Verlag, 1988, pp. 489-501.

Modified ElGamal Cryptosystem

Daisuke NAKAMURA and Kunikatsu KOBAYASHI

Department of Electrical and Information Engineering, Faculty of Engineering,
Yamagata University, 4-3-16 Jonan, Yonezawa, 992 Japan
E-mail: paka@ee5.yz.yamagata-u.ac.jp
E-mail: kobayash@ee5.yz.yamagata-u.ac.jp

Abstract. We propose a modified ElGamal cryptosystem which can broadcast communicate by encrypting every different plaintext (same plaintext is also acceptable) for plural users, and is also applicable to the systems which have hierarchical structures. And, we show that the security of this cryptosystem is based on difficulties of solving discrete logarithm problems , it maintains equivalent security with the original ElGamal cryptosystem. The transmission efficiency of this cryptosystem is improved.

1   Introduction

In recent years, the necessity for information security technologies has ever intensified, and, as such , the public key cryptosystem is now commonly utilized in the business world. One system, the ElGamal cryptosystem [1] has high security since its security is based on difficulties of discrete logarithm problems. However, it has some problems as the transmission efficiency of ciphertext is one half of other cryptosystems, and, in the case of communication, from security aspects, it has to use different random numbers for each user among plural users.

This paper proposes a modified ElGamal cryptosystem which can broadcast communicate by encrypting every different plaintext (same plaintext is also acceptable) for plural users, and is also applicable to the systems which have hierarchical structures. This cryptosystem has applied the Chinese remainder theorem to (cryptogram) polynomials, and has its security based on difficulties of discrete logarithm problems. And also, unlike the ElGamal cryptosystem, in the case of communicating among plural users, it successfully works by utilizing only one random number.

At first, the cryptosystem which is proposed in this paper is shown below, followed by the algorithm of key generation, encryption and decryption with some simple numerical examples. And finally, the security of this cryptosystem will be discussed.

2   The Cryptosystem

This cryptosystem has applied the Chinese remainder theorem to (cryptogram) polynomials, and its security is based on difficulties of discrete logarithm problems. A general formula in the case of number of users at n, and a concrete example in the case number of users at 4 are shown below:

2.1 Key Generation

$$\left\{ \begin{array}{ll} \text{public keys of the system} & : \text{prime } p, \text{primitive root } \alpha \\ \text{user } i\text{'s secret key} & : x_i \ (1 \leq i \leq n) \\ \text{user } i\text{'s public key} & : y_i \equiv \alpha^{x_i} \bmod p \\ \text{a secret information of a sender} & : \text{random number } r \\ \text{plaintext to user } i & : M_i \end{array} \right. \quad (1)$$

2.2 Encryption

The cryptogram polynomial is shown next. The generalized (number of users at n) cryptogram polynomial $c(x)$ is:

$$c(x) = \sum_{i=1}^{n} \left[M_i(y_i^r)^e \left\{ \prod_{k=1, k\neq i}^{n} (y_i^r - y_k^r) \right\}^{-1} \prod_{k=1, k\neq i}^{n} (x - y_k^r) \right] \bmod p. \quad (2)$$

Here, e is a constant that satisfies arbitrary $e \geq n$, and employ e that will become $e = 2^a$ (a is arbitrary natural number), for speeding-up. Ciphertexts will, in all, become $n + 1$ piece of:

$$\left\{ \begin{array}{ll} C & = \alpha^r \bmod p \\ C_i & = \sum_{j=1}^{n} A_j \left\{ \binom{n-1}{n-1-i} \prod_{k=1, k\neq j}^{n-1-i} Y_k \right\} \bmod p, \ (i = 0, 1, 2, \cdots, n-2) \\ C_{n-1} & = \sum_{j=1}^{n} A_j \bmod p. \end{array} \right. \quad (3)$$

Here, $\left\{ \binom{n-1}{n-1-i} \prod_{k=1, k\neq j}^{n-1-i} Y_k \right\}$ means lump total, while there are $\binom{n-1}{n-1-i}$ combination of product consisted of $n - 1 - i$ pieces that do not contain Y_j exist. Compare this with in the case when $n = 4$. Also, A_j, Y_j are as shown below:

$$\left\{ \begin{array}{l} A_j = M_j Y_j^e \left\{ \prod_{k=1, k\neq j}^{n} (Y_j - Y_k) \right\}^{-1} \bmod p \\ Y_j \equiv y_j^r \bmod p. \end{array} \right. \quad (4)$$

Next, a case when number of users are 4 is shown below. The cryptogram polynomial will be:

$$\begin{aligned}
c(x) = {} & M_1(y_1^r)^e\{(y_1^r - y_2^r)(y_1^r - y_3^r)(y_1^r - y_4^r)\}^{-1}(x - y_2^r)(x - y_3^r)(x - y_4^r) \\
& + M_2(y_2^r)^e\{(y_2^r - y_1^r)(y_2^r - y_3^r)(y_2^r - y_4^r)\}^{-1}(x - y_1^r)(x - y_3^r)(x - y_4^r) \\
& + M_3(y_3^r)^e\{(y_3^r - y_1^r)(y_3^r - y_2^r)(y_3^r - y_4^r)\}^{-1}(x - y_1^r)(x - y_2^r)(x - y_4^r) \\
& + M_4(y_4^r)^e\{(y_4^r - y_1^r)(y_4^r - y_2^r)(y_4^r - y_3^r)\}^{-1}(x - y_1^r)(x - y_2^r)(x - y_3^r)
\end{aligned} \tag{5}$$

and, its ciphertexts will be:

ciphertexts
$$\begin{cases}
C \equiv \alpha^r \bmod p \\
C_0 \equiv A_1 y_2^r y_3^r y_4^r + A_2 y_1^r y_3^r y_4^r + A_3 y_1^r y_2^r y_4^r + A_4 y_1^r y_2^r y_3^r \bmod p \\
C_1 \equiv A_1(y_2^r y_3^r + y_2^r y_4^r + y_3^r y_4^r) + A_2(y_1^r y_3^r + y_1^r y_4^r + y_3^r y_4^r) \\
\qquad + A_3(y_1^r y_2^r + y_1^r y_4^r + y_2^r y_4^r) + A_4(y_1^r y_2^r + y_1^r y_3^r + y_2^r y_3^r) \bmod p \\
C_2 \equiv A_1(y_2^r + y_3^r + y_4^r) + A_2(y_1^r + y_3^r + y_4^r) \\
\qquad + A_3(y_1^r + y_2^r + y_4^r) + A_4(y_1^r + y_2^r + y_3^r) \bmod p \\
C_3 \equiv A_1 + A_2 + A_3 + A_4 \bmod p.
\end{cases} \tag{6}$$

Here,

$$\begin{cases}
A_1 \equiv M_1(y_1^r)^e\{(y_1^r - y_2^r)(y_1^r - y_3^r)(y_1^r - y_4^r)\}^{-1} \bmod p \\
A_2 \equiv M_2(y_2^r)^e\{(y_2^r - y_1^r)(y_2^r - y_3^r)(y_2^r - y_4^r)\}^{-1} \bmod p \\
A_3 \equiv M_3(y_3^r)^e\{(y_3^r - y_1^r)(y_3^r - y_2^r)(y_3^r - y_4^r)\}^{-1} \bmod p \\
A_4 \equiv M_4(y_4^r)^e\{(y_4^r - y_1^r)(y_4^r - y_2^r)(y_4^r - y_3^r)\}^{-1} \bmod p.
\end{cases} \tag{7}$$

2.3 Decryption

The decryption of generalized (number of users at n) will be, at first as:

$$C^{x_i} = (\alpha^r)^{x_i} = (\alpha^{x_i})^r \equiv y_i^r \bmod p \tag{8}$$

and using:

$$M_i \equiv (C^{x_i})^{-e} \left\{ \sum_{i=0}^{n-1} C_i (C^{x_i})^i (-1)^{n-i+1} \right\} \bmod p. \tag{9}$$

M_i could be decrypted.

And next, in case of number of users at 4, find:

$$C^{x_i} \equiv (\alpha^r)^{x_i} \equiv y_i^r \bmod p \tag{10}$$

and, next calculate:

$$C_3(C^{x_i})^3 - C_2(C^{x_i})^2 + C_1 C^{x_i} - C_0 \equiv M_i(y_i^r)^e \bmod p \tag{11}$$

and finally:

$$M_i \equiv (C^{x_i})^{-e}[C_3(C^{x_i})^3 - C_2(C^{x_i})^2 + C_1 C^{x_i} - C_0] \bmod p \tag{12}$$

decrypt M_i.

3 Numerical Examples

Following shows numerical examples in the case of the number of users at 4. Here, let $e = 4$.

3.1 In the Case of $M_1 = M_2 = M_3 = M_4$

$$\left\{ \begin{array}{ll} \text{public keys of the system} & : \text{prime } p = 127, \text{primitive root } \alpha = 3 \\ \text{user } i\text{'s secret keys} & : x_1 = 35, x_2 = 17, x_3 = 22, x_4 = 46 \\ \text{user } i\text{'s public keys} & : y_1 = 90, y_2 = 86, y_3 = 70, y_4 = 31 \\ \text{a secret information of a sender} & : \text{random number } r = 100 \\ \text{plaintexts to user } i & : M_1 = M_2 = M_3 = M_4 = 10 \end{array} \right. \quad (13)$$

Ciphertexts will be:

$$\text{Ciphertexts} \left\{ \begin{array}{l} C = 79 \\ C_0 = 126 \\ C_1 = 101 \\ C_2 = 8 \\ C_3 = 22. \end{array} \right. \quad (14)$$

As decrypt this:

$$\left\{ \begin{array}{l} M_1 = 10 \\ M_2 = 10 \\ M_3 = 10 \\ M_4 = 10 \end{array} \right. \quad (15)$$

can be obtained, and could decrypt.

3.2 In the Case of $M_1 \neq M_2 \neq M_3 \neq M_4$

$$\left\{ \begin{array}{ll} \text{public keys of the system} & : \text{prime } p = 127, \text{primitive root } \alpha = 3 \\ \text{user } i\text{'s secret keys} & : x_1 = 35, x_2 = 17, x_3 = 22, x_4 = 46 \\ \text{user } i\text{'s public keys} & : y_1 = 90, y_2 = 86, y_3 = 70, y_4 = 31 \\ \text{a secret information of a sender} & : \text{random number } r = 100 \\ \text{plaintexts to user } i & : M_1 = 10, M_2 = 11, M_3 = 12, M_4 = 13 \end{array} \right. \quad (16)$$

Ciphertexts will be:

$$\text{Ciphertexts} \left\{ \begin{array}{l} C = 79 \\ C_0 = 29 \\ C_1 = 79 \\ C_2 = 67 \\ C_3 = 37. \end{array} \right. \quad (17)$$

As decrypt this:

$$\left\{ \begin{array}{l} M_1 = 10 \\ M_2 = 11 \\ M_3 = 12 \\ M_4 = 13 \end{array} \right. \quad (18)$$

can be obtained and could decrypt.

4 Examination of Security

To begin with, we consider the current ElGamal cryptosystem. Ciphertexts will be given as follows:

$$\begin{cases} C \equiv \alpha^r \\ C_0 \equiv My^r \equiv M(\alpha^x)^r \equiv MC^x \bmod p. \end{cases} \tag{19}$$

The security ground is that finding r from C, or finding M and r from C_0 is difficult. That is, its difficulty is equivalent to that of a discrete logarithm problem. Therefore, that the discrete logarithm should be difficult to be solved is a necessary condition of the ElGamal cryptosystem being secure. On the other hand, whether there are any ways to cryptanalyze ElGamal cryptosystem without solving a discrete logarithm problem is a question to be answered. That is, whether a discrete logarithm problem being difficult is a sufficient condition of ElGamal cryptosystem being secure or not is still a question to be answered.

This cryptosystem is considered to have less security in case where $M_1 = M_2 = \cdots = M_i = M, (i = 2, 3, \cdots, n)$ than $M_1 \neq M_2 \neq \cdots \neq M_i, (i = 2, 3, \cdots, n)$. Because in this case, numbers of information that is only known by a sender (unknown quantity) M, r is less than numbers of information made public (relational formula). We will conclude in the following Table 1 in the case that $n = 2$ simply. Various attack methods could be considered to this cryptosystem.

Table 1. Relationship between the state of plaintext and each variable

The states of plaintext	Unknown quantity	Relational formula
$M_1 = M_2 = M$	M, r	C, C_0, C_1
$M_1 \neq M_2$	M_1, M_2, r	C, C_0, C_1

Table 2 shows briefly the security for the possible attack methods, respectively. The detail information of each attack will be given later.

4.1 In the Case of $n = 2$

First, we show the case that $n = 2$.

A Third Party's Attack with Ciphertexts in the Case that $n = 2$, $M_1 = M_2$. Here, we consider the case that somebody gets the ciphertexts and attack with the public key. We assume the plaintexts unchanged, as $M_1 = M_2 = M$, and $e = 2$, the ciphertexts become

$$\begin{cases} C \equiv \alpha^r \bmod p \\ C_0 \equiv My_1^r y_2^r \equiv MC^{x_1}C^{x_2} = MC^{x_1+x_2} \bmod p \\ C_1 \equiv M(y_1^r + y_2^r) \equiv M(C^{x_1} + C^{x_2}) \bmod p. \end{cases} \tag{20}$$

Table 2. Relationship between the attack method and the cryptoanalyzed results

Attack method	Result
A third party's attack with ciphertexts in the case that $n = 2, M_1 = M_2$	×
U_1's attack with U_1's secrets and ciphertexts in the case that $n = 2, M_1 = M_2$	×
A third party's attack with ciphertexts in the case that $n = 2, M_1 \neq M_2$	×
U_1's attack with U_1's secrets and ciphertexts in the case that $n = 2, M_1 \neq M_2$	×
A third party's attack with ciphertexts in the case of n users	×
Attack with conspiracy and ciphertexts in the case of n users	×
Fault-based attack (get a random number r)	○

† If $n = 3$, result is same as $n = 2$ too.

If M, r can be obtained from these three ciphertexts, this cryptosystem will not be safe. Here we consider finding M, r, or M, x_1, x_2 from three ciphertexts, C, C_0, C_1. If we suppose $GCD(C_0, C_1) = M$, where GCD means Greatest Common Divisor, both $MC^{x_1+x_2}, M(C^{x_1} + C^{x_2})$ are smaller than p, we can find M. However, since $GCD(C_0, C_1) = M$ never occurs in general, there is no need to consider it. If $GCD(C_0, C_1) \neq M$, (i) finding r from C, (ii) finding M, r, or $M, x_1 + x_2$ from C_0, and (iii) finding M, r, or M, x_1, x_2 from C_1, are difficult because they are the same problems as those of discrete logarithms. The combination of them can hardly reduce the difficulty of finding M, r, or M, x_1, x_2, because all the forms of exponents of C, C_0, C_1 are different from one another. Hence, this cryptosystem is secure against this attack method.

U_1's Attack with U_1's Secret Information and Ciphertexts in the Case that $n = 2$, $M_1 = M_2$. Next we consider whether one user (user U_1) can obtain any secret information of another user (user U_2), from the secret information x_1 and a plaintext M of the U_1 and U_2 themselves. We assume the plaintexts unchanged, as $M_1 = M_2 = M$. This problem is equal to a question whether r or x_2 can be obtained from C, C_0, C_1, M, and x_1. From the ciphertexts, if $e = 2$, the following equations can be obtained:

$$\begin{cases} M(C^{x_2})^2 - C_1 C^{x_2} + C_0 \equiv 0 \bmod p \\ C^{-x_2} + C^{-x_1} \equiv \frac{C_1}{C_0} \bmod p. \end{cases} \tag{21}$$

Although user U_1 can obtain the value of C^{x_2} from either equation, in order to obtain the secret information x_2 of user U_2 from C^{x_2}, they have to solve a discrete logarithm problem. That is, finding the other user's secret key by this cryptosystem is equal to solving a discrete logarithm problem, it is hard to obtain the other user's secret key x_2 from three equations. Hence, this cryptosystem is secure against this attack method.

A Third Party's Attack with Ciphertexts in the Case that $n = 2$, $M_1 \neq M_2$. Next, we consider the case that somebody gets the ciphertexts and attack with the public key. We assume the plaintexts changed, namely $M_1 \neq M_2$. Then, the ciphertexts when $e = 2$ can be shown as:

$$\begin{cases} C = \alpha^r \bmod p \\ C_0 = (M_1 C^{x_1} - M_2 C^{x_2})(C^{x_1} - C^{x_2})^{-1} C^{x_1} C^{x_2} \bmod p \\ C_1 = (M_1 C^{2x_1} - M_2 C^{2x_2})(C^{x_1} - C^{x_2})^{-1} \bmod p. \end{cases} \quad (22)$$

Finding M, r, or M, x_1, x_2 from ciphertexts C, C_0, C_1 in this case is considered to be more difficult than in the case of $M_1 = M_2 = M$, because the former is more complex.

By combining two ciphertexts C_0 and C_1, we can get the following equation:

$$M_2(C^{x_2})^2 + C_1 C^{x_2} + M_1 C^{2x_1} - C_1 C^{x_1} \equiv 0 \bmod p. \quad (23)$$

Since this equation contains two unknown numbers, M_2 and C^{x_2}, it is impossible to obtain the value of M_2 or C^{x_2} from this equation. In the same manner, from the equation below

$$\frac{C_0}{C_1} = \frac{(M_1 C^{x_1} - M_2 C^{x_2}) C^{x_1} C^{x_2}}{M_1 C^{2x_1} - M_2 C^{2x_2}} \quad (24)$$

we cannot get the value of M_2 and C^{x_2} for the same reason. In short, in order to obtain other user's plaintext M_2, we have to solve a discrete logarithm problem. In other words, this cryptosystem is secure against this attack method.

U_1's Attack with U_1's Secret Information and Ciphertexts in the Case that $n = 2$, $M_1 \neq M_2$. Next, we consider whether one user (user U_1) can obtain any secret information of another user (user U_2), from the secret information x_1 and a plaintext M of the U_1 and U_2 themselves. We assume the plaintexts changed, as $M_1 \neq M_2$, and $e = 2$. In this case, by combining the ciphertexts, we can obtain following equations.

$$\begin{cases} C_0(y_1^r - y_2^r) = M_1 y_1^{2r} y_2^r - M_2 y_1^r y_2^{2r} \\ C_1(y_1^r - y_2^r) = M_1 y_1^{2r} - M_2 y_2^{2r} \end{cases} \quad (25)$$

If U_1 can evaluate y_2^r, then U_1 can also calculate M_2, so it can be said that it is not secure. But, from (25), the next relation can be obtained.

$$\underline{(C_0 - C_1 y_1^r + M_1 y_1^{2r})}(y_1^r - y_2^r) \equiv 0 \bmod p. \quad (26)$$

The under-lined part is always equal to 0, therefore, it is impossible to calculate y_2^r. From this, it is secure against this attack method.

4.2   In the Case of $n = 3$

Next, we show the case that $n = 3$.

A Third Party's Attack with Ciphertexts in the Case that $n = 3$, $M_1 = M_2 = M_3 = M$. First, we consider the case that somebody gets the ciphertexts and attack with the public key. We assume the plaintexts unchanged, as $M_1 = M_2 = M_3 = M$, and $e = 3$, the ciphertexts become

$$\begin{cases} C = \alpha^r \bmod p \\ C_0 = M(AY_1^4 Y_2 Y_3 + BY_1 Y_2^4 Y_3 + DY_1 Y_2 Y_3^4) \bmod p \\ C_1 = M\{AY_1^4(Y_2 + Y_3) + BY_2^4(Y_1 + Y_3) + DY_3^4(Y_1 + Y_2)\} \bmod p \\ C_2 = M(AY_1^4 + BY_2^4 + DY_3^4) \bmod p. \end{cases} \quad (27)$$

Here,

$$\begin{cases} Y_1 \equiv y_1^r \bmod p \\ Y_2 \equiv y_2^r \bmod p \\ Y_3 \equiv y_3^r \bmod p, \end{cases} \quad (28)$$

and,

$$\begin{cases} A \equiv \{(Y_1 - Y_2)(Y_1 - Y_3)\}^{-1} \bmod p \\ B \equiv \{(Y_2 - Y_1)(Y_2 - Y_3)\}^{-1} \bmod p \\ D \equiv \{(Y_3 - Y_1)(Y_3 - Y_2)\}^{-1} \bmod p. \end{cases} \quad (29)$$

First, we consider finding M, r, or M, x_1, x_2, x_3 from four ciphertexts, C, C_0, C_1, C_2. However, this problem is equal to solving a discrete logarithm problem, that is, it is difficult. And, if these are combined, it is also difficult to find four unknown numbers from three ciphertexts (We regard C as the useless data for cryptoanalyzing, because finding r from C is completely equivalent to the discrete logarithm problem).

Attack with Conspiracy (U_1 and U_2) and Ciphertexts in the Case that $n = 3$, $M_1 = M_2 = M_3 = M$. Next, we consider whether two conspiring users (U_1 and U_2) can obtain any secret information of remaining user (U_3), from the secret information x_1, x_2 and a plaintext M of the U_1, U_2 and U_3 themselves. In this case, U_1 and U_2 can only find a value of $Y_3 (= y_2^r \equiv C^{x_3} \bmod p)$. However, it is difficult to find x_3 from Y_3 because this problem is as same as discrete logarithm problem. Therefore, this cryptosystem is secure.

Only U_1's Attack in the Case that $n = 3$, $M_1 = M_2 = M_3 = M$. Next, we consider whether a user (U_1) can obtain any secret information of other users by himself. We assume the plaintexts same, namely $M_1 = M_2 = M_3 = M$.

In this case, U_1 can calculate the Y_i ($i = 2, 3$), but it is difficult to find x_i ($i = 2, 3$) from Y_i because this problem is as same as discrete logarithm problem. Hence, this cryptosystem is secure against this attack method.

A Third Party's Attack with Ciphertexts in the case that $n = 3$, $M_1 \neq M_2 \neq M_3$. Here, we consider the case that somebody gets the ciphertexts and attacks with the public key. We assume the plaintexts changed, as $M_1 \neq M_2 \neq M_3$, and $e = 3$, the ciphertexts become

$$
\begin{cases}
C \equiv \alpha^r \bmod p \\
C_0 \equiv M_1 A Y_1^4 Y_2 Y_3 + M_2 B Y_1 Y_2^4 Y_3 + M_3 D Y_1 Y_2 Y_3^4 \bmod p \\
C_1 \equiv M_1 A Y_1^4 (Y_2 + Y_3) + M_2 B Y_2^4 (Y_1 + Y_3) + M_3 D Y_3^4 (Y_1 + Y_2) \bmod p \\
C_2 \equiv M_1 A Y_1^4 + M_2 B Y_2^4 + M_3 D Y_3^4 \bmod p.
\end{cases}
$$

$$(30)$$

Where, Y_1, Y_2, Y_3, A, B, D is same variable in the case of $M_1 = M_2 = M_3 = M$.

First, we consider finding M, r, or M, x_1, x_2, x_3 from four ciphertexts, C, C_0, C_1, C_2. However, this problem is equal to solving a discrete logarithm problem, that is, it is hard. And, if these are combined, it is difficult to find four unknown numbers from three ciphertexts (We regard C as the useless data for cryptoanalyzing, because finding r from C is completely equivalent to the discrete logarithm problem). From this, this cryptosystem is secure by this attack method.

Attack with Conspiracy (U_1 and U_2) and Ciphertexts in the Case that $n = 3$, $M_1 \neq M_2 \neq M_3$. Next, we consider whether two conspiring users (U_1 and U_2) can obtain any secret information of remaining user (U_3), from the secret information x_1, x_2 and the plaintext M_1, M_2. We assume the plaintexts changed, as $M_1 \neq M_2 \neq M_3$.

If user U_1 and user U_2 can evaluate Y_3 then they can calculate M_3, so it is not secure. And in this case, since there are three ciphertexts (here we ignore C because it is completely equivalent to the discrete logarithm problem) to the two unknowns (plaintext M_3 and secret information Y_3), we can predict that decryption is possible.

Here, from the ciphertext formula, we get

$$
\begin{cases}
\qquad\qquad C = \alpha^r \bmod p \\
(Y_1 - Y_2)(Y_2 - Y_3)(Y_3 - Y_1)C_0 = -M_1 Y_1^4 Y_2 Y_3 (Y_2 - Y_3) \\
\qquad\qquad\qquad - M_2 Y_1 Y_2^4 Y_3 (Y_3 - Y_1) \\
\qquad\qquad\qquad - M_3 Y_1 Y_2 Y_3^4 (Y_1 - Y_2) \\
(Y_1 - Y_2)(Y_2 - Y_3)(Y_3 - Y_1)C_1 = -M_1 Y_1^4 (Y_2 + Y_3)(Y_2 - Y_3) \\
\qquad\qquad\qquad - M_2 Y_2^4 (Y_1 + Y_3)(Y_1 - Y_3) \\
\qquad\qquad\qquad - M_3 Y_3^4 (Y_1 + Y_2)(Y_1 - Y_2) \\
(Y_1 - Y_2)(Y_2 - Y_3)(Y_3 - Y_1)C_2 = -M_1 Y_1^4 (Y_2 - Y_3) - M_2 Y_2^4 (Y_3 - Y_1) \\
\qquad\qquad\qquad - M_3 Y_3^4 (Y_1 - Y_2).
\end{cases}
$$

$$(31)$$

Let's combine the above formulas in order to disappear M_3.
(i) For combination of C_2 and C_1
    We get

$$(Y_2 - Y_3)(Y_3 - Y_1)[\underline{(Y_1 - Y_2)\{C_1 - (Y_1 + Y_2)C_2\} + M_1 Y_1^4 - M_2 Y_2^4}] = 0. \quad (32)$$

But, the under-lined part of (32) is always equal to 0, therefore it is impossible to calculate Y_3 from this formula.

(ii) For combination of C_1 and C_0

We get

$$(Y_2-Y_3)(Y_3-Y_1)[\underline{(Y_1 - Y_2)\{C_0(Y_1 + Y_2) - C_1 Y_1 Y_2\} + M_1 Y_1^4 Y_2^2 - M_2 Y_1^2 Y_2^4}] = 0. \tag{33}$$

But, the under-lined part of (33) is always equal to 0, therefore it is impossible to calculate Y_3 from this formula.

(iii) For combination of C_2 and C_0

We get

$$(Y_2 - Y_3)(Y_3 - Y_1)[\underline{(Y_1 - Y_2)(C_0 - C_2 Y_1 Y_2) + M_1 Y_1^4 Y_2 - M_2 Y_1 Y_2^4}] = 0. \tag{34}$$

But, the under-lined part of (34) is always equal to 0, therefore it is impossible to calculate Y_3 from this formula.

In the end, even if the ciphertexts are combined perfectly, the secret information can not be calculated.

More, we consider whether two users (U_1 and U_2) can evaluate the random number r. From their secret keys, following relation can be got.

$$Y_1 Y_2 = y_1^r y_2^r = (y_1 y_2)^r \bmod p. \tag{35}$$

However, r can not be computed from this formula, because (35) is equivalent to the discrete logarithm problem. So, it is secure against this attack.

Only U_1's Attack in the Case that $n = 3$, $M_1 \neq M_2 \neq M_3$. Next, we consider whether a user (U_1) can obtain any secret information of other users by himself. We assume the plaintexts changed, namely $M_1 = M_2 = M_3 = M$.

In this case, from the ciphertext formula, we get

$$\begin{cases} (Y_2 - Y_3)(Y_3 - Y_1)[(Y_1 - Y_2)\{C_1 - (Y_1 + Y_2)C_2\} + M_1 Y_1^4 - M_2 Y_2^4] = 0 \\ (Y_2 - Y_3)(Y_3 - Y_1)[(Y_1 - Y_2)(C_0 - C_2 Y_1 Y_2) + M_1 Y_1^4 Y_2 - M_2 Y_1 Y_2^4] = 0. \end{cases} \tag{36}$$

By combining these equations, we get

$$\begin{aligned} &(Y_2 - Y_3)(Y_3 - Y_1)[(Y_1 - Y_2)(C_1 Y_1 - Y_1^2 C_2 - C_0) + M_1 Y_1^4(Y_1 - Y_2)] \\ &= (Y_1 - Y_2)(Y_2 - Y_3)(Y_3 - Y_1)\underline{(C_1 Y_1 - Y_1^2 C_2 - C_0 + M_1 Y_1^4)} = 0. \end{aligned} \tag{37}$$

If the attacker can find Y_2, Y_3 from this (37), this cryptosystem is not secure. But, under-lined part of (37) equal to decryption formula of user U_1. In the end, attacker can not find Y_2, Y_3. Hence, this cryptosystem is secure against this attack method.

4.3 Attack in the Case of n Users

Now, we consider a case where the number of general users is n. Finding M, r, or $M, x_1, \cdots, x_n$ only from ciphertexts $(C, C_0, C_1, \cdots, C_{n-1})$ is as difficult as it is in the case of $n = 2$. The only problem is whether $n - 1$ users out of n users conspiring together can obtain the secret of the n-th user. In this case, however, as understood from (3), since the coefficients C_i $(i = 0, 1, \cdots, n - 1)$ of each order of the variable x in cryptogram polynomials $c(x)$ are all given in the form of different exponents, any combination of them can only lead to such equation as (21), and thus it is difficult for $n - 1$ users to find the secret key of the n-th user.

After all, this cryptosystem has its security based on the difficulty of solving a discrete logarithm problem, which makes it as secure as the ElGamal cryptosystem.

4.4 Fault-based Attack (get a random number r)

Next, when attackers can get a random number r, an fault-based attack [4] on ElGamal cryptosystem becomes possible. That is, provided that the random number r is obtained, the plaintext M can be obtained from the ciphertext C_0 and a public key y as follows:

$$M = \frac{C_0}{y^r} \bmod p \tag{38}$$

and thus, care should be taken to generate random numbers. This cryptosystem is not secure from fault-based attacks either, and so in order to generate the random number, care should be taken.

4.5 Condition e

Then we consider the condition of the constant e. Let it be $e < n$. For example, when $n = 2, e = 0, M_1 = M_2 = M$ always leads to $C_1 \equiv 0, C_0 \equiv -M \bmod p$, and therefore it is not secure. In the same way when $n = 2, e = 1, M_1 = M_2 = M$ always leads to $C_1 \equiv M, C_0 \equiv 0 \bmod p$, and thus it is not secure. On the other hand, when $e \geq n$, the plaintext does not appear in a fixed form in the ciphertext even when $M_1 = M_2 = M$. Therefore, the condition $e \geq n$ is necessary in order to maintain security.

4.6 Answers to Reviewers' Comments

Finally, a comment by one of the reviewers said that if the same random number is used for all receivers in the original ElGamal cryptosystem, it requires only $n + 1$ pieces of ciphertexts. The original ElGamal cryptosystem will be more efficient than this proposed cryptosystem. In the original ElGamal cryptosystem, however, security problems occur if the same random number is used twice. On the other hand, when the plaintexts are not all the same, this cryptosystem can uses the same random number twice. Hence, with this cryptosystem, we do not have to take into account the time for checking the random number used once. Moreover, the processing speed of this cryptosystem is faster than the current ElGamal cryptosystem. For example, we consider the case that a user communicates with two users (U_1, U_2) twice. The ciphertexts of the original ElGamal cryptosystem becomes $(M_1 \neq M_2)$

$$\begin{cases} C = \alpha^r \ , \ C_1 = M_1 y_1^r \ , \ C_2 = M_2 y_2^r & \text{First Communication} \\ C' = \alpha^{r'} \ , \ C_1' = M_1' y_1^{r'} \ , \ C_2' = M_2' y_2^{r'} & \text{Second Communication.} \end{cases} \quad (39)$$

If $r = r'$, the following equations can be obtained:

$$\frac{C_1'}{C_1} = \frac{M_1'}{M_1} \quad , \quad \frac{C_2'}{C_2} = \frac{M_2'}{M_2}. \quad (40)$$

And, this is not secure. But, the ciphertexts of this cryptosystem becomes $(e = 2)$

$$\begin{cases} C = \alpha^r \ , \ C_0 = y_1^r y_2^r (y_1^r - y_2^r)^{-1} (M_1 y_1^r - M_2 y_2^r) \\ \qquad , \ C_1 = (y_1^r - y_2^r)^{-1} (M_1 y_1^r - M_2 y_2^r) & \text{First Communication} \\ C' = \alpha^r \ , \ C_0' = y_1^{r'} y_2^{r'} (y_1^{r'} - y_2^{r'})^{-1} (M_1' y_1^{r'} - M_2' y_2^{r'}) \\ \qquad , \ C_1' = (y_1^{r'} - y_2^{r'})^{-1} (M_1' y_1^{r'} - M_2' y_2^{r'}) & \text{Second Communication.} \end{cases} \quad (41)$$

If $r = r'$, the following equations can be obtained:

$$\frac{C_0'}{C_0} = \frac{M_1' y_1^r - M_2' y_2^r}{M_1 y_1^r - M_2 y_2^r} \quad , \quad \frac{C_1'}{C_1} = \frac{M_1' y_1^{2r} - M_2' y_2^{2r}}{M_1 y_1^{2r} - M_2 y_2^{2r}}. \quad (42)$$

But, the attacker cannot calculate the plaintext from (42), because (42) includes two unknown numbers (r and plaintext). As the result, this cryptosystem does not have the limit of the random number in the case that the plaintexts are not all the same (that is, it permits the same random number use). For this reason, this cryptosystem is more efficient.

5 Conclusion

In this paper, we have proposed a modified ElGamal cryptosystem that can encrypt different plaintexts (same plaintext is also acceptable) and can broadcast communicate to plural users as well as applicable to hierarchical structured systems. While the ElGamal cryptosystem requires $2n$ pieces of ciphertexts when communicating in cryptogram with n users, this cryptosystem only requires $n+1$ pieces, so transmission efficiency has been improved. Also, for random numbers r, while the ElGamal cryptosystem requires n pieces, this cryptosystem requires only one piece. As for the security aspect, since the security of this cryptosystem is based on difficulties of discrete logarithm calculations, its security level can be assumed as equivalent to the original ElGamal cryptosystem. And furthermore, by holding plural pieces of secret keys, this cryptosystem can be utilized with the systems which have hierarchical structure.

References

1. T.E.ElGamal, "A public key cryptosystem and a signature scheme based on discrete logarithm," Proc. Crypto 84, 1985.
2. N.Ikeno and K.Koyama, "Modern cryptography," The Institute of Electronics, Information and Communication Engineers, 1986.
3. E.Okamoto, "Introduction to cryptography," Kyoritsu Syuppan, 1993.
4. Y.Zheng and T.Matsumoto, "Breaking real-world implementations of cryptosystems by manipulating their random number generation," SCIS'97-6B, 1997.

Remarks on Blind Decryption

Kazuo Ohta

NTT Laboratories
Nippon Telegraph and Telephone Corporation
1-1 Hikari-no-oka, Yokosuka, Kanagawa, 239 Japan
E-mail: ohta@isl.ntt.co.jp

Abstract. This paper describes two attacks against blind decryption (decode) based on the commutative random-self reducibility and RSA systems utilizing the transformability of digital signatures proposed in [2]. The transformable digital signature was introduced in [8, 2] for defeating an oracle attack, where the decrypter could be abused as an oracle to release useful information for an attacker acting as a requester of blind decryption. It was believed in [8, 2] that the correctness of a query to an oracle was ensured by the transformable signature derived from an original signature issued by the decrypter in advance, and a malicious query to an oracle could be detected before the blind decryption by the decrypter or would lead to release no useful information to an attacker. The first attack can decrypt *all* encrypted data with *one* access to an oracle. The second one generates a valid signature for an arbitrary message selected by an attacker abusing the validation check procedure.

Keywords: digital signature, blind decryption, oracle attack, transformability, RSA scheme, ElGamal scheme, commutative random-self reducible problem

1 Introduction

In pay magazines and software delivery systems using Internet or CD-ROM, wherein many encrypted articles and programs are common, a subscriber selects an article or program after browsing the summaries. If the subscriber requests a decryption key corresponding to his selection from the pay magazine or software company directly, there exists a threat to his privacy, that is, the company could become a big brother in the digital world [1].

To ensure the privacy of the subscriber, *blind decryption* was introduced [14]; the subscriber can obtain a decrypted message for a ciphertext selected by the subscriber without telling the company the ciphertext to be decrypted. Hence, the subscriber can read the selected article or software while the company can charge for the decryption. Hereafter, the company is called the decrypter, and the subscriber is called the requester of the blind decryption.

Blind decryption suffers from the *oracle problem*: the decrypter (a company) can be abused as an oracle into releasing useful information for an attacker acting as a requester (a subscriber).

A countermeasure to the oracle problem that utilizes a *transformable digital signature* was discussed in [8, 2] : Reference [8] for ElGamal [3] system, Reference [2] for both RSA [11] and ElGamal systems utilizing the *transformability* of RSA digital signature and ZKIP-digital signature [6, 5] based on commutative random self-reducibility [9].

The notion of *transformable digital signature* was introduced in [8, 2] to solve an oracle problem. The transformability of a signature is where an original signature can be transformed into another valid signature of the same signature scheme. A decrypter distributes encrypted data (an article or program) together with a transformable signature such that no one can generate a transformed signature without the original signature issued by the decrypter in advance, a requester shows the *transformable digital signature* of a query when it requests the decryption step. It seems an interesting approach for defeating an oracle attack. The plausible reason is as follows: the correctness of a query to an oracle is ensured by the transformable signature derived from an original signature issued by the decrypter, and a malicious query to an oracle will be discovered before the decryption step by the decrypter. The query must be very restricted, if its signature is to pass the validity check.

Reference [2] utilized two pairs of public-secret keys for the same RSA modulus, one for the encryption and the other for the signature. It also utilized a *special* hash function in order to construct the *transformable digital signature* generally based on the commutative random self-reducible (CRSR) problem. The CRSR problem covers various ZKIP protocols, for example, Fiat-Shamir [5] and Schnorr [12] schemes etc.

This paper will describe two attacks against blind decryption utilizing the transformability of digital signature based on both commutative random-self reducibility systems and RSA system proposed in [2]. The first attack can decrypt *all* encrypted data with *one* access to an oracle, which proceeds a decryption step after validating the transformed signature. The second attack generates a signature for an arbitrary message selected by an attacker.

2   Analyzed Schemes

This paper will analyze the following schemes proposed in [2] in order to defeat an oracle attack.

2.1   Blind Decryption using a Special Hash Function

Key generation: Let p and q be large primes such that $q \mid p - 1$, $\alpha \in (Z/pZ)^*$ has order q. A decrypter B chooses a secret key $x \in Z/qZ$ and publishes the public key (y, α, p, q), where $y = \alpha^x \bmod p$. B also has a public-secret key pair for transformable signatures based on a hash function with a special property, and publishes its public key.

Here the *special property* of the hash function is as follows:

(1) Given (m, e), it is difficult to find x satisfying $e = g(m, x)$.

(2) Given $(m, x, e, \tilde{x}, \tilde{e})$, $\tilde{m}$ can be computed easily where $e = g(m, x)$ and $\tilde{e} = g(\tilde{m}, \tilde{x})$.

This property is required to construct a transformable digital signature based on CRSR problems. Examples of g are given in [2]: $g(m, x) = mh(x) \bmod q$ for a prime q and $g(m, x) = m \oplus h(x)$, where h is an ideal hash function. Note that a message should be transformed and a hash function h is not applied to m in transformable signatures.

Step 1 Preliminary (Distribution of encrypted data together with signatures): B encrypts data m_i using different random keys $k^{(i)}$ as follows $(1 \le i \le L)$: B generates a random integer $k^{(i)} \in Z/qZ$, calculates $c_1^{(i)} = k^{(i)}x \bmod q$, and $c_2^{(i)} = m_i \alpha^{k^{(i)}} \bmod p$, and generates a signature $s^{(i)} = (z_1'^{(i)}, \ldots, z_t'^{(i)}, e'^{(i)})$ for $c_1^{(i)}$ by any CRSR-based signature scheme where $g(c_1^{(i)}, x) = c_1^{(i)}h(x) \bmod q$. B distributes L encrypted data $(c_1^{(i)}, c_2^{(i)}, s^{(i)})$ to requester A. A checks the validity of each signature. If it is not valid, A requests B to issue a valid one. A does not proceed to the next step until A receives all valid encrypted data with signatures.

Step 2 Signature transformation and request: When A wants to decrypt $(c_1^{(i_0)}, c_2^{(i_0)})$, A computes the transformation $(\tilde{c}, \tilde{s})$ from $(c_1^{(i_0)}, s^{(i_0)})$. Then a transformed $(X, \tilde{s})$ is sent to B, where $X = \tilde{c}$. This message indicates a request for blind decryption.

Step 3 Signature check, exponentiation and return: Upon receiving the pair, B first checks the signature for X. If the check is not valid, B does not proceed to the next step and returns nothing or a warning message. If the check is valid, B computes $Y = \alpha^{\{Xx^{-1} \bmod q\}} \bmod p$, and returns Y to A.

Step 4 Final decryption: Upon receiving Y, A calculates $Z = Y^{\{\overline{c_1}^{-1} \bmod q\}}$ $\bmod p$, where $\overline{c_1} = \frac{g(\tilde{c_1}, \tilde{x}_1, \ldots, \tilde{x}_t)}{c_1 h(x_1, \ldots, x_t)} \bmod q$ and $\tilde{x}_j$'s are computed during the signature transformation. Since $Z \equiv \alpha^{k^{(i_0)}}$ (mod p), A can determine m_{i_0} by computing $c_2^{(i_0)}/Z \bmod p$.

The reason that $Z \equiv \alpha^{k^{(i_0)}}$ (mod p) was given in Section 5.1 of [2], and $\tilde{x}$'s were also explained in Section 4.2 there.

2.2 Blind Decryption using the RSA Systems

Key generation: Decrypter B prepares two pairs of RSA exponents (e_1, d_1) and (e_2, d_2) for the same RSA modulus, where $\gcd\{e_1, e_2\} = 1$. (e_1, d_1) is for the encryption and (e_2, d_2) is for the signature. (e_1, e_2, n) is a public key of B and (d_1, d_2, p, q) is his secret key.

Step 1 Preliminary (Distribution of encrypted data together with signatures): B encrypts data m_i using public key e_1 and secret key

d_2 as follows ($1 \leq i \leq L$): B calculates $c^{(i)} = m_i^{e_1} \bmod n$, and $s^{(i)} = c^{(i)^{d_2}} \bmod n$. B distributes L encrypted data $(c^{(i)}, s^{(i)})$ to requester A. A checks the validity of each signature. If it is not valid, A requests B to issue a valid one. A does not proceed to the next step until A receives all valid encrypted data with signatures.

Step 2 **Signature transformation and Request**: When A wants to decrypt $(c^{(i_0)}, s^{(i_0)})$, A generates $r \in Z/nZ$ and computes the transformation $(\tilde{c}, \tilde{s})$ from $(c^{(i_0)}, s^{(i_0)})$ as follows:

$$\tilde{c} = c^{(i_0)} r^{e_1 e_2} \bmod n,$$
$$\tilde{s} = s^{(i_0)} r^{e_1} \bmod n.$$

Transformed $(X, \tilde{s})$ is then sent to B, where $X = \tilde{c}$. This message indicates a request for blind decryption.

Step 3 **Signature check, exponentiation and return**: Upon receiving the pair, B first checks the signature for $\tilde{c}$, that is, $X \stackrel{?}{\equiv} \tilde{s}^{e_2} \pmod{n}$. If the check is not valid, B does not proceed to the next step and returns nothing or a warning message. If the check is valid, B computes $Y = X^{d_1} \bmod n$, and returns Y to A.

Step 4 **Final decryption**: Upon receiving Y, A calculates $Z = \frac{Y}{r^{e_2}} \bmod n$. Since $Z \equiv \frac{(c^{(i_0)} r^{e_1 e_2})^{d_1}}{r^{e_2}} \equiv \frac{((c^{(i_0)})^{d_1} r^{e_2})}{r^{e_2}} \equiv m_{i_0} \pmod{n}$, A can determine m_{i_0}.

3 Attacks

We will describe two attack procedures against blind decryption using transformable signatures.

3.1 Blind Decryption Using a Special Hash Function

Existential forgery of a signature scheme Since the discussed signature scheme is based on the ZKIP protocol, the ZKIP simulation technique is also applicable here, that is, the simulator guesses the challenge value of e and the z-components at first, then the value of x-components that satisfy the check equation can be calculated. For example, in the Schnorr scheme [12], the check equation is $\alpha^z \stackrel{?}{\equiv} xy^e \pmod{p}$.

If a hash function g is *ideal*, the ZKIP protocol can be transformed into a *secure* digital signature scheme by Fiat-Shamir's transformation technique, where $e = g(m, x)$. [*]

If a hash function has the special property described in Section 2, the second property ensures the effective calculation of $\tilde{m}$ satisfying $\tilde{e} = g(\tilde{m}, \tilde{x})$, where $\tilde{e}$

---

[*] It is proven in [10, 4] that the signature scheme derived in this way is *existentially unforgeable under an adaptive chosen-message attack* [7].

and $\tilde{x}$ are given in advance, which means the digital signature is *existentially forgeable under a known-message attack* with knowledge of (m, x, e).

Moreover if the special hash function is defined by $g(m, x) = mh(x) \bmod q$, then $\tilde{m}$ is calculated effectively satisfying $\tilde{e} = g(\tilde{m}, \tilde{x})$ without knowledge of (m, x, e), which means the digital signature is *existentially forgeable under a key-only attack* combining the ZKIP simulation technique.

Hereafter $\tilde{m}$ is denoted by X^*.

Attack Procedure

Step 1 Query generation: An attacker generates $(X^*, \tilde{s})$, where $\tilde{s} = (\tilde{x}, \tilde{e})$. This message indicates a request for blind decryption.

Step 2 Oracle procedure: Upon receiving the pair, B first checks the signature for $\tilde{c}_1$. If the check is valid, B computes $Y^* = \alpha^{\{X^* x^{-1} \bmod q\}} \bmod p$, and returns Y^* to A.

Step 3 Decryption: The attacker calculates $Z^{(i)} = (Y^*)^{\frac{c_1{}^{(i)}}{X^*} \bmod q} \bmod p$ upon receiving Y^*, and determines m_i by computing $\frac{c_2{}^{(i)}}{Z^{(i)}} \bmod p$ for all i $(1 \le i \le L)$.

Since $Y^* = \alpha^{\{X^* x^{-1} \bmod q\}} \equiv \alpha^{\{\frac{X^*}{x} \bmod q\}}$ (mod p), all $Z^{(i)}$ can be calculated as follows:

$$Z^{(i)} = (Y^*)^{\frac{c_1{}^{(i)}}{X^*} \bmod q} \equiv \left\{\alpha^{\{\frac{X^*}{x} \bmod q\}}\right\}^{\frac{c_1{}^{(i)}}{X^*} \bmod q}$$
$$\equiv \alpha^{\{\frac{c_1{}^{(i)}}{x} \bmod q\}} \equiv \alpha^{\{\frac{k^{(i)} x}{x} \bmod q\}} \equiv \alpha^{k^{(i)}} \pmod{p}.$$

Thus

$$\frac{c_2{}^{(i)}}{Z^{(i)}} \equiv \frac{m_i \alpha^{k^{(i)}}}{\alpha^{k^{(i)}}} \equiv m_i \pmod{p}.$$

Note that since this attack yields Y^* which is independent of i, *all* distributed data encrypted by the decrypter can be decrypted with one access to an oracle, which is a serious flaw.

3.2 Blind Decryption using RSA Systems

Existential forgery of an original signature scheme Since the RSA scheme is existential forgeable under a key-only attack, that is, after fixing signature s, we can calculate *forged* message m by $m = s^e \bmod n$, it is not so surprising that an attacker can calculate the signature of unspecified message. The second attack described here generates a valid signature for an arbitrary message selected by an attacker even if the query must undergo a validation check.

Attack Procedure

Step 1 **Query generation**: An attacker generates $(X^*, \widetilde{s}^*)$, where M is the target message which will be signed, $r \in Z/nZ$ is a random integer, $\widetilde{s}^* = r^{e_1} M \bmod n$ and $X^* = (\widetilde{s}^*)^{e_2} \bmod n$. This message indicates a request for blind decryption.

Step 2 **Oracle procedure**: Upon receiving the pair, B first checks the signature for X^*, that is, $X^* \overset{?}{\equiv} (\widetilde{s}^*)^{e_2} \pmod{n}$. If the check is valid, B computes $Y^* = (X^*)^{d_1} \bmod n$, and returns Y^* to A.

Step 3 **Calculation of useful information**: Upon receiving Y^*, the attacker calculates s^* satisfying both equations:

$$(s^*)^{e_2} \bmod n = Y^*,$$
$$(s^*)^{e_1} \bmod n = \widetilde{s}^*,$$

because of $\gcd\{e_1, e_2\} = 1$ [13]** , and calculates $s = \frac{s^*}{r} \bmod n$ as the useful information of target message M.

Since $\widetilde{s}^* = r^{e_1} M \bmod n$ and $(s^*)^{e_1} \bmod n = \widetilde{s}^*$, the equation $s^{e_1} \equiv (\frac{s^*}{r})^{e_1} \equiv \frac{\widetilde{s}^*}{r^{e_1}} \equiv \frac{r^{e_1} M}{r^{e_1}} \equiv M \pmod{n}$ holds. Thus s is a signature of target message M corresponding to the public key (e_1, n).

Note that the value of M can be selected by an attacker arbitrarily and it is impossible for a decrypter to trace the origin of signature s by comparing the value of Y^*.

4   Concluding Remarks

It was believed in [8, 2] that if the signature check was valid, the correctness of a query to an oracle had to be ensured by the transformable signature, and this constraints of a query would defeat an oracle attack.

As described in this paper, the special property of the hash function introduced in [2] is very dangerous, and the treatment of the key values embedded in the c_1-component, where $c_1 = kx \bmod q$ comparing to $c_1 = \alpha^{\{kx \bmod q\}} \bmod p$ in [8], must also be dangerous.

As a result of these problems, blind decryption with transformable digital signature proposed in [2] is more insecure against an oracle attack than the scheme proposed in [8].

The second attack is not so serious in actual terms, since the obtained signature is not a true signature in the case the first key pair (e_1, d_1) is for the

---

** If $\gcd\{e_1, e_2\} = 1$ holds, a and b such that $ae_1 + be_2 = 1$ are calculated easily by the extended Euclidian algorithm. Thus s^* is calculated using a and b as follows: $s^* = (Y^*)^b (\widetilde{s}^*)^a \bmod n$. If $\gcd\{e_1, e_2\} = \beta$ holds, $(s^*)^\beta$ is calculated similar way, which means that the partial knowledge on s^* is revealed abusing the validation check procedure.

encryption, not for the signature. The existence of such an attack, however, implies the weakness of using the transformability of digital signatures in order to defeat the oracle attack.

It is an interesting approach for solving an oracle attack to adopt transformable digital signatures. It is an open question whether the scheme proposed in [8] is secure against an oracle attack.

References

1. Chaum, D.: "Security without Identification: Transaction Systems to Make Big Brother Obsolete," Communications of the ACM, 28, 10, pp.1030-1044, (1985).
2. Damgård, I., Mambo, M. and Okamoto, E. "Further Study on the Transformability of Digital Signatures and the Blind Decryption," The 1997 Symposium on Cryptography and Information Security, SCIS97-33C, (1997).
3. ElGamal, T. "A Public Key Cryptosystem and a Signature Scheme Based on Discrete Logarithms," IEEE Transactions on Information Theory, IT-31, 4, pp.469–472, (1985).
4. Feig,U., Fiat, A. and Shamir, A. "Zero-Knowledge Proofs of Identity," Journal of Cryptology, 1, p.77–94.
5. Fiat, A. and Shamir, A. "How to Prove Yourself," Lecture Notes in Computer Science 263, Advances in Cryptology –CRYPTO'86, Springer-Verlag, pp.186–194, (1987).
6. Goldwasser, S., Micali, S. and Rackoff, C. "The Knowledge Complexity of Interactive Proof Systems," SIAM Journal on Computing, 18, pp.186-208, (1989).
7. Goldwasser, S., Micali, S. and Rivest, R. "A Digital Signature Scheme Secure Against Adaptive Chosen-Message Attacks," SIAM Journal on Computing, 17, pp.281–308, (1988).
8. Mambo, M., Sakurai, K. and Okamoto, E. "How to Utilize the Transformability of Digital Signatures for Solving the Oracle Problem, " Lecture Notes in Computer Science 1163, Advances in Cryptology –Asiacrypt'96, Springer-Verlag, pp.322–333, (1996).
9. Okamoto, E. and Ohta, K. "Divertible Zero Knowledge Interactive Proofs and Commutative Random Self-Reducibility," Lecture Notes in Computer Science 434, Advances in Cryptology –Eurocrypt'89, Springer-Verlag, pp.134–149, (1990).
10. Pointcheval, D. and Stern, J. "Security Proofs for Signature Schemes," Lecture Notes in Computer Science 1070, Advances in Cryptology –Eurocrypt'96, Springer-Verlag, pp.387–398, (1996).
11. Rivest, R., Shamir, A. and Adleman, L. "A Method for Obtaining Digital Signatures and Public Key Cryptosystems," Communications of ACM, 21, 2, pp.120-126, (1978).
12. Schnorr, C.P. "Efficient Signature Generation by Smart Card," Journal of Cryptology, 14, 4, pp.161-174, (1991).
13. Simmons, G. J.: "A "weak" privacy protocol using the RSA crypto algorithm," CRYPTOLOGIA, 7, 2, pp.180-182, (1983).
14. Sakurai, K. and Yamane, Y. "Blind Decoding, Blind Undeniable Signature, and their Applications to Privacy Protection," Lecture Notes in Computer Science 1174, Information Hiding, Springer-Verlag, pp.257–264, (1996).

High-Speed Cryptography
(Extended Abstract)

George Davida   René Peralta

CCCNS,
Electrical Engineering and Computer Science Department,
University of Wisconsin-Milwaukee, P.O. Box 784,
Milwaukee 53201
USA
(davida@cs.uwm.edu)   (peralta@cs.uwm.edu)

Abstract. We present a new method for achieving high speed encryption and decryption using large-block cryptosystems. The method applies to both private and public key cryptosystems. The method amplifies the encrypting speed of any cryptosystem, and it is provably reducible to the latter.

1   Introduction

Cryptologists divide encryption algorithms into block ciphers and stream ciphers. One of the most important types of stream ciphers is the "one-time-pad". In this cipher, the key K is a binary random string that is as long as the message being enciphered. The key is used only once. To encipher a new message, a new random string K is used. This scheme is information-theoretically secure.

RSA and the Data Encryption Standard are examples of block ciphers. DES encrypts a block of 64 bits, which is quite small. RSA typically encrypts data in blocks of 512 or (in newer implementations) 1024 bits. However, it is not known how many of those bits are simultaneously secure (even under the assumption that the RSA is not polynomial-time invertible).[1]

The speed of encryption/decryption is critical for applications. For example, many people who "trust" RSA more than DES, are still forced to use the slower RSA only for exchanging a secret key to be used with the faster DES. The same holds for PGP, perhaps the most widely used cryptosystem these days.

Some of the efforts in speeding up cryptosystems have involved improvements in the implementation of the basic iterations, as in the case of DES [3, 14, 4]. In the case of RSA, improvements in speed have been hard to come by, mainly because the underlying algorithms are part of a long-established field and hence have already been optimized over many decades of work. Symptomatic of the need for such speed-ups is the fact that people have been proposing the use of less well-understood methods, like elliptic-curves [11, 7, 8, 10]. Other

---

[1] Simultaneous security of bits is a subtle concept. We choose not to discuss it at length here as it would distract the reader from the main topic of this paper. For a definition see [13]

proposals, including the use of low-exponent RSA to speed up encryption, have been floated around. How dangerous this trend can be has been exposed by the works of Hastad [5], Coppersmith, Franklin,Patarin, and Reiter [2] and Patarin [12] among others.

2 The cryptosystem

Let $\{R_1, R_2, ...R_n\}$ be a set of random bit row vectors of length b each. These strings are *public* and form an n x b matrix R. To encrypt a block M of length b, the user selects a random row-vector I over $GF(2)$ of size n. The user then computes $F(M) = I\,R + M$. To obtain M from $F(M)$ and R, the string I is clearly sufficient. Now the user sends I encrypted with a secure public or private key cryptosystem. For convenience we will assume the use of RSA to encrypt I, although we see no a priori reasons to avoid other systems. The computational cost of encrypting a string of size $b >> n$ using RSA is proportional to $O(n^{2.6} \cdot b/n)$.[2] The cost of our technique is $O(n^{2.6} + b \cdot n) = O(b \cdot n)$ for $b > n^{1.6}$). Letting $b = n^k$, the speed-up of our method is $\Theta(n^{k+1.6}/n^{k+1}) = \Theta(n^{.6})$. The hidden constants in the assymptotic expressions make the speed-up much larger than $n^{.6}$.

Note that each block encryption requires a different string I. If the crypt-analyst correctly guesses the string I then he/she has decrypted the block corresponding to that string. However, this has *no implications* about the security of other blocks (assuming blocks are independent). Thus $n = |\,I\,|$ should be moderately large (say $n \geq 100$). Note that the security is *independent* of the block length b.

2.1 Security

It is not hard to show that our system is as secure as the underlying method used to encrypt I. We will denote by $E(x)$ the encryption of x. We assume E is bijective.

Theorem 1. *Obtaining I from $E(I)$ is random poly-time reducible to obtaining M from $E(I), R$, and $I \cdot R + M$.*

Proof. Suppose you have access to an oracle function F such that $F(E(I), R, I \cdot R + M) = M$. Now suppose that you are given $E(I)$, where I is an n-bit vector. To obtain I you can do the following:

1. Create a random n x b matrix R.
2. Create a random b-bit vector U.
3. Obtain $F(E(I), R, U) = \theta$ (note that θ exists because the function $f(\theta) = I \cdot R + \theta$ is a bijection on $(GF(2)\,)^b$).

---

[2] this is assuming the use of practical fast multiplication techniques. e.g. Karatsuba-Ofman [6].

4. Now solve the linear equation $I \cdot R + \theta = U$ for I.

In step 4, the number of unknowns is n (i.e. the number of bits in I). The number of equations is b (the number of bits in U). Since $n << b$ the equation is over-determined. I is a solution, so at least one solution exists. Since R is random and $n << b$, the probability that multiple solutions exist is negligible.

2.2 Partial information

The issue of partial information about the plaintext or the private key is a thorny one (witness Maurer's result implying that RSA is asymptotically breakable given ϵN bits of information about N for any $\epsilon > 0$ [9]).[3] In the scheme proposed here, particular attention should be paid to the case where partial information is available about a particular block. If any n bits of the plaintext block are known, then it is highly likely that the whole block can be obtained (the problem reduces to solving a system of equations over $GF(2)$). Furthermore, if I is encrypted using a public-key system, then about $n - 32$ bits may suffice to obtain I (taking 2^{32} as an approximation to the number of operations feasible in reasonable time by modern computers). This is because the unknown 32 bits can be guessed and then the guess can be checked against the encryption of I (once more, the good news is that decryption of one block has no implications about the security of other blocks). Note however, that this would only be true if the size n of I is about the same size as the size of the full plaintext in the public-key system. Although it is not known how many RSA bits are simultaneously secure, typical applications assume all of them are. The alternative is to put the plaintext in a sub-block of RSA plaintext whose bits are deemed simultaneously secure. It is known that such blocks of size $\Omega(\log n)$ exist in RSA. However, doing this would clearly decrease the speed of encryption of an already slow enciphering technique. However, in our construction the speed of RSA is of little consequence, hence we can use a very large RSA key to encrypt a much smaller piece of plaintext. On this issue, the best asymptotic result known is due to Alexi et.al. [1], where it is proven that the $\log \log N$ least significant bits of RSA are simultaneously secure. This essentially means that we should put I in the least significant bits of RSA and use random bits for the remaining portion of the plaintext. Doing this effectively removes the "$n - 32$" problem referred to above: the cryptanalyst must obtain at least n bits of a block plaintext to obtain the remaining $b - n$ bits of the block plaintext. If we use this technique then having only $n - 1$ bits of the block plaintext gives *no information* about the remaining bits (since a guess of the missing bit can no longer be checked).

Nevertheless it remains true that, whereas in RSA we don't know how much damage partial information does, in our scheme we do know that partial information definitely makes the system breakable. Therefore the user of our system should use a cheap (computation-wise) compression algorithm on the plaintext as a first step. However, we don't believe this to be a serious burden since doing the latter is recommended no matter what encryption algorithm is used.

---

[3] Of course Maurer's bits are not any bits, but particular bits of information.

3 Encryption/decryption speed

The reader may have already surmised the next feature of our construction: *use as big a block as your memory resources allow*. As the length b of the blocks increase, the cost of encrypting/decrypting the index I becomes negligible. In a software implementation on a machine with register size r, the speed of our system is essentially $n/(2r)$ XOR operations per bit. With $n = 128$ and $r = 64$ this expression is 1. Thus the cost per bit is one XOR operation. Constructing special purpose hardware amounts to increasing the length r, with the corresponding linear increase in encryption/decryption speed. Either in software or hardware, and either used with secret keys or public keys, we believe our system to be *much* faster than anything else that has been proposed.

References

1. Alexi, W., Chor, B., Goldreich, O., Schnorr, C.: RSA and /Rabin functions: certain parts are as hard as the whole. Siam Journal on Computing **17** (1988) 194–209.
2. Coppersmith, D., Franklin, M., Patarin, J., Reiter, M.: Low-exponent RSA with related messages. In Advances in Cryptology - Proceedings of EUROCRYPT 96 (1996) vol. 1070 of Lecture Notes in Computer Science, Springer-Verlag pp. 1–9.
3. Davio, M., Desmedt, Y., Goubert, J., Hoornaert, F., Quisquater, J.-J.: Efficient hardware and software implementations for the DES. In Advances in Cryptology - Proceedings of CRYPTO 84 (1985) Springer-Verlag pp. 144–146.
4. Everle, H.: A high-speed DES implementation for network applications. In Advances in Cryptology - Proceedings of CRYPTO 92 (1993) vol. 740 of Lecture Notes in Computer Science, pp. 521–539.
5. Hastad, J.: Solving simultaneous modular equations of low degree. SIAM Journal on Computing **17** (1988) 336–341.
6. Karatsuba, Ofman: Multiplication of multidigit numbers on automata (in russian). Doklady Akademii Nauk SSSR **145** (1962) 293–294.
7. Koblitz, N.: Elliptic curve cryptosystems. Mathematics of Computation **48** (1987) 203–209.
8. Koyama, K., Maurer, U. M., Okamoto, T., Vanstone, S. A.: New public-key schemes based on elliptic curves over the ring z_n. In Advances in Cryptology - Proceedings of CRYPTO 91 (1992) vol. 576 of Lecture Notes in Computer Science, pp. 252–266.
9. Maurer, U.: Factoring with an oracle. In Advances in Cryptology - Proceedings of EUROCRYPT 92 (1993) vol. 658 of Lecture Notes in Computer Science, Springer-Verlag pp. 429–436.
10. Menezes, A. J.: Elliptic curve public key cryptosystems. Kluwer Academic Publishers 1993.
11. Miller, V. S.: Use of elliptic curves in cryptography. In Advances in Cryptology - Proceedings of CRYPTO 85 (1986) vol. 218 of Lecture Notes in Computer Science, Springer-Verlag pp. 417–426.
12. Patarin, J.: Some serious protocol failures for RSA with exponent e of less than $\simeq$ 32 bits. Cryptography conference, CIRM, Luminy, France 1995.

13. Peralta, R.: Simultaneous security of bits in the discrete log. In Advances in Cryptology - Proceedings of EUROCRYPT 85 (1986) Lecture Notes in Computer Science, Springer-Verlag pp. 62–72.
14. Verbauwhede, I., Hoornaeert, F., Vandewalle, J., Man, H. D.: Security and performance optimization of a new DES data encryption chip. IEEE journal of solid-state circuits **23** (1988) 647–656.

Secure Applications of Low-Entropy Keys

John Kelsey   Bruce Schneier   Chris Hall

Counterpane Systems
101 E. Minnehaha Parkway
Minneapolis, MN 55419
{kelsey,schneier,hall}@counterpane.com

David Wagner
U.C. Berkeley
Soda Hall, C.S. Division
Berkeley, CA 94720-1776
daw@cs.berkeley.edu

Abstract. We introduce the notion of key stretching, a mechanism to convert short s-bit keys into longer keys, such that the complexity required to brute-force search a $s + t$-bit keyspace is the same as the time required to brute-force search a s-bit key stretched by t bits.

1 Introduction—Why Stretch a Key?

In many real-world cryptographic systems, we are, for various reasons, limited to encryption keys with relatively low-entropy. In other words, we are limited to a key that is unlikely to take on more than (say) 2^{40} different values. This can happen for a variety of reasons: legacy systems that force the use of outdated 56- or 64-bit key lengths, keys that must be remembered and typed in by users, keys generated from realtively poor random bit sources, or various countries' restrictions on key-length.

In the realm of user-entered keys and passphrases, it has become common to carry out some kind of computationally expensive calculation to derive the actual key or secret value. This is intended to increase the cost of exhaustive search against a large portion of the possible keyspace. One problem with these ad hoc methods is that it's not always clear how much additional security they add. We are interested in explicitly answering a question of "how hard is this brute-force search," in terms of either dollars or bits.

In this paper, we describe a general kind of procedure, called *key stretching*, which adds a known number of bits to the expected difficulty of an exhaustive search attack. That is, we can make a 40-bit search as expensive as a 56-bit search would normally be.

The remainder of the paper is organized as follows. In Section 2 we describe a general framework for key-stretching algorithms. In Section 3 we describe various classes of attack that are possible on key-stretching algorithms, and some design principles that allow us to resist these attacks. In Section 4 we describe two different key stretching algorithms: one based on a one-way hash function, and the other on a block cipher. We are able to give proofs, under some reasonable assumptions, that any attacks on the hash-based scheme translate into attacks on the underlying cryptographic primitive. Finally, in Section 5, we discuss extensions to frustrate brute-force attacks which make use of massively parallel devices.

2   A General Model for Key Stretching

Key stretching is about adding a specific number of bits to a keysearch or brute-force attack of some kind. In a cryptographic context, what we'd like is for the following two things to be equally difficult:

A brute-force search of a key-stretching scheme that stretches a s-bit key to $s + t$ bits, and

A keysearch of the actual cipher, with $s + t$ bits of key.

All of our methods for doing this involve finding some function $F()$ which approximates a random function and which requires roughly 2^t work to compute. We must then convince ourselves that there are no shortcuts for the attacker, and that this function is roughly as hard for him to compute as it is for a user.

A general method for key-stretching is as follows:

1. We start with some low-entropy key, K_{short}. We want to derive a hard-to-search key, K_{long}, so that searching all possible values of K_{long} takes 2^{s+t} rekeyings and trial encryptions, where s is the number of bits of entropy of K_{short}, and t is the number of bits of stretching being done.
2. Let $Salt$ be an occasionally changing salt value. For some applications, $Salt$ changes once every year or few months. For others, it may never change. For still others, it changes with each new message.
3. Let $F()$ be some function that approximates a random function. We require that computing $F()$ is guaranteed to take about the same amount of work as searching 2^t keys in a brute-force exhaustive keysearch.
4. Let $K_{long} = F(K_{short}, Salt)$.

Once we have this algorithm, we must then convince ourselves that an attacker carrying out a keysearch of the stretched key has to carry out nearly all 2^t computations for each short key stretched to a long key. That is, there must be no significant "economies of scale" in doing the keysearch.

2.1   Salt

In Section 3, various precomputation attacks on key-stretching schemes are discussed. To resist these, we use a salt. The purpose of a salt value is to make it impossible for an attacker to precompute a list of all or a large portion of the possible long keys used for all messages.

There are three ways we can use salt values:

1. *Per System.* If we have many noninteroperable systems, we can use a different salt for each, perhaps based on the hash of the programmer's full name, the program's or system's name, and the date on which the code was completed. This forces the attacker to do a separate precomputation for each system attacked. If 2^{s+t} work-factor searches are sufficiently expensive, this may, in practice, mean that only a few such systems are ever attacked.

2. *Per Time Period.* For interoperable systems, we may wish to use a salt that changes periodically and unpredictably. For example, we might have a salt that changes once per year, and that is defined as the hash of all the stock prices of the stocks in the S&P 100, on the last active trading day in November. This is unpredictable by any attacker, so precomputations can't start until November for the next year's messages. Again, this works well if $s + t$ bit keysearches are sufficiently expensive.

3. *Per Message.* We can make precomputation attacks much less rewarding for passive eavesdroppers by changing the salt for each message sent, and deriving the salt randomly. Unfortunately, this makes a chosen-ciphertext attack possible, in which a precomputation with any salt allows the recovery of a given message's long key. This works because the attacker can simply replace the sender's salt with his own salt.

A *Hybrid* scheme is the best way to do this. If the system can handle the additional requirements, use two different values to derive each message's salt: a per-message random salt component, along with a long-term salt which is either changed each year or is set to different values for different non-interoperable systems. This forces the attacker to do a new precomputation each year (or for each noninteroperable system), in order to be able to successfully use even an active attack.

In our general scheme, described in this section, and in our two schemes described in Section 4, the salt value used is assumed to be the hash of whatever inputs were chosen for the salt value.

3 Attacks on Key Stretching

3.1 Economies of Scale

Keysearch attacks typically benefit from certain "economies of scale": optimizations that are not available or useful to an ordinary user, but that make an attacker's job easier. For example, in a straightforward brute-force search of DES [NBS77] with known plaintext and ciphertexts, an attacker can omit computation of the last round of DES in each trial encryption, optimize the order of the keys searched to minimize the work involved in changing keys, and build massively parallel hardware useful only for DES key searching.

In designing a key-stretching algorithm, the most important economies of scale attacks are the following:

Narrow-Pipe Attacks A "narrow-pipe" attack occurs when some intermediate stage of the key-stretching computation has too few bits of state. It is obvious that having an intermediate state of less than $s + t$ bits will leave us with less security than we expect, because an attacker can just guess this intermediate state. As will be described below, however, repeated intermediate values can also give an attacker economies of scale: he can reuse the repeated results. If any intermediate stages have fewer than $s + t + 6$ bits of state, then this becomes an issue.[1]

Reuse of Computed Values In the generic construction given above, to make any strong statements about how much difficulty is added to a keysearch attack, we must know whether or not an attacker ever gets to reuse final or intermediate $F()$ computations. An attacker who can reuse these computations may be able to do a keysearch much more cheaply than we would otherwise expect. The issue is making sure that the intermediate computations have enough bits of state, as discussed above. However, we also need to review our specific choice of $F()$ to ensure that it can't be sped up substantially by reuse of intermediate values.

Special-Purpose Massively Parallel Keysearch Machines In some keysearch attacks, massively parallel computers are built to cheaply try all possible keys. Wherever possible, our choice of $F()$ should be influenced by the desire to make such attacks more expensive without making the function significantly more expensive for legitimate users on general-purpose computers to compute.

3.2 Cherry Picking

Even if the whole keysearch is guaranteed to take up at least (say) 2^{80} work, it may be that some part of the keyspace can be searched very cheaply. If this is the case for a significant portion of the keyspace in our key stretching scheme, then this becomes an important weakness. Just as it should cost 2^{72} trial encryptions and rekeyings to search 2^{-8} of all possible 80-bit keys, a 56-bit key stretched to 80 bits of effective strength should cost 2^{72} encryptions and rekeyings to search any 2^{-8} of the keyspace. In practice, this means that nearly all short keys should take about the same number of actual operations to stretch.

3.3 Nonrandom Long Keys

Ideally, the long keys should be indistinguishable from random bit strings for anyone who doesn't know the corresponding short keys. If this isn't the case, then some attacks may be possible based on guessing the long keys directly from these patterns. In particular, if there is some relationship between pairs (or k-tuples) of short keys that leads to some relationship between the corresponding pairs

---

[1] There's nothing magical about the number 6, it just ensures less than one percent reuse of the intermediate values. Note that this concern applies only to cryptographic mechanisms that approximate random functions rather than random permutations. A random permutation won't ever suffer an internal collision with itself when a different input value has been used.

(or k-tuples) of long keys, an attacker may be able to mount a kind of related-key attack on our key-stretching scheme. If long keys are highly nonrandomly distributed, it may even be possible to guess a significant subset of the possible long keys without any stretching computations.

3.4 Full and Partial Precomputations

In ordinary keysearch attacks, if an attacker can force the use of some chosen plaintext, or can count on the use of some known plaintext in almost all cases, he can carry out a single precomputation of all possible keys, and index them by the expected ciphertext block from the chosen or known plaintext.

In attacking a key-stretching algorithm, a slightly better alternative is available. An attacker can carry out the full 2^{s+t} trial encryptions and rekeyings once, and wind up with a list of 2^s possible long keys. Each message can now be attacked using an s-bit search. (Note that this can even be done on massively parallel hardware under some circumstances, e.g. by sorting the long key list, and preloading a different subset of the long keys to each parallel search machine.)

Similarly, an attacker can carry out a partial precomputation, computing some subset of 2^{s-u} possible long keys, to get a 2^{s-u} search per message, with a 2^{-u} probability of getting the correct key in any message.

This is an inherent problem with key-stretching algorithms: they all are slightly more susceptible to precomputation in this way. The best that any key-stretching algorithm can do is not to be any more vulnerable than this to pre-computation or partial precomputation attacks. In practice, it is more practical to do a $s+y$-effective-keylength precomputation attack, with a chosen- or known-plaintext that will appear in almost all messages the attacker wishes to break. One goal of key stretching is that we can set t large enough that an $s+t$-bit search is no longer practical. Otherwise, we will need to use a salt value as described in Section 2.1.

4 Key Stretching Algorithms

4.1 A Hash-Function-Based Key Stretching Algorithm

Let $H()$ be a secure, collision-resistant one-way hash function, such as SHA1 [NIST93] or RIPE-MD160 [DBP96], and let S be a salt value.
The basic scheme works as follows:

$X_0 = H(K_{short}, S)$.
For $i = 1$ to 2^t:
$\qquad X_i = H(X_{i-1})$.
$K_{long} = X_{2^t}$.

We are computing the 2^t-th iterate of $H()$. We will denote the ith iterate of $H()$ as $H^i()$. Hence,

$$K_{long} = H^{2^t}(K_{short}, S).$$

Considering each of our design criteria in turn, we can make the following statements of security:

Time to Compute: One crucial requirement is that naive iteration must be the fastest way to compute $H^{2^t}(x)$ for random inputs x. In other words, there must be no shortcuts available to implement $H^{2^t}()$. Fortunately, we have some theoretical results which assure us that such shortcuts can't exist, if H has sufficient resistance to collision attacks.

We say that an m-bit hash function $H()$ is strongly collision-resistant if the best way to find an unknown collision is with a naïve birthday attack. Normally this requires at least $2^{m/2}$ work (where the unit of time is how long it takes to compute $H(x)$ for a randomly chosen m-bit string x). We must be careful, though: a permutation fits this definition, yet our proof of security depends on the ability to find collisions using a naïve birthday attack. Hence we add the additional technical requirement that a naïve birthday attack is likely to find a collision for $H()$. We expect that a truly random function would admit a birthday attack, so if $H()$ is a pseudorandom function then we also expect that it will admit a birthday attack. In other words, this second requirement should be satisified in practice for most reasonable hash functions; it is primarily technical in nature.

Given these two properties of $H()$, we have the following result.

Theorem 1. *If $H()$ is a strongly collision-resistant hash function that admits a naïve birthday attack, then computing the i-th iterate of H requires time at least $i/2$.*

We leave the proof for the appendix.

This theorem shows that one cannot really compute the 2^t-th iterate of $H()$ any faster than by straightforward iteration, as the ability to find a shortcut would imply a weakness in the underlying hash function. In short, we get very close to the amount of strength from key stretching that one would expect intuitively: the theorem says that iterating the hash function 2^t times adds at least $t - 1$ bits of extra "strength" to the key.

In fact, our proof yields an even stronger result, which is applicable even in the case that there is a way to slightly speed up collision attacks on the hash function. We prove that if finding a collision takes at least $2^{m/2-c}$ time, for some $c > 0$, then iterating the hash function 2^t times adds at least $t-c-1$ bits of "strength." Note that for some hash functions which have slight weaknesses against collision search, it may be possible to truncate the hash and achieve even better proofs of security, though there are some limits to when this is possible.

We should emphasize that the theorem assumes that the input X is chosen at random. Hence, it shows that the *average-case* time-complexity for computing the stretched key is close to 2^t.

Cherry Picking: Unfortunately we are not able to show that the *best-case* time-complexity is also 2^t. In fact, given X and $H^{2^t}(X)$, one can compute $H^{2^t}(Y)$ for a different Y in time 1. Simply let $Y = H(X)$, for then

$H^{2^t}(Y) = H(H^{2^t}(X))$. Therefore it is difficult for us to make a statement about the security of this scheme against cherry picking. Because of the redundancy in the input to the hash function, we believe it will be secure given a secure hash function, but cannot prove it. This issue is related to the reuse of internal values, discussed below.

Non-Random Long Keys: There should not be any significant number of non-random long keys. By assumption, $H()$ is a strongly collision-resistant hash function. If one could predict $H(Y)$ without knowing Y, with better than random chance, then one could produce collisions for $H()$ faster than with a naïve birthday attack.

Reusing Internal Values: If the output of our hash function is large enough, then we are unlikely to produce duplicate values X, X' along with i and j $(1 \leq i, j \leq 2^t)$ such that $H^i(X) = H^j(X')$ where $X \neq X'$ or $i \neq j$. Hence we expect that an attacker will not be able to reuse values in order to speed up a brute force search.

4.2 A Block-Cipher-Based Key Stretching Algorithm

Let $E_K(X)$ be the encryption under some block cipher, E, of X under key K. In this case E should have a key length and block length which are each at least K_{long} bits long. Then, this method is:

$K_0 = (K_{short}, S)$.
For $i = 1$ to 2^t:
    $K_i = E_{K_{i-1}}(0)$.
$K_{long} = K_{2^t}$.

For ease of notation, let $f(k) = E_k(0)$. Then

$$K_{long} = f^{2^t}(K_{short} \| S)$$

Remark: *Note that we run into some practical problems with this scheme when we want to stretch a key to more bits than the block size of the cipher. We can easily get around this by using two independent blocks in our computation, though this makes it harder to prove the security of the resulting key-stretching scheme. Alternatively, we may try to find a block cipher of appropriate size.*

Considering each of our design criteria in turn, we can make the following statements of security:

Time to Compute: Unfortunately we are not able to make as strong a statement for this approach as for the hash-based approach. One observation we have made is that the ability to compute $f^{2^t}()$ in time faster than 2^t would speed up a time/memory trade-off attack [H80]. It will not be a significant speed-up, but a speed-up nonetheless.

If we can prove that $f^1()$ is a strongly-collision resistant hash, then we can apply the analysis from the previous section. However, there is no guarantee that this property will hold.

Cherry Picking: As with the hash function approach, it is difficult to make assertions about the strength of this cipher against cherry picking. We expect that a set of keys for which computing $Stretch_{E,2^t}()$ can be done in time significantly less than 2^t would also point out a weakness in the underlying cipher. However, we are not able to make a formal proof to this effect.

Non-Random Long Keys: Suppose it is possible to learn K_{i+1} without knowing K_i. Therefore, it is possible to know $E_K(X)$ given X but not K. This is a major weakness in the block cipher. In fact, if we can reliably guess $E_K(X)$ without knowledge of any u bits of K, then we have just found a way to reduce the effective keyspace of E by u bits.

Reusing Internal Values: A secure block cipher can be viewed as a pseudorandom permutation family. Therefore one would expect that $E_{k_1}(0) = E_{k_2}(0)$ with at most slightly better than random chance (otherwise this would provide a method for distinguishing the permutation family from a random permutation family contradicting its pseudorandomness). So provided that $s + t$ is sufficiently small compared to the block length, we expect that there will not be any repeated internal values.

5 Making Massively Parallel Hardware More Expensive

Just as with ordinary keysearch attacks, one concern we have with attacks against a key-stretching algorithm is whether or not it is feasible for an attacker to build a special-purpose massively-parallel keysearch machine. For example, we may have a secure key-stretching scheme which stretches 40-bit keys to an effective strength of 56 bits. Unfortunately, it is feasible for a moderately well-funded attacker to build a machine to carry out a 56-bit keysearch of some cipher like DES [Wie94, BDRSSTW96]. We would like our key-stretching algorithms to be hard implement on very cheap hardware, the kind that would most likely be used in building a keysearch machine.

In making cheap hardware implementations of our scheme more difficult, it is important to keep our ultimate goal in mind: We want to raise the cost of keysearch machines to the point where it is too expensive to build. However, we must remember not to do this at the cost of usability of the key-stretching scheme. If a user must choose to stretch her 40-bit key to only 56-bits, instead of 64, because of the added expense of our hardware-frustrating techniques, then we've most likely made the attacker's job easier. Typically, we will be interested in hardware-frustrating techniques that don't cost more than one or two extra bits of stretching, but make the parallel search engines significantly more expensive to build.

5.1 Modifying the Hash-Based Approach

In Section 4.1 we proposed a scheme using hash functions. Most hash functions proposed—SHA-1, MD5, etc.—are designed for efficient implementations. One approach is to use hash functions which do not yield efficient implementations;

however, people are not likely to design such hash functions. Instead we can modify existing hash functions to yield expensive hash functions, without voiding their security warranty.

Let $f()$ be a one-way, strongly collision-resistant hash function with an m-bit output and $E()$ an m-bit permutation. Then we define a new hash function F as

$$F(X) = E(f(X)).$$

It is easy to show that $F()$ is also a one-way, strongly collision-resistant hash function. Suppose that $O(Y)$ was an oracle which could invert $F()$, then we can turn this into an oracle $O'(Y)$ for inverting $f()$ by setting $O'(Y) = O(E(Y))$. Similarly, if $F(X) = F(X')$ for some $X \neq X'$, then $f(X) = f(X')$. Hence it is no easier to find collisions for $F()$ than it is to find collisions for $f()$.

So we can make an expensive hash function $F()$ by making $E()$ an expensive permutation. Using the resulting hash function $F()$ we can apply the analysis of Section 4.1.

Note that in order for these arguments to be valid, $E()$ must not depend on the input to $F()$.

5.2 A Design for a Computationally Expensive Permutation

Our permutation $E()$ needs to involve operations that are expensive to provide on cheap hardware, but not on a general-purpose processor. Two obvious places to look for this are 32-bit arithmetic and use of moderately large amounts of RAM.

Let C0,M0 and C1,M1 be parameters for a linear congruential generator, such that the generator never overflows a 32-bit register. (In other words, $(M0 - 1) * C0 + 1 < 2^{32}$ and $(M1 - 1) * C1 + 2 < 2^{32}$.) Let $T[0..255]$ be a 256-element table of 32-bit unsigned values.

One might build the permutation using an involution (up to replacement of f by $-f$):

$$t = w[0] + w[1] + w[2] + w[3] + w[4]$$

$$w[0] = w[0] + f(0, t)$$

$$w[1] = w[1] + f(1, t)$$

$$w[2] = w[2] + f(2, t)$$

$$w[3] = w[3] + f(3, t)$$

$$w[4] = w[4] - f(0, t) - f(1, t) - f(2, t) - f(3, t)$$

This has the effect of altering every bit of the hash output with a minimum number of operations. The whole permutation might be computed as follows:

```
temp = word[0]+word[1]+word[2]+word[3]+word[4];
A0 = temp % M0;
A1 = temp % M1;
u = temp;
for(i=0;i<256;i++){
A0 = (A0 * C0 + 1) % M0;
A1 = (A1 * C1 + 1) % M1;
T[i] = A0^A1^u;
u = rol(u,13)+T[i];
}
j = 255;
sum = 0;
for(i=0;i<256;i++){
u = rol(u,6)^T[j];
word[i%4] += u;
sum += u;
j = (j+T[j])%256;
}
word[4] -= sum;
```

Note that this is intended as a discussion of a possible way to do this. We have not spent enough time researching this algorithm to make any strong claims about it, other than that it is reversible. However, it is useful to remember that, because we have hash functions on both sides of it, it doesn't need too much cryptographic strength.

The basic purpose of this permutation is to require the availability of 256 32-bit words of RAM and 32-bit arithmetic operations in order to carry out a key-stretching.

6 Related Work

Some work on key stretching for block ciphers was independently done by [QDD86]. Also, our techniques are similar in spirit to the technique of using repeated iterations of DES to make UNIX password-guessing attacks more expensive [MT79].

Other authors have also independently examined the problem of hardening password-protection schemes based on one-way functions. Manber proposed one simple approach based on hashing a random "salt" with the password; the resulting hash digest is stored, but the salt is securely deleted [Man96]. Abadi, Lomas, and Needham recently independently proposed a scheme for strengthening passwords which is very similar to Manber's [Aba97]; Abadi et. al. also show how to apply that approach to communication security in a setting similar to the one we envision for key stretching. They point out several important differences between key stretching and password strengthening, which are worth repeating:

- Strengthening requires extra work from only one party; key stretching adds to the workload of both endpoints to the communication. In some applications, these computational savings could be a critical factor. Also, if the endpoints have access to multiple CPUs, strengthening can be easily parallelized, whereas stretching a key is an inherently sequential process.
- Strengthening actually adds information-theoretic entropy, while stretching does not, so with key stretching thorough use of salts is especially important to prevent dictionary-style attacks.
- The two approaches seem to rely on somewhat different properties of the underlying hash function. Local one-wayness seems to be critical for password strengthening. In contrast, the analysis of Section 4 suggests that key stretching may rely most heavily on the hash function's resistance to collision attacks.

  The collision-resistance properties of today's cryptographic hash functions are arguably somewhat better-analyzed than their local one-wayness properties. On the other hand, our proofs make extremely strong assumptions of collision-resistance, so our theoretical analysis may not be as strong as we'd like for practical use.

Finally, there has been much work on using public-key techniques to strengthen cryptosystems that must rely on low-entropy shared secrets. However, these require heavy-weight public-key algorithms and complex protocols. In contrast, one of our central design requirements was that our key stretching schemes should not require implementation of any new cryptographic primitives: if both endpoints already have a shared block cipher, where possible we should re-use that cipher to stretch keys, or if a hash function is already available, it should be used, but no new primitives should be introduced. In short, key stretching provides a simpler and lighter-weight version of the public-key approaches; the power of key stretching is not as great as that achievable with public-key cryptography, but it is still substantial.

7 Summary, Conclusions, and Further Directions

In this paper, we have introduced the concept of *key-stretching*: a method of increasing the difficulty of trying all possible values for some low-entropy variable by a fixed, well-understood amount. We have also given constructions for two key-stretching schemes, one based on a block cipher and the other on a hash function. The hash-based construction was shown to have the property that a method for speeding up the exhaustive search of the low-entropy variable translates into a significant weakness in the underlying hash function.

Of course, key stretching is no substitute for long keys. Key stretching only reduces a short key's resistance to certain attacks. If at all possible, system designers should use long keys.

Several open questions remain. It would be nice to see an analysis of various key schedules' economies of scale for keysearch attacks. For example, Peter

Trei [Tre97] has recently demonstrated that a software DES keysearch can step through the DES key schedule in Gray code order, making each new key much cheaper to schedule for the keysearcher than a key is to schedule for an ordinary user. What other ciphers have this or worse properties, which make keysearch attacks easier to carry out? What design principles can a cipher designer follow to ensure that there aren't economies-of-scale for keysearch attacks on his cipher? What design principles exist for designing permutation algorithms that will require certain hardware support to compute efficiently?

8 Acknowledgments

The authors would like to thank Matt Blaze and Martín Abadi for their helpful comments.

References

[Aba97]   M. Abadi, personal communication.

[BDRSSTW96] M. Blaze, W. Diffie, R. Rivest, B. Schneier, T. Shimomura, E. Thompson, and M. Wiener, "Minimal Key Lengths for Symmetric Ciphers to Provide Adequate Commercial Security," January 1996.

[DBP96]   H. Dobbertin, A. Bosselaers, and B. Preneel, "RIPEMD-160: A Strengthened Version of RIPEMD," *Fast Software Encryption: Third International Workshop, Cambrdige, UK, February 1996 Proceedings*, Springer-Verlag, 1996, pp. 71–82.

[H80]   M.E. Hellman, "A Cryptanalytic Time-Memory Trade Off," *IEEE Transactions on Information Theory*, v. 26, n. 4, Jul 1980, pp. 401–406.

[Knu81]   D. Knuth, *The Art of Computer Programming: Volume 2, Seminumerical Algorithms*, Addison-Wesley, 1981.

[Man96]   U. Manber, "A Simple Scheme to Make Passwords Based on One-Way Functions Much Harder to Crack," *Computers & Security*, v. 15, n. 2, 1996, pp. 171–176.

[MT79]   R.H. Morris and K. Thompson, "UNIX Password Security," *Communications of the ACM*, v. 22, n. 11, Nov 1979.

[NBS77]   National Bureau of Standards, NBS FIPS PUB 46, "Data Encryption Standard," National Bureau of Standards, U.S. Department of Commerce, Jan 1977.

[NIST93]   National Institute of Standards and Technology, NIST FIPS PUB 180, "Secure Hash Standard," U.S. Department of Commerce, May 93.

[QDD86]   J.-J. Quisquater, Y. Desmedt, and M. Davio, "The Importance of 'Good' Key Schemes (How to Make a Secure DES with $\leq$ 48 Bit Keys?)," *Advances in Cryptology—CRYPTO '85 Proceedings*, Springer-Verlag, 1986, pp. 537-542.

[Sch96]   B. Schneier, *Applied Cryptography, Second Edition*, John Wiley & Sons, 1996.

[Tre97]   Peter Trei, *personal communication*, 1997.

[Wie94]   M. Wiener, "Efficient DES Key Search," TR-244, School of Computer Science, Carleton Unversity, May 1994.

A   Theoretical analysis of hash iteration

We give the proof of Theorem 1 here. First, we must prove the following lemma:

Lemma 2. *Suppose we can evaluate the 2^m-th iterate of a b-bit hash function h in $2^m/l$ time on average, for some $m < b/4$. Then we can find a collision in h about $l/2$ times as fast as a naive birthday attack.*

Proof: Let $k = 2^{b/2}$. Define $f(j) = h^j(a)$ for some fixed starting point a. Suppose that computing the 2^m-th iterate h^{2^m} of h can be done in $2^m/l$ work, for some $l > 1$. We know $2^m < \sqrt{k}$, so assume $l < \sqrt{k}$. We show how to find a collision in h with $2k/l$ work.

Note first that computing $f(i + j)$ from $f(i)$ takes only j/l work, if $j \geq 2^m$. Compute $f(i + 2^m)$ from $f(i)$ with $2^m/l$ work, then compute $f(i + 2 \cdot 2^m)$ from that with $2^m/l$ work, and so on, until you reach $f(i + j)$; you'll need $j/2^m$ steps, and each step takes $2^m/l$ time, so the total time needed is j/l.

The typical method of finding a collision is as follows: by the birthday paradox, the sequence $f(0)$, $f(1)$, $f(2)$, ..., $f(k)$ will hit a cycle with very high probability. This leads immediately to a collision in h. (If i, j are the least $i < j$ with $f(i) = f(j)$, then $f(i-1)$ and $f(j-1)$ are two colliding preimages of h.)

In our optimized attack, we compute the following values:

$$f(k), f(k+\sqrt{k}), f(k+2\sqrt{k}), \ldots, f(2k), f(2k+1), f(2k+2), \ldots, f(2k+\sqrt{k}).$$

Now we claim that this optimized sequence has two powerful properties. First, if the original sequence $f(0), \ldots, f(k)$ has a collision, then the optimized sequence will too. Moreover, the optimized sequence can be enumerated significantly more efficiently than the original sequence.

First we establish that if the original sequence $f(0), \ldots, f(k)$ cycles and gives a collision, then the optimized sequence will too. Note that the optimized sequence can be viewed as an application of the baby-step giant-step method. The second half of the sequence, namely the values $f(2k), \ldots, f(2k + \sqrt{k})$ form a sort of "landing pad": if the original sequence enters a cycle of period less than k, then one of the values $f(k + j\sqrt{k}), j = 0, \ldots, \sqrt{k} - 1$ will hit the landing pad and cause a collision in the optimized sequence. (Why? Let p be the period of the cycle. If $p \leq \sqrt{k}$, then the second half of the optimized sequence will have a collision. Otherwise, $\sqrt{k} < p < k$, and there must be some i, j with $0 \leq i, j < \sqrt{k}$ such that $i = j\sqrt{k} \bmod p$. The latter statement follows just because it is impossible to have $\sqrt{k}$ mutually disjoint subsets of values modulo p, if each subset has cardinality $\sqrt{k}$ and if $k > p$.)

We see that the optimized sequence yields a collision whenever the original sequence does. Furthermore, finding collisions in the optimized sequence is easy, when they exist. For example, it suffices to use a hash table with $2\sqrt{k}$

entries, or to sort the $2\sqrt{k}$ values; the time required for setting up the data structure will be small compared to complexity of computing the sequence.

Next we examine how long it takes to compute the optimized sequence. Computing $f(k)$ can be done in k/l time from $f(0)$. (See above.) Also, $f(k + \sqrt{k})$ can be computed in $\sqrt{k}/l$ time from $f(k)$, and $f(k + 2\sqrt{k})$ can be gotten in another $\sqrt{k}/l$ time, and so on. Therefore, computing the first half of the optimized sequence requires $2k/l$ work. Also, we can compute $f(2k + 1), f(2k + 2), \ldots, f(2k + \sqrt{k})$ from $f(2k)$ with $\sqrt{k}$ time.

Therefore, the total time to compute the optimized sequence is $2k/l + \sqrt{k}$. The latter term will be negligible, so for simplicity we call it $2k/l$.

This means that we can find a collision in $2k/l$ time by taking advantage of the oracle for evaluating the 2^m-th iterate of h. A naive birthday attack would take time $2^{b/2} = k$, so our optimized technique is $l/2$ times faster than that.

QED.

Corollary 3. *Suppose you're given a b-bit hash function h where finding a collision takes at least $2^{b/2-c}$ time, for some c. Suppose further that a naïve birthday attack works against this hash. Then you can't evaluate h^{2^m} in less than 2^{m-c-1} time on average, and key-stretching with h^{2^m} adds at least $m - c - 1$ bits of "strength" to the key.*

The theorem then follows directly from the corollary.

Theorem 4 1. *If $H()$ is a strongly collision-resistant hash function that admits a naïve birthday attack, then computing the i-th iterate of H requires time at least $i/2$.*

A Key Escrow System
of the RSA Cryptosystem

Yoshiki Sameshima

e-mail: `same@ori.hitachi-sk.co.jp`

R & D Department, Hitachi Software Engineering Co., Ltd.
6-81 Onoe-cho Naka-ku Yokohama Japan 231

Abstract. This paper focuses a key escrow system of the RSA cryptosystem that protects user privacy with the following properties; (1) neither investigation agency nor key escrow agent accesses private key of user directly, (2) investigation agency can decrypt user data of restricted time period and communication entities, and (3) split private keys of user are deposited correctly in multiple key escrow agents without any information leakage of the private key with help of a zero-knowledge interactive protocol. The security of the whole system is discussed as well as the performance of the zero-knowledge interactive protocol.

1 Introduction

As an infrastructure of various kinds of activities such as business, education, health care, public service, a global scale network must support security services, which are based on the cryptographic technology. In order to realize secure network, strong cryptography is desirable basically, however such technology might be used by criminals to prevent the police from investigation on their communications.

An alternative is key escrow encryption, which is a combination of strong encryption and emergency decryption capability by third parties. The Clinton Administration announced the first and most famous key escrow encryption in April 1993 [11], other countries such as U.K. [10] proposed such policies, and OECD also referred to lawful access to plain text or cryptographic keys [7].

The basic technique of the key escrow encryption is simple; single or multiple third parties, called Key Escrow Agents (KEAs), have (split) secret keys of citizens, and under proper court or other legal order an investigative agency (IA) gathers the split secret keys from the KEAs to decrypt data with the keys to access communications and/or computer files of target users or suspects.

From the view of user privacy, several methods of restricting such law-enforced access to plain data have been proposed. In the Fair Public Key Cryptosystems [6], restriction on decryption with condition of time and communication parties was realized, however the system required handshake between communication parties, which did not suit messaging system. A system with warrant bounds [5] realized restriction on decryption with condition of time by a method that KEAs provided the IA key information that was effective only limited time period; the system, which was based on the Diffie-Hellman key exchange [2], permitted both node surveillance, in which communications involving a particular target could be decrypted, and edge surveillance, in which communications between particular two targets could be decrypted. The system assumed that all users shared same Diffie-Hellman key exchange parameters, that is, a base field Z_p and a generator $g \in Z_p^*$. However, such assumption is not realistic in a global network; each domain or nation will use different system parameters. Yamane [12] proposed a system realizing non-disclosure of target user name under investigation to KEAs. The system introduced a key factory that generated key pairs of the ElGamal cryptosystem [3] of all users, which was a single point of failure.

This paper focuses two points. The first is that the deposited key is a private key of the RSA cryptosystem [8], while the deposited keys in the previous works were a private key of the ElGamal or Diffie-Hellman cryptosystem [5] [12]. Since the system does not require the handshake protocol [6], it can be applied to messaging system. The second is protection of user privacy; first nobody except owner user has access to its private key directly, secondly investigation agency can decrypt user data which is restricted with time period and communication entities, and thirdly split private keys of user are deposited in multiple KEAs without any information leakage of the keys, however the correctness of the split is guaranteed in arbitrary assurance.

First Chapter 2 describes basic requirements of key escrow system. Next Chapter 3 proposed a new key escrow system of the RSA cryptosystem, that is, the registration procedure of user to the system, validation process, communication between users and investigation procedure. Chapter 4 discusses security and performance of the system, and finally Chapter 5 concludes the paper.

2 Requirements to Key Escrow System

The followings are general requirements for key escrow system. Some of them were satisfied by the previous works [6] [5] [12].

1. **Guarantee of Decryption**
   There must be guarantee that the deposited private key of a user corresponds to the public key of the user so that an investigation agency can decrypt data sent to/from the user.

2. **Non Disclosure of Private Key Information**
   Only the owner of public key knows the corresponding private key. Single KEA is off course not desirable, because the break of the agent leads to the collapse of the whole system. Even if the private key information is divided and shared by multiple KEAs, the partial key information should not go out from the agents, because the original private key may be reconstructed through the collection of such partial information.

3. **Restriction of Decryption**
   For the purpose of protection of user privacy, decryption executed for investi-

gation should be restricted by condition, such as time period of investigation, peer entities of encrypted communication, etc.

4. **Non Disclosure of Decrypted Data**

   Disclosure of decrypted data should be restricted as much as possible. It is desirable that even the KEA should not know user data, because it does not need to know.

5. **Non Disclosure of Target User Name**

   Disclosure of target user (suspect) name and/or peer communication entity should be restricted. It is desirable that even KEA should not know the names of them.

3 Overall Architecture

The proposed system consists of seven kinds of entities, and each role of them is described briefly in the followings:

- **User**: Users exchange encrypted messages with the cryptosystem. Before use of the system each user generates two pairs of private and public keys of the RSA cryptosystem, one for data encryption and the other for digital signature. Then the user splits the private key for data encryption, and presents them in encrypted form to the RA with the public keys. The private key for digital signature is kept secret.
- **RA**: Registration Authority certifies the user and distributes the key information to the KEAs, VA, CJ and CA.
- **KEA**: Key Escrow Agent holds one of the split private keys. It also processes decryption request from the IA.
- **VA**: Validation Authority executes a validation protocol with the KEAs in order to confirm correctness of the combination of the split private and public keys that the user presented.
- **CA**: Certification Authority issues public key certificates of the user on the request from the RA.
- **IA**: Investigation Agency intercepts encrypted data sent to and/or from a target user and decrypts them with help of the KEAs under order of the CJ.
- **CJ**: Court of Justice admits the IA the access to user data and gives a certificate of the permission of decryption.

It is assumed that the RA, KEA, VA, CA and CJ are trusted, that is, they fulfill their tasks correctly as described in this chapter. Users might not be honest; they may not behave correctly during the registration procedure or communication phase described in this chapter. The IA may try to decrypt user communications not permitted from the CJ.

3.1 Registration of User

The following steps show the registration process of a user to the system. Figure 1 illustrates the entities described above and how information is passed between them. The numbers in the figure correspond to the indexes of the registration steps except I1 and I2, which are referred to in Section 3.4.

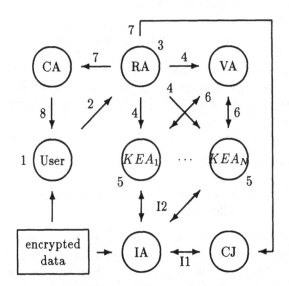

Figure 1: Entities and Data Flow

1. A user generates a pair of private and public keys of the RSA cryptosystem (n, d) and (n, e) for data encryption; the user chooses two large prime numbers p and q, calculates the least common multiplier l of $p - 1$ and $q - 1$, and chooses d and e satisfying $e \times d = 1 \pmod{l}$. The user splits the private key into $d_1, \ldots, d_N$, which sum equals to d under modulus l: $d = \sum d_i$ $\pmod{l}$. [1] Then the user chooses KEAs $(KEA_i)_i$ that she/he deposits the split private keys, and encrypts split private key d_i with the public key of KEA_i. The user also generates a key pair for digital signature (n', e') and (n', d'), however the private key never be deposited.
2. The user goes to the RA possibly with her/his identification card and presents the public keys, encrypted split private keys and the names of KEAs.
3. The RA certifies the user with the identification card and stores the public keys, encrypted split private keys with KEA names, her/he name, address, etc. in its local database.
4. The RA sends the public key for data encryption and KEA names to the VA, and also sends each of encrypted split private keys with the public key of the user to the corresponding KEA.
5. Each KEA decrypts the data to get the split private key for data encryption, and stores it with the public key.
6. The VA and KEAs execute the validation protocol described in the next section, and the VA sends the result to the RA, that is, whether the sum of the split private keys corresponds to the public key or not.

---

[1] The basic idea of division of RSA private key was given in [1], in which product form was adopted, that is, $d = \prod d_i \pmod{l}$.

7. If the validation goes well, the RA sends the combination of the user name, KEA names, and public keys, $\{user, (KEA_i)_i, (n, e), (n', e')\}$, to the CJ, the public keys with the user name to the CA securely, and then destroys the information stored in Step 3.

8. The CA issues the public key certificates including the keys and user name.

After the registration process, the CJ has the following information got in Step 7:

Table 1: Information hold by CJ

user name	public key for data encryption	public key for digital signature	KEA names
user	(n, e)	(n', e')	$(KEA_i)_i$
⋮	⋮	⋮	⋮

and KEA_i has the following information of split private keys indexed by public key:

Table 2: Information hold by KEA_i

public key for data encryption	split private keys
(n, e)	(n, d_i)
⋮	⋮

in which no user name/identifier appears explicitly.

3.2 Validation Protocol

Figure 2 is a diagram illustrating one round of the validation protocol between the VA and KEAs. The number of the round depends on assurance of the validation, which will be discussed in Section 4.3. The protocol is executed through a secure connection from the VA to each KEA, that is, the VA and the KEA authenticate mutually and the integrity and origin of transmitted data are guaranteed. Before the execution of the rounds the VA sends the corresponding public key in order to let KEA_i know which split private key is about to be validated.

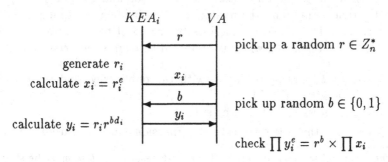

Figure 2: One Round of Validation Protocol

1. VA generates a random number $r \in Z_n^* = \{1, 2, \ldots, n-1\}$ sends it all KEAs.
2. KEA_i picks up a random number $r_i \in Z_n^*$, calculates $x_i = r_i^e \pmod{n}$, and sends x_i to VA. The random number r_i should be large enough so that the calculation of r_i from x_i is computationally infeasible.
3. After reception of all x_i, VA generates a random numbers $b \in \{0, 1\}$ and sends it to all KEAs.
4. KEA_i calculates $y_i = r_i r^{bd_i} \pmod{n}$ where d_i is the deposited split private key under validation, and sends y_i to VA.
5. VA confirms $\prod y_i^e = r^b \times \prod x_i \pmod{n}$.

3.3 Communication between Users

The following steps describe the procedure of an originator user, that is, the originator O sends an encrypted message to a recipient R.

1. gets the public key certificate for data encryption of the recipient user from the CA, verifies it with the public key of the CA, extracts the public key of the recipient (n_R, e_R),
2. generates a random number r and calculates $k_1 = r^{e_R} \pmod{n_R}$, and then
3. gets current date and time $date$ and calculates $k_2 = (hash(k_1) \parallel date)^{d'_O} \pmod{n'_O}$ with a hash function and the originator's private key for digital signature (n'_O, d'_O), [2]
4. calculates $k = r \oplus date$ to use as a session key of a symmetric cryptosystem and finally,
5. sends k_1, k_2, and a message encrypted with k to the recipient.

The recipient decrypts k_1 with its private key for data encryption (n_R, d_R) to get r, k_2 with the originator's public key for digital signature (n'_O, e'_O) to get $date$, and then finds the session key $k = r \oplus date$.

3.4 Investigation Procedure

Initially the CJ gives permission the IA to decrypt data sent from and/or to a target user with the signed certificate of the permission (labelled I1 in Figure 1), which includes the public keys of originator and recipient, the permitted investigation period, and the names of KEAs holding the split private keys of the recipient. The following describes the protocol between the IA and KEAs (labelled I2 in Figure 1), which is protected through secure connections.

1. IA sends k_1 and k_2 to KEA_i with the public keys and the certificate of permission from the CJ.
2. KEA_i processes the following steps:
   (a) verifies that the certificate of permission was issued from the CJ,

---

[2] The length of the concatenation of the hash result and $date$ must be shorter than the length of n_O.

(b) calculates $k_2^{e'_O}$ (mod n'_O) and checks that the first part of the result equals to $hash(k_1)$, and the second part *date* is included in the permitted investigation period, and then

(c) computes $k_1^{d_i}$ (mod n_R) with the split private key of the recipient that is retrieved from its local database with the public key as key, and sends it back to the IA.

3. *IA* calculates the products of all responses from KEA_i to get r:

$$\prod(k_1)^{d_i} = (k_1)^{\sum d_i} = (k_1)^{d_R} = r^{e_R d_R} = r \pmod{n_R}.$$

The agency calculates $k_2^{e'_O}$ (mod n'_O) to get *date* and then finds the session key $k = r \oplus date$.

4 Discussions

4.1 Consideration on Requirements

In this section it is shown that the proposed system satisfies the requirements described in Chapter 2, and also refers to the security of registration of user, communication between users and investigation procedure.

1. **Guarantee of Decryption**

   Through the validation protocol, it is proven that the private key is correctly split and deposited to KEAs, and the IA can decrypt messages with the cooperation of the KEAs. However, conspired users might use another protocol than that described in Section 3.3 to communicate without fear of decryption of the IA; for example they might use another RSA key pair not registered to the system, or complete different encryption algorithms. The author considers that such attacks cannot be prevent with key escrow technology in general, and it must be prescribed by law that such communication itself is illegal.

2. **Non-Disclosure of Private Key Information**

   Since a private key is generated by the owner user, each split private key is transmitted securely to each KEA, the validation protocol is a zero-knowledge interactive proof as proven in Section 4.3, and the IA gets only (partial) decrypted data, therefore only KEA knows the split private key information. Because the user can split the private key randomly, single KEA does not have any information of the private key. As a consequence, no single entity except the user knows the private key information, and there is no single point of failure in the system.

3. **Restriction on Decryption**

   Two conditions are realized about restriction on decryption for investigation. The first restriction is that only communication during permitted time period by the CJ is decrypted through request from the IA, because each KEA extracts the date and time information from k_2 and checks against the certificate from the CJ. Nobody can forge k_2 since it is generated with the private key of the originator, which only the originator knows. The originator might use wrong *date* to disorder the investigation, however this is unlikely, because if the date information is wrong, the recipient cannot get the correct session key that is computed from the date information.

The second is restriction on originator and recipient of transmitted data. Each KEA uses a split private key of the recipient and a public key of the originator during the decryption requested from the IA, and the key are selected from the information contained the certificate from the CJ. As a result only communication between entities permitted by the certificate is decrypted, unless the certificate is forged.

4. **Non-Disclosure of Decrypted Data**

The IA sends the encrypted data to the KEAs and the KEAs send back *partially* decrypted data through secure connections. Therefore each KEA knows only the partially decrypted data, and this shows that the system satisfies the Non-Disclosure of Decrypted Data requirement.

5. **Non-Disclosure of Target User Name**

The name of a target user under investigation is known to the CJ and IA. The KEAs are let known the public keys of the target users, therefore the KEA do not know the user name. However, if a KEA executes the full search of the public key certificates issued from the CA, it can find the target user name from the public key information contained in the certificates, and this remains a problem.

4.2 Security of Communication between Users

In order to find the session key k, r is required, which can be got only through calculation $k_1^{d_R}$ (mod n_R), therefore only the owner of (n_R, d_R) knows the session key, and the confidentiality of the communication is satisfied.

4.3 Security of Validation Protocol

This section proves the validation protocol is a zero-knowledge interactive proof [4], actually it has the three properties, completeness, soundness and zero-knowledge, which ensure the followings:

- the private key is correctly split and deposited to KEAs, therefore, the IA can decrypt messages with the cooperation of the KEAs.
- Neigher VA nor a third party can get any information about the private key and split keys, and a KEA cannot get any information about the split private keys that the other KEAs hold.

The proof of security of the validation protocol assumes the security of the RSA cryptosystem; it is computationally infeasible to calculate m from $c = m^e$ (mod n) without knowledge of the private key d.

Lemma 1 Completeness. *If the private key is correctly split, deposited, and all KEA_i and VA follow the protocol, then VA accepts the split keys are as valid.*

Proof: Since $y_i^e = (r_i \times r^{bd_i})^e = r_i^e \times (r^{d_i})^{eb} \pmod{n}$,

$$\prod y_i^e = \prod r_i^e \times \prod (r^{d_i})^{eb} = \prod x_i \times (\prod r^{d_i})^{eb} = \prod x_i \times (r^{\sum d_i})^{eb} = \prod x_i \times (r^d)^{eb}$$
$$= \prod x_i \times r^b \pmod{n}$$

and thus Step 5 of the protocol (Section 3.2) is always true. $\square$

Lemma 2 Soundness. *Assume that some KEA_i^*s are unjust and/or that some of them do not have the correct split private keys. If VA follows the protocol and KEA_i^*s perform arbitrary polynomial time computations, VA accept the proof as valid with probability bounded by 2^{-k}, where k is the number of rounds.*

Proof (Sketch): KEA_i^*s can cheat VA by guessing b and sending

$$x_1 = r_1^e \times r^{-b} \pmod{n} \text{ and } y_1 = r_1$$

from KEA_1^* to VA and

$$x_i = r_i^e \pmod{n} \text{ and } y_i = r_i (i \neq 1)$$

from KEA_i^*s to VA where r_1 and r_i are random numbers in Z_n^*. However the probability of this event is $1/2$ for one round and 2^{-k} for the whole protocol.

In order to increase the probability, KEA_i^*s must choose x_i in such a way that they can computer the e-th logarithms y' and y'' of $r^b \times \prod x_i$ for $r \in Z_n^*$ and $b \in \{0,1\}$, that is,

$$(y')^e = r^0 \times \prod x_i \quad \text{and} \quad (y'')^e = r^1 \times \prod x_i \pmod{n}.$$

Then the ratio of y'' and y' is the e-th logarithm of r, because

$$(y''/y')^e = (y'')^e/(y')^e = (r^1 \times \prod x_i)(r^0 \times \prod x_i) = r \pmod{n}$$

As a result KEA_i^*s can decrypt any encrypted data r without knowing the private key d and this shows the RSA cryptosystem is broken. $\square$

Lemma 3 Zero-Knowledge. *Any VA including an unjust VA^* does not increase any information except whether the split private keys are correctly deposited or not.*

Proof (Sketch): It is enough to prove the existence of probabilistic polynomial algorithm that simulates the protocol with VA^* and to show that the simulation cannot be distinguished from the protocol between VA^* and $(KEA_i)_i$ with any polynomial algorithms.

Assume that VA^* sends b by calculating a fixed random tape RT, data from sent from KEAs, the public key information, and data got through the protocol before sending b. The simulators KEA_i^* are constructed as follows:

1. Give VA^* RT and the public key.
2. Repeat the following steps until the number of the outputs (y_i)s becomes k:

   (a) Receive r from VA^*.
   (b) Pick randomly $y_i \in Z_n^*$ and $b' \in \{0, 1\}$.
   (c) Calculate
   $$x_1 = y_1^e \times r^{-b'} \pmod{n}$$
   and
   $$x_i = y_i^e \pmod{n}(i \neq 1)$$
   and send $(x_i)_i$ to VA^*.
   (d) Get b from VA^*.
   (e) If $b = b'$ then output $(y_i)_i$, otherwise go back to Step (b).

In the following it is shown that the simulators satisfy the property stated in the beginning of the proof.

First it is shown that the above calculation time is probabilistic polynomial by proving that the probability of $b = b'$ is $1/2$. Since b' and y_i are generated randomly, $x_1 = y_1^e \times r^{-b'} \pmod{n}$ and $x_i = y_i^e \pmod{n}(i \neq 1)$ are distributed uniformly in Z_n^*. On the other hand b output from V^* depends on RT, the public key and data got through the protocol before sending b, which are independent from b'. As a result b and b' are mutually independent, and thus the probability of $b = b'$ is $1/2$.

Next it is shown that the probability distribution of the communication between VA^* and KEA_is cannot be distinguished from that between VA^* and KEA_i^*s. The former is
$$Probability(((x_i)_i, b, (y_i)_i)) = Probability((r_i^e)_i, b, (r_i r^{bd_i})_i)$$
$$= 1/2(n-1)^{N+1},$$
while the latter is
$$Probability((x_i)_i, b, (y_i)_i) = Probability((y_1^e \times r^{-b'}, y_2^e, \ldots), b', (y_i)_i)$$
$$= 1/2(n-1)^{N+1}.$$
Since y_is are generated randomly, $y_1^e \times r^{-b'}$ and $y_i^e(i \neq 1)$ are distributed uniformly in Z_n^*, and thus these two expressions cannot be distinguished. $\square$

4.4 Performance of Validation Protocol

The most computationally consuming parts of one round of the protocol are the calculations of the powers under modulus n, which appear three times: two e-th powers and one d_i-th power: [3] r_i^e, r^{bd_i} and $\prod y_i^e = (\prod y_i)^e$. An RSA cryptosystem implementation on SparcII executes 17 bit public encryption with 1,024 bit modulus in 0.01 second, and it is estimated to take 0.60 second to calculate 1,024 bit private key operation. As a result it will take about 0.62 second for the three calculations for 1,024 bit RSA cryptosystem.

---

[3] Actually there are $2N$ e-th and d_i-th powers, but the calculations by the KEAs are executed parallelly, therefore it seems to be one time respectively.

The proof of soundness shows that the probability of accept of wrong split private keys is 2^{-k} where k is the number of the rounds. If the system accepts of a wrong key with probability up to one million-th, the number of the rounds should be larger than twenty, and the protocol takes longer than 12 seconds.

For the purpose of the estimation of the scalability, let calculate the number of users that single VA machine can serve with the M/M/1 queueing model. The average response time (μ) is $1/12 = 0.083$. Let X be the total number of users and assume that a user goes to the RA once a year. The average request arriving period (λ) is $X/(3600 \times 8 \times 312)$ where the RA opens 8 hours per day and closes on Sundays.

The average response time T is calculated with the equation $T = 1/(\mu - \lambda)$. If it is required that the average response time T should be less than one minute, then the total number of users X must be less than about 600 thousands.

For the purpose of increase the performance, it is possible to widen the range of the challenge b; actually b can be chosen randomly from $\{0, 1, \ldots, l-1\}$ where l is the least common multiplier of $p-1$ and $q-1$, and the possibility of acceptance of wrong split keys can be decreased to l^{-k}. [4] The order of l is bigger than that of the square root of $n = p \times q$, and one round is enough. As a consequence the number of users increases up to 140 millions, which is sufficiently large.

4.5 Performance of Investigation

The major computationally consuming part of the investigation procedure is the computation of $k_1^{d_i}$ and $k_2^{e'_o}$ of KEA_i, while verification of certificate from CJ will not affect the performance, because the result of checking of the first decryption request can be cached and used for the later requests. As a result there is no extra computation comparing with the other key escrow systems [5] [12].

5 Conclusions

The author has proposed a key escrow system of the RSA cryptosystem that satisfies non-disclosure of private key to an investigation agency and restricts decryption by the IA with conditions of time period and originator and/or recipient. It is also described that the security and performance of the system as well as those of the validation protocol, which confirms correctness of the split of the private key.

For the purpose of the development of a global network, a key infrastructure and a key recovery/escrow system that satisfies governments, citizens, organizations are desired. Key escrow technology can be applied to self-escrow or key recovery in an organization; in case that an employee or crypto-token is missing, encrypted data is restored. However there might be different requirements of such system from those of the key escrow system; for example, the private

---

[4] In this case the zero-knowledgeness of the validation protocol is lost.

key is split and deposited to managers, and only some of them are required to decrypt data, not all of them. Another requirement might be inter-operability between the key recover within the organization and key escrow organized by government. International key escrow is also a very controversial issue. Much study is needed to make clear requirements and real systems implementing the requirements.

Acknowledgements

The author would like to thank to Professor Tsutomu Matsumoto for his advice and comments on this paper.

References

1. C.Boyd, "Some Applications of Multiple Key Ciphers," Advances in Cryptology: Proceedings of Crypto 88, Springer-Verlag, pp. 455-467 (1989)
2. W.Diffie and M.Hellman, "New Directions in Cryptography," IEEE Transactions of Information Theory, 22 pp. 644-654 (1976)
3. R.ElGamal, "A public key cryptosystem and a signature scheme based on discrete logarithms," IEEE Transactions on Information Theory, 31, pp.469-472 (1985)
4. A.Fiat and A.Shamir, "How To Prove Yourself: Practical Solutions to Identification and Signature Problems," Advances in Cryptology: Proceedings of Crypto 86, Springer-Verlag, pp. 186-194 (1987)
5. A.K.Lenstra, P.Winkler and Y.Yacobi, "A Key Escrow System with Warrant Bounds," Advances in Cryptology: Proceedings of CRYPTO'95, Springer-Verlag, pp. 197-207 (1995)
6. S.Micali, "Fair Public-Key Cryptosystems," Advances in Cryptology: Proceedings of CRYPTO'92, Springer-Verlag, pp. 113-138 (1992)
7. Organization for Economic Co-operation and Development, "OECD Adopts Guidelines for Cryptography Policy," (http://www.oecd.org/news_and_events/release/nw97-24a.htm) (March 1997)
8. R.L.Rivest, A.Shamir and L.Adleman, "A method for obtaining digital signatures and public key cryptosystems," Communications of ACM, 21, pp. 120-126 (1978)
9. B.Schneier, *Applied Cryptography, Second Edition*, John Wiley & Sons, Inc. (1996)
10. I.Taylor (MBE MP Minister for Science & Technology), "Licensing of Trusted Third Parties for the Provision of Encryption Services," Public Consultation Paper on Detailed Proposals for Legislation (http://dtiinfo1.dti.gov.uk/pubs/) (March 1997)
11. The White House, Office of the Press Secretary, "Statement by the Press Secretary," (http://www.eff.org/pub/Privacy/Key_escrow/Clipper/Clipper_II/Clipper /Key_escrow/Clipper_Capstone_EES_Tessera_Skipjack/wh_crypto_original.announce) (16th April 1993)
12. Y.Yamane and K.Sakurai, "How to restrict investigators' tapping in Key Escrow Systems," (in Japanese) The 1996 Symposium on Cryptography and Information Security 7C, The Institute of Electronics, Information and Communication Engineers (January 1996)

A Key Escrow System with Protecting User's Privacy by Blind Decoding

Kouichi SAKURAI[1], Yoshinori YAMANE[1]
Shingo MIYAZAKI[1] Tohru INOUE[2]

[1] Kyushu University, Dept. of Computer Science,
Hakozaki, Higashi-ku, Fukuoka, 812-81, JAPAN
`sakurai@csce.kyushu-u.ac.jp`
[2] Advanced Mobile Telecomm. Security Tech. Research Lab. Co.,Ltd.
3-20-8, Shin-Yokohama, Yokonaha, Kanagawa, 222, JAPAN
`t-inoue@amsl.co.jp`

Abstract. We propose a new key recovery system with satisfying the following properties:

1. The court-authorized eavesdropping by the investigator is limited both in tapping time and in tapped conversation.
2. Trustees, who are cooperating with the investigator to eavesdrop a user's communication, cannot know whom the investigator is intercepting.
3. No investigator can obtain illegally the secret key of users against which no legitimate court order has been issued.

Our system utilizes the blind decoding: a client has a message encrypted with a server's secret key and the client asks the server to decode the message without revealing what is the decoded plaintext nor learning the server's secret key. Our system also introduces two agencies besides the trustees. These are related to the mechanism of registering users and of distributing the user's escrowed keys, named "Key Producer," and "Registration Center." Our system can be implemented by using only the discrete-log based cryptosystems (the Diffie-Hellman and the ElGamal).

1 Introduction

1.1 The Key Escrow and Fair Cryptosystems

The KEY ESCROW The White House announced the Escrowed Encryption Initiative on April 16th, 1993, and Subsequently the National Institute of Standards and Technology approved Escrowed Encryption Standard. While the several discussion on the Key Escrow, the implementation, and improvements of the technique and system have been development.

Designing key escrow systems, a dilemma exists between law enforcement agencies and rights advocates protecting the privacy of the citizens. This paper investigates how to protect user's privacy in key escrow/recovery systems, and propose a system with increasing the effectiveness of digital surveillance not only as an anti-crime measure but also as commercial applications while making better protection of user's privacy.

FAIR PUBLIC-KEY CRYPTOSYSTEMS Micali proposed a fair public-key cryptosystem [Mic92], which is an alternative approach to the key escrow system, and mentioned some variants of the basic notion of a fair public-key cryptosystem, two of which are as follows:

Time-bounded court-authorized eavesdropping: One of the main drawbacks of the key escrow system is that once interception is allowed, the active investigator can intercept all further messages and also decrypt the monitored older messages, as they obtain the unit key U from the escrow agents. The similar problem is also pointed out in the Micali's original fair cryptosystem.

Making trustees oblivious: Micali gives an idea called "oblivious trustees" for preventing trustees from giving advance warning to the person whose line are tapping (or to be tapped). At the same time, however, Micali alarms that making trustees oblivious might introduce a new danger that one could obtain illegally the secret key of users against which no legitimate court order has been issued.

1.2 Previous work

There are previous works on the first problem of making court-authorized tapping time-bounded. As Micali mentioned [Mic92], a solution is to use a tamper proof hardware module, and another is to use time-bounded keys. However, the latter solution requires many keys for long time communications, then it is not practical. Lesntra, Winkler, and Yacobi [LWY95] developed a system with time-bounded warrant. Several approaches are discussed for solving this problem [Diff94, BKOSW94, HMP95].

However, no exact discussion has been done on the second problem of an illegal extraction of users' secret key without no legitimate court order when we make trustees oblivious.

1.3 Our approach and resulted solution

We propose a new key recovery system which solves both the 1st and 2nd problem.

OUR BASIC IDEA Our basic approach is to make investigators oblivious of users' secret key, whereas Micali's Fair Cryptosystems [Mic92] making trustees oblivious of the user's name.

After tapping the encrypted message of the target user, the investigator asks the trustees to decode the encrypted message without revealing what is the decoded original text nor learning user's secret key. We realize such a system by applying a blind decoding protocol, which Micali also used for making trustee oblivious.

In our proposed system, before eavesdropping communication among users, the investigator first have to get an authorized permission from the court. After checking the court-authorized permission supplied from the investigator, the trustees decode the encrypted message via a blind decoding protocol with the investigator. Thus, eavesdropping by the investigator is restricted to the message under the court-authorized permission and is not possible without on-line cooperating with the trustees.

OUR APPROACH for MAKING TRUSTEES OBLIVIOUS The system described above does not yet achieve oblivious trustees. Then, for making trustees oblivious of the user's name, our system introduces two agencies, which are related to the mechanism of registering users and of distributing the user's escrowed keys, named "Key Producer," and "Registration Center." The blind decoding plays again an important role for user's getting the keys generating from the Key Producer.

In the system proposed in [Sam97], each trustee preserves the shared user's secret key related to its public key. So, trustees can know whom the investigator is intercepting by searching the target user's name corresponding to the public key. On the other hand, in our system, trustees cannot disclose the target user's name except their collusion attack.

THE BLIND TECHNIQUE The origin of the blind technique is Chaum's blind signature scheme [Cha82], in which Alice obtains a valid signature for a message from a signer Alice without her seeing the message nor the signature. The blind signature scheme is defined for public-key based signature schemes, whereas the blind decoding scheme is defined for a (public-key) encryption scheme.

A blind decoding scheme is a protocol between Alice and Bob, in which Alice has a message encrypted with Bob's secret key and Alice asks Bob to decode the message without revealing what is the decoded original text nor learning Bob's secret key. A blind decoding can be implemented using the RSA encryption scheme via the similar protocol as the RSA-based blind signature scheme of Chaum [Cha82]. Micali [Mic92] applied the blind decoding protocol based on RSA scheme into fair cryptosystems for making trustees oblivious.

Our system can use blind decoding scheme for ElGamal Encryption scheme [SY96]. Thus, we can make the fair Diffie-Hellman scheme [Mic92] oblivious by using only the discrete logarithm based cryptosystems, and our system can be constructed based only on the Diffie-Hellman and the ElGamal.

2 Our applied blind decoding for ElGamal Encryption

2.1 ElGamal's Public-Key Cryptosystem

Now we consider the ElGamal's public-Key cryptosystem [ElG85]. Bob sets $g \in Z_p^*$ as the base, picks $x \in Z_{p-1}$ at random, and computes $y = g^x \bmod p$. Bob publishes y, g, p as his public key whereas he keeps x as his secret key. Suppose Alice wants to send a string m to Bob. Alice picks $r \in Z_{p-1}$ at random, computes $C_1 = g^r \bmod p, C_2 = my^r \bmod p$ and sends (C_1, C_2) to Bob. On receiving (C_1, C_2), Bob uses his secret key to compute $m = C_2/(C_1)^x \bmod p$.

2.2 The protocol

We apply the technique of Shamir's 3-pass message transmission scheme, which is originally proposed as a tool for mental poker by Shamir et al. [SRA79] and independently proposed as Massey-Omura's cryptosystem (see, e.g. [Kob87]), for making blind the ElGamal Encryption. A similar technique for making a discrete-log based cryptosystem blind is used in [CP92].

Suppose that Bob's public key is (P_B, g, p) and his secret key is S_B. Also assume that Alice has a cipher text C, which is encrypted by Bob. Namely,

$$C = (C_1, C_2) = (g^r \bmod p, P_B^r \cdot M \bmod p)$$

for a text M and a Bob's randomly selected r.

Step 1: Alice picks $a \in Z_{p-1}^*$ at random, computes $X = C_1{}^a$, and sends X to Bob.

Step 2: On receiving X, Bob computes $Y = X^{S_B}$, and sends Y to Alice.

Step 3: On receiving Y, Alice uses her secret a to compute $Z = Y^{a^{-1}}$, which is

$$Y^{a^{-1}} \equiv (X^{S_B})^{a^{-1}} \equiv X^{S_B \cdot a^{-1}} \equiv C_1^{a \cdot S_B \cdot a^{-1}} \equiv C_1^{S_B} \pmod{p}.$$

Then, Alice obtain the original message M by computing $C_2/Z = C_2/C_1^{S_B} \pmod{p}$.

2.3 Avoiding decoder's cheating

In the RSA-based blind decoding scheme, the correctness the decrypted message is checked by anybody with the encrypted message and the public key, namely it has a self-verification property. However, in the case of the ElGamal encryption scheme, Alice cannot verify the correctness of decrypted message by herself, because the encrypted message is randomized then is not unique in the ElGamal encryption scheme. Therefore, in the proposed protocol, Bob has a chance to cheat Alice by sending $\tilde{Y} = X^T$, where $T \neq S_B$. To avoid such a cheating by Bob, we consider an additional subprotocol, in which Bob shows indeed that he correctly computes Y from X. The confirmation protocol of undeniable signature scheme [CvA89] achieves the requirement, in which the prover shows that $Y := X^S \bmod p$ by using public information $(g, X, P = g^S \bmod p)$. Here we assume that the modulus p has the form $2q + 1$, where q is also prime, and the base g has the prime order q.

Step 1: Alice picks $e_1, e_2 \in \mathbf{Z}_q^*$ at random, and computes $c := Y^{e_1} P_B^{e_2} \bmod p$, then sends c to Bob.

Step 2: Bob computes $d := c^{S_B^{-1} \bmod q} \bmod p$, and sends d to Alice.

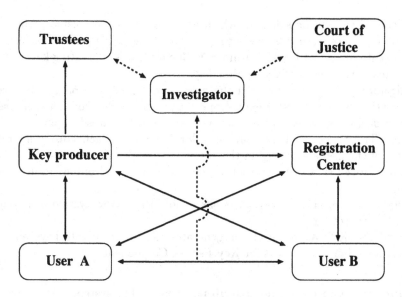

Fig. 1. The configuration of our system

Step 3: Alice accepts Y as a correctly computed result if and only if the equation $d \equiv X^{e_1} g^{e_2} \pmod{p}$ holds.

The correctness of this protocol is shown in [CvA89].

Remark. A technical comment on perfect undetectability against Bob is given in [SY96], and a countermeasure against the abuse of the blind decoding called "oracle spotting problem" [AN95] is investigated in [MOS96].

3 Our proposed recovery key system

3.1 Describing of our system

The System configuration Our proposed system consists of the following components (see Figure 1), each of which has a pair of public and private keys. We denote the public key, and private key, P_x and S_x respectively, where x indicates the party (e.g. User U, Trustee T etc.).

User (U) Users join the system, and communicate with other users via encrypted messages. Each user has a pair of the public key and the private key (of

ElGamal encryption scheme), which are ecrowed in the trustees, while the individual user encrypts messages to be sent the the other user by using a conventional secret key algorithm E with each user's generating keys, which is mixed with the receiver's public key.

Investigator (I) For the purpose of the electronic surveillance on criminal conversation, an investigator eavesdrops digital communication between users, then deciphers the encrypted messages obtained by eavesdropping.

Trustees (Ti, i=1,2,···) There could be plural trustees. Each trustee shares a part of the user's escrowed in the system.

Court of Justice (J) A court issues the permission of eavesdropping to investigators.

Registration Center (RC) When users ask to join the escrow system, this center make registration.

Key Producer (KP) A key producer generates the user's private keys and the corresponding public keys for Key Escrow Component.

Producer's generating and distributing keys The systems concerning for the initialization for generating and distributing keys are the key producer, the registration center, and the trustees.

The key producer (KP) executes the following.

1. KP generates a private key S_U for users, then KP splits S_U into n pieces for the n trustees as: $S_U = S_U^1 + S_U^2 + \cdots + S_U^n \bmod p$. Next KP computes $P_U := g^{S_U} \bmod p$.

   Remark: No user U is registered yet at this point.

2. KP sends the following information related to S_U, S_U^i to the key registration center and to the trustees respectively.

   To the Registration Center: KP encrypts S_U and P_U by KP's own public key P_{KP}: $S_U, P_U \rightarrow E_{P_{KP}}[S_U, P_U]$. Then, KP sends the registration center

   $$(P_U, E_{P_{KP}}[S_U, P_U]).$$

   To the trustees: The KP computes K_{KP-J} by Diffie-Hellman scheme [DH76] using KP's private key S_{KP} and the court's public key P_J as $K_{KP-J} := (P_J)^{S_{KP}} \bmod p$. Then, KP encrypts the public key P_U by using K_{KP-J} and sets the result as ID_U: $ID_U := E_{K_{KP-J}}[P_U]$. The KP sends via a secure channel each trustee T_i a pair of each user's ID, ID_U and a part of split private key S_{U^i}: (ID_U, S_U^i).

Registering users and distributing user's key The registration of the users and distribution of user's key are executed among users, the registration center (RC) and the key producer (KP).

1. When a user requests the RC to join the system, the user can selects a favorite public key among the RC's public key list like selecting the telephone number. Suppose the user selects a public key P_U.

2. RC sends the user the encrypted key corresponding to the selected public key P_U, $E_{P_{KP}}[S_U, P_U]$.
3. The user U asks the key producer KP to decipher the encrypted key $E_{P_{KP}}[S_U, P_U]$ via a blind decoding protocol. Thus, the user finally obtains the public key P_U and the corresponding private key S_U.

Users' encrypted communication When a user A make ciphering communication with user B, user A sends the following cipher text to user B

$$C = (C_1, C_2, C_3) = (g^r \bmod p, K_A \times P_B^r \bmod p, E_{K_A}[m]),$$

where K_A is a user A's selecting secret key used for a conventional secret-key algorithm E and m is a plain text.

For identifying the targeted person's name from the eavesdropped conversation, a law enforcement access field (LEAF) is attached as the Clipper.

Generating LEAF The Clipper has a constant value as unit number UID, and has a variable value as session keys K. To affect that contents to LEAF, Clipper inserts session key K in LEAF. On the other hand, in our system, the public key P_B, and the corresponding private key S_B, are constant values, while the cipher text C is variable. Thus our system inserts the computed result of the cipher text C and the data via a one-way hash function for identifying the targeted person, and also inserts the public key P_B for identifying the receiver B into the LEAF.

Verifying LEAF: User B verifies the received LEAF as follows;
1. Compute his public key P_B from his inserted private key S_B, as $P_B := g^{S_B} \bmod p$.
2. Compute the hash value of a cipher text C with the date *date* by using the one-way hash function h, then obtain $h(C, data)$.
3. Confirm the correctness of

$$E_{KF_{pub}}[h(C, date)\|P_B]$$

by the device-stored (or programmed) embedded family public key KF_{pub} with the received LEAF.

Confirmation OK: Regard the received cipher text C as decoded by the private key S_B.

Confirmation NoGood: stop decoding as a false-LEAF is used.

Investigator's tapping users' communication The eavesdropping users' encrypted communication is executed by investigators with on-line-help of trustees after court's permission. Suppose that the investigator try to intercept an encrypted message from user A to user B.

1. The investigator first takes out the targeted person's public key P_B received from cipher text, between user A and B, eavesdropped from LEAF. The investigator eavesdrops a cipher text C and LEAF, then decode LEAF using private key KF_{priv} of family keys:

$$LEAF \to h(C, date), P_B.$$

2. The investigator sends P_B to the court.
3. The court considers whether eavesdropping to the targeted person B is legitimate or not. In case of giving the permission, the court first computes the common key K_{KP-J} for Diffie-Hellman scheme between the key producer KP and the court J. Next, the court obtains ID_B by encypting the user B's public key P_B with K_{KP-J}. Finally, the court signs ID_B and the date with the court's private key S_J and publishes the result $Perm$ as the warrant of the tapping.

$$K_{KP-J} := P_{KP}^{S_J} \equiv g^{S_{KP}S_J} \equiv P_J^{S_{KP}} \pmod{p}.$$
$$ID_B := E_{K_{KP-J}}[P_B].$$
$$Perm := Sig_{S_J}[ID_B, date].$$

4. The court sends the investigator $Perm$, a permission of eavesdropping.
5. The investigator sends each key trustee, $Perm$ then after trustee confirming signature and date, search private key S_B^i corresponding to ID_B.
6. The investigator ask the trustees to decode the tapped cipher text C via a blind decoding.

4 Remarks on our proposed system

4.1 On the correctness of the decrypted message in blind decoding with distributed servers

We have remarked that the correctness of the decrypted message in blind decoding can be done by applying the confirmation protocol of undeniable signature scheme [CvA89] (See Subsection 2.3). However, we should note that this technique is applicable only to the case of the single prover. The application fails in the case with the distributed provers, if our system adopts the distributed trustees.

In fact, when the investigator asks the *multiple* trustee the decryption of the tapping message, the investigator cannot check whether blind decoding is correctly executed or not, because the investigators do no know $g^{S_B^i}$. Further the techniques in [CvA89] can not proceed unless anyone knows $S_B = S_B^1 + \cdots + S_B^n$. Pederson's protocol [Ped91] answers to this problem, though the key producer splitting S_U have to be changed to be a more complicated manner, which is based on a verifiable secret sharing [Fel87].

Here, we describe the protocol for verifying the correctness of the decrypted message for multiple provers. Firstly, in key generation, KP computes the inverse

$V_U = S_U^{-1} \mod q$ of a secret key S_U, and then splits V_U into n prices for the n trustees: $V_U = V_U^1 + V_U^2 + \cdots + V_U^n \mod p$. Each trustee T_i stores V_U^i related to S_U^i on his database.

In tapping user B's communication, the investigator can verify the correctness of the decrypted message by trustees below. Here, similarly in Section 2.2, let $C_1^{S_B}$ (mod p) be the correct message decrypted by trustees and $X = C_1^a \mod p$. In blind decoding protocol, each trustee computes $Y_i = X^{S_B^i} \mod p$ and sends it to the investigator;

$$Y = \prod_{i=1}^{k} Y_i \mod p$$
$$= X^{S_{B1}+S_{B2}+\cdots+S_{Bk}} \mod p$$
$$= X^{S_B} \mod p$$

Step 1: The investigator picks $e_1, e_2 \in \mathbf{Z}_q^*$ at random, and computes $c := Y^{e_1} P_B^{e_2} \mod p$, then sends c to all trustees.

Step 2: Each trustee T_i computes $d_i := c^{V_B^i} \mod p$, and sends d_i to the investigator.

Step 3: The investigator accepts Y as a correctly computed result if and only if the equation $\prod_{i=1}^{n} d_i \equiv X^{e_1} g^{e_2} \pmod{p}$ holds.

The soundness of this protocol is shown below.

$$\prod_{i=1}^{n} d_i = Y^{e_1(V_1+V_2+\cdots+V_n)} P_B^{e_2(V_1+V_2+\cdots+V_n)} \mod p$$
$$= X^{S_B e_1 V_B} g^{S_B e_2 V_B} \mod p$$
$$= X^{e_1} g^{e_2} \mod p$$

4.2 Why the Key Producer is introduced

Two methods are typical for making (private) keys. One is that owner himself makes his own private key (e.g. in the Micali's fair cryptosystem [Mic92]). The other is that a specific organization for key generating service makes user's private keys (e.g. in Clipper [BDKMT93]). Our system takes the latter approach.

We could construct a simpler system with only one key management center, while the proposed system divides the organization related to registering users and distributing keys into three: Key Producer, Registration Center, Trustees.

The problems of the system without the Key Producer are the following:

1. In the user's registration stage, Registration Center and Trustees have to communicate with each other. This might induce some collision attack by these two agencies.
2. If the system has not so many registered users, then an exhaustive computation could attack the Registration Center's database, then disclose the name of the users, which breaks the user's privacy.

We solve these problems by introducing the Key Producer.

5 Concluding remarks

In this paper, we proposed a key escrow system based on blind decoding techniques. The detailed version of this paper will make further discussion on security of the proposed system from several aspects remarked in [FY95].

References

[AN95] R.J.Anderson and R.Needham, "Robustness principles for public key protocols," Proc. CRYPTO'95, pp.236-247 (1996).

[BDKMT93] E. F. Brickell, D. E. Denning, S. T. Kent, D. P. Maher, W. Tuchman, "SKIPJACK Review Interim Report," July 28 (1993).

[BGK95] E. F. Brickell, P. Gemmell, and D. Kravitz, "Trustee-based tracing extensions to anonymous cash and the making of anonymous change" Proc. SODA'95. pp.457-466 (1995).

[BELW94] D. M. Balenson, C. M. Ellison, S. B. Lipner, S. T. Walker, "A New Approach to Software Key Escrow Encryption," Trusted Information Systems, Inc., (1994). (also in [Hof95]).

[BKOSW94] T. Beth, H. J. Knobloch, M. Otten, G. J. Simmons, P. Wichmann, "Towards Acceptable Key Escrow Systems," Proc. of The 2nd ACM Conf. on Computer and Communications Security, pp.51-58 (1994).

[Bla94] M. Blaze, "Protocol Failure in the Escrowed Encryption Standard," In the Proceedings of The 2nd ACM Conference on Computer and Communications Security, November 1994,59-67.(also in [Hof95]) August 20, (1994).

[CBHMS89] D. Chaum, B. den Boer, E. van Heyst, S. Mjolsners, A. Steenbeek, "Efficient Offline Electronic Checks, Advances in Cryptology, Eurocrypt '89, LNCS 434, Springer Verlag, pp.294-301.

[Cha82] D. Chaum, "Blind Signatures for untraceable payments," Advances in Cryptology Proceedings of Crypto '82, (1983).

[CP92] D. Chaum and T. Pederson, "Wallet databases with observers," Advances in Cryptology - CRYPTO'92, (1993) pp.89-105.

[CPS94] J. L. Camenisch, J. -M. Piveteau, M. A. Stadler, "Blind signatures Based on the Discrete Logarithm Problem," Advances in Cryptology - EUROCRYPT '94, (1994).

[CvA89] D. Chaum, H. van Antwerpen, "Undeniable Signatures," Advances in Cryptology-CRYPTO '89, (1989).

[DH76] Diffie, W. and Hellman, M.E., "New Directions in Cryptography," IEEE Trans. Inf. Theory, IT-22, 6, pp.644-654 (1976).

[Diff94] Diffie, W. presented in Proc. of E.I.S.S. Workshop on Escrowed-Key Cryptography Edi. by Beth and Otten (1994).

[DS94] D. E. Denning, M. Smid, "Key Escrowing Today," IEEE Communications Magazine, Vol.32, No.9 (Sept.1994), pp.58-68.

[ElG85] T. ElGamal, "A public key cryptosystem and a signature scheme based on discrete logarithms," IEEE Trans. on IT, 31, pp.469-472 (1985).

[Fel87] P.Feldman, "A practical scheme for non-interactive verifiable secret sharing," Proc. IEEE FOCS97 pp.427-437.

[FY95] Y.Frankel, and M.Yung, "Escrow Encryption Systems Visited: Attacks, Analysis, and Designs," Advances in Cryptology-CRYPTO '95, (1995).

[HMP95] P. Horster, M. Michels, H. Peterson, "A new key escrow system with active investigator," Technical Report, TR-95-4-F, University of Technology Chemnitz-Zwickau, April 18, (1995).

[Hof95] L. J. Hoffman ed, *Building in Big Brothers:* the cryptographic policy debate, Springer Verlag, (1995).

[Kob87] N. Koblitz, "Elliptic curve cryptosystems," Math. Comp., vol.48, No.177, pp.203-209 (1987).

[LWY95] A.K.Lenstra, P.Winkler, Y.Yacobi, "A key escrow system with warrant bounds," Advances in Cryptology- CRYPTO '95, (1995), pp.197-207.

[MOS96] M.Mambo, E.Okamoto, and K.Sakurai, "How to utilize the transformability of digital signatures for solving the oracle problem," Advances in Cryptology- ASIACRTPT '96, (1996), pp.322-333.

[Mic92] S. Micali, "Fair public key cryptosystems," Laboratory for Computer Science, Massachusetts Institute of Technology, Cambridge, Mass.; MIT/ LCS/ TR-579.b; November (1993). (also in [Hof95])

[Mil85] V. S. Miller, "Use of elliptic curves in cryptography," Proc. of CRYPTO'85, pp. 417-426 (1985).

[Ped91] T.P.Pedersen, "Distributed Provers with Applications to Undeniable Signatures," Advances in Cryptology-EUROCRYPT'91, pp.221-242, (1991).

[RSA78] R. L. Rivest, A. Shamir, and L. Adleman, "A method for obtaining digital signatures and public key cryptosystems," *Comm. ACM*, **21**, pp.120-126 (1978).

[Sam97] Y. Sameshima, "A Key Escrow System of the RSA cryptosystem," Pre-Proceedings of 1997 Information Security Workshop, pp. 75-85 (1997).

[SRA79] A. Shamir, L. Rivest, and L. Adleman, "Mental Poker," MIT/LCS, TM-125 (1979).

[SY96] K.Sakurai, and Y.Yamane, "Blind decoding, blind undeniable signatures, and their applications to privacy protection," Proc. 1st Information Hiding Workshop, Cambridge, U.K. Springer LNCS 1174 (1996), pp.257-264.

Some Recent Research Aspects of Threshold Cryptography

Yvo Desmedt*

Department of Electrical Engineering and Computer Science, and
the Center of Cryptography, Computer and Network Security
University of Wisconsin–Milwaukee
PO Box 784, Milwaukee, WI 53201, U.S.A.
e-mail: desmedt@cs.uwm.edu

Department of Mathematics
Royal Holloway
University of London
U.K.

Abstract. In the traditional scenario in cryptography there is one sender, one receiver and an active or passive eavesdropper who is an opponent. Depending from the application the sender or the receiver (or both) need to use a secret key. Often we are not dealing with an individual sender/receiver, but the sender/receiver is an organization. The goal of threshold cryptography is to present practical schemes to solve such problems without the need to use the more general methods of mental games.

In this paper we survey some recent research results on this topic. In particular on: DSS based threshold signatures, robust threshold cryptography, threshold cryptography without a trusted dealer, more optimal secret sharing schemes for threshold cryptography, proactive threshold cryptography and its generalizations.

1 Introduction

Public key [31] allows any sender to send private data to a known receiver (or to a receiver whose public key is authentic [58]). A public key system can also be used to digitally sign documents. Any receiver who knows the authentic public key of the sender can check whether data originated from the sender, or that it was created or modified by an outsider. Conventional cryptography achieves similar properties in a weaker sense [55, 64].

Traditionally, cryptography considers the case where there is one sender and one receiver. However, a lot of communication is between an individual and an organization, *e.g.*, a company, a governmental agency, a non-profit organization,

* A part of this work has been supported by NSF Grant NCR-9508528, the E.P.S.R.C. and by CNR AI n.94.00011.

etc. Examples are utility bills, tax forms, newsletters from professional organizations, etc. Organizations need also to communicate to each other. Moreover, many, and certainly security related, actions are taken by a group of people instead of by an individual. Indeed, the authority to sign a document is often *not* in the hands of a single person. In a bank wholesale transactions need to be signed by two co-signers. In the parliament (house) it is not the speaker who votes on a proposal for a new law, but a majority and this is also true in other democratic institutes (*e.g.*, a board of directors).

So there is a need for guaranteeing the authenticity of messages sent by a group of individuals to another group (or person) and this without enormous expansion of keys and/or messages. One often knows an organization (and its public key), but not necessarily who works in this organization or even less who has the power to sign in the name of the organization. So, to avoid a key management problem and to allow distribution of power an organization should have mainly one public key, instead of relying on the many public keys of the individuals inside that organization, who are unknown to the outside world. If the organization has one public key, the power to sign (or to decrypt, or to use a cryptosystem) should then be shared, to avoid abuse and to guarantee reliability. In our mechanical society such properties are often achieved. The goal of threshold cryptography is to make this possible in an electronic society. It combines threshold schemes [7, 62] (or secret sharing schemes [46]) with cryptography.

In this paper, we first discuss some of the first attempts to address the aforementioned issues, see Section 2. We then give a brief survey of some basic schemes that achieve this goal, see Section 3. Recent research results are briefly surveyed in Section 4. Finally in Section 5 we give some further details.

2 Early attempts

Shamir [62] was the first to discuss that a company's secret key, used to digitally sign documents, should not be given to a single entity. He noted that:

> Consider, for example, a company that digitally signs all checks (see RSA
> ...). If each executive is given a copy of the company's secret signature
> key, the system is convenient but easy to misuse. If the cooperation of
> all the company's executives is necessary in order to sign each check,
> the system is safe but inconvenient. The standard solution requires at
> least three signatures per check, and it is easy to implement with a $(3,n)$
> threshold scheme. Each executive is given a small magnetic card with
> one D_i piece, and the company's signature generating device accepts
> any three of them in order to generate (and later destroy) a temporary
> copy of the actual signature key D. The device does not contain any
> secret information and thus need not be protected against inspection.
> An unfaithful executive must have at least two accomplices in order to
> forge the company's signature in this scheme.

The solution suffers from many problems, the company's signature generating device can:

- leak the master key,
- modify the message being signed (indeed the co-signers have no control over the message that is allegedly being signed), and
- sign extra messages.

So full trust is necessary in the manufacturer of the device and the one who operates it. So this solution is not very secure.

The fact that sometimes a ciphertext needs to be decrypted jointly by a group of users, instead of by a single user, was addressed in [17] and later in [26]. The first solution presented is not very secure and the second one is far from practical since it relies on mental games (general secure distributed computation) mechanisms [43, 4, 13].

3 Basic schemes

In this section, for simplicity, we mainly follow the description used in [19], and discuss a generalization of it in Section 4.4.

A cryptosystem corresponds to evaluate a function with two inputs. One of them is the key, and the other one varies from application to application, examples being: the plaintext, the ciphertext, the text to sign, a seed, etc. Often this function is written as having one input with a key as parameter, $e.g.$, $f_{\text{key}}(\text{input})$. In our context it is useful to view that input as a parameter, so that we have

$$f_{\text{key}}(\text{input}) = g_{\text{input}}(\text{key}), \tag{1}$$

where f and g are functions.

Some important cryptographic schemes have the property that a function g, playing a major component, is homomorphic [47], $i.e.$,

$$g_b(k_1 + k_2) = g_b(k_1) * g_b(k_2), \tag{2}$$

where b is the aforementioned input, and k_1, k_2 belong to the key space. As a first example consider the ElGamal encryption scheme [32]. First the public key is (g, y, p) where g has a large enough order, p is a large enough prime, $y = g^a \bmod p$, and a is the secret key. The ciphertext is $(c_1, c_2) = (g^k \bmod p, M \cdot y^k \bmod p)$, where $M \in Z_p$ is the message. Now, a major component is the computation of $g_{c_1}(a) = c_1^a \bmod p$, since, given c_2, it allows the computation of the plaintext M [21]. As a second example we consider RSA signature generation and decryption. When signing or decrypting one computes $g_b(d) = b^d \bmod n$, where b is the (hashed and processed) text to sign or respectively the ciphertext, d is the secret key and n is the public modulus, $i.e.$, the product of two primes.

Now Shamir's secret sharing scheme [62] satisfies the property that:

$$\text{key} = \sum_{i \in B} (\text{constant}_{i,B}) \cdot (\text{share}_i), \tag{3}$$

where B is a subset of the set of all participants, called A, and $|B| = t$, the threshold. So, if Shamir's secret sharing scheme is used and g is homomorphic we obtain, using (3) and (2) that

$$g_{\text{input}}(\text{key}) = g_{\text{input}} \left(\sum_{i \in B} (\text{constant}_{i,B}) \cdot (\text{share}_i) \right) \tag{4}$$

$$= \prod_{i \in B} g_{\text{input}} (\text{constant}_{i,B} \cdot \text{share}_i)$$

$$= \prod_{i \in B} (g_{\text{input}}(\text{share}_i))^{\text{constant}_{i,B}} . \tag{5}$$

So, in (5) $g_{\text{input}}(\text{share}_i)$ can be evaluated by the shareholder and sent together with his identity (*i.e.*, i) to a reliable combiner. If enough shareholders responded, the combiner, knowing the identities, can compute a set B' which cardinality must be at least as large as the threshold t, *i.e.*, $|B'| \geq t$. The combiner chooses a $B \subseteq B'$ such that $|B| = t$, computes $\text{constant}_{i,B}$ for all $i \in B$ and then evaluates (5).

Originally $g_{\text{input}}(\text{share}_i)$ was called the partial result, but now one also refers to it as partial signature, partial decryption, etc., depending from the context.

Let us now discuss the security aspects. The combiner needs to be reliable, otherwise a fault tolerant implementation is required. If the final result of the computation will be public (*e.g.*, when signing), the combiner is allowed to reveal all the information he receives, otherwise (*e.g.*, when decrypting ciphertext) he cannot. The security goal is that the resulting scheme is as secure as the original one. It should be observed that a cryptanalyst may now receive as extra information:

- up to $t - 1$ shares, given by up to $t - 1$ corrupted shareholders,
- up to $l = |A|$ partial results, and this for each $g_{\text{input}_j}(\text{key})$ that was revealed to the cryptanalyst.

So the task of the cryptanalyst should be as hard regardless whether he received this extra information or not. This is usually achieved by requiring that any $t-1$ shares can be simulated (zero-knowledge [44]) and that the partial results can be simulated when $g_{\text{input}_j}(\text{key})$ is given (minimal-knowledge [39]).

It should be noted that Shamir's original secret sharing scheme only works over a finite field. However, the secret key in RSA belongs to $Z_{\phi(n)}(+)$, which is not a finite field. The additive property of (3) is desirable since it allows one to obtain threshold cryptography as we explained in Equations (4)–(5). An extension of Shamir's secret sharing, presented in [25] works over any Abelian group (by viewing the secret as belonging to an "extended" key space). The equality:

$$g_{\text{input}} (\text{constant}_{i,B} \cdot \text{share}_i) = (g_{\text{input}}(\text{share}_i))^{\text{constant}_{i,B}}$$

should then be viewed as the multiplicative notation of a scalar operation in a module [47] and not as an exponentiation. Other secret sharing schemes have been presented to satisfy (3), as will be surveyed in Section 4.3 and discussed in more details in Section 5.2. Finally, $\phi(n)$ must remain secret, which implies that the shareholders should not know $Z_{\phi(n)}$. The reader interested in detailed descriptions of how these technical issues in these basic schemes have been solved can consult [10, 9, 33, 29, 22, 34, 19].

4   Recent research: a brief survey

For several cryptoschemes and applications one has developed threshold crypto variants, such as threshold zero-knowledge proofs, threshold pseudorandom generators, etc. The concept of threshold cryptography has also been extended to general access structures [46], so that the subsets of A (the set of the participants) authorized to jointly use the cryptoscheme are not necessarily specified by a threshold. Note that the security of these schemes varies. One has unconditionally secure schemes, proven secure (under a computational complexity assumption) ones, some are (proven) as secure as the original cryptoscheme, and finally some threshold cryptoschemes have heuristic security. We refer the reader to [24] for a survey of research done by 1994 on these topics. While that survey was very general, we restrict ourselves to discuss only a few topics and discuss threshold cryptography in a more narrow context. So, for example, we will not discuss group signatures [14]. We refer the reader interested in that topic to [12].

Recent research has mainly focused on:

1. **reliability**. Threshold cryptoschemes that are reliable are called *robust* and we briefly discuss those in Sections 4.1 and 5.3.
2. **security enhancements**, such as:
   (a) **no trusted dealer** (see Sections 4.2 and 5.4).
   (b) **proactive security and its generalization** (see Sections 4.2 and Section 5.5).
   (c) **insiders' anonymity** (see Section 4.2).
3. **efficiency**, as discussed in Sections 4.3 and 5.2.
4. **generalizations**, such as
   (a) **threshold DSS** (see Sections 4.4).
   (b) **abstraction**, (see Section 4.4).

We now briefly survey these issues.

4.1   Reliability

To analyze the reliability aspect, let us focus on (5). It is clear that if one (or more) shareholder sends one wrong partial result, $g_{\text{input}}(\text{share}_i)$ the result will (likely) be wrong. If a public key system is used, one can using the public key verify that the result is wrong. When the numbers of wrong partial results is small, and a public key system is used, an exhaustive search will evidently find out who sent the wrong partial result [61]. One can then recompute the result

g_{input}(key) ignoring the wrong partial results, provided one has at least $t + e$ partial results, where e is the number of wrong ones.

Recent research has focused on the computation of g_{input}(key) without an exhaustive search [28, 42, 37, 41].

4.2 Security enhancements

Several security enhancements have been proposed, which we now briefly discuss.

No trusted dealer One can wonder who computes the share of a participant. In the first schemes a single trusted dealer was often used. It is clear that such an approach can best be avoided, however this is not always that easy. We refer the reader to [57, 42, 8, 16] and to Section 5.4 for some details.

Proactive security and its generalizations One can wonder what should happen when a share is stolen or lost. Worse, what happens when an outsider collects more shares than the threshold? As already observed in [26], it is a bad idea to change the public key of a group, in particular when this group is well known. Those who have not updated their public key database will use the old one. Also the new public key must be certified enough times independently before it can be trusted.

The solution that has been proposed to address this problem is to get new *guaranteed correct* shares without relying on a trusted dealer and to keep the old public key as long as is reasonable possible. The old shares should be destroyed and the update should be done frequently enough, taken the power of the enemy who may collect shares into account.

The following is a more general problem. How given shares for authorized subsets of the participants in A, specified by an access structure Γ_A, can one, without a dealer, distribute new shares for an access structure $\Gamma'_{A'}$, where A' is the new set of participants. If $\Gamma_A \not\subseteq \Gamma'_{A'}$ it is clear that some shareholders must destroy their shares.

The concept of proactive secret sharing is based on [56] and its combination with threshold cryptography has been studied in [45, 36, 59]. The generalization has been studied independently in [23] and [35]. Prior work on redistributing secret shares was done outside the scope of threshold cryptography, as can be found in [15, 2].

Insiders' anonymity An outsider, not receiving the help of insiders nor of the combiner, sees only g_{input}(key), and therefore is unable to find out who was active in the computation as observed in [19]. However, insiders and the combiner may (*e.g.*, in threshold signatures) see g_{input}(share$_i$) and i. Therefore they may find out who the active insiders are. In voting, for example, this is not desired and one needs to guarantee the anonymity of the insiders. A first solution has been proposed in [40]. Note that the opposite problem, the one of tracing who was involved, was already studied in [52] and that this problem can usually be solved in robust threshold cryptosystems.

4.3 Efficiency

For several unconditionally secure threshold authentication schemes, *e.g.*, [30] and for ElGamal based threshold decryption [21] each share is as long as the key. However, when one uses the extended Shamir's secret sharing scheme [25] for threshold RSA one has:

$$l * \text{length(key)} \leq \text{length(share}_i) < 2 * l * \text{length(key)},$$

where l is the number of shareholders. (Note that when $t = l$ one has that length(share$_i$) = length(key) [10, 33]). Secret sharing schemes have been developed that allow more efficient threshold RSA schemes. Two approaches have been followed: the one is guaranteed to work, while the other one is likely to work. In the last approach it is possible that although a certain set of participants has a cardinality larger or equal to t, they will not be able to perform the threshold computation in (5). We refer the reader to [20, 1, 6, 49].

4.4 Generalizations

g is not homomorphic What if the function g is not homomorphic? This problem in its generality corresponds with the mental games problem [43, 4, 13]. In its generality no practical solution has been proposed to address this problem. For some algorithms, such as DSS, a practical approach may be desirable. This was studied in [50, 42]. It should be noted that, even for the non-robust schemes, there is a significant difference between those solutions and the RSA solution. In threshold RSA, if one trusts t shareholders (or more), but not $t - 1$ (or less), t (non-faulty) shareholders are sufficient to jointly compute the result. However, in the threshold DSS schemes more than t are required to co-sign. In fact, in the Gennaro-Jarecki-Krawczyk-Rabin scheme at least $2t - 1$ participants are required, which implies that if l is even and t corresponds to majority, (*i.e.*, $\lfloor l/2 \rfloor + 1$) no practical threshold DSS signature scheme has been presented so far.

Abstraction One can wonder whether there is a need that g is a homomorphism. More general approaches have been discussed in [3]. We briefly focus on one of those (see also [11]).

Suppose that shareholders of a key want to compute $g_{\text{input}}(\text{key})$ in a practical distributed way. This is, for example, possible if there exist a recomputation function η' and functions g' such that

$$g_{\text{input}}(\text{key}) = \eta' \left(g'_{\text{input}}(\text{share}_{i_1}), \ldots, g'_{\text{input}}(\text{share}_{i_t}) \right).$$

5 Some details

It is clear that seeing the large number of papers that have appeared on threshold cryptography, that a book is needed to profoundly cover the aforementioned subtopics. To avoid giving no details whatsoever, a few topics will be chosen and discussed in some depth. We do no longer order the subtopics as we did in Section 4.

We first remind the reader when a secret sharing scheme is called homomorphic [5].

5.1 Homomorphic secret sharing

Let $(s_1, s_2, \ldots, s_l)$ be a share assignment of the key k and similarly $(s'_1, s'_2, \ldots, s'_l)$ be the shares of the key k'. Assume operations, denoted using "+", are defined on the share spaces and the key space. A secret sharing scheme is called homomorphic [5] if $((s_1 + s'_1), (s_2 + s'_2), \ldots, (s_l + s'_l))$ is a possible share assignment of the key $k + k'$. Shamir secret sharing scheme is homomorphic. In fact any secret sharing scheme satisfying (3) in which the shares belong to a module [47] (an Abelian group with scalars belonging to a ring), the constant$_{i,B}$ are scalars, and the keys belong to a submodule, is homomorphic, as is easy to verify.

5.2 More efficient schemes

As we surveyed in Section 4.3, the problem of making more efficient secret sharing schemes useful for threshold cryptography is in particular important for threshold RSA.

We only discuss here a variant for $t = 2$ of a scheme given in [20] and then generalize it using Kurosawa-Stinson interpretation of the scheme given in [6]. We use the occasion to explain how to use these schemes for threshold RSA.

We first explain the case $t = 2$.

An example Let l be the number of participants. Let $K(+)$ be a group and $k \in K$ be the secret. We number the participants i from 0 till $l - 1$ and represent i in binary representation, i.e., i corresponds to the bits $(i_1, \ldots, i_{\lceil \log_2(l) \rceil})$.

When creating shares, the dealer will choose $\lceil \log_2(l) \rceil$ independent uniformly random elements $r_c \in K$ ($1 \le c \le \lceil \log_2(l) \rceil$). Through a secure channel participant i receives as sub-share $s_{i,c} = r_c$ when $i_c = 0$ and otherwise $s_{i,c} = k - r_c$. So, a participant i receives $\lceil \log_2(l) \rceil$ sub-shares.

We now discuss how i and j can reconstruct the key. If $i \ne j$ then in their binary representation there will be at least one column c in which they differ, i.e., $i_c \ne j_c$. Assume that $i_c = 0$, then $k = s_{j,c} + s_{i,c}$. If the group $K(+)$ is Abelian, then the scheme is homomorphic and the reconstruction works regardless whether $i_c = 0$ or not.

Now we explain how to use this scheme for threshold RSA [20]. Assume, as in [19], that n is the product of primes of equal length[2]. The distributor chooses the shares as we explained using $K = Z_{\phi(n)}(+)$ and $k = d$. When co-signing, assume that m is the hashed and processed message. Each participant i sends the number i and the sub-partial signatures $\sigma_{i,c} = m^{s_{i,c}} \bmod n$ for all c. Assume that this was done by participants, let say i and j. Giving correct shares, knowing i and j, one can find a column c where $i_c \neq j_c$ and compute the signature since $\sigma_{i,c} * \sigma_{j,c} = m^{s_{i,c}+s_{j,c}} = m^d$. If participants i and j know in advance that they will be co-signing, then they only need to send one $\sigma_{i,c}$ instead of $\lceil \log_2(l) \rceil$ many.

Note that the shares in [20] are as long as in the variant we discussed here, but that more randomness is required.

A generalization The 2-out-of-l previous scheme is based on $\lceil \log_2(l) \rceil$ independent 2-out-of-2 sharing schemes. The scheme in [6] satisfies a similar property. This scheme inspired Kurosawa and Stinson and they gave a generalization we now discuss [49].

Let A and A' be finite sets, B a subset of A, $l = |A|$ and $l' = |A'|$ and F be a set of functions from A to A'. We assume that $l' < l$. A function f from A to A' is a perfect hash for B if f restricted to B is one-to-one. F is a Perfect Hash Family (l, l', t) if for all subsets $B \subset A$ with cardinality t there is at least one function f in F such that f is a perfect hash for B. Note that the binary representation defines such a Perfect Hash Family from the set A to $A' = \{0, 1\}$.

A Perfect Hash Family can now be used to construct new secret sharing schemes from old ones. Suppose that one is given a t-out-of-l' sharing scheme and F, a Perfect Hash Family (l, l', t). One can then construct a t-out-of-l secret sharing scheme. Let us first discuss how to distribute shares. For each $f \in F$, the dealer uses the share generation algorithm of the t-out-of-l sharing scheme producing l shares $s_{a'}$ for all $a' \in A'$. If $f(i) = f(j) = a'$ participant i and j receive as subshare $s_{a'}$. The randomness used when distributing shares corresponding to f is independent of the randomness utilized for the f' iteration. The total number of subshares is $|F|$ and the length of the share of a participant is the sum of the length of his subshares.

When t shareholders, let us say in $B \subset A$, want to reconstruct the secret, they find which $f \in F$ is a perfect hash for B and they use subshares corresponding with that f. The reconstruction algorithm of the t-out-of-l' is then used.

If the original t-out-of-l' sharing scheme can be used for threshold RSA, then so can the t-out-of-l one.

5.3 Robustness

A simple example as an introduction We start by discussing an unconditionally secure threshold cryptosystem. In 1974 Gilbert, MacWilliams and

---

[2] Otherwise, work modulo $\phi(n)\lfloor n^2/\phi(n) \rfloor$ instead of modulo $\phi(n)$, similar as in [34].

Sloane proposed the following authentication scheme. The sender and receiver have a common $a, b \in_R GF(q)$, which describes a secret line in the vectorspace $GF(q) \times GF(q)$ of points with coordinates (x, y) satisfying the equation $y = a \cdot x + b$. (The original description of this scheme was over a projective space instead of over a vector space.) To authenticate a message $m \in GF(q)$ the sender sends the point (m, MAC) on the line, *i.e.* the Message Authentication Code is $\text{MAC} = a \cdot m + b$. The receiver accepts the received message m' as authentic if (m', MAC') is on the secret line. If the secret is used only once the probability of a successful impersonation or substitution attack if $1/q$.

If q is a prime, then any homomorphic secret sharing scheme might be used to transform this scheme into a threshold authentication one. Indeed, let s_i be a share of a and s_i' be a share of b, then $\text{MAC}_i = m \cdot s_i + s_i'$ is a share of the MAC, called a partial MAC [22, 30, 27]. If Shamir's secret sharing scheme is used, as in [30], this scheme is not robust.

Using the connection between threshold schemes and error-correcting codes [18, 54, 48] this scheme can easily be made robust. Indeed, let the shares of a, *i.e.*, $(s_1, s_2, \ldots, s_l)$, and the shares of b, *i.e.*, $(s_1', s_2', \ldots, s_l')$, be chosen as codewords in an appropriate linear code over $GF(q)$. If this is a good error-correcting code, then one can correct errors provided sufficiently many participants compute their partial MAC, *i.e.*, MAC_i. For security purposes it is necessary that the scheme is perfect and composite [5]. Perfectness means that $t - 1$ shares do not reveal anything about the key and compositeness that the revelation of *all* the shares of $k_1 + k_2$, where $k_1 + k_2 \in GF(q)$, does not reveal anything more about (k_1, k_2) than what $k_1 + k_2$ does. Reed-Solomon error-correcting codes [60] codes satisfy these properties when used as in [54].

Making threshold RSA robust From [54] it is rather obvious that the generalization of Shamir secret sharing scheme implies a generalization of Reed-Solomon codes. It therefore seems that RSA could be made robust using this generalized Reed-Solomon code. However, when the number of errors is rather large, no algorithm is known to locate the errors in this generalized Reed-Solomon code. Note that it is easy to prove that if one could efficiently generalize the Berlekamp-Massey algorithm [53] to work for this generalized Reed-Solomon code, that the discrete log problem and factoring problem would both be easy [28]. Whether there exists a polynomial-time algorithm to detect the error locations is still an open problem. However, the problem need not to be addressed to obtain robust threshold RSA.

The common method used to achieve robust RSA is to send more data and to rely on the fact that RSA is a public key algorithm. If each of t participants proves that he has sent the correct partial result, then one can ignore all other partial results. This implies that one only needs $t + e$ partial results, where e is the number of incorrect partial results. Note that in the McEliece-Sarwate's use of Reed-Solomon codes one needs $t + 2e$ shares to recompute the key. Several methods have been developed (see Section 4.1) and we only discuss one of those.

Gennaro-Jarecki-Krawczyk-Rabin [41] developed two methods to achieve robust threshold RSA. One is interactive and the other one is non-interactive. We discuss the non-interactive one which is based on the Gilbert-MacWilliams-Sloane authentication scheme.

The scheme assumes that $n = pq$ is the product of safe primes (a prime p is safe if $p = 2p' + 1$ where p' is a prime). To detect an error the combiner will receive extra information $a_{i,j}$ and $b_{i,j}$, where i indicates the participant and j the subshare (see Section 5.2). In fact, for each subshare $s_{i,j}$ the dealer chooses uniformly random an $a_{i,j}$, such that $1 \leq a_{i,j} \leq n^{\delta_1}$ and an $b_{i,j}$ such that $1 \leq b_{i,j} \leq n^{1+\delta_1+\delta_2}$, where δ_1 and δ_2 are appropriately chosen [41]. The dealer gives participant i privately, the subshare $s_{i,j}$ and the integer $y_{i,j}$, where $y_{i,j} = a_{i,j} \cdot s_{i,j} + b_{i,j}$, for all j. The dealer also gives the combiner privately the integers $a_{i,j}$ and $b_{i,j}$ for all i and j. We trust that the combiner will keep these values secret and that the combiner will perform the verifications we now describe. Otherwise more combiners might be used as described in [41].

When co-signing participant i computes the sub-partial signatures $\sigma_{i,j}$ of m and sub-mac $Y_{i,j} = m^{y_{i,j}} \bmod n$ for each j and send those to the combiner. We now explain how the combiner can locate the correct partial signatures. To verify whether it is correct the combiner verifies if

$$(\sigma_{i,j})^{a_{i,j}} \cdot m^{b_{i,j}} = Y_{i,j} \bmod n,$$

for all received $\sigma_{i,j}$. The combiner now uses these partial signatures for which the verification was successful. Note that it is still possible that the correct sub-partial signature is $-\sigma_{i,j}$. For all existing threshold RSA schemes this implies that the actual signature may have to be multiplied by -1. Knowing e the combiner can easily check whether this is necessary.

5.4 Avoiding a trusted dealer

If the secret key can be chosen randomly, as is usually the case in a discrete log setting, then the following use of homomorphic secret sharing can be utilized towards abolishing the need for a trusted dealer.

The first participant chooses a uniformly random key k_1 and plays distributor of this key generating shares $(s_{1,1}, s_{1,2}, \ldots, s_{1,l})$. The first participant sends, using a secure channel, the shares $s_{1,i}$ to participant i and $1 \leq i \leq l$. Now, t participants, let say those in $B \subset A$, will perform similar operations (choosing the randomness independently) and create shares $s_{j,i}$ instead of $s_{1,i}$ and send those privately to participant i. A participant i can then compute the share $s_i = \sum_{j \in B} s_{j,i}$. Since the sharing scheme is homomorphic, s_i is a share of the key $k = \sum_{j \in B} k_j$. If the keys k_j belong to an Abelian group (see also [38]) and the secret sharing scheme is perfect, then $t - 1$ shareholders have no information about the secret key k.

The first use of this idea in the context of threshold cryptography was in [57]. Pedersen's scheme also guarantees that the distribution is verifiable, i.e., that the shares the shareholders received will always recompute the same secret key. Pedersen's scheme also guarantees that this secret key corresponds to the public key that is made public.

Note that the problem of avoiding a trusted dealer is much more complex in the context of RSA [8].

5.5 Proactive

We briefly explain how the use of homomorphic secret sharing is useful towards achieving proactive threshold cryptography. We assume that the secret sharing scheme is homomorphic.

If $(s_1, s_2, \ldots, s_l)$ is a share assignment for the key k and $(s'_1, s'_2, \ldots, s'_l)$ is a uniformly random share assignment for the "key" 0, then $(s''_1, s''_2, \ldots, s''_l) = (s_1 + s'_1, s_2 + s'_2, \ldots, s_l + s'_l)$ is a new share assignment for the same key k. Assume that one trusts t shareholders. Then t participants, denoted by j, can each contribute their own random $(s'_{j,1}, s'_{j,2}, \ldots, s'_{j,l})$. This is done in a similar way as in Section 5.4, however the shares correspond with the "keys" 0. When working in an Abelian group (see also [38]) and when the secret sharing scheme is perfect, the resulting share $s''_i = s_i + \sum_{j \in B} s'_{j,i}$ will be guaranteed independent of the original share s_i, due to the properties of the one-time-pad [63]. Both s_i and s''_i are shares of the same key k.

One should note that the schemes are more complex since each contributing shareholder needs to prove that his contribution $(s'_1, s'_2, \ldots, s'_l)$ consists of shares of 0. Also, achieving proactive threshold RSA is more complex (see Section 4.2).

6 Final comments

As mentioned, we did not discuss all aspects of threshold cryptography in this survey. For example, some threshold cryptoschemes (not cited in this paper) have some security problems as was pointed out in [51].

Acknowledgment

The author thanks the many researchers with whom he had discussions on the topic.

References

1. N. Alon, Z. Galil, and M. Yung. Efficient dynamic-resharing "verifiable secret sharing" against mobile adversary. In P. G. Spirakis, editor, *Algorithms — ESA '95, Third Annual European Symposium, Proceedings (Lecture Notes in Computer Science 979)*, pp. 523–537. Springer-Verlag, 1995. Corfu, Greece, September 25–27.

2. F. Bao, R. Deng, Y. Han, and A. Jeng. Design and analysis of two basic protocols for use in ttp-based key escrow. In V. Varadharajan, J. Pieprzyk, and Y. Mu, editors, *Information Security and Privacy, Second Australian Conference, ACISP '97, (Lecture Notes in Computer Science 1270)*, pp. 261–270. Springer-Verlag, 1997. Sydney, NSW, Australia, July 7–9.

3. A. Beimel, M. Burmester, Y. Desmedt, and E. Kushilevitz. Computing functions of a shared secret. Manuscript, 1995.

4. M. Ben-Or, S. Goldwasser, J. Kilian, and A. Wigderson. Multi-prover interactive proofs: How to remove intractability assumptions. In *Proceedings of the twentieth annual ACM Symp. Theory of Computing, STOC*, pp. 113–131, May 2–4, 1988.

5. J. C. Benaloh. Secret sharing homomorphisms: Keeping shares of a secret secret. In A. Odlyzko, editor, *Advances in Cryptology, Proc. of Crypto '86 (Lecture Notes in Computer Science 263)*, pp. 251–260. Springer-Verlag, 1987. Santa Barbara, California, U.S.A., August 11–15.

6. S. R. Blackburn, M. Burmester, Y. Desmedt, and P. R. Wild. Efficient multiplicative sharing schemes. In U. Maurer, editor, *Advances in Cryptology — Eurocrypt '96, Proceedings (Lecture Notes in Computer Science 1070)*, pp. 107–118. Springer-Verlag, 1996. Zaragoza, Spain, May 12–16.

7. G. R. Blakley. Safeguarding cryptographic keys. In *Proc. Nat. Computer Conf. AFIPS Conf. Proc.*, pp. 313–317, 1979. vol.48.

8. D. Boneh and M. Franklin. Efficient generation of shared RSA keys. In B. S. Kaliski, editor, *Advances in Cryptology — Crypto '97, Proceedings (Lecture Notes in Computer Science 1294)*, pp. 425–439. Springer-Verlag, 1997. Santa Barbara, California, U.S.A., August 17–21.

9. C. Boyd. Some applications of multiple key ciphers. In C. G. Günther, editor, *Advances in Cryptology, Proc. of Eurocrypt '88 (Lecture Notes in Computer Science 330)*, pp. 455–467. Springer-Verlag, May 1988. Davos, Switzerland.

10. C. Boyd. Digital multisignatures. In H. Beker and F. Piper, editors, *Cryptography and coding*, pp. 241–246. Clarendon Press, 1989. Royal Agricultural College, Cirencester, December 15–17, 1986.

11. M. Burmester. Homomorphisms of secret sharing schemes. In U. Maurer, editor, *Advances in Cryptology — Eurocrypt '96, Proceedings (Lecture Notes in Computer Science 1070)*, pp. 96–106. Springer-Verlag, 1996. Zaragoza, Spain, May 12–16.

12. J. Camenish and M. Stadler. Efficient group signature schemes for large groups. In B. S. Kaliski, editor, *Advances in Cryptology — Crypto '97, Proceedings (Lecture Notes in Computer Science 1294)*, pp. 410–424. Springer-Verlag, 1997. Santa Barbara, California, U.S.A., August 17–21.

13. D. Chaum, C. Crépeau, and I. Damgård. Multiparty unconditionally secure protocols. In *Proceedings of the twentieth annual ACM Symp. Theory of Computing, STOC*, pp. 11–19, May 2–4, 1988.

14. D. Chaum and E. van Heyst. Group signatures. In D. W. Davies, editor, *Advances in Cryptology, Proc. of Eurocrypt '91 (Lecture Notes in Computer Science 547)*, pp. 257–265. Springer-Verlag, April 1991. Brighton, U.K.

15. L. Chen, D. Gollmann, and C. Mitchell. Key escrow in mutually mistrusting domains. In M. Lomas, editor, *Security Protocols (Lecture Notes in Computer Science 1189)*, pp. 139–153. Springer-Verlag, 1997. Cambridge, United Kingdom April 10–12, 1996.

16. C. Cocks. Split knowledge generation of RSA paremeters. Presented at the 6th IMA Conference on Coding and Cryptography, Cirencester, England, to appear in the proceedings, December 17–19, 1997.

17. R. A. Croft and S. P. Harris. Public-key cryptography and re-usable shared secrets. In H. Beker and F. Piper, editors, *Cryptography and coding*, pp. 189–201. Clarendon Press, 1989. Royal Agricultural College, Cirencester, December 15–17, 1986.

18. G. I. Davida, R. DeMillo, and R. Lipton. Protecting shared cryptographic keys. In *Proceedings of the 1980 Symposium on Security and Privacy*, pp. 100–102. IEEE Computer Society, April 1980. IEEE Catalog No. 80 CH1522-2.

19. A. De Santis, Y. Desmedt, Y. Frankel, and M. Yung. How to share a function securely. In *Proceedings of the twenty-sixth annual ACM Symp. Theory of Computing (STOC)*, pp. 522–533, May 23–25, 1994. Montréal, Québec, Canada.

20. Y. Desmedt, G. Di Crescenzo, and M. Burmester. Multiplicative non-abelian sharing schemes and their application to threshold cryptography. In J. Pieprzyk and R. Safavi-Naini, editors, *Advances in Cryptology — Asiacrypt '94, Proceedings (Lecture Notes in Computer Science 917)*, pp. 21–32. Springer-Verlag, 1995. Wollongong, Australia, November/December, 1994.

21. Y. Desmedt and Y. Frankel. Threshold cryptosystems. In G. Brassard, editor, *Advances in Cryptology — Crypto '89, Proceedings (Lecture Notes in Computer Science 435)*, pp. 307–315. Springer-Verlag, 1990. Santa Barbara, California, U.S.A., August 20–24.

22. Y. Desmedt and Y. Frankel. Shared generation of authenticators and signatures. In J. Feigenbaum, editor, *Advances in Cryptology — Crypto '91, Proceedings (Lecture Notes in Computer Science 576)*, pp. 457–469. Springer-Verlag, 1992. Santa Barbara, California, U.S.A., August 12–15.

23. Y. Desmedt and S. Jajodia. Redistributing secret shares to new access structures and its applications. Tech. Report ISSE-TR-97-01, George Mason University, July 1997. ftp://isse.gmu.edu/pub/techrep/97_01_jajodia.ps.gz.

24. Y. G. Desmedt. Threshold cryptography. *European Trans. on Telecommunications*, 5(4), pp. 449–457, July-August 1994. (Invited paper).

25. Y. G. Desmedt and Y. Frankel. Homomorphic zero-knowledge threshold schemes over any finite abelian group. *SIAM Journal on Discrete Mathematics*, 7(4), pp. 667–679, November 1994.

26. Y. Desmedt. Society and group oriented cryptography : a new concept. In C. Pomerance, editor, *Advances in Cryptology, Proc. of Crypto '87 (Lecture Notes in Computer Science 293)*, pp. 120–127. Springer-Verlag, 1988. Santa Barbara, California, U.S.A., August 16–20.

27. Y. Desmedt. Threshold cryptography. In W. Wolfowicz, editor, *Proceedings of the 3rd Symposium on: State and Progress of Research in Cryptography*, pp. 110–122, February 15–16, 1993. Rome, Italy, invited paper.

28. Y. Desmedt. Extending Reed-Solomon codes to modules. In *Proceedings 1995 IEEE International Symposium on Information Theory*, p. 498, Whistler, BC, Canada, September 17–22, 1995.

29. Y. Desmedt and Y. Frankel. Perfect zero-knowledge sharing schemes over any finite Abelian group. In R. Capocelli, A. De Santis, and U. Vaccaro, editors, *Sequences II (Methods in Communication, Security, and Computer Science)*, pp. 369–378. Springer-Verlag, 1993. Positano, Italy, June 17–21, 1991.

30. Y. Desmedt, Y. Frankel, and M. Yung. Multi-receiver / multi-sender network security: efficient authenticated multicast/ feedback. In *IEEE INFOCOM '92, Eleventh Annual Joint Conference of the IEEE Computer and Communications Societies*, pp. 2045–2054, Florence, Italy, May 4–8, 1992. .

31. W. Diffie and M. E. Hellman. New directions in cryptography. *IEEE Trans. Inform. Theory*, IT-22(6), pp. 644–654, November 1976.

32. T. ElGamal. A public key cryptosystem and a signature scheme based on discrete logarithms. *IEEE Trans. Inform. Theory*, 31, pp. 469–472, 1985.

33. Y. Frankel. A practical protocol for large group oriented networks. In J.-J. Quisquater and J. Vandewalle, editors, *Advances in Cryptology, Proc. of Eurocrypt '89 (Lecture Notes in Computer Science 434)*, pp. 56–61. Springer-Verlag, 1990. Houthalen, Belgium, April 10–13.

34. Y. Frankel and Y. Desmedt. Parallel reliable threshold multisignature. Tech. Report TR-92-04-02, Dept. of EE & CS, Univ. of Wisconsin–Milwaukee, April 1992. ftp://ftp.cs.uwm.edu/pub/tech_reports/desmedt-rsa-threshold_92.ps.

35. Y. Frankel, P. Gemmell, P. D. MacKenzie, and M. Yung. Optimal resilience proactive public key cryptosystems. In *38th Annual Symp. on Foundations of Computer Science (FOCS)*. IEEE Computer Society Press, October 20–22, 1997. Miami Beach, Florida, U.S.A.

36. Y. Frankel, P. Gemmell, P. D. MacKenzie, and M. Yung. Proactive RSA. In B. S. Kaliski, editor, *Advances in Cryptology — Crypto '97, Proceedings (Lecture Notes in Computer Science 1294)*, pp. 440–454. Springer-Verlag, 1997. Santa Barbara, California, U.S.A., August 17–21.

37. Y. Frankel, P. Gemmell, and M. Yung. Witness-based cryptographic program checking and robust function sharing. In *Proceedings of the Twenty-Eighth Annual ACM Symp. on Theory of Computing*, pp. 499–508, May, 22–24, 1996.

38. Y. Frankel, Y. Desmedt, and M. Burmester. Non-existence of homomorphic general sharing schemes for some key spaces. In E. F. Brickell, editor, *Advances in Cryptology — Crypto '92, Proceedings (Lecture Notes in Computer Science 740)*, pp. 549–557. Springer-Verlag, 1993. Santa Barbara, California, U.S.A., August 16–20.

39. Z. Galil, S. Haber, and M. Yung. Minimum-knowledge interactive proofs for decision problems. *SIAM J. Comput.*, 18(4), pp. 711–739, August 1989.

40. C. Gehrmann and Y. Desmedt. Truly anonymous secret sharing. Manuscript.

41. R. Gennaro, S. Jarecki, H. Krawczyk, and T. Rabin. Robust and efficient sharing of RSA functions. In N. Koblitz, editor, *Advances in Cryptology — Crypto '96, Proceedings (Lecture Notes in Computer Science 1109)*, pp. 157–172. Springer-Verlag, 1996. Santa Barbara, California, U.S.A., August 18–22.

42. R. Gennaro, S. Jarecki, H. Krawczyk, and T. Rabin. Robust threshold DSS signatures. In U. Maurer, editor, *Advances in Cryptology — Eurocrypt '96, Proceedings (Lecture Notes in Computer Science 1070)*, pp. 354–371. Springer-Verlag, 1996. Zaragoza, Spain, May 12–16.

43. O. Goldreich, S. Micali, and A. Wigderson. How to play any mental game. In *Proceedings of the Nineteenth annual ACM Symp. Theory of Computing, STOC*, pp. 218–229, May 25–27, 1987.

44. S. Goldwasser, S. Micali, and C. Rackoff. The knowledge complexity of interactive proof systems. *SIAM J. Comput.*, 18(1), pp. 186–208, February 1989.

45. A. Herzberg, S. Jarecki, H. Krawczyk, and M. Yung. Proactive secret sharing. In D. Coppersmith, editor, *Advances in Cryptology — Crypto '95, Proceedings (Lecture Notes in Computer Science 963)*, pp. 339–352. Springer-Verlag, 1995. Santa Barbara, California, U.S.A., August 27–31.

46. M. Ito, A. Saito, and T. Nishizeki. Secret sharing schemes realizing general access structures. In *Proc. IEEE Global Telecommunications Conf., Globecom'87*, pp. 99–102. IEEE Communications Soc. Press, 1987.

47. N. Jacobson. *Basic Algebra I.* W. H. Freeman and Company, New York, 1985.

48. E. D. Karnin, J. W. Greene, and M. Hellman. On secret sharing systems. *IEEE Tr. Inform. Theory*, 29(1), pp. 35–41, January 1983.

49. K. Kurosawa and D. Stinson, June 1996. Personal communication.

50. S. K. Langford. Threshold DSS signatures without a trusted party. In D. Coppersmith, editor, *Advances in Cryptology — Crypto '95, Proceedings (Lecture Notes in Computer Science 963)*, pp. 397–409. Springer-Verlag, 1995. Santa Barbara, California, U.S.A., August 27–31.

51. S. K. Langford. Weaknesses in some threshold cryptosystems. In N. Koblitz, editor, *Advances in Cryptology — Crypto '96, Proceedings (Lecture Notes in Computer Science 1109)*, pp. 74–82. Springer-Verlag, 1996. Santa Barbara, California, U.S.A., August 18–22.

52. C. Li, T. Hwang, and N. Lee. Threshold-multisignature schemes where suspected forgery implies traceability of adversarial shareholders. In A. De Santis, editor, *Advances in Cryptology — Eurocrypt '94, Proceedings (Lecture Notes in Computer Science 950)*, pp. 194–204. Springer-Verlag, May 9–12, 1995. Perugia, Italy, May 9–12.

53. F. J. MacWilliams and N. J. A. Sloane. *The theory of error-correcting codes.* North-Holland Publishing Company, 1978.

54. R. J. McEliece and D. V. Sarwate. On sharing secrets and Reed-Solomon codes. *Comm. ACM*, 24(9), pp. 583–584, September 1981.

55. A. Menezes, P. van Oorschot, and S. Vanstone. *Applied Cryptography.* CRC, Boca Raton, 1996.

56. R. Ostrovsky and M. Yung. How to withstand mobile virus attacks. In *Proceedings of the 10-th Annual ACM Symp. on Principles of Distributed Computing*, pp. 51–60, August 19–21, 1991. Montreal, Quebec, Canada.

57. T. P. Pedersen. A threshold cryptosystem without a trusted party. In D. W. Davies, editor, *Advances in Cryptology, Proc. of Eurocrypt '91 (Lecture Notes in Computer Science 547)*, pp. 522–526. Springer-Verlag, April 1991. Brighton, U.K.

58. G. J. Popek and C. S. Kline. Encryption and secure computer networks. *ACM Computing Surveys*, 11(4), pp. 335–356, December 1979.

59. T. Rabin. A simplified approach to threshold and proactive RSA. Manuscript.

60. I. S. Reed and G. Solomon. Polynomial codes over certain finite fields. *SIAM Journal on Applied Mathematics*, 8, pp. 300–304, 1960.

61. M. K. Reiter and K. P. Birman. How to securely replicate services. *ACM Transactions on programming languages and systems*, 16(3), pp. 986–1009, 1994.

62. A. Shamir. How to share a secret. *Commun. ACM*, 22, pp. 612–613, November 1979.

63. C. E. Shannon. Communication theory of secrecy systems. *Bell System Techn. Jour.*, 28, pp. 656–715, October 1949.

64. D. R. Stinson. *Cryptography: Theory and Practice.* CRC, Boca Raton, 1995.

A High-Speed Small RSA Encryption LSI
with Low Power Dissipation

A. Satoh[1], Y. Kobayashi[1], H. Niijima[1], N. Ooba[1], S. Munetoh[1], and S. Sone[2]

[1] IBM research, Tokyo Research Laboratory, IBM Japan Ltd., 1623-14,
Shimotsuruma, Yamato-shi, Kanagawa 242, Japan
{akashi, kobayasy, nijima, ooba, munetoh} @ trl.ibm.co.jp
[2] IBM Microelectronics Division, Yasu Plant, IBM Japan Ltd., 800, Ichimiyake,
Yasu-cho, Yasu-gun, Shiga 520-23, Japan
ssone@jp.ibm.com

Abstract. A 1024-bit RSA encryption LSI with DES and MD5 functions was developed. An RSA accelerator core implemented in the LSI is 4.9 mm^2 in area, and has three 1024-bit adders that perform doubling, squaring, and exponential operations simultaneously. A 1024-bit RSA operation takes 23 msec with 100-mA peak current at the maximum frequency of 45 MHz. A 1024-bit RSA key is generated in 0.3 sec by using arithmetic functions supported by the LSI. The throughputs of DES and MD5 at 45 MHz are 18.9 MB/sec and 29.7 MB/sec, respectively.

1 Introduction

With the constant expansion of network systems, electronic commerce applications such as online shopping and banking are rapidly gaining popularity. RSA public-key method [1] is an indispensable encryption algorithm for authenticating the identity of the person at the other end of a communication line and for exchanging secret data safely, and is also the de facto standard. Encryption using 512-bit RSA used to be considered safe enough, but improvements in computer power and cryptanalysis techniques made it vulnerable and 1024-bit RSA is now strongly recommended for high-security systems. In electronic commerce systems, high-speed RSA hardware accelerators are essential to smartcards, and especially to authentication servers, which have vast numbers of accesses.

The bottleneck of the RSA operation is its modular exponentiation for very long numbers. Many techniques [2]-[6], such as the Montgomery's method, are used in RSA accelerators to simplify modulo reduction. In any techniques, addition and subtraction are the basic operations, and the performance of the long adder is the key to the overall chip performance. Many mechanisms for improving the adder performance have been proposed. However, carry-detection circuits [4],[7]-[8] requiring asynchronous control may involve a timing problem, and carry-save adders [9] and redundant binary adders [10] need extra cycles for conversion between binary and redundant forms.

To minimize the number of operation cycles, the LSI described in this paper uses a straightforward algorithm for modular exponentiation, which is executed by performing a sequence of 1M additions, and background adjustment. Each addition cycle is then speeded up by a new carry-skip adder in which a carry fully propagates. This approach realizes a fast, small, low-power implementation of an RSA encryption accelerator.

2 Chip Features

The 1024-bit RSA encryption LSI was fabricated by using three-metal-layer 0.5-μm CMOS technology. The 5.31 × 5.31 mm^2 chip is mounted on a 0.65 mm-pitch 160-pin package. Several 1024-bit arithmetic functions, DES [11][12], MD5 [13], a random-number seed generator, and a low-frequency generator are also implemented in the chip, as shown in Table I. There are two sets of I/O and clock pins: one for the RSA block and the other for the rest of the functions. The I/Os of these two blocks are isolated. The RSA block accepts key lengths from 8 to 1024 bits with 8-bit granularity, and the operation time is 23 msec for 1024-bit RSA and 6 msec for 512-bit RSA without using

Table 1. Chip Features.

Process Technology	3.3 V, 3 metals 0.5-μm CMOS
Package	0.65-mm pitch 160-pin
Die Size	5.31 × 5.31 mm^2
RSA Circuit Size	4.9 mm^2 (accelerator) 1.1 mm^2 (controller)
Maximum Frequency	45 MHz
RSA Operation Time (1024 bits)	23 msec @ 45 MHz 210 msec @ 5 MHz
Max. Power Dissipation (1024 bits)	330 mW @ 45 MHz 50 mW @ 5 MHz
Peak Current (1024 bits)	100 mA @ 45 MHz 15 mA @ 5MHz
Key Length	8-1024 bits
Arithmetic Functions	A mod N, A+B mod N A × B mod N , A^B mod N
DES	18.9 MB/sec @ 45 MHz ECB, CBC, CFB, OFB
MD5	29.7 MB/sec @ 45 MHz
Others	Random-number seed generator Low-frequency oscillator

the Chinese Remainder Theorem (CRT). The LSI supports burst transfer modes with 8-bit and 16-bit data width, and the throughputs of DES and MD5 are 18.9 MB/sec and 29.7 MB/sec, respectively, in 45-MHz operation

Fig. 1 shows a microphotograph of the chip, which consists of custom macros (an RSA accelerator, adders for MD5, a 1024-bit register, and oscillators) and a gate array. A 1024-bit register with an area of 1.27 mm^2 is used as a data I/O buffer in DES and MD5 operation. The chip was mounted on an experimental ISA card, shown in Fig. 2, and its power dissipation was measured. Fig. 3 shows the maximum power consumed in consecutive 1024-bit RSA operation as a function of the clock frequency. Low power dissipation levels of 330 mW at 45 MHz operation and 50 mW at 5 MHz were measured at room temperature, with a 3.3-V power supply.

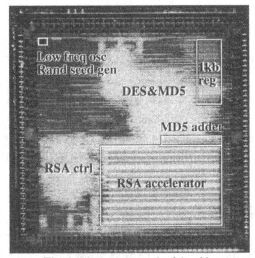

Fig. 1. Microphotograph of the chip.

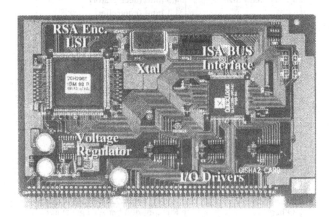

Fig. 2. Experimental ISA card.

Fig.4 shows a comparison of 1024-bit RSA operation times without CRT; the data were collected from Web sites [14]-[19] and tables in [6]. The items at the top three are discrete RSA chips, while the others are smartcard chips whose maximum frequency is 5 MHz. The IBM chip is the fastest at 45-MHz operation, and is 1.7 times faster than the PCC200. The power dissipation of both the PCC200 and the NL0048 at maximum frequency is 1 W, which is 3 times higher than that of the IBM chip. At 25-MHz operation, the IBM chip requires only 190 mW, which is 1/5 of the power used by the PCC200.

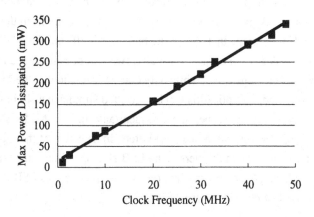

Fig. 3. Power dissipation vs. clock frequency for consecutive 1024-bit RSA.

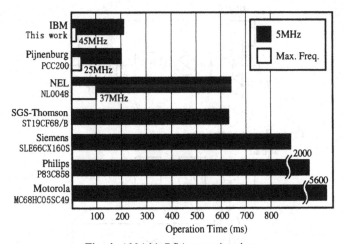

Fig. 4. 1024-bit RSA operation time.

3 Modular Exponentiation

A plain text M is encrypted as a cipher text C according to the modular exponentiation shown below by using a public key e in the RSA encryption.

$$C \equiv M^e \pmod{n}$$

This operation is performed by repeating a sequence of squaring and modular multiplication steps. There are two ways to compute C: one is to search for '1' bits in e from the MSB side, and the other is to search for such bits from the LSB side. Fig. 5 (a) shows a modular exponentiation circuit in which '1' bits are searched for form the MSB side, and Fig. 5 (b) shows a circuit in which they are searched for from the LSB side. In Fig. 5 (a), M is set to a register as an initial value, and squaring and modular multiplication are then performed alternately by a multiplier, although modular multiplication can be skipped when $e_i = 0$, where e_i is the i-th bit from the LSB-side of the exponent e. If we assume that half of the bits in e are '0' and the other half are '1', an m-bit operation takes $1.5m$ cycles. Basically, two sets of multiplier and register are required in the LSB-side operation, while only one set is required in the MSB-side one. However, squaring and multiplication can be executed simultaneously in the LSB-side operation, whereas they must be done sequentially in the MSB-side operation. Therefore, the LSB-side operation takes $m+1$ steps irrespective of the bit-pattern in e. In addition, a part of the two multipliers in the LSB-side operation can be shared, which is effective for reducing the power dissipation. Consequently, this LSB-side algorithm was chosen for the LSI described here.

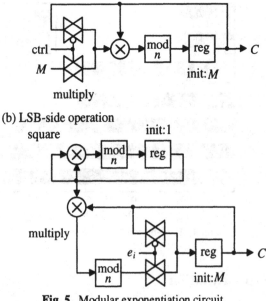

Fig. 5. Modular exponentiation circuit.

4 High-Speed Adder

Modular exponentiation is executed by repetition of addition and subtraction in the LSI. The adders designed for the operation are 1035 bits long, but the critical path has only 47 gates, that is, a $0.4 \text{ ns} \times 47 = 18.8$ ns delay.

Since addition in a higher block cannot be executed until a carry comes up from a lower block, the key to performance is to speed up carry propagation. Fig. 6 shows the 9-bit composition of the high-speed adder, which has the same structure as in the LSI implementation. To balance block-internal and carry-propagation delays, every higher block is one bit longer than the block directly below.

A carry input $c_i = 1$ propagates to the higher adder as a carry $c_{i+1} = 1$: only when the i-th adder inputs x_i and y_i satisfy the formula below:

$$x_i \oplus y_i = 1 \quad (\oplus : \text{XOR})$$

Before C_j (a carry input of the block j) comes, calculate the logical product of all $x_i \oplus y_i$ in the block,

$$P_{j+1} = \prod_i x_i \oplus y_i .$$

When $P_{j+1} = 1$, the carry input $C_j = 1$ can skip the block immediately [20]. A carry generated in each block propagates from g_i to g_{i+1} at the i-th adder, and

$$p_i = \prod_k^{k<i} x_k \oplus y_k$$

is ANDed with $x_i \oplus y_i$, then fed to p_{i+1}. An output z_i initially holds a sum assuming the block carry $C_j = 0$, and is inverted by the XOR gate if $C_j = 1$ comes up later [21].

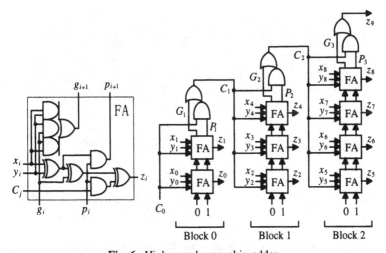

Fig. 6. High-speed carry-skip adder.

5 RSA Encryption Circuit

Fig. 7 shows a block diagram of an RSA circuit, which consists of one 1024-bit adder (ADR_D), two 1035-bit adders (ADR_S and ADR_P), three 1024-bit registers (DB, SQ and PW), two 1035-bit registers (S and P) and three 3:1 multiplexers. An RSA operation of less than 1024 bits can be executed by filling the higher bits of the registers with '0' and reducing the loop counts. A 1024-bit operation is is explained below. One multiplication is performed by carrying out 1k additions, and one exponentiation by repeating the multiplication 1k times.

The value in the DB register is shifted by one bit in the MSB direction during each addition cycle, and $\times 2$ modulo n is calculated by the adder ADR_D. The multiplication result is stored in the S register by selecting and adding DB when the i-th bit of the SQ register $SQ_i = 1$. The result is selected and multiplied by the bit PW_i and the bit e_j, which is the j-th bit of the exponent e used in the j-th multiplication cycle, is then stored in the P register. In each addition cycle, modulo n is calculated to prevent overflow.

In order to calculate $C = M^e \pmod{n}$, M is squared repeatedly and the value for which $e_j = 1$ is multiplied in the LSB-side operation. Thus, the procedure starts with the operation $x^2 \pmod{n}$, where x is the value in the S register. The same value x is fed from S to the 1024-bit registers DB and SQ at the beginning of the multiplication, and the product of the two registers is then calculated followed by modulus n, and the result is stored back to S. In this operation, a 1024-bit value $2^i x \pmod{n}$ generated in DB is added up to 1024 times according to the formula

$$x^2 \pmod{n} = \sum_{0}^{1023} (2^i x \pmod{n}) \cdot x_i .$$

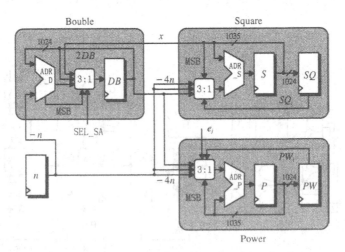

Fig. 7. Block diagram of the RSA encryption circuit.

The maximum value of n is $2^{1024} - 1$, and hence $2^i x \pmod{n}$ is equal to or less than $2^{1024} - 2$; this gives

$$\sum_0^{1023} (2^i x \pmod{n}) \cdot x_i < \sum_0^{1023} (2^{1024} - 2)$$

$$= (2^{1024} - 2) \cdot 1024 = 2^{1034} - 2^{11}$$

One sign bit, explained later, is required, and thus the total bit length of the S register is 1035.

According to Algorithm 1, $2^i x \pmod{n}$ is computed by the "Double" part of Fig. 7.

Algorithm 1: $DB \leftarrow 2^i x \pmod{n}$
$\quad DB \leftarrow x$;
$\quad$ for $i = 0$ to 1023 do {
$\quad\quad$ if $2DB - n \geq 0$
$\quad\quad\quad DB \leftarrow 2DB - n$;
$\quad\quad$ else
$\quad\quad\quad DB \leftarrow 2DB$;
$\quad$ }

Asserting the select signal SEL_SA of the 3:1 multiplexer, an initial value x is set in the 1024-bit register DB from the 1035-bit register S. To avoid overflow, x should be kept less than n. The details of this operation are explained later. The value x in DB is less than n, and thus $2DB$ is less than $2n$. By subtracting n when $2DB$ is equal to or greater than n, and keeping $2DB$ when it is less than n, $2^i x \pmod{n}$ is obtained. In the block diagram shown in Fig. 7, the 1024-bit adder ADR_D executes $2DB - n$, and $2DB$ or $2DB - n$ is selected and restored to DB according to the sign bit MSB. Repeating this operation always satisfies the condition $0 \leq DB < n$, and $2^i x \pmod{n}$ is obtained in DB at the end of the i-th addition cycle.

Algorithm 2 computes $x^2 \pmod{n}$ by using the result $2^i x \pmod{n}$ in the DB register.

Algorithm 2: $S \leftarrow x^2 \pmod{n}$
$\quad SQ \leftarrow x$;
$\quad$ if $SQ_0 = 0$
$\quad\quad S \leftarrow 0$;
$\quad$ for $i = 1$ to 1023 do {
$\quad\quad$ if $SQ_i = 1$
$\quad\quad\quad S \leftarrow S + DB$;
$\quad\quad$ else if $S \geq 0$
$\quad\quad\quad S \leftarrow S - 4n$;
$\quad$ }

An initial value x is set to the 1024-bit register SQ from the S register. If $SQ_i (= x_i) = 1$, $2^i x \pmod{n}$ from DB is added to S during the i-th cycle. During the first addition cycle

$i = 0$, the initial value of S is x, and thus x is kept in S when $SQ_0 (= x_0) = 1$, or S is reset to 0 when $SQ_0 = 0$.

A 1024-bit value from DB is added to S up to 1024 times, resulting in a 1034-bit positive number. This value should be adjusted to obtain a 1024-bit positive number by subtracting n many times in the adder ADR_S. Incidentally, ADR_S is used for addition only when $SQ_i = 1$, and can therefore be used for the adjustment S when $SQ_i = 0$. The frequencies of '0' and '1' bits in SQ_i are approximately equal, and thus the intermediate value S can be adjusted around the 1024-bit value by executing $S \leftarrow S - n$ when $S \geq n$ and $SQ_i = 0$. However, since the frequencies of '0' and '1' are not always equal, subtracting $4n$ can adjust S around the 1024-bit value even if the ratio of '0' to '1' bits is 1:4. Subtracting $4n$ when $S \geq 0$ rather than when $S \geq 4n$ makes it easier to control the sequence, because the execution of the adjusting operation can be determined by checking the MSB of the S register without a trial subtraction $S - 4n$. The intermediate value may be a negative number, as a result of the $4n$ subtraction; this is why the size of SQ and PW is 1035 bits including the sign bit. When one multiplication cycle (that is, 1K additions) is finished, the value is adjusted within the limits of $0 \leq S < n$. If there is a possibility that S is greater than n, S is converted into a negative value by repeating the $-4n$ operation, then adding n a few times and stopping when S becomes greater than zero.

$x^{e_j} \cdot PW (\mathrm{mod} n)$ is calculated by the "Power" part of Fig. 7, according to Algorithm 3.

> Algorithm 3: $P \leftarrow x^{e_j} \cdot PW (\mathrm{mod}\ n)$
> while $e_j = 1$ do {
> $PW \leftarrow P$;
> $P \leftarrow 0$;
> for $i = 0$ to 1023 do {
>   if $PW_i = 1$
> $P \leftarrow P + DB$;
>   else if $P \geq 0$
> $P \leftarrow P - 4n$;
> } }

Starting from M, $x = M$, M^2, M^4, M^8, $\cdots$ $(\mathrm{mod}\ n)$ is obtained in the S register, and the modular multiplication is executed by multiplying the integer $x = M^{2^j} (\mathrm{mod}\ n)$ and PW when $e_j = 1$. At the beginning of the j-th cycle, the 1035-bit register P holds the result of the previous $j-1$-th cycle,

$$\prod_k^{k<j} M^{e_k 2^k} (\mathrm{mod}\ n),$$

which is transferred to the 1024-bit register PW. To perform the operation $P \leftarrow x \times PW$, the multiplicand x is doubled modulo n, and the value $2^i x \pmod{n}$ is added to P when $PW_i = 1$. By this time, $2^i x \pmod{n}$ has already been calculated in DB by the adder ADR_D for the square operation. Consequently, ADR_D can be shared between the square and the exponential operations.

The first addition cycle in the S register can be skipped, because x has already been set to S, but P should be reset to 0 and the DB output $2^i x \pmod{n}$ is added, starting from $i = 0$ when $PW_i = 1$, because the initial value of P is not x. The rest of the operations, such as the $-4n$ adjustment in the adder ADR_P when $PW_i = 0$, follow the same pattern as in Algorithm 2.

Incidentally, the bit lengths of M, e, and n in the modular exponentiation $M^e \pmod{n}$ are not always the same. Even if they are the same, there is no guarantee that the condition $M < n$ is satisfied. When $M > n$, DB becomes greater than n as a result of the operation

$$DB \leftarrow 2DB - n$$

and repeating this operation causes overflow. The operation

$$S \leftarrow 1 \times M \pmod{n}$$

is executed by storing the integer 1 to the registers DB and S, and storing M to SQ. The result $M \pmod{n}$ is used as the initial value of DB.

1024-bit RSA encryption takes 1025 multiplication cycles, and one multiplication requires 1024 additions followed by a few (about 4) adjustment cycles. Therefore the RSA operation time at 45 MHz (22-nsec cycle) is

$$1025 \times (1024 + 4) \times 22 \text{ nsec} \cong 23 \text{ msec}$$

6 RSA Key Generation

Two prime numbers of around 512 bits in length are needed to generate a 1024-bit key. Eratosthenes' sieve and Fermat's test are used for the primality test. The sieve uses the function $C = A \pmod{n}$, and if the result is $C = 0$ for at least one of $n = 3, 5, 7, \cdots$, then A is a composite. Because of the memory limitation, the 1st to 256th odd primes (3-1633) are used for the sieve, and thus about one out of 6.6 odd numbers passes through. Once a modular table $A \pmod{n}$ for all 256 primes is generated, remainders of the next candidate $A+2 \pmod{n}$ are easily obtained by $+2$ and $-n$ operations on the table. From the prime number theorem, the prime density around 2^{512} is

$$\frac{d}{dn}\frac{n}{\ln n} = \frac{\ln n - 1}{(\ln n)^2} = \frac{\ln 2^{512} - 1}{(\ln 2^{512})^2} \cong \frac{1}{356}$$

Therefore, one out of $356 \div 2 = 178$ odd numbers is a prime on average, and one out of $178 \div 6.6 \cong 27$ odd numbers (that passed the sieve) is a prime. Thus, 27 Fermat's tests are required to find one 512-bit prime number, and one Fermat's test (that is, one modular exponentiation $C = A^B \pmod{n}$) in 45-MHz operation takes

$$513 \times (512 + 4) \times 22 \text{ nsec} \cong 5.9 \text{ msec}$$

In comparison, the operation time for the sieve is short enough. As a result, it takes about

$$5.9 \text{ msec} \times 27 \times 2 \cong 0.32 \text{ sec}$$

to find two prime numbers.

It is possible that these numbers that passed Fermat's test are not primes. However the probability that a randomly chosen odd number smaller than $x = 2^{512}$ is a pseudoprime is lower than [22]

$$\frac{1}{2} x^{-\frac{\ln \ln \ln x}{2 \ln \ln x}} \cong 2^{-77}$$

Therefore, one Fermat's test is sufficient for this purpose.

After that, a private key d is calculated from a public key e by using the extended Euclidean algorithm, for which a divide function not yet supported in this LSI, is required. However, the function can be executed very fast, even in ordinary MPUs.

7 DES and MD5 Circuits

Fig. 8 shows a block diagram of the DES encryption circuit. The thick lines are 64-bit data buses and the fine lines are 32-bit buses except in the key scheduling part on the right side of the figure. A 64-bit plain-text Din is divided into two 32-bit parts and stored in registers L and R through 2:1 and 4:1 multiplexers. After the initial permutation IP, the operation shown in the formula below is executed 16 times with the scheduling 56-bit key K in the gray area of the figure.

$$\begin{cases} L_i \leftarrow R_{i-1} \\ R_i \leftarrow L_{i-1} \oplus f(R_{i-1}, K_i) \end{cases}$$

Then, the inverse permutation IP^{-1} is done and the cipher text is output to Dout through the 2:1 multiplexer. As a result, 18 cycles (IP, 16 iterations and IP^{-1}) are required to encrypt 64-bit data, and the throughput at 45-MHz operation is

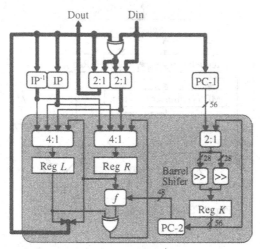

Fig.8. Block diagram of the DES circuit.

$$8\,B \div 18\,\text{cycles} \times 45\,\text{MHz} = 20\,\text{MB/sec}$$

Decryption requires one extra cycle for key scheduling. As a result, its throughput is

$$8\,B \div 19\,\text{cycles} \times 45\,\text{MHz} = 18.9\,\text{MB/sec}$$

In addition to the ECB mode, CBC, CFB, and OFB modes are supported by switching a 64-bit XOR gate and two 2:1 multiplexers, shown in the upper center of the figure.

Fig. 9 shows a block diagram of the MD5 hash function circuit. All data buses have 32-bit width. Four adders are implemented by custom macros and the others by gate arrays. Constant values $Ti = |\sin(i) \cdot 2^{32}|$ ($i = 1, \cdots, 64$) are also held by gate arrays. At the beginning of hashing, registers $A\sim D$ are initialized as follows:

$$\{A, B, C, D\} = \{01234567\,\text{h}, 89\text{ABCDEF h}, \text{FEDCBA98 h}, 76543210\,\text{h}\}$$

It takes 16 cycles to feed a 512-bit message M to the nonlinear function block through a 32-bit data bus. Four different functions are applied to M, and therefore $16 \times 4 = 64$ cycles are required to generate 128-bit hash data from a 512-bit message. The hash data in registers A~D are output through a selector, and if the following message input exists, the current hash value is added to the previous initializing data and restored to the four registers again as a new initial value.

Data input and output takes 24 cycles in 16-bit data transfer mode, and issue of the start command takes one cycle. Assuming that there are 8 cycles for four 32-bit additions to generate the initial value, MD5 throughput at 45-MHz operation is

$$64\,B \div (64 + 24 + 1 + 8)\,\text{cycles} \times 45\,\text{MHz} = 29.7\,\text{MB/sec}$$

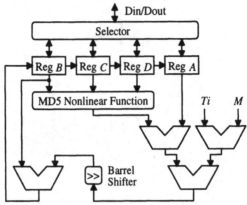

Fig. 9. Block diagram of the MD5 circuit.

8 Conclusion

An RSA encryption LSI with DES and MD5 function was developed. It has 4.9-mm² accelerator core that calculates a 1024-bit RSA in 23 msec at 45 MHz. It is suitable not only for smart cards but also for authentication servers. In addition, its low-power features of 100-mA peak current at 45 MHz and 15-mA at 5 MHz can be integrated into various mobile gears. A 2048-bit RSA accelerator is being developed, in which the bit length of the adder is doubled, and the critical path delay is reduced from 47 gates to 18 gates through the introduction of a new carry-skip technique. Multiplication and modular multiplication for $2048\text{-}bit \times 2048\text{-}bit$ operands and division and modulo functions for $4096\text{-}bit \div 2048\text{-}bit$ operands will also be supported.

Acknowledgement

The authors would like to thank Mr. K. Sugimoto and Dr. S. Shimizu for their encouragement and support throughout this work.

References

[1] R. Rivest, A. Shamir and L. Adelman: "A Method for Obtaining Digital Signatures and Public-key Cryptosystems," Comm. ACM, vol. 21, no. 2, pp. 120-126, 1978.

[2] P. Montgomery: "Modular Multiplication without Trial Division," Mathematics of Computation, vol. 44, no. 170, pp. 519-521, 1985.

[3]   P. Barret: "Implementing the Rivest Shamir and Adelman Public Key Encryption Algorithm on a Standard Digital Signal Processor," Advances in Cryptology - Crypto '86, LNCS 263, Springer-Verlag, pp. 311-323, 1987.

[4]   H. Sedlak: "The RSA Cryptography Processor," Advances in Cryptology - Eurocrypt '87, LNCS 293, Springer-Verlag, pp. 95-105, 1988.

[5]   D. de Waleffe and J-J.Quisquater: "CORSAIR: A Smart Card for Public Key Cryptosystems," Advances in Cryptology - Crypto '90, LNCS 537, Springer-Verlag, pp. 503-513, 1990.

[6]   D. Naccache and D. M'Raihi: "Cryptographic Smart Cards," IEEE Micro, vol. 16, no. 3, pp. 14-24, June 1996.

[7]   P. A. Ivey, A. L. Cox, J. R. Harbridge and J. K. Oldfield: "A Single-Chip Public Key Encryption System," IEEE J. Solid-State Circuits, vol. 24, no. 4, pp. 1071-1075, Aug. 1989.

[8]   M. Shand and J. Vuillemin: "Fast Implementations of RSA Cryptography," Proceedings of the 11th IEEE Symp. on Computer Arithmetic, pp. 252-259, 1993.

[9]   P. A. Ivey, S. N. Walker, J. M. Stern and S. Davidson: "An Ultra-High Speed Public Key Encryption Processor," Proceedings of IEEE 1992 Custom Integrated Circuits Conf. pp.19.6.1-19.6.4, May 1992.

[10] A. Vandemeulebroeck, E. Vanzieleghem, T. Denayer, and P. G. A. Jespers: "A New Carry-Free Division Algorithm and its Application to a Single-Chip 1024-b RSA Processor," IEEE J. Solid-State Circuits, vol. 25, no. 3, pp. 748-756, June 1990.

[11] FIPS PUB 46, "Data Encryption Standard," National Bureau of Standards, 1977.

[12] FIPS PUB 81, "DES Modes of Operation," National Bureau of Standards, 1980.

[13] R. Rivest: "The MD5 Message-Digest Algorithm," RFC 1321, Apr. 1992.

[14] http://www.pijnenburg.nl, Pijnenburg Beheer N.V.

[15] http://www.nel.co.jp, NTT Electronics Co.

[16] http://www.siemens.de, Siemens AG.

[17] http://www.st.com, SGS-Thomson Microelectronics.

[18] http://www.philps.com, Philips.

[19] http://www.mcu.motsps.com, Motorola.

[20] M. Lehman and N. Burla: "Skip Techniques for High-Speed Carry Propagation in Binary Arithmetic Units," IRE Trans. Elec. Comput., vol. EC-10, pp. 691-698, Dec. 1961.

[21] O. J. Bedrij: "Carry-Select Adder," IRE Trans. Elec. Comput., vol. EC-11, pp. 340-346, June 1962.

[22] C. Pomerance: "On the Distribution of Pseudoprimes," Mathmatics of Computation, vol. 34, no. 156, pp. 587-593, Oct. 1981.

The Case for a Secure Multi-Application Smart Card Operating System

Constantinos Markantonakis
Information Security Group, Computer Science Department,
Royal Holloway, University of London, Egham,
Surrey, TW20 OEX, United Kingdom.
Email: costasm@dcs.rhbnc.ac.uk

27 October 1997

Abstract : The idea of a multi-application smart card operating system is not a new one, but only recently the smart card industry is catching up with proper software and hardware architectures that contribute in the anticipated evolution. In this paper we survey some of the proposed software architectures and comment on their applicability and performance, along with investigating the entirely new demands imposed both in the smart card operating system and the application level. We also present a slightly different more decentralized view of a secure smart card multi-application operating system with some interesting new features.

Keywords: Smart card, multi-application, operating system, interpreter, applet, objects, Java, JavaCard.

1   Introduction

The smart card, this small microprocessor found in many plastic cards, is believed to play a very important role in the area of Information Technology (IT) security. Taking into account the advertised [1] features of the smart card processors people believed they found the solution to all security related problems. This is partially true, in a sense that smart cards are addressing some specific security issues, but not every single one.

Among the key issues in the acceptance of the smart card technology are security, upgradability and programmability. These features are the consequences of improvements both in the performance of the current smart card microprocessors [7,8,9,19] and also in the new advanced operating system architectures [10,11,12]. In smart cards, as in many computerized devices, the operating system is considered as a security critical system component that determines the internal and external behavior of the whole system. The development of the Smart Card Operating Systems (SCOS's) offered the same advantages as the development of operating systems in the early computers. The application developers are free from any concerns about the specific hardware constraints of their device and users benefit from a variety of new applications (transport, banking, retail, health care, etc.)

Most SCOS's [10,11,12,18] are largely concerned with the management and protection of data files along with the provision of cryptographic algorithms [13]. Current SCOS's offer data structuring methods organized in files and directories [14]. Although [14] claims that provides an abstract view of a multi-application operating system, it is obvious that SCOS's built around this proposed methodology will be single application oriented. Currently, if more than one application will have to reside in the same card, application developers will have to agree and define their application structures in advance. Moreover if inter-application communication is required then all the necessary inter application relationships should be defined in advance.

Soon afterwards smart card application developers realized the need for new techniques that will enable smart cards to securely host multiple applications [15,16,17]. Furthermore this implies, that applications might originate from different companies, run on different smart card processors, share certain information and more importantly they could be installed at any later stage in the card lifecycle without reference to the existing applications. Moreover strong guarantees should be present that applications will not interfere with each other and that resources should be accessible only through the operating system calls.

In this paper we survey the current status of the multi-application smart card operating system technology. We provide a brief survey of the concepts of object code interpretation on smart card processors and how it is achieved by using the Java language. Finally, we introduce some new concepts and ideas that will strengthen the overall notion of a secure multi-application smart card operating system.

2 Object Code Interpretation in Smart cards

In February 1997 Schlumberger and Gemplus announced the introduction of a smart card that will run programs written in Sun Microsystems' Java programming language [25] and will adhere to the Java Card Application Program Inteface (API) Ver. 1.0 [26,27]. The API presents the java.iso7816 package which defines the basic commands and error codes as defined in [14]. The minimum smart card environment needed to run the Java card API is 300 (KIP) CPU, 12KB ROM, 4KB EEPROM and 512B of RAM. The Java card API supports the following data types needed for Smart card applications: Boolean, byte and short data types - all object oriented scope and binding rules - all flow of control statements - all operators and modifiers - unidimensional arrays or supported data types. Current work in the Java Card Forum [2] suggests that a new version of the Java card API Ver 2.0 is under development with more advanced features and extended functionality.

In May 1997 Schlumberger announced the availability of the of the Cyberflex [28] smart card prerelease series which supports the above features. Currently Cyberflex is based on Motorola's M68HC055SC49 processor [23,24] and it contains the Solo Virtual Machine and the General Purpose Operating system. The Solo Virtual Machine translates the Java Bytecodes into instructions that the microprocessor on the smart card could understand. The General Purpose Operating System (GPOS) implements the operations presented in [14]. Furthermore the Solo Virtual Machine is considered small enough, only 4 Kbytes, and it resides on top of the GPOS which is about 8Kbytes.

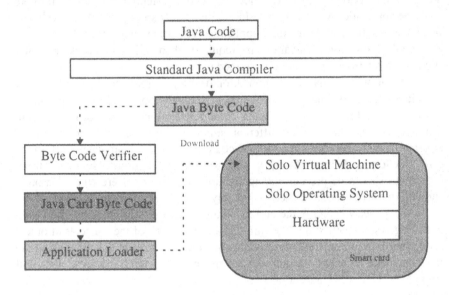

Figure 1. The Smart card Java application development and installation

The steps in order to create a Java application, download it and execute it on the smart card are the following: Firstly, the application programmer must take into account [14] and develop, compile the Java smart card application by using a standard Java development environment. Secondly the application developer must also take into account the following space constraints for the Pre-Release Series: application size - 2.8 Kbytes, Java stack size -16 bytes, card library size 1.2 Kbytes. Due to the fact that there is no byte code verifier in the card, the newly created Java code classes should be verified externally. As soon as the Java classes are verified, the Java card classes are created and the application code is ready to be installed in the card. The whole procedure is summarized in Fig. 1. Currently the fact that the Java Card bytecode is only a subset of the whole Java bytecode, it should be regarded as an advantage, since it will help to maintain a small and manageable problem structure which is easier to handle. If this basic and redundant structure works properly, at later stages it will be easier to proceed with adding more functionality.

Another issue that requires further discussion is the following: First of all, how Java cards are identified when they are introduced into systems ? Some proposals suggest to use the ATR (Answer to Reset) feature, supported almost by every smart card. The Java card forum suggests an alternative solution with the introduction in the class loader level, a command that will return specific JavaCard related information. The new command is called GET_INFORMATION and is actually a variation of the GET_RESPONSE command defined in [14] by using an existing instruction (INS) code, INS=0xC0 and new P1, P2 values P1=0xAA, P2=0x55. This new proposal will avoid the incompatibilities encountered in current smart cards responses to reset and it will also allow the card to return Java related information.

The notion of Java code interpretation in the smart cards is relatively new and many issues like inter-application communication, sharable files and their access relationships still have to be addressed. Other issues like transaction integrity [21], loading of applications [22], errors and exception handling [4], file management interface specifications [3] are actually defined but not in a great detail. Further issues require cautious examination and proper definition in order to minimize any applicable attacks. We will further analyze some of these issues in Chapter 3.

Although the JavaCard prerelease series is successfully addressing some issues of the multi-application smart cards, it is not the ideal solution. We believe that a lot of functionality needs to be removed from the Java Interpreter and placed in the underlying operating system or even in the application level. This will improve application execution times and it will also help to achieve a formally verified trusted environment. Actually this cannot easily be achieved taking into account that Java applications run approximately 200 times slower than non interpreted applications and due to the fact that Java language has neither formal semantics nor a formal description of its type system [20].

3   Reviewing the Issues for Secure Download and Execution of Application Code in Smart Cards

In this section we present the core idea of this paper by commenting some of the features offered by current smart card architectures along with highlighting some additional issues that need to be taken into serious consideration. Our proposals cover both the application level and the operating system level.

At the bottom level of the smart card architecture we encounter the smart card microprocessor. It is obvious that if the smart card chip cannot be trusted then there is very little benefit in building other software structures on top of it. Up to date, there are no reported cases of smart card manufacturers fabricating chips containing back doors or any undocumented instructions. Certainly more evidence is required that chips are manufactured with trusted engineering methods. In our study we assume that smart card chips are reasonable trustable.

Moving to the next layer (in ROM memory) on top of the trusted silicon, we encounter the Smart Card Operating System layer. We will classify smart card operating systems into two categories, single application and multi-application oriented. The multi-application operating systems can be subdivided into further two categories, those with pre-installed applications and those providing run-time application installation and execution. It is obvious that the later category, which also includes the Java cards, it is still open for further debates and proposals.

In the case of the JavaCard we have the Java interpreter which is responsible for translating the Java bytecodes into commands that would make sense for the underlying processor. In [28] the Java interpreter is considered as part of the operating system and is placed in ROM memory during the chip manufacturing phase. This is a rather solid and centralized view of a smart card operating system and a Java interpreter. We certainly accept that the proposed architecture supports the multi-application characteristics of smart cards, but we believe that it offers very little towards their upgradability. This is true since any "middle-level" future improvements will require change of the underlying ROM of the card. The term "middle-level" improvements refer for example to changes in the inter-application communication features, cryptographic features, etc.

For these reasons we propose a more decentralized view of a smart card Java interpreter. In order to achieve our goal, we will have to extract some functionality of the interpreter and place it somewhere else. We suggest that the Java interpreter should only translate higher level commands into lower level machine code understandable by the processor. Furthermore the interpreter should be coupled with various "...*Managers*" like a *Inter-Application Manager* (IAM) responsible for the inter application communication, a *Signature Manager* (SM) described later on in this chapter, a *Cryptography Manager* (CM) responsible for handling any cryptographic operations, *Installation Manager* that will install new applications in the card. Basically the interpreter will consult these *Managers* and authorize them to complete and manage certain operations.

The interesting feature of all these M*anagers* is that they will not be part of the interpreter masked in ROM memory but they will be stored in EEPROM. This will allow the smart card to easily adopt any changes and future improvements. *Managers* will be implemented and distributed only by authorized entities like smart card manufacturers, etc. Prior to the installation of a latest version of a *Manager* its signature should be verified. Furthermore, the card should install any *Managers* only if they come from certain "trusted" origins. These *Managers* will help smart cards to successfully cope with any future improvements without being necessary to modify their whole ROM architecture, but on the other hand they might introduce further vulnerabilities.

It is true that interpreting Java code in smart cards is time consuming. Thus we ought to investigate possible means of reducing execution times. One can immediately suggest that improvements in chip architectures (Reduced Instruction Set Computer RISC processors) or even improvements on compilation and interpretation techniques is a good starting point. These are absolutely true, but in the case of smart cards a further easier method could adequately reduce the execution time of interpreted code. The categorization of Applets into trusted and non-trusted is a crucial step. This can be easily achieved through checking the Applet signatures. Once the Applets are classified, the next step requires to place them under different boundaries and assign them different privileges. The *Manager* entities analyzed previously could help a lot. The idea is for the interpreter to consult different *Managers* for different categories of Applets. Trusted Applets will require certain *Managers* to perform minimal checks and thus run faster, whereas in contrast, untrusted Applets will require different *Managers* that will perform thorough checks and as a result they will be executed slower. The whole idea can be summarized in the following sentence, depending on the Applet's origin introduce two different levels of interpretation from two different *Managers*.

In [32] the Java Card Forum suggests the introduction of a Transaction Integrity Mechanism (TIM) which ensures at the virtual machine level that non-volatile memory updates are either not performed at all, or fully performed. We will extend the notion of TIM's and introduce the notion of an Applet activity Log Mechanism (ALM). The ALM refer to the appropriate mechanisms that will allow the interpreter to log certain Applet operations. The existence of ALM and TIM will help to maintain the integrity of the system or at least discover after an incident what values are changed and by whom.

We are aware of the fact that specifying what Applet activities should be audited is a rather difficult task. In a Java smart card environment this statement is even more paradoxical because it is both easy and difficult. It is relatively easy due to the restricted variety of smart card commands. Among the Java Card API Ver 1.0 commands that could be audited are the following: write and update operations on files, construction of subclasses, signature generation, Applet names or even a signed hash function on an Applet's code etc. The whole auditing procedure requires a runtime tracing mechanism. This tracing mechanism could be designed in the form of a Java class. A more advanced solution would require that this tracing mechanism would be part of the operating system and more specifically a major component of the Java interpreter called the *Tracing Manager*. By placing calls of this tracing mechanism at the right places operations could be monitored.

A further important issue in the construction of the *Tracing Manager* (TM) is that it should work very closely with the TIM. This is necessary, because some times certain operations might be canceled and the transaction integrity cache might need to be rolled back. The *Tracing Manager* should be aware of all these facts in order to update the *Applet activity Log File* (ALF).

Among the most important issues which govern the implementation of a *Tracing Manager* are the size and the access permissions of the ALF. In a smart card environment where the storage of a single byte is of significant importance, the storage of a large log file could be a major problem. On the other hand, if the ALF is small enough then malicious Applets could overwrite their actions. Moreover, if the access permissions for the (ALF) are not properly defined then it might be vulnerable to unauthorized alterations. Is there a solution then, that will provide both functionality and assurance ?

Our proposal suggests to allocate a small cyclic log file of limited size 0.5-1.0KByte that will record some of the aforementioned operations. Ideally the ALF should be a system file with update and write operations only allowed to the *Tracing Manager* whereas read access should be public. Every time the file is getting full and it is about to overwrite itself, it will raise an exception and provide the user with the ability to sign and download itself in a diskette or in the terminals hard drive. We see then how the secondary storage memory of the users terminal can be used as storage repository for the ALF. Although in the Cyberflex Pre-Release series due to CRC computation failure there are limitations preventing the use of Cyclic files for logging purposes, we believe that our approach is feasible and effective.

The description of a problem often encountered in the smart card application level is the following: A user is required to pay some amount of money (Correct Payment, CP) in order to receive some kind of service from an Internet shop. Consequently the user downloads in her/his card and web browser the appropriate Applets that will handle both the offered service and the means of payment. Now let us assume that both Applets are rogue and although they prompt the user to authorize a CP request, in reality they are going to withdraw a larger amount (False Payment, FP). How can we guard against this ?

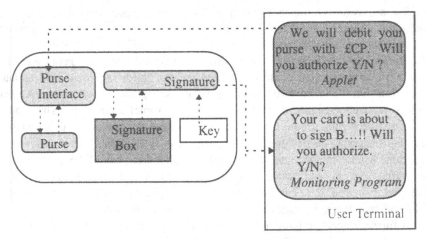

Figure 2. Description of the Signature Manager

At a certain stage the card has to sign the payment request in order to authorize it. But since the user communicates with the card through the rogue Applet and currently there is no direct interface in the card to check what is actually being signed, there is no straight forward solution. In order to overcome this problem new features should be added both in the operating system and the application level. In the application level we assume that all communication with the *Purse* is handled by a *Purse Interface,* specially designed by the purse provider. We further assume that Applet communication with the *Purse Interface* is performed through standardized messages. Moreover the *Purse Interface* will be also responsible for communicating, again in a standardized syntax, with the *Signature Manager.* The *Signature Manager* should be part of the operating system or the interpreter and masked in ROM during the manufacturing phase. Its main responsibility is to serve the role of a security guard for every message that is going to be signed by the card. The *Signature Manager* is going to be monitored by the user, with a dedicated monitoring program running in the users terminal Fig 2.

Back in our example the Applet will try to authorize the FP request, by sending it to the *Purse Interface* demanding from the card to authorize it. As soon as the *Purse Interface* receives this message it will consult the *Signature Manager*. The *Signature Manager* will raise an exception and will also prompt the user (via the monitoring program) to authorize the FP request. The user, by verifying that FP is different from CP, he/she will realize that the Applet is malicious. In case FP and CP are the same, the user has to provide a signature key which will be verified by the card and used to sign the payment request.

The *Signature Manager* should be able to communicate with other entities (interfaces) that need to use the signature box (e.g. a File Encryption Interface). This is the main reason why communication with these interfaces should take place in a standardized format. Java language provides the opportunity to various application providers to write their own application interfaces and download them in the card. Since these interfaces will communicate with the *Signature Manager* in a standardized form, they will enable the monitoring program running in the users terminal, to clarify the actual messages which are going to be signed. The monitoring program in the users terminal should be provided by the smart card manufacturers and should be trustable and formally verified. Furthermore communication between the monitoring program and the Signature Manager should take place via a separate communication channel (optionally encrypted) and established every time the card is inserted in the reader. Since the program will reside in the users terminal, it is up to the user to make sure that it is adequately protected.

We see that in order to circumvent the lack of direct monitoring capabilities on the cards, we use the users terminal. With our proposed solution users would feel confident that they have control on what is exactly being singed by their cards.

4   Conclusions and Future Work

In a smart card environment operating systems and code interpreters should be seen as security critical system components. Our view of a smart card environment regards the smart card as the hosts being communicated by clients. Current smart card architecture suggest that protection in the application level is closely related with how well protected are the components of the underlying operating system. Our suggestions successfully address some specific problems, but we generally believe that in order to achieve higher smart card upgradability and true multi-functionality we have to securely un-hide certain parts of both the Operating System and the code interpreter. Furthermore, we claim that the code interpreter should be divided into smaller components that will be easier to handle, extendible and they could be easier verified.

The Java card technology is major step towards supporting the multi-application aspect of smart cards, but on the other hand it introduces new uncertainties that need to be taken into serious consideration. Thorough tests and risks analysis need to be taken into consideration in order examine every aspect of smart card security, and finally provide more adequate protection mechanisms.

References

[1]   Ruth Cherneff, John Griffin, Dave Outcalt, Dr. Carmen Pufialito, Rhonda Kaplan Singer, Michelle Stapleton, *"Smart Cards 97"*, http://www1 .shore.net/~bauster /cap/s-card/index.html#top, 1997.

[2]   *Java Card Forum*, http://www.javacardforum.org/

[3]   Bull, *"Java Card Application Program Interface (API), File Management Interface Specication"*, http://www.javacardforum.org/jcf/jcftech/FileSys. doc, 1997

[4]   Fabien Thiriet, Schlumberger Electronic Transactions, *"Java Card Application Program Interface (API), Errors and Exception Handling"*, http://www.javacard forum.org/jcf/ jcftech/eandf.doc,1997

[5]   Patrice Peyret, *"Application-Enabling Card Systems with Plug-and-Play Applets"*, Smart Card'96, 1996.

[6]   Schlumberger, *"Cyberflex"*, http://www.smartcardsys.com/slb/index .htm

[7]   Philips Semiconductors, "Integrated Circuits and Modules for Chip Cards", PG Identification & Automotive Hamburg, 1997.

[8]   Philips Semiconductors, "The New Generation Crypto Controller P83C858 ", 1996

[9]   Motorola, "Microcontroller literature",http://www.mcu.motsps.com/lit/, 1997.

[10]   General Information Systems Ltd., *"OSCAR, Specification of a smart card filling system incorporating data security and message authentication"*, http://www.gis.co .uk/ oscman1.htm, 1993.

[11]   Gemplus, *"MCOS 16 K EEPROM DES Reference Manual Ver 2.2"*, 1990.

[12]   Gemplus, *"MPCOS Multi Application Payment Chip, Reference Manual Ver 4.0"*,1994.

[13]   B. Schneier, Applied Cryptography, Second Edition, John Wiley & Sons, 1996.

[14]   International Standard Organization, *"ISO/IEC 7816-4"*, 1995.

[15]   Stephen Lee, *"The Case for Multifunctional Smart cards"*, Smartcard Technology International, 1995.

[16]   IBM, *"IBM Multi Functional Card General Information"*, Smart Card'96, 1996.

[17]   Card Europe UK-Background Paper, *"Smartcard Technology Leading to Multi Service Capability"*, 1994.

[18]   General Information Systems Ltd, UK, *"ISOS- The industry Standard Operating System, Introduction"*, 1995.

[19]   Ian Blythe, *"Smarter, More Secure Smartcards"*, Byte Magazine, June 1997.

[20]   Drew Dean, *"Java Security:From HotJava to Netscape And Beyond"*, Computer Science Department Princeton University, 1996.

[21]   Jacques Soussana, *"Java Card Application Program Interface, Transaction integrity"*, http://www.javacardforum.org/jcf/jcftech/transact.doc, 1997

[22]   Dominique Bolignamo, Dyade, *"Java Card Application Program Interface (API), Loading"*, http://www.javacardforum.org/jcf/ jcftech /JCFLoadingV1.doc, 1997

[23]   Motorola, *"M68HC05SC Family - At a Glance"*,http://design-net.com /csic /SMARTCRD/sctable .htm, 1997

[24]   Motorola,*"Motorola's M68HC05SC family microcontrollers."*, http:// designnet.com/csic/SMARTCRD/smartcrd.htm , 1997

[25]   Java*"Java Programming Language "*,http://java.sun.com/

[26]   Sun Microsystems, "The Java Card API specification", http://java.sun. com:80/products/commerce/, 1996

[27]   Java Soft, "Java Card API Frequently asked Questions", http://www. javasoft.com/products/commerce/doc.javacard_faq.htm

[28]   Schlumberger, *"Cyberflex Smart card: Prelease Series Developers manual"*,http://www.cyberflex.austin.et.slb.com/cyberflex/cyberhome.ht ml

An Augmented Family of Cryptographic Parity Circuits

Kenji Koyama[1] and Routo Terada[2]

[1] Nippon Telegraph and Telephone C.S. Labs, Hikari-dai 2-2 (Inuidani, Sanpeidani), Seika-cho, Souraku-gun, Kyoto 619-02, Japan (e-mail: koyama@progn.kecl.ntt.jp)
[2] University of S. Paulo, Computer Science Dept., Rua do Matao, 1010 S. Paulo-SP, Bra[sz]il, ZIP 05508-970 (e-mail: rt@ime.usp.br)

Abstract. A computationally inexpensive involution called *value dependent swapping* is introduced. This involution is included in the non-linear cryptographic family of functions called Parity Circuits to increase its non-affineness and thus increase its strength against cryptanalysis. Our analysis shows that this augmented version of Parity Circuits still has fundamental cryptographic properties. The addition of this involution introduces a new type of randomization while preserving the invertibility of the functions being defined. We formulate affineness for a general function, and introduce a normalized non-affineness measure. We prove some non-affineness conditions for the augmented Parity Circuits, and evaluate their non-affineness. We suggest the value-dependent swapping can also be incorporated into DES-like cryptographic functions as well to make them stronger against cryptanalysis.

1 Introduction

We introduce a random involution called *value-dependent swapping*, *VDS*. In the *VDS*, the left half and the right half of a sequence of bits are swapped if its weight is odd. *VDS* is included in the cryptographic family of functions called Parity Circuits $C(n, d)$ [3] to obtain an augmented version called $C_+(n, d)$, where n is the plaintext input length, and d is the depth of the circuit. Cryptographic properties of $C_+(n, d)$ are analyzed. In particular, we prove that $C_+(n, d)$ for $n \geq 4$ is *not* affine. We also show the degree of the non-affineness of $C_+(n, d)$ increases as n or d increases.

This work is in response to a very recent short note by Youssef and Tavares [6] in which they show our original Parity Circuits [3] are affine and hence insecure.

In Section 2, we introduce *VDS*, and in Sections 3 and 4, we summarize the Parity Circuits $C(n, d)$ and define the augmented circuits $C_+(n, d)$. In Section 5, the swapping properties for $C_+(n, d)$ are clarified. In Section 6.1, we formulate affineness for a general function, and introduce a normalized non-affineness measure. In Section 6.2, we prove non-affineness conditions for $C_+(n, d)$. In Section 6.3, we evaluate the non-affineness measure for the circuits $C_+(n, d)$ when n or d increases. In Section 7 and 8, other cryptographic properties are briefly described.

2 Value-dependent swapping

We propose a random involution called value-dependent swapping (VDS). A function called *value-dependent swapping* is generally defined as follows.

Definition 1. Let $x = L \parallel R$ be a sequence of $2k$ $(k > 0)$ bits, where L stands for left half of x, and R stands for right, $length(L) = length(R) = k$. A *value-dependent swapping*, or $V(x)$, is defined to be

$$V(x) = \begin{cases} R \parallel L & if \ h(x) = 0, \\ \\ L \parallel R & if \ h(x) = 1, \end{cases}$$

where $h(x) \in \{0, 1\}$.

Notice that $V(x)$ is an involution: $V(V(x)) = x$ if $h(L \parallel R) = h(R \parallel L)$. Among various candidates for $h(x)$ satisfying $h(L \parallel R) = h(R \parallel L)$, we can define a particular involutional value-dependent swapping called VDS.

Definition 2. (VDS) Let $x = L \parallel R$ be a sequence of $2k$ $(k > 0)$ bits, where $length(L) = length(R) = k$. A VDS, which is an involutional *value-dependent swapping* based on the parity of the weight of x, is defined to be

$$V(x) = V(L \parallel R) = \begin{cases} R \parallel L & if \ \ weight(x) \ \ is \ odd, \\ \\ L \parallel R & otherwise \ , \end{cases}$$

where $weight(x)$ is the number of 1's in the bit-sequence x.

Notice that if $L = R$, then $weight(x)$ is even and no swapping occurs.

From now on in this paper, we will assume that n is even, unless otherwise noticed.

3 Summary of Parity Circuits C(n,d)

We summarize in this section the basic concepts defined in [3] which will be used later.

Definition 3. A *parity circuit layer with length* n, or simply an $L(n)$ circuit layer, is a Boolean device with an n-bit input and an n-bit output, characterized by a *key* that is a sequence of n symbols from $\{0, 1, +, -\}$.

The symbols 0 and 1 are called *testers*, the symbol $+$ is called *even inverter*, and $-$ is called *odd inverter*.

Definition 4. A function $B = f(K, A)$ computed by an $L(n)$ circuit layer with key $K = k_1 k_2 \cdots k_n \in \{0, 1, +, -\}^n$ is the relation from an n-bit input sequence $A = a_1 a_2 \cdots a_n \in \{0, 1\}^n$ to an n-bit output sequence $B = b_1 b_2 \cdots b_n \in \{0, 1\}^n$

defined below. An $L(n)$ circuit layer computes first the variable T modulo 2 such that:

$$T = \sum_{j=1}^{n} t_j \bmod 2 \quad \text{where } t_j = \begin{cases} 1 \text{ if } (k_j = 0 \text{ and } a_j = 0) \text{ or } (k_j = 1 \text{ and } a_j = 1) \\ 0 \text{ otherwise.} \end{cases}$$

Note that $T = 0$ if there are no testers in K. When $T = 0$ we will say an *even parity event* ocurred; otherwise, an *odd parity event* occurred.

The output $B = b_1 b_2 \cdots b_n$ of the circuit layer is then

$$b_j = \begin{cases} \overline{a}_j \text{ if } \begin{cases} k_j = + \text{ and } T = 0 \text{ (even event)} \\ \text{or} \\ k_j = - \text{ and } T = 1 \text{ (odd event)} \\ \text{or} \\ k_j = 1 \end{cases} \\ a_j \text{ otherwise.} \end{cases}$$

It is shown in [3] that every circuit layer $L(n)$ computing f has an inverse layer $L^{-1}(n)$ to compute f^{-1} i.e., $f^{-1}(K, f(K, A)) = A$, for any n-bit input A and any key K.

Definition 5. A *parity circuit of width n and depth d*, or simply a $C(n, d)$ *circuit*, is a matrix of d $L(n)$ circuit layers with keys denoted by $\mathbf{K} = K_1 \parallel K_2 \parallel \cdots \parallel K_d$ for which the n output bits of the $(i-1)$-th circuit layer are the n input bits for the i-th circuit layer, for $2 \leq i \leq d$. The *key* for the $C(n, d)$ circuit is a $d \times n$ matrix with its d lines containing the circuit layer keys.

Let $F(.)$ be the function from $\{0, 1\}^n$ to $\{0, 1\}^n$ computed by a circuit $C(n, d)$ with key $K_1 \parallel K_2 \parallel \cdots \parallel K_d$. That is, $F(\mathbf{K}, A)$ is defined as

$$F(\mathbf{K}, A) = f(K_d, f(K_{d-1}, \cdots f(K_1, A) \cdots)).$$

It is also shown in [3] the inverse function $F^{-1}(.)$ is computed by the "inverted" circuit $C^{-1}(n, d)$ with key $K_d \parallel K_{d-1} \parallel \cdots \parallel K_1$.

Table 1 shows the behavior of an example of $C(n, d)$ circuit [3] with width $n = 10$ and depth $d = 3$ that will be referred to as Example 1 with key $\mathbf{K}^*$ in the later sections.

4 Augmented Non-affine Parity Circuits $C_+(n,d)$

Definition 6. A function $B = f_+(K, A)$ computed by an *augmented $L(n)$ circuit layer* with key K, or simply $L_+(n)$ *layer*, is the function $V(f(K, A))$, where V is the VDS function as in Defintion 2, and f is the function computed by an $L(n)$ circuit layer.

Table 1. Example 1: $C(n,d)$ when $n = 10$ and $d = 3$

Input	1	0	1	1	0	0	1	0	0	1
K_1	–	0	1	–	+	+	1	1	–	+
Output	0	0	0	0	0	0	0	1	1	1
K_2	+	1	0	1	1	+	0	–	+	–
Output	1	1	0	1	1	1	1	0	1	0
K_3	–	0	1	+	+	0	–	+	+	–
Output	1	1	1	0	0	1	0	0	1	1

We will see next that $L_+(n)$ layer is still invertible: for invertion just compute $V(x)$ *before* computing the inverse of $L(n)$ (as pointed out, $V(x)$ is an involution).

Theorem 7. *Every function* $B = f_+(K, A)$ *computed by an* $L_+(n)$ *layer is invertible, i.e., for any n-bit input sequence* A, *and any key* K, *there is an inverse layer,* $L_+^{-1}(n)$ *layer, to compute* f_+^{-1} *so that* $f_+^{-1}(K, f_+(K, A)) = A$.

Proof First, we have from Lemma 1 in [3] that every function $f(K, A)$ computed by an $L(n)$ layer has an inverse f^{-1}. From the definition, we have $f_+ = V \circ f$ and $f_+^{-1} = f^{-1} \circ V$. Since V is an involution, we have

$$f_+^{-1} \circ f_+ = f^{-1} \circ V \circ V \circ f$$
$$= identity \quad \square$$

$L_+(n)$ layers are composed as $L(n)$ layers are in Section 3:

Definition 8. An *augmented parity circuit of width n and depth d*, or simply a $C_+(n, d)$ *circuit*, is a matrix of d $L_+(n)$ layers with keys denoted by $\mathbf{K} = K_1 \parallel K_2 \parallel \cdots \parallel K_d$ for which the n output bits of the $(i - 1)$-th circuit layer are the n input bits for the i-th circuit layer, for $2 \le i \le d$. The *key* for the $C_+(n, d)$ circuit is a $d \times n$ matrix with its d lines containing the circuit layer keys. A function $F_+(\mathbf{K}, A)$ is computed by a $C_+(n, d)$ circuit as:

$$F_+(\mathbf{K}, A) = f_+(K_d, f_+(K_{d-1}, \cdots, f_+(K_1, A) \cdots)$$

where each $f_+(K_i, .)$ is computed by a $L_+(n)$ circuit layer as defined before.

Since each function computed by $L_+(n)$ layers is invertible, as we have seen, the functions F_+ computed by $C_+(n, d)$ circuits are also invertible.

Table 2 shows the behavior of a $C_+(10, 3)$ circuit with the same input and the same key $\mathbf{K}^*$ in Example 1.

5 Swapping Properties for C_+ Circuits

The swapping properties for C_+ are clarified in the following Theorems 9, 10 and 12.

Table 2. $C_+(n,d)$ when $n = 10$ and $d = 3$

Input	1	0	1	1	0	0	1	0	0	1	swap ?
K_1	$-$	0	1	$-$	$+$	$+$	1	1	$-$	$+$	
Output	0	0	1	1	1	0	0	0	0	0	yes
K_2	$+$	1	0	1	1	$+$	0	$-$	$+$	$-$	
Output	0	1	1	0	0	0	0	1	0	1	no
K_3	$-$	0	1	$+$	$+$	0	$-$	$+$	$+$	$-$	
Output	0	0	0	1	1	0	1	0	1	1	yes

Theorem 9. *Let n be a positive integer ($n \geq 1$), let $A = a_1\, a_2\, \cdots\, a_n \in \{0,1\}^n$ be an n-bit input sequence to a circuit $C(n,d)$ with key $\mathbf{K}$ and let $B = b_1 b_2 \cdots b_n \in \{0,1\}^n$ be the n-bit output sequence. If A is uniformly generated, then*

$$Prob\{weight(B) \text{ is odd}\} = \frac{1}{2}, \quad Prob\{weight(B) \text{ is even}\} = \frac{1}{2}.$$

Proof By hypothesis, $Prob\{a_j = 0\} = 1/2$ and $Prob\{a_j = 1\} = 1/2$, for $1 \leq j \leq n$.

Let $p = Prob\{a_j \text{ is complemented by } \mathbf{K}\}$. Then:

$$Prob\{b_j = 0\} = Prob\{a_j = 1\} \cdot p + Prob\{a_j = 0\} \cdot (1 - p)$$
$$= (1/2)p + (1/2)(1 - p) = 1/2.$$

Similarly, one can show $Prob\{b_j = 1\} = 1/2$, for $1 \leq j \leq n$.

By mathematical induction, we show $Prob\{weight(B) \text{ is odd}\} = 1/2$ for any positive integer n. When $n = 1$, we have $Prob\{weight(B) \text{ is odd}\} = 1/2$. Let $B \in \{0, 1\}^k$ and $B^+ = (B \parallel b_{k+1}) \in \{0, 1\}^{k+1}$. If $Prob\{weight(B) \text{ is odd}\} = 1/2$, then we have

$$Prob\{weight(B^+) \text{ is odd}\} = Prob\{weight(B) \text{ is odd}\} \cdot Prob\{b_{k+1} = 0\}$$
$$+ Prob\{weight(B) \text{ is even}\} \cdot Prob\{b_{k+1} = 1\}$$
$$= (1/2) \cdot (1/2) + (1/2) \cdot (1/2)$$
$$= 1/2. \quad \square$$

From Theorem 9, a swapping occurs in an $L_+(n)$ layer with probability $1/2$. If A is uniformly generated, then we have the following formulas from well known results of binomial distribution,

$$Prob\{\text{one or more swappings occur in } C_+(n,d) \text{ circuit}\} = 1 - \left(\frac{1}{2}\right)^d.$$

$$\text{The average number of swappings in } C_+(n,d) \text{ circuit is} : \frac{d}{2}.$$

$$\text{The variance of the number of swappings in } C_+(n,d) \text{ circuit is} : \frac{d}{4}.$$

Let p be the probability that the swapping occurs in one layer. Considering now d layers, we have: the first formula is derived from the equation:

$$Prob\{\text{one or more swappings occur in } d \text{ layers}\}$$

$$= 1 - Prob\{\text{no swappings occur in } d \text{ layers}\}$$

The average and the variance are derived from well known results of binomial distribution: the average number of swappings in d layers is dp, and its variance is $dp(1-p)$. Since $p = 1/2$, we have the above formulas.

By randomization through VDS, the output of $F_+(\mathbf{K}, A)$ coincides with the output of $F(\mathbf{K}, A)$ with the following probability.

Theorem 10. *Let $P(n, d) = Prob\{F_+(\mathbf{K}, A) = F(\mathbf{K}, A)\}$ for a common set of input A and key $\mathbf{K}$, where $F_+(\mathbf{K}, A)$ is computed by $C_+(n, d)$, and $F(\mathbf{K}, A)$ is computed by $C(n, d)$. If A and $\mathbf{K}$ are uniformly generated, then*

$$P(n, 1) = \frac{1}{2},$$

$$P(n, d) = \left(\frac{1}{4} - \frac{1}{2^{n+1}} - \frac{1}{2^{n-1}+1}\right)\left(\frac{1}{2} - \frac{1}{2^n}\right)^{d-2} + \frac{1}{2^{n-1}+1} \quad \text{if } d \geq 2.$$

Proof

Case 1 $(d = 1)$: If the weight of $f(K, A)$ is odd, then $L \neq R$ and $f_+(K, A) = V \circ f(K, A) \neq f(K, A)$. Since $Prob\{f_+(K, A) \neq f(K, A)\} = 1/2$, we have $P(n, 1) = 1/2$.

Case 2 $(d \geq 2)$: Let $\mathbf{K_d}$ be the key of d layers. If $d = 2$, $f_+(K_1, A) = f(K_1, A)$ $(= A')$ and $f_+(K_2, A') \neq f(K_2, A')$, then $F_+(\mathbf{K_2}, A) \neq F(\mathbf{K_2}, A)$ with probability 1. If $f_+(K_1, A) \neq f(K_1, A)$, then $F_+(\mathbf{K_2}, A) = F(\mathbf{K_2}, A)$ with probability $1/2^n$. Thus, when $d = 2$, we have

$$
\begin{aligned}
&P(n, 2) \\
&= Prob\{F_+(\mathbf{K_2}, A) = F(\mathbf{K_2}, A)\} \\
&= Prob\{f_+(K_2, f_+(K_1, A)) = f(K_2, f(K_1, A))\} \\
&= Prob\{f_+(K_1, A) = f(K_1, A) \ (= A')\} \cdot Prob\{f_+(K_2, A') = f(K_2, A')\} \\
&\quad + Prob\{f_+(K_1, A) \neq f(K_1, A)\} \cdot \frac{1}{2^n} \\
&= \frac{1}{4} + \frac{1}{2}\frac{1}{2^n}
\end{aligned}
$$

More generally, when $d \geq 2$, we have

$$
\begin{aligned}
&P(n, d) \\
&= Prob\{F_+(\mathbf{K_d}, A) = F(\mathbf{K_d}, A)\} \\
&= Prob\{F_+(\mathbf{K_{d-1}}, A) = F(\mathbf{K_{d-1}}, A) \ (= A'')\} \cdot \\
&\quad Prob\{f_+(K_d, A'') = f(K_d, A'')\} \\
&\quad + Prob\{F_+(\mathbf{K_{d-1}}, A) \neq F(\mathbf{K_{d-1}}, A)\} \cdot \frac{1}{2^n} \\
&= P(n, d-1)\frac{1}{2} + (1 - P(n, d-1))\frac{1}{2^n} \\
&= P(n, d-1) \cdot \left(\frac{1}{2} - \frac{1}{2^n}\right) + \frac{1}{2^n}.
\end{aligned}
$$

By obtaining a finite geometric sum, we have the above formula. $\qquad\square$

6   Non-affineness

6.1   Non-affineness Measure

In general, for any fixed key $\mathbf{K}$, a cryptographic function $\mathcal{F}(\mathbf{K}, .)$ is affine if and only if the following equation holds for any input $A = (a_1, a_2, \cdots, a_n)$, $a_i \in \{0, 1\}$.

$$\mathcal{F}(\mathbf{K}, A) = \mathcal{F}(\mathbf{K}, 0) \oplus a_1 \mathcal{D}(\tilde{A}_1) \oplus a_2 \mathcal{D}(\tilde{A}_2) \oplus \cdots \oplus a_n \mathcal{D}(\tilde{A}_n), \qquad (1)$$

where $\mathcal{D}(\tilde{A}_i) = \mathcal{F}(\mathbf{K}, \tilde{A}_i) \oplus \mathcal{F}(\mathbf{K}, 0)$, and $\tilde{A}_i$ $(1 \le i \le n)$ denotes an input with only the i-th bit equal to 1, and $\oplus$ denotes the exclusive-or operation.

If there is a nonempty set of inputs A and a nonempty set of keys $\mathbf{K}$ for which equation (1) does not hold, then $\mathcal{F}$ is *non-affine*. A measure of non-affineness can be defined by the number of pairs (A, K) for which equation (1) does not hold. It is similar to a measure of non-linearity which is often defined by the order of the Boolean canonical form of the nonlinear function [5]. Thus, we introduce a normalized non-affineness measure as follows.

Definition 11. Let $\mathcal{A}$ be the input set, and $|\mathcal{A}|$ be the number of elements in $\mathcal{A}$. Let H be the number of elements in $\mathcal{A}$ for which equation (1) does not hold. A *key-dependent non-affineness measure* $N_{\mathbf{K}}$ for a cryptographic function $\mathcal{F}$ with key $\mathbf{K}$ is defined by

$$N_{\mathbf{K}} = \frac{H}{|\mathcal{A}|}.$$

Let $\mathcal{K}$ be the key set, and $|\mathcal{K}|$ be the number of elements in $\mathcal{K}$. A *non-affineness measure* N is defined by an average of $N_{\mathbf{K}}$ over the key set $\mathcal{K}$ as

$$N = \frac{\sum_{\mathcal{K}} N_{\mathbf{K}}}{|\mathcal{K}|}.$$

Note that $\mathcal{F}$ is affine if and only if $N = 0$. Even if $\mathcal{F}$ is non-affine, there may exist keys implying $N_{\mathbf{K}} = 0$. If $\mathcal{F}$ is $F_+(\mathbf{K}, A)$ computed by $C_+(n, d)$, then N is evaluated by all of the combinations of 2^n inputs and 4nd keys. In general the bounds for N are evaluated as follows.

Theorem 12. *Let $\mathcal{F}$ be a bijection from $\{0, 1\}^n$ to $\{0, 1\}^n$. A non-affineness measure N is bounded as*

$$0 \le N \le 1 - \frac{n+1}{2^n}.$$

Proof For any cryptographic function $\mathcal{F}$ and any key $\mathbf{K}$, equation (1) holds for the inputs $\tilde{A}_i$ $(1 \le i \le n)$ and the input equal to zero. That is, $n + 1$ inputs always satisfy equation (1). Thus, we have $H \le 2^n - (n + 1)$. Consequently, we have the above inequality.   □

Theorem 13. *Let $\mathcal{F}$ be a bijection from $\{0, 1\}^n$ to $\{0, 1\}^n$. If $n = 2$, then $\mathcal{F}$ is affine.*

Proof If $\mathcal{F}$ is a bijection from $\{0,1\}^2$ to $\{0,1\}^2$, then the function $\mathcal{F}$ has four outputs such as $B_1 = (0,0)$, $B_2 = (0,1)$, $B_3 = (1,0)$ and $B_4 = (1,1)$. Since $B_i = B_j \oplus B_k \oplus B_\ell$ for any combination of distinct subscripts (i, j, k, ℓ), equation (1) always holds. □

6.2 Non-affineness for C_+ Circuits

The non-affine conditions for $L_+(n)$ and $C_+(n,d)$ will be shown in Theorems 14 and 15.

Theorem 14. *A function $f_+(.)$ based on $L_+(n)$ is not affine if $n \geq 4$.*

Proof: We prove that there is a key K so that $f_+(K, A)$ is not affine. Consider four input sets A_0, A_1, A_2, A_3 and their outputs such that

$$B_i = (b_{i,1}, b_{i,2}, ..., b_{i,n}) = f_+(K, A_i) = f_+(K, (a_{i,1}, a_{i,2}, ..., a_{i,n})),$$

$$(0 \leq i \leq 3, \ n \geq 4).$$

$$
\begin{aligned}
A_0 &= (0,0,0,...,0), & (a_{0,j} &= 0 \ (1 \leq j \leq n)), \\
A_1 &= (1,0,0,...,0), & (a_{1,1} &= 1, \ a_{1,j} = 0 \ (j \neq 1)), \\
A_2 &= (0,1,0,...,0), & (a_{2,2} &= 1, \ a_{2,j} = 0 \ (j \neq 2)), \\
A_3 &= (1,1,0,...,0), & (a_{3,1} &= a_{3,2} = 1, \ a_{3,j} = 0 \ (j \neq 1,2)).
\end{aligned}
$$

If the function $f_+(.)$ is affine, then the following equation must hold for any key.

$$B_3 = B_0 \oplus B_1 \oplus B_2.$$

However, when the key K is all zero, we have

$$
\begin{aligned}
B_0 &= (0,0,0,...,0,0,...,0), & (b_{0,j} &= 0 \ (1 \leq j \leq n)), \\
B_1 &= (0,0,0,...,1,0,...,0), & (b_{1,n/2+1} &= 1, \ b_{1,j} = 0 \ (j \neq n/2+1)), \\
B_2 &= (0,0,0,...,0,1,...,0), & (b_{2,n/2+2} &= 1, \ b_{2,j} = 0 \ (j \neq n/2+2)), \\
B_3 &= (1,1,0,...,0,0,...,0), & (b_{3,1} &= b_{3,2} = 1, \ b_{3,j} = 0 \ (j \neq 1,2)),
\end{aligned}
$$

and

$$B_3 \neq B_0 \oplus B_1 \oplus B_2.$$

Thus, the function $f_+(.)$ is not affine if $n \geq 4$. □

Theorem 15. *A function $F_+(.)$ based on $C_+(n,d)$ is not affine if $n \geq 4$.*

Proof: Without loss of generality, we show the case when $n = 4$. We prove that we can construct keys $\mathbf{K} = K_1 \| K_2 \| \cdots \| K_d$ so that $F_+(\mathbf{K}, A)$ is not affine. To check non-affineness simply consider the four input sets A_0, A_1, A_2 and A_3 such that

$$A_0 = (0,0,0,0), \quad A_1 = (1,0,0,0), \quad A_2 = (0,1,0,0), \quad A_3 = (1,1,0,0)$$

Let B_i^ℓ be the output of the ℓ-th circuit layer $L_+(4)$ for input A_i.

$$B_i^\ell = f_+(K_\ell, f_+(K_{\ell-1}, \cdots f_+(K_1, (a_{i,1}, a_{i,2}, a_{i,3}, a_{i,4})), \quad (0 \le i \le 3).$$

If the function $F_+(.)$ is affine, then the following equation must hold for any key.

$$B_3^d = B_0^d \oplus B_1^d \oplus B_2^d.$$

However, we can choose key $\mathbf{K}$ so that this equation does not hold.
(1) If d is odd, each layer key is chosen as

$$K_\ell = (0, 0, 0, 0) \quad (1 \le \ell \le d).$$

Thus, we have

$$B_0^{d-1} = (0,0,0,0), \quad B_1^{d-1} = (1,0,0,0), \quad B_2^{d-1} = (0,1,0,0), \quad B_3^{d-1} = (1,1,0,0),$$

$$B_0^d = (0,0,0,0), \quad B_1^d = (0,0,1,0), \quad B_2^d = (0,0,0,1), \quad B_3^d = (1,1,0,0).$$

Consequently,

$$B_3^d \ne B_0^d \oplus B_1^d \oplus B_2^d.$$

(2) If d is even, each layer key is chosen as

$$K_\ell = (0,0,0,0), \quad (1 \le \ell \le d-2), \quad K_{d-1} = (+,-,0,0), \quad K_d = (+,0,0,0).$$

Thus, we have

$$B_0^{d-2} = (0,0,0,0), \quad B_1^{d-2} = (1,0,0,0), \quad B_2^{d-2} = (0,1,0,0), \quad B_3^{d-2} = (1,1,0,0),$$

$$B_0^{d-1} = (0,0,1,0), \quad B_1^{d-1} = (0,0,0,0), \quad B_2^{d-1} = (1,1,0,0), \quad B_3^{d-1} = (0,0,0,1),$$

$$B_0^d = (1,0,1,0), \quad B_1^d = (0,0,0,0), \quad B_2^d = (0,0,0,1), \quad B_3^d = (1,0,0,1).$$

Consequently,

$$B_3^d \ne B_0^d \oplus B_1^d \oplus B_2^d.$$

From cases (1) and (2), we conclude that function $F_+(.)$ is not affine when $n = 4$. The general case when $n \ge 6$ is similarly formalized as in the proof of Theorem 14. $\qquad\Box$

6.3 Evaluation of Non-affineness Measure for C_+ Circuits

6.3.1. Example We use here the same key $\mathbf{K}^*$ used in $C(10, 3)$ of Example 1 in Section 3 for comparison reasons.

Putting $\mathcal{F} = F_+$ and $D(\tilde{A}_i) = F_+(\mathbf{K}^*, 0) \oplus F_+(\mathbf{K}^*, \tilde{A}_i)$, we have checked whether or not equation (1) holds for all of 1024 inputs. There are only 64 inputs satisfying the affine equation (1) as shown in Table 3. Therefore, the function computed by this $C_+(n, d)$ circuit is *not affine*.

Since $|A| = 1024$ and $H = 960 (= 1024 - 64)$, we have $N_{\mathbf{K}^*} = 960/1024 = 0.9375$. Note that equation (1) holds for the inputs $\tilde{A}_i$ with only the i-th bit equal to 1 $(1 \le i \le 10)$, as shown in underlined numbers in Table 3.

Table 3. Inputs satisfying the affine equation for $C_+(10,3)$ with $\mathbf{K}^*$

000	008	023	062	070	0e3	117	174	19f	200	24c	284	2eb	31f	397	3f4
001	010	040	063	073	0ef	11b	178	1f0	20c	24f	288	2ef	370	399	3f8
002	013	043	067	080	100	160	193	1f4	22c	263	28c	313	378	39a	3f9
004	020	061	06b	08c	103	163	197	1fc	22f	26f	2ee	31b	37c	39b	3fc

6.3.2. Total Properties of Non-affineness By computer simulation, we have estimated the non-affineness measure N for $C_+(n,d)$ when $2 \leq n \leq 16$ and $1 \leq d \leq 10$. Table 4 shows the range of the values of $N_\mathbf{K}$, which have been exhaustively computed for all keys. For example, if $n = 4$ and $d = 1$, then $N_\mathbf{K} = N = 1/4 = 0.250$ for any key among all of $256(= 4^4)$ keys. From Table 4, we can observe that circuits $C_+(n,d)$ may imply $N_\mathbf{K} = 0$ for some keys if $n = 4$, $1 \leq d \leq 2$. However, $N_\mathbf{K} \neq 0$ otherwise. Table 5 shows the values of N obtained by an extensive computer simulation. From Table 5, we can observe that the degree of non-affineness N for $C_+(n,d)$ increases as n or d increases.

Table 4. Key-dependent non-affineness measure $N_\mathbf{K}$

n	d	Range of $N_\mathbf{K}$	No. of tested keys	Comments
4	1	$N_\mathbf{K} = 0.250$	$256(= 4^4)$	
4	2	$0.000 \leq N_\mathbf{K} \leq 0.500$	$65536(= 4^8)$	$N_\mathbf{K} = 0$ for 25.00% keys
4	3	$0.000 \leq N_\mathbf{K} \leq 0.625$	$16777216(= 4^{12})$	$N_\mathbf{K} = 0$ for 3.125% keys
6	1	$0.375 \leq N_\mathbf{K} \leq 0.750$	$4096(= 4^6)$	
8	1	$0.438 \leq N_\mathbf{K} \leq 0.813$	$65536(= 4^8)$	

Table 5. Non-affineness measure N (*: results of exhaustive tests)

	$n = 2$	$n = 4$	$n = 6$	$n = 8$	$n = 10$	$n = 16$
$d = 1$	0.00	0.250*	0.445*	0.566*	0.605	0.999
$d = 2$	0.00	0.266*	0.548	0.823	0.913	0.999
$d = 3$	0.00	0.350*	0.683	0.886	0.946	0.999
$d = 4$	0.00	0.405	0.740	0.901	0.969	0.999
$d = 6$	0.00	0.440	0.810	0.921	0.980	0.999
$d = 8$	0.00	0.492	0.853	0.939	0.983	0.999
$d = 10$	0.00	0.527	0.866	0.952	0.986	0.999

7 Other Cryptographic Properties for C_+ Circuits

Besides involution and non-affineness, other cryptographic properties such as nonlinearity, the probability of bit complementation, avalanche effect for $C_+(n, d)$ circuits can be clarified. These properties (except non-affineness) are similar to those for $C(n, d)$ circuits, which were described in [3]. For $C_+(n, d)$ circuits, the n and d values can be increased as necessary to properly secure a cryptosystem.

8 Conclusions

We have proposed a family of augmented non-affine parity circuits $C_+(n, d)$ by introducing a random involution called value-dependent swapping (VDS).

We also incorporated *VDS* into DES to make it stronger against differential [1] and linear cryptanalysis [2, 4].

References

1. Biham, E. and A. Shamir: Differential Cryptanalysis of DES-like Cryptosystems. presented at CRYPTO'90 (Aug.), 1990.
2. Kaneko, T., Koyama, K. and R. Terada: Dynamic swapping schemes and Differential Cryptanalysis. IEICE Transactions on Fundamentals, vol. E77-A, pp 1328-1336, 1994.
3. Koyama, K. and R. Terada: Nonlinear Parity Circuits and Their Cryptographic Applications. Proceedings of CRYPTO'90, 1990.
4. Nakao, Y., Kaneko, T., Koyama, K. and R. Terada: The security of an RDES cryptosystem against Linear Cryptanalysis. IEICE Transactions on Fundamentals, vol. E79-A, pp 12-19, 1996.
5. Rueppel, R.A.: Analysis and Design of Stream Ciphers. Springer-Verlag, Berlin, 1986.
6. Youssef, A.M., and S.E. Tavares: Cryptanalysis of 'nonlinear- parity circuits'. Electronic Letters, vol. 33 (7), pp. 585-586, 1997.

A New Byte-Oriented Block Cipher

X. Yi and K. Y. Lam
Department of Information Systems and Computer Science
National University of Singapore, Lower Kent Ridge Road, Singapore 119260
E-mail: {yix,lamky}@iscs.nus.edu.sg

S. X. Cheng and X. H. You
National Mobile Communications Research Laboratory
Southeast University, Nanjing, 210096, P.R.China
E-mail: {sxcheng,xhyou}@seu.edu.cn

Abstract. In this paper, a new byte-oriented block cipher with a key of length 64 bits is proposed. In the proposed cipher, the block length is 64 bits and only byte operations are utilized. The cipher structure is composed of two simple operations (exclusive-or and addition) and three cryptographically strong S-boxes (one is 8×8 S-box, two are 8-bit involution S-boxes) and chosen to provide necessary confusion and diffusion and facilitate both hardware and software implementation. The design principles of the proposed cipher are explained and a sample data is given.

1 Introduction

SAFER K-64 (for Secure And Fast Encryption Routine with a Key of length 64 bits) was developed for Cylink Corporation (Sunnyvale, CA, USA) as a non-proprietary cipher by J.L.Massey in reference [1]. The cipher uses only byte operations in the processes of encryption and decryption, which makes it particularly useful in applications such as smart cards where very limited processing power is available. The diffusion in SAFER K-64 is provided by an unorthodox linear transform called the Pseudo-Hadamard Transform. The use of the non-involution transform resulted in slightly different encryption and decryption processes. This is in contrast to most recently proposed iterated block ciphers. From the point of view of implementation, it has to be regarded as a blemish in an otherwise perfect design.

In this paper, we propose a new byte-oriented block cipher with a key of length 64 bits in according with Shannon's principles of confusion and diffusion for obtaining security in secret-key cipher [2]. The proposed cipher reserves some advantages of SAFER K-64, such as only byte operations in the processes of encryption and decryption, and overcomes the blemish of non-similarity of encryption and decryption processes of SAFER K-64.

The proposed cipher encrypts data in 64-bit blocks. A 64-bit block plaintext goes in one end of the algorithm, and a 64-bit block ciphertext comes out the other end. The cipher structure is composed of two simple operations (exclusive-or and addition) and three cryptographically strong S-boxes (one is 8×8 S-box, two are 8-bit involution S-boxes) and chosen to provide necessary confusion and diffusion and facilitate both hardware and software implementation. The deciphering process is the same as the enciphering process once the decryption key subblocks have been computed from the encryption key subblocks. It satisfies confusion and diffusion requirements.

The user-selected key of the cipher is 64 bits long. The key can be any 64-bit number and can be changed at any time. The 112 key subblocks of 8 bits used in the encryption process are generated from the 64-bit user-selected key. In its key schedule, the cipher is utilized to confuse the 64-bit user-selected key so as to produce the "independent" key subblocks.

The proposed cipher is introduced in Section 2. Some design principles of the cipher are revealed in section 3. Security of the cipher is considered in section 4.

2 Description of the proposed block cipher

The encryption process of the proposed cipher consists of 6 similar rounds followed by an output transformation. The complete first round and the output transformation are depicted in Fig.1 and Fig.2 respectively.

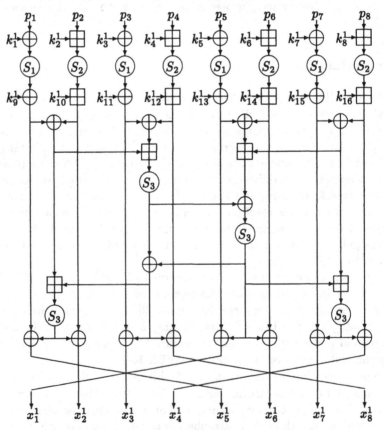

Fig.1: Computational graph of the complete first round

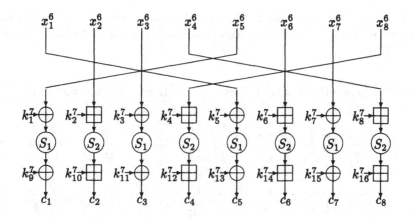

Fig.2: Computational graph of the output transformation

Each symbol in Fig.1 and Fig.2 is illustrated as follows:

(1) $\oplus$: bit-by-bit exclusive-OR of 8-bit subblocks.

(2) $\boxed{+}$: addition modulo 2^8 of 8-bit integers.

(3) S_1 and S_2: two involution boxes from 8 bits to 8 bits which are constructed based on the method proposed in reference [3].

(4) S_3: 8×8 substitution box which is obtained in the way introduced in reference [4].

(5) $(p_1, p_2, \cdots, p_8)$: plaintext of the cipher.

(6) $(k_1^i, k_2^i, \cdots, k_{16}^i)$: key subblocks of the i-th round.

(7) $(x_1^i, x_2^i, \cdots, x_8^i)$: output of the i-th round.

(8) $(c_1, c_2, \cdots, c_8)$: ciphertext of the cipher.

2.1 Encryption process

Fig.1 and Fig.2 are the overview of the proposed cipher. The 64-bit data block is firstly divided into eight 8-bit subblocks: $p_1, p_2, p_3, p_4, p_5, p_6, p_7, p_8$. These eight subblocks become the input to the first round of the algorithm. There are six rounds total. In each round shown in Fig.1, the eight subblocks are permuted and substituted by S_1, S_2 and S_3 and XORed and added with one another and with two 8-bytes (64-bit) of key material. Between each round, the first subblock and the fifth subblock are swapped and so are the fourth subblock and the eighth subblocks. After the sixth round, there is a final output transformation as shown in Fig.2. Finally, the eight 8-bit subblocks are reattached to produce the ciphertext.

2.2 Decryption process

The computational graph of the decryption process is essentially the same as that of the encryption process shown in Fig.1 and Fig.2, the only change being the decryption key subblocks are computed from the encryption key subblocks as shown in Table 1, where $-k_j^i$ denotes the additive inverse (modulo 2^8) of k_j^i, i.e., $-k_j^i \boxed{+} k_j^i = 0$.

Round	Encryption key subblocks	Decryption key subblocks
1-st	$k_1^1,\ k_2^1,\ k_3^1,\ k_4^1,\ k_5^1,\ k_6^1,\ k_7^1,\ k_8^1$	$k_9^7,\ -k_{10}^7, k_{11}^7, -k_{12}^7, k_{13}^7, -k_{14}^7, k_{15}^7, -k_{16}^7$
	$k_9^1, k_{10}^1, k_{11}^1, k_{12}^1, k_{13}^1, k_{14}^1, k_{15}^1, k_{16}^1$	$k_1^7,\ -k_2^7,\ k_3^7,\ -k_4^7,\ k_5^7,\ -k_6^7,\ k_7^7,\ -k_8^7$
2-nd	$k_1^2,\ k_2^2,\ k_3^2,\ k_4^2,\ k_5^2,\ k_6^2,\ k_7^2,\ k_8^2$	$k_{13}^6, -k_{10}^6, k_{11}^6, -k_{16}^6, k_9^6,\ -k_{14}^6, k_{15}^6, -k_{12}^6$
	$k_9^2, k_{10}^2, k_{11}^2, k_{12}^2, k_{13}^2, k_{14}^2, k_{15}^2, k_{16}^2$	$k_5^6,\ -k_2^6,\ k_3^6,\ -k_8^6,\ k_1^6,\ -k_6^6,\ k_7^6,\ -k_4^6$
3-rd	$k_1^3,\ k_2^3,\ k_3^3,\ k_4^3,\ k_5^3,\ k_6^3,\ k_7^3,\ k_8^3$	$k_{13}^5, -k_{10}^5, k_{11}^5, -k_{16}^5, k_9^5,\ -k_{14}^5, k_{15}^5, -k_{12}^5$
	$k_9^3, k_{10}^3, k_{11}^3, k_{12}^3, k_{13}^3, k_{14}^3, k_{15}^3, k_{16}^3$	$k_5^5,\ -k_2^5,\ k_3^5,\ -k_8^5,\ k_1^5,\ -k_6^5,\ k_7^5,\ -k_4^5$
4-th	$k_1^4,\ k_2^4,\ k_3^4,\ k_4^4,\ k_5^4,\ k_6^4,\ k_7^4,\ k_8^4$	$k_{13}^4, -k_{10}^4, k_{11}^4, -k_{16}^4, k_9^4,\ -k_{14}^4, k_{15}^4, -k_{12}^4$
	$k_9^4, k_{10}^4, k_{11}^4, k_{12}^4, k_{13}^4, k_{14}^4, k_{15}^4, k_{16}^4$	$k_5^4,\ -k_2^4,\ k_3^4,\ -k_8^4,\ k_1^4,\ -k_6^4,\ k_7^4,\ -k_4^4$
5-th	$k_1^5,\ k_2^5,\ k_3^5,\ k_4^5,\ k_5^5,\ k_6^5,\ k_7^5,\ k_8^5$	$k_{13}^3, -k_{10}^3, k_{11}^3, -k_{16}^3, k_9^3,\ -k_{14}^3, k_{15}^3, -k_{12}^3$
	$k_9^5, k_{10}^5, k_{11}^5, k_{12}^5, k_{13}^5, k_{14}^5, k_{15}^5, k_{16}^5$	$k_5^3,\ -k_2^3,\ k_3^3,\ -k_8^3,\ k_1^3,\ -k_6^3,\ k_7^3,\ -k_4^3$
6-th	$k_1^6,\ k_2^6,\ k_3^6,\ k_4^6,\ k_5^6,\ k_6^6,\ k_7^6,\ k_8^6$	$k_{13}^2, -k_{10}^2, k_{11}^2, -k_{16}^2, k_9^2,\ -k_{14}^2, k_{15}^2, -k_{12}^2$
	$k_9^6, k_{10}^6, k_{11}^6, k_{12}^6, k_{13}^6, k_{14}^6, k_{15}^6, k_{16}^6$	$k_5^2,\ -k_2^2,\ k_3^2,\ -k_8^2,\ k_1^2,\ -k_6^2,\ k_7^2,\ -k_4^2$
output	$k_1^7,\ k_2^7,\ k_3^7,\ k_4^7,\ k_5^7,\ k_6^7,\ k_7^7,\ k_8^7$	$k_9^1,\ -k_{10}^1, k_{11}^1, -k_{12}^1, k_{13}^1, -k_{14}^1, k_{15}^1, -k_{16}^1$
trans.	$k_9^7, k_{10}^7, k_{11}^7, k_{12}^7, k_{13}^7, k_{14}^7, k_{15}^7, k_{16}^7$	$k_1^1,\ -k_2^1,\ k_3^1,\ -k_4^1,\ k_5^1,\ -k_6^1,\ k_7^1,\ -k_8^1$

Table 1: The encryption key subblocks and decryption key subblocks

2.3 Key schedule

The 112 key subblocks of 8 bits used in the encryption process are generated from the 64-bit user-selected key K_0 (sixteen for each of the six rounds and sixteen more for the output transform).

Similar to the design decision employing precomputable subkeys in reference [5], these subkeys are required to be precomputed for faster operation because not precomputing the subkeys will result in slower operation.

In our key schedule, the proposed cipher is utilized to confuse the 64-bit user-selected key so as to produce the "independent" key subblocks in the sense that the given key subblocks can not deduce the uncertain key subblocks, i.e., protecting the cipher from cryptanalytic attacks using related keys (see [6], [7] and [8]).

The procedure for generating the encryption subkeys K_1^1 and K_2^1 that are required within the first round (where K_1^1 and K_2^1 act as $(k_1^1, k_2^1, \cdots, k_8^1)$ and $(k_9^1, k_{10}^1, \cdots, k_{16}^1)$ respectively) from the 64-bit user-selected key K_0 is shown in Fig.3.

In Fig.3, K_C denotes the constant encryption key of the generation process, in which the key subblock k_j^i is supposed to be $j + i \times 16$ for all i, j.

Just as the design decision regarding to subkeys in reference [5], these subkeys generated by using the above method are the one-way hash values of the user-selected key.

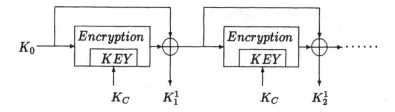

Fig.3: Computational graph of the generation process of the key subblocks

By analogy, the encryption key subblocks in the other round and output transformation can be generated. After 14 hashes, 112 key subblocks of the encryption process are finally produced.

Ideally, one wishes the entire subkeys sequence $K_1^1, K_2^1, \cdots, K_1^7, K_2^7$ to have the character of a sequence independently-chosen uniformly-random subkeys. Of course, this cannot be achieved in a strict sense because all of the subkeys in the sequence are determined entirely by the user-selected K_0. The real goal in the design of the key schedule is to make the departure from independence so complicated that it cannot be exploited by an attacker.

From the key schedule, we can know that no other equipment than the existing cipher is utilized, in other words, no attachment is required to generate the key subblocks.

3 Design principles for the proposed cipher

3.1 Similarity of encryption and decryption

The similarity of encryption and decryption means that decryption is essentially the same process as encryption, the only difference being that different key subblocks are used. This similarity results from

1. Using the output transformation in the encryption process so that the effect of $(k_1^1, k_2^1, \cdots, k_{16}^1)$ can be cancelled by the using inverse key subblocks $(k_9^1, -k_{10}^1, k_{11}^1, -k_{12}^1, k_{13}^1, -k_{14}^1, k_{15}^1, -k_{16}^1, k_1^1, -k_2^1, k_3^1, -k_4^1, k_5^1, -k_6^1, k_7^1, -k_8^1)$ in the decryption process.
2. Using an involution (i.e., a self-inverse function) with 32 bits input and 32 bits output within the cipher. The involution used in the cipher is shown in Fig.4. The self-inverse property is a consequence of the fact that the exclusive-OR of (A_1, A_3, A_5, A_7) and (A_2, A_4, A_6, A_8) is equal to the exclusive-OR of (B_1, B_3, B_5, B_7) and (B_2, B_4, B_6, B_8); Thus, the input to the $C\&D$ (Confusion and Diffusion) structure in Fig.4 is unchanged when $A_1, A_3, A_5, A_7,$ A_2, A_4, A_6 and A_8 are replaced by $B_1, B_3, B_5, B_7, B_2, B_4, B_6$ and B_8. Thus, if $B_1, B_3, B_5, B_7, B_2, B_4, B_6$ and B_8 are the inputs to the involution, the left half of the output is

$$(B_1, B_3, B_5, B_7) \oplus S((B_1, B_3, B_5, B_7) \oplus (B_2, B_4, B_6, B_8))$$
$$= (A_1, A_3, A_5, A_7) \oplus S((A_1, A_3, A_5, A_7) \oplus (A_2, A_4, A_6, A_8))$$

$$\oplus S((A_1, A_3, A_5, A_7) \oplus (A_2, A_4, A_6, A_8))$$
$$= (A_1, A_3, A_5, A_7)$$

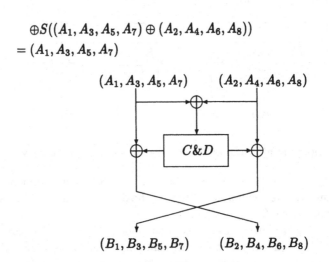

Fig.4: Computational graph of the involution function

Similarly, the right half of the output is (A_2, A_4, A_6, A_8).

3.2 Confusion and diffusion

The new byte-oriented block cipher is designed in accordance with Shannon's principles of confusion and diffusion for obtaining security in secret-key ciphers.

3.2.1 Confusion Confusion (see [2] [9] [10]) means that the ciphertext depends on the plaintext and key in a complicated and involved way.

The confusion in the proposed cipher is achieved by using the two 8-bit involution boxes S_1 and S_2 and the 8×8 substitution box S_3 and by mixing the two "incompatible" group operations $\oplus$ and $\boxed{+}$ with the signal.

It is well-known that S-boxes provide a DES-like crytposystem with the confusion property. They are the only nonlinear components of these ciphers. In order to achieve good confusion property, the two involution boxes and the substitution box in the cipher are chosen to have high nonlinearities (the nonlinearity of each output bit for these boxes is usually about 100).

In addition, the two algebraic group operations $\oplus$ and $\boxed{+}$ are incompatible in the sense that they do not satisfy the associative law, i.e.,

$$a\boxed{+}(b\oplus c) \neq (a\boxed{+}b)\oplus c$$

The use of these boxes and the mix of the two "incompatible" operations with the signal make the statistics of the ciphertext depend in a complicated way on the statistics of the plaintext.

3.2.2 Diffusion The diffusion requirement on a cipher (see [2] [9] [10]) is that each plaintext bit should influence every ciphertext bit and each key bit should influence every ciphertext bit.

For the proposed cipher, a check by computer has shown that the diffusion requirement is satisfied after the first round, i.e., each output bit of the first round depends on every bit of the plaintext and on every bit of the user-selected key.

Diffusion is provided by the two 8-bit involution boxes S_1 and S_2, the 8×8 substitution box S_3 and the $C\&D$ structure shown in Fig.5.

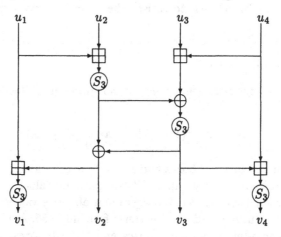

Fig.5: Computational graph of the $C\&D$ structure

The structure has a "complete diffusion" effect in the sense that each output subblock depends on every input subblock and the transformation denoted by the structure is invertible.

S_1, S_2 and S_3 are chosen to approximatively satisfy strict avalanche criterion, which also contribute to diffusion property of the cipher.

In a word, the cipher structure is chosen to provide the necessary diffusion for the cipher.

3.3 Implementations of the cipher

The cipher structure is chosen to facilitate both hardware and software implementations. In the encryption process, a regular modular structure is chosen so that the cipher can be easily implemented in hardware.

When implementing the cipher in hardware, the two 8-bit involution boxes S_1 and S_2 and the substitution box S_3 can be realized with three look-up tables of 256 bytes each, i.e., simple byte-in byte-out look-up tables. In view of only byte operations in the cipher, the cipher in particular suits for for applications such as smart cards where very limited processing power is available.

The cipher can also be easily implemented in software because only two basic operations on pair of 8-bit subblocks and three group of arrays are used in the encryption process.

4 Security considerations for the cipher

The two involution boxes S_1, S_2 and the S-box S_3 are the only nonlinear components of the cipher. In reference[13], Biham and Shamir showed that DES could be broken if poor S-boxes were used. For the DES-like cryptosystems to be cryptographically strong, so must their S-boxes. In other word, the security of DES-like cryptosystems depends heavily on the strength of the S-boxes used. Therefore, the choice of cryptographically strong S-boxes is an important concern in design of secure cryptosystems.

S_1, S_2 and S_3 are chosen to satisfy the following cryptographically strong properties.

4.1 High nonlinearity

The relation between nonlinearity and Walsh spectrum of Boolean function $f(x)$ is

$$N_f = 2^{n-1}(1 - 2^{-n} \max_{\omega \in GF(2^n)} | S_{<f>}(\omega) |) \tag{1}$$

For some 8-bit involution S-boxes and 8×8 S-boxes randomly produced by our procedure in reference [3] and [4], all Walsh spectrum values of eight output bits of them are computed out and the maximum absolute values among them are sought out. They usually fall into the range from 48 to 56. Among these S-boxes, we choose some 8-bit involution S-boxes and 8×8 S-boxes, the nonlinearities of eight output bits of which are greater than 100, as S_1, S_2 and S_3. It will guarantee that Rueppel's "closest linear approximation" [11] to S_1, S_2 and S_3 is of no much help to cryptanalysis.

4.2 Strict avalanche criterion and output bits independence criterion

The lack of accuracy of lower-dimensional approximations is a desirable property for a S-box, i.e., it should fulfill strict avalanche criterion (SAC) [12].

In order to choose some 8-bit involution S-boxes S_1, S_2 and 8×8 S-boxes S_3 which fulfill SAC from the above chosen S-boxes, the dependence matrices of the above chosen S-boxes are calculated out. Among them, we further choose some 8-bit involution S-boxes and 8×8 S-boxes, each element in the dependence matrices of which has a value close to 0.5, as S_1, S_2 and S_3. Therefore, S_1, S_2 and S_3 chosen in this step are ensured to approximately to fulfill SAC.

Another desirable property for a S-box is that output bit independence criterion (BIC) [12] should be satisfied. This will guarantee that every pair of output bits will have a correlation as close as possible to zero when any single input bit is inverted.

For these 8-bit involution S-boxes S_1, S_2 and 8×8 S-boxes S_3 chosen above, the correlation coefficient of every pair of the output bits is computed out. Among them, we further choose some 8-bit involution S-boxes and 8×8 S-boxes, the correlation coefficient of every pair of the output bits of which is less than 0.01, as S_1, S_2 and S_3. Hence, S_1, S_2 and S_3 chosen in this step are ensured to approximately to fulfill BIC.

4.3 Equiprobable input/output XOR distribution

Differential cryptanalysis introduced by Biham and Shamir [13] is based on using the imbalances in the input/output XOR distribution table, for a S-box, to predict the output XOR from the input XOR. If no information about the output changes can be gained from the knowledge of the input changes, each output XOR must occur with equal probability for each input XOR.

For these 8-bit involution S-boxes and 8×8 S-boxes which pass the above screen, their input/output XOR distributions are constructed. In most of their input/output XOR distributions matrices, the maximum entries are usually about 12, which is much less than 256. It is an evidence that large S-boxes have better cryptographic properties than small S-boxes. Finally, we choose these 8-bit involution S-boxes and 8×8 S-boxes as S_1, S_2 and S_3. An example of S_1, S_2 and S_3 chosen in the above way is shown in Appendix A.

In view of the cryptographically strong properties of S_1, S_2 and S_3, good confusion and good diffusion, the two basic features that contribute to the security of a block cipher, can be provided to the proposed cipher.

The best measure of security available today for an iterated cipher is its resistance to attack by differential cryptanalysis [13]. It is easy to show that, for the appropriate definition of difference between a pair of plaintext blocks (or a pair of ciphertext blocks), the new byte-oriented block cipher is a Markov cipher [14]. The preliminary results available today suggest that the proposed cipher appears to be secure against the differential cryptanalysis after 3 round.

5 Conclusion

A new byte-oriented block cipher with a key of length 64 bits has been proposed above. In the new cipher, the block length is 64 bits and only byte operations are utilized. Therefore, it is particularly useful in applications such as smart cards where very limited processing power is available. The cipher structure is composed of two simple operations (exclusive-or and addition) and three cryptographically strong S-boxes (one is 8×8 S-box, two are 8-bit involution S-boxes) and chosen to provide necessary confusion and diffusion and facilitate both hardware and software implementation.

A software implementation of the cipher is being carried out on a personal computer (486SX). The enciphering data rate of the algorithm reachs about 3.5Mbits per second. The sample data of encryption and decryption subkeys and the interior results of encryption and decryption processes are illustrated in Appendix B.

The security of the proposed cipher needs furth intensive investigation. The authors invite interested parties to attack this proposed cipher and will be grateful to receive the result of any such attacks.

Acknowledgement

The authors would like to thank Bruce Schneier for his helpful suggestions and valuable references.

References

1. J.L.Massey, "SAFER K-64: A byte-oriented block-ciphering algorithm", Proceedings of the Cambridge Algorithm Workshop'93, Lecture Notes in Computer Science **809**(1994)1-17.
2. C.E.Shannon, "Communication theory of secrecy system", Bell Systems Technical Journal, Vol.28, (1949)656–715.
3. X.Yi, S.X.Cheng, "A method for obtaining cryptographically strong 8-bit involution boxes", submitted to IEEE Communications Letters.
4. X.Yi, S.X.Cheng, X.H.You, K.Y.Lam, "A method for obtaining cryptographically strong 8x8 s-boxes", Proceedings of IEEE Global Communications Conference, Globecom'97.
5. B.Schneier, "Description of a new variable-length key, 64-bit block cipher (Blowfish)", Proceedings of 1994 Fast Software Encryption, Lecture Notes in Computer Science **809** (1994)191–204.
6. E.Biham, "New types of cryptanalytic attacks using related keys", Proceedings of Eurocrypt'93, LNCS **765**. Journal of Cryptology, **Vol.7, No.4**, (1993)229-246
7. J. Kelsey, B. Schneier, and D. Wagner, "Key-schedule cryptanalysis of 3-WAY, IDEA, G-DES, RC4, SAFER, and Triple-DES," Advances in Cryptology, Proceedings of CRYPTO 96, Lecture Notes in Computer Science **1109** (1996)237-251.
8. J. Kelsey, B. Schneier, and D. Wagner, "Related-key cryptanalysis of 3-WAY, Biham-DES, CAST, DES-X, newDES, RC2, and TEA", Proceedings of ICICS'97, Springer-Verlag, November 1997.
9. X.Lai, J.L.Massey, "A proposal for a new block encryption standard", Advances in Cryptology, Proceedings of EUROCRYPT'90, Lecture Notes in Computer Science **473** (1991)389–404.
10. X.Lai, "On the design and security of block cipher", ETH Series in Information Processing, **V.1**, Konstanz: Hartung–Gorre Verlag, 1992.
11. A.Rueppel, "Analysis and design of stream ciphers", Springer-Verlag, Heidelberg and New York, 1986.
12. A.Webster, S.Tavares, "On the design of S-boxes", Advances in Cryptology, Proc. of CRYPTO'85, Lecture Notes in Computer Science (1986)523–534.
13. E.Biham, A.Shamir, "Differential cryptanalysis of DES-like cryptosystems", Journal of Cryptology, **Vol.4, No.1**, (1991)3-72
14. X.Lai, J.L.Massey, "Markov ciphers and differential cryptanalysis", Advances in Cryptology, Proceedings of EUROCRYPT'91, Lecture Notes in Computer Science **547** (1991)17-38.

$$S_1 = \begin{bmatrix}
143 & 187 & 199 & 104 & 217 & 170 & 243 & 234 & 119 & 180 & 200 & 203 & 101 & 50 & 94 & 83 \\
117 & 90 & 136 & 148 & 71 & 63 & 32 & 181 & 245 & 125 & 122 & 169 & 248 & 87 & 225 & 80 \\
22 & 163 & 92 & 57 & 250 & 140 & 255 & 150 & 223 & 45 & 153 & 47 & 249 & 41 & 178 & 43 \\
78 & 152 & 13 & 142 & 164 & 204 & 141 & 215 & 196 & 35 & 102 & 195 & 172 & 105 & 131 & 21 \\
186 & 91 & 103 & 69 & 236 & 67 & 93 & 20 & 210 & 247 & 113 & 212 & 194 & 155 & 48 & 235 \\
31 & 229 & 149 & 15 & 189 & 110 & 165 & 29 & 231 & 137 & 17 & 65 & 34 & 70 & 14 & 211 \\
201 & 240 & 146 & 246 & 128 & 12 & 58 & 66 & 3 & 61 & 161 & 193 & 190 & 157 & 85 & 244 \\
177 & 74 & 198 & 124 & 207 & 16 & 241 & 8 & 220 & 226 & 26 & 238 & 115 & 25 & 176 & 224 \\
100 & 171 & 183 & 62 & 160 & 254 & 167 & 239 & 18 & 89 & 227 & 219 & 37 & 54 & 51 & 0 \\
191 & 216 & 98 & 228 & 19 & 82 & 39 & 218 & 49 & 42 & 221 & 77 & 251 & 109 & 184 & 205 \\
132 & 106 & 168 & 33 & 52 & 86 & 206 & 134 & 162 & 27 & 5 & 129 & 60 & 175 & 192 & 173 \\
126 & 112 & 46 & 208 & 9 & 23 & 252 & 130 & 158 & 209 & 64 & 1 & 233 & 84 & 108 & 144 \\
174 & 107 & 76 & 59 & 56 & 237 & 114 & 2 & 10 & 96 & 253 & 11 & 53 & 159 & 166 & 116 \\
179 & 185 & 72 & 95 & 75 & 214 & 213 & 55 & 145 & 4 & 151 & 139 & 120 & 154 & 232 & 40 \\
127 & 30 & 121 & 138 & 147 & 81 & 242 & 88 & 222 & 188 & 7 & 79 & 68 & 197 & 123 & 135 \\
97 & 118 & 230 & 6 & 111 & 24 & 99 & 73 & 28 & 44 & 36 & 156 & 182 & 202 & 133 & 38
\end{bmatrix}$$

$$S_2 = \begin{bmatrix}
29 & 228 & 120 & 45 & 37 & 103 & 207 & 254 & 208 & 76 & 89 & 135 & 246 & 167 & 80 & 236 \\
175 & 234 & 206 & 150 & 137 & 32 & 109 & 82 & 212 & 193 & 106 & 252 & 180 & 0 & 186 & 138 \\
21 & 68 & 71 & 94 & 160 & 4 & 128 & 172 & 183 & 73 & 223 & 130 & 97 & 3 & 255 & 145 \\
96 & 100 & 98 & 147 & 182 & 166 & 184 & 93 & 119 & 117 & 238 & 222 & 83 & 154 & 191 & 244 \\
224 & 194 & 215 & 115 & 33 & 75 & 81 & 34 & 148 & 41 & 189 & 69 & 9 & 226 & 225 & 210 \\
14 & 70 & 23 & 60 & 118 & 122 & 104 & 209 & 139 & 10 & 232 & 230 & 211 & 55 & 35 & 249 \\
48 & 44 & 50 & 239 & 49 & 161 & 188 & 5 & 86 & 153 & 26 & 162 & 203 & 22 & 155 & 217 \\
132 & 158 & 123 & 67 & 240 & 57 & 84 & 56 & 2 & 190 & 85 & 114 & 136 & 227 & 250 & 140 \\
38 & 221 & 43 & 187 & 112 & 142 & 165 & 11 & 124 & 20 & 31 & 88 & 127 & 213 & 133 & 149 \\
245 & 47 & 216 & 51 & 72 & 143 & 19 & 251 & 241 & 105 & 61 & 110 & 218 & 185 & 113 & 237 \\
36 & 101 & 107 & 235 & 229 & 134 & 53 & 13 & 177 & 205 & 196 & 179 & 39 & 201 & 220 & 16 \\
181 & 168 & 202 & 171 & 28 & 176 & 52 & 40 & 54 & 157 & 30 & 131 & 102 & 74 & 121 & 62 \\
248 & 25 & 65 & 200 & 170 & 253 & 214 & 243 & 195 & 173 & 178 & 108 & 233 & 169 & 18 & 6 \\
8 & 87 & 79 & 92 & 24 & 141 & 198 & 66 & 146 & 111 & 156 & 247 & 174 & 129 & 59 & 42 \\
64 & 78 & 77 & 125 & 1 & 164 & 91 & 242 & 90 & 204 & 17 & 163 & 15 & 159 & 58 & 99 \\
116 & 152 & 231 & 199 & 63 & 144 & 12 & 219 & 192 & 95 & 126 & 151 & 27 & 197 & 7 & 46
\end{bmatrix}$$

$$S_3 = \begin{bmatrix}
82 & 134 & 32 & 54 & 135 & 38 & 250 & 81 & 174 & 245 & 110 & 44 & 203 & 153 & 19 & 164 \\
120 & 136 & 169 & 115 & 197 & 146 & 220 & 26 & 137 & 112 & 205 & 247 & 30 & 232 & 60 & 222 \\
133 & 64 & 73 & 179 & 55 & 74 & 3 & 198 & 180 & 241 & 2 & 25 & 45 & 31 & 97 & 102 \\
240 & 100 & 140 & 252 & 75 & 111 & 161 & 217 & 178 & 206 & 10 & 186 & 237 & 157 & 229 & 6 \\
7 & 61 & 68 & 195 & 156 & 132 & 243 & 0 & 53 & 87 & 80 & 95 & 148 & 131 & 141 & 123 \\
201 & 208 & 149 & 124 & 159 & 88 & 175 & 183 & 51 & 173 & 171 & 230 & 253 & 219 & 9 & 193 \\
78 & 76 & 216 & 228 & 106 & 63 & 218 & 214 & 226 & 72 & 192 & 251 & 166 & 128 & 182 & 255 \\
92 & 22 & 43 & 224 & 113 & 59 & 20 & 139 & 163 & 121 & 101 & 191 & 185 & 151 & 41 & 83 \\
56 & 86 & 67 & 11 & 176 & 172 & 248 & 158 & 15 & 187 & 207 & 152 & 84 & 12 & 177 & 122 \\
189 & 143 & 118 & 4 & 96 & 170 & 91 & 223 & 89 & 27 & 1 & 145 & 79 & 23 & 167 & 246 \\
94 & 14 & 46 & 204 & 150 & 108 & 168 & 103 & 16 & 138 & 200 & 13 & 42 & 107 & 154 & 69 \\
98 & 162 & 70 & 65 & 37 & 184 & 104 & 50 & 126 & 155 & 52 & 236 & 165 & 35 & 190 & 233 \\
244 & 85 & 238 & 18 & 235 & 196 & 127 & 231 & 194 & 93 & 33 & 130 & 29 & 47 & 58 & 227 \\
211 & 160 & 40 & 114 & 99 & 249 & 242 & 66 & 209 & 117 & 144 & 181 & 28 & 210 & 17 & 225 \\
105 & 49 & 36 & 213 & 202 & 234 & 129 & 239 & 5 & 147 & 57 & 48 & 142 & 221 & 34 & 125 \\
254 & 90 & 116 & 212 & 24 & 21 & 8 & 188 & 109 & 215 & 119 & 39 & 199 & 77 & 62 & 71
\end{bmatrix}$$

Appendix A: S-boxes

The entry of the i-th row and the j-th column in the above matrixes S_1, S_2 and S_3 denotes the substitution result of $16 \cdot (i-1) + (j-1)$ by S_1, S_2 and S_3, where $i, j = 1, 2, \cdots, 16$.

Appendix B: Sample data

For the proposed cipher, according to the key schedule, when the user-selected key is 64-bit all-zero block, the encryption key subblocks are generated and the decryption key subblocks are computed as follows:

ROUND	ENCRYPTION KEY								DECRYPTION KEY							
1	8	17	180	219	26	111	1	193	243	177	243	159	247	55	217	212
	172	219	11	82	165	156	156	168	202	104	242	188	223	3	44	156
2	27	108	232	64	79	88	232	223	28	57	178	15	38	46	253	56
	45	84	193	177	32	191	219	60	78	81	27	193	58	139	87	80
3	79	144	70	147	63	221	120	170	1	64	95	128	29	227	84	177
	61	174	234	71	80	151	53	9	243	216	240	197	94	86	157	57
4	128	99	140	122	180	184	129	118	226	136	219	85	96	206	114	182
	96	120	219	74	226	50	114	171	180	157	140	138	128	72	129	134
5	94	40	240	199	243	170	157	59	80	82	234	247	61	105	53	185
	29	192	95	79	1	29	84	128	63	112	70	86	79	35	120	109
6	58	175	27	176	78	117	87	63	32	172	193	196	45	65	219	79
	38	199	178	200	28	210	253	241	79	148	232	33	27	168	232	192
output	202	152	242	68	223	253	44	100	172	37	11	174	165	100	156	88
transform.	243	79	243	97	247	201	217	44	8	239	180	37	26	145	1	63

By using the above encryption key subblocks and decryption key subblocks, the ciphertext and interior encryption results corresponding to 64-bit plaintext $(0, 0, 0, 0, 0, 0, 0, 0)$ and the interior decryption results corresponding to the ciphertext are shown as follows:

ROUND	ENCIPHERING								DECIPHERING							
plaintext	0	0	0	0	0	0	0	0	161	56	99	190	233	35	120	13
1	14	247	155	243	233	164	21	208	98	189	224	68	214	183	232	94
2	187	236	184	10	189	143	87	65	151	28	158	33	191	227	42	237
3	99	157	153	13	249	230	191	246	121	149	228	118	234	163	241	85
4	246	171	155	170	212	44	45	42	231	54	111	172	82	98	30	0
5	91	93	142	99	254	47	104	253	238	67	189	76	18	218	17	68
6	95	52	77	243	62	235	70	234	219	197	2	73	223	117	39	193
ciphertext	161	56	99	190	233	35	120	13	0	0	0	0	0	0	0	0

Practice-Oriented Provable-Security

Mihir Bellare[1]

Dept. of Computer Science & Engineering, University of California at San Diego, 9500 Gilman Drive, La Jolla, CA 92093, USA. E-Mail: `mihir@cs.ucsd.edu`. URL: `http://www-cse.ucsd.edu/users/mihir`.

1 Introduction

This short article is intended to complement my invited talk at this conference.[1] I would like to try to introduce you to a certain, relatively new, sub-area of cryptography that we have been calling *practice-oriented provable-security*. It is about applying the ideas of "provably security" to the derivation of practical, secure protocols. I believe it is a fruitful blend of theory and practice that is able to enrich both sides and has by now had some impact on real world security.

I will begin by describing the basic idea behind provable security. (For many of you, this will be mostly recall, but some novel viewpoints or examples may enter.) Next, I will illustrate practice-oriented provable security by providing an overview of a treatment of symmetric (ie. private key) encryption in this setting. Finally I will point briefly to the many other topics treated in this area. I hope to leave you feeling there is scope here both for interesting research and for application.

2 Protocols, primitives, proofs and practice

The basic task in cryptography is to enable to parties to communicate "securely" over an insecure channel, namely in a way that guarantees privacy and authenticity of their transmissions. (There are many other tasks as well, but we will begin by thinking about this basic one.)

2.1 Protocols and primitives: the problem

PROTOCOLS: THE END GOAL. To enable secure communication, one wants cryptographic *protocols* or *schemes*. For example, an encryption scheme enables users to communicate privately. Such a scheme is specified by a pair $(\mathcal{E}, \mathcal{D})$ of algorithms. The first, run by the sender, takes a *key* and the *plaintext* M to create a *ciphertext* C, which is transmitted to the receiver. The latter applies $\mathcal{D}$, which takes a key and the received ciphertext to recover the plaintext. (Roughly, the security property desired is that an adversary can't learn anything useful about

---

[1] The bulk of my talk was about the materiel in [4]. This article is intended to provide some background and tell you about the bigger picture.

the plaintext given the ciphertext, but we will get into this more later.) They key could be a shared one (this is the private key or symmetric setting) or the keys for encryption and decryption could be different (the public key or asymmetric setting). Designing an encryption scheme means designing the two algorithms $\mathcal{E}$ and $\mathcal{D}$.

Similarly, a message authentication scheme (or protocol) enables parties to tag their data so that the recipient is assured that the data originates with the person claiming to have sent it and has not been tampered with on the way.

The design of such protocols is the end goal for the cryptographer. However, it is not an easy one to reach. What makes it reachable at present is that we have very good *primitives* on which to *base* these protocols.

PRIMITIVES: THE TOOLS. Julius Caesar also wanted to design protocols. He had a much harder time than we do today, because he didn't have DES or the RSA function.

The latter are examples of what I will call *atomic primitives*. Certainly, they are cryptographic objects of some sort. What is it that distinguishes them from protocols? The distinction is that in their purest and rawest state, atomic primitives don't solve any cryptographic problem we actually care about. We must *use* them appropriately to construct protocols to solve the problems that matter. For example, DES based CBC encryption is a way of using DES to do symmetric encryption. By first hashing a message and then decrypting under RSA we have a possible way to do digital signatures based on the RSA function. (Whether these ways are good or bad ways of accomplishing the goal is another question, to be addressed later.) Thus, atomic primitives are simple building blocks that must be put together to yield protocols.

Good atomic primitives are rare, as are people who understand their workings. Certainly, an important effort in cryptography is to design new atomic primitives and cryptanalyze them and old ones. This, however, is not the part of cryptography I want to talk about. The reason is that the design (or discovery) of good atomic primitives is more an art than a science. On the other hand, I'd like to claim that the design of protocols can be made a science.

THE QUESTION. We will view a cryptographer as an engine for turning atomic primitives into protocols. That is, we focus on protocol design under the assumption that good atomic primitives exist. Some examples of the kinds of questions we are interested in are these. What is the best way to encrypt a large text file using DES, assuming DES is secure? What is the best way to design a signature scheme using the RSA function, assuming the latter is one-way? How "secure" are known methods for these tasks? What do such questions even mean, and can we find a scientific framework in which to ask and answer them?

THE PROBLEM. The problem with protocol design is that a poorly designed protocol can be insecure *even though the underlying atomic primitive is good*. An example is ECB (Electronic Code-Book) mode encryption with a block cipher. It is not a good encryption scheme because partial information about the plaintext leaks. Yet this is no fault of the underlying atomic primitive (typically DES). Rather, the atomic primitive was mis-used.

Indeed, lots of protocols are broken. Yet the good atomic primitives, like DES and RSA, have never been convincingly broken. We would like to build on the strength of atomic primitives in such a way that protocols can "inherit" this strength, not loose it!

2.2 Provable security: Reductions

The idea of provable security was introduced in the pioneering work of Gold-wasser and Micali [17]. They developed it in the particular context of asymmetric encryption, but it soon spread to be applied to other tasks. (Of these, the most basic were pseudorandomness [13,27,16] and digital signatures [18]).

WHAT IS PROVABLE SECURITY? The paradigm is as follows. Take some goal, like achieving privacy via encryption. The first step is to make a formal adversarial model and *define* what it *means* for an encryption scheme to be secure. With this in hand, a particular scheme, based on some particular atomic primitive, can be analyzed from the point of view of meeting the definition. Eventually, one shows that the scheme "works" via a *reduction*. The reduction shows that the *only way* to defeat the protocol is to break the underlying atomic primitive. In other words, there is no need to directly cryptanalyze the protocol: if you were to find a weakness in it, you would have unearthed one in the underlying atomic primitive. So you might as well focus on the atomic primitive. And if we believe the latter is secure, we *know*, without further cryptanalysis of the protocol, that the protocol is secure.

An important sub-part of the last step is that in order to enable a reduction one must also have a formal notion of what is meant by the security of the underlying atomic primitive: what attacks, exactly, does it withstand? For example, we might assume RSA is a one-way function.

Here is another way of looking at what reductions do. When I give you a reduction from the one-wayness of RSA to the security of my protocol, I am giving you a transformation with the following property. Suppose you claim to be able to break my protocol. Let P be the program that does this. My transformation takes P and puts a simple "wrapper" around it, resulting in a protocol P'. This protocol P' provably breaks RSA. Conclusion? As long as we believe you can't break RSA, there could be no such program P. In other words, my protocol is secure.

Those familiar with the theory of NP-completeness will recognize that the basic idea of reductions is the same. When we provide a reduction from SAT to some problem we are saying our problem is hard unless SAT is easy; when we provide a reduction from RSA to our protocol, we are saying the latter is secure unless RSA is easy.

Here, I think, is a beautiful and powerful idea. Some of us by now are so used to it that we can forget how innovative it was. And for those not used to it, it can be hard to understand (or, perhaps, believe) at first hearing, perhaps because it delivers so much. Protocols designed this way truly have superior security guarantees.

NOMENCLATURE. In some ways the term "provable security" is misleading. As the above indicates, what is probably the central step is providing a model and definition, which does not involve proving anything. And one does not "prove a scheme secure:" one provides a reduction of the security of the scheme to the security of some underlying atomic primitive. For that reason, I sometimes use the term "reductionist security" to refer to this genre of work.

THE COMPLEXITY-THEORETIC APPROACH. The precise formalization of provable security can take many forms. The theoretical literature has chosen, for the most part, to develop it in a complexity theoretic framework where one talks about "polynomial time" adversaries and transformations, and "negligible success probabilities." This approach was convenient for a field striving to develop a technical idea of great depth. Complexity-based cryptography has been remarkably successful, coming up with definitions for many central cryptographic primitives, and constructions based on "minimal assumptions." For a brief introduction to this body of work, refer to the recent survey by Goldreich [15].

IN PRACTICE? The potential for the idea of provable security to impact practice is large. Yet its actual impact had been disappointingly small, in the sense that these ideas were reflected almost not at all in protocols used in practice. Here are some possible reasons.

In practice, block ciphers are the most popular atomic primitive, especially for private key cryptography. Yet the provable security line of work (prior to the development of the practice-oriented variant) omitted any treatment of schemes based on block ciphers: only number-theoretic atomic primitives were deemed adequate as a basis for protocol design. In particular some of the world's most used protocols, such as CBC MAC [1] or encryption [21,2], seemed to be viewed as outside the domain of provable security.[2]

·The main generic disadvantage of the schemes delivered by the traditional provable security approach is that they are inefficient.[3] This is due in part to the complexity of the constructions. But it is also due in part to a reliance on inefficient atomic primitives. For example, a MAC would be constructed out of a one-way function like RSA rather than out of a block cipher. This takes us back to the above.

Finally, some aspects of the complexity-theoretic approach unfortunately distanced provable security from practice. For example, practioners need numbers: how many cycles of adversary computation can the scheme withstand, how many bits is the security parameter? These are only loosely captured by "polynomials" or "negligible probabilities." To make provable security useful, reductions and security analyses must be concrete. Theoreticians will say, correctly, that this

---

[2] Luby and Rackoff [20] studied the Feistel structure behind DES, but what I am talking about is to look at protocols that use DES and ask about their security.

[3] Typically the gap relative to what is desirable in practice is enormous. In some cases it is small, but still seems enough to preclude usage.

information can be obtained by looking at their proofs. But this view obscures the importance of working on improving the security of reductions.[4]

Practice-oriented provable security attempts to remedy this by appropriate paradigm shifts.

3 Practice-oriented provable security

Practice-oriented provable security as I discuss it was introduced in a set of papers authored by myself and Phil Rogaway [7,6,5]. We preserve and focus on the two central ideas of the provable security approach: the introduction of *notions*, or *definitions* that enable us to think about protocols and atomic primitives in a systematic way, and the idea of doing reductions. But we modify the viewpoints, models, and problems treated. Here are some elements of the approach and work to date.

3.1 Using block ciphers

Block ciphers like the DES are the most ubiquitous tool in practical cryptographic protocol design. However, as indicated above, traditionally nothing was proved about protocols that use them. An important element of our line of work is to integrate block ciphers into the fabric of provable security. On the one hand we analyze existing schemes that use block ciphers to assess how well they meet strong, formal notions of security; on the other hand we design new schemes based on block ciphers and show they meet such notions. In the first category are our analyses of the CBC MAC [6] and analyses of various modes of operation of a block cipher [4]. In the second category are constructions like the XOR MAC [5] or the cascade [3].

Key to these results (and perhaps more important than any individual result) is that we treat block ciphers systematically by formally modeling them in some way. Specifically, the suggestion of [6], followed in the other works, was to model a block cipher as a *finite pseudorandom function* (FPRF) family. (The fundamental notion of a pseudorandom function family is due to Goldreich, Goldwasser and Micali [16]. The finite variant was introduced in [6].) Roughly, we are assuming that as long as you don't know the underlying key, the input-output behavior of a block cipher closely resembles that of a random function.

Thus, the theorems in the mentioned papers say that a scheme (eg. CBC MAC) is secure unless one can detect some deviation from random behavior in the underlying block cipher. Underlying this claim is a reduction, as usual in the provable security approach, showing how to break the cipher given any way to break the scheme based on it.

The idea of treating block ciphers as pseudorandom functions provides a fresh way of looking at block ciphers from both the design and usage perspective. On

---

[4] This is not to say concrete security has always been ignored. One person who from the beginning has systematically addressed concrete security in his works is Claus Schnorr. See any of his papers involving cryptographic reductions.

the one hand, this view can form the basis for analyses of many other block cipher based schemes. On the other hand, we suggest it be a design criterion for future block ciphers (a view that new efforts such as AES do seem to support) and that existing ciphers should be cryptanalyzed to see how well they meet this goal.

3.2 Concrete security

Practice oriented provable security attempts to explicitly capture the inherently *quantitative* nature of security, via a *concrete* or *exact* treatment of security. Rather than prove asymptotic results about the infeasability of breaking a protocol in polynomial time, we present and prove "exact" or "concrete" reductions. Our results have the form: "If DES withstands an attack in which the adversary gets to see 2^{36} plaintext-ciphertext pairs, then our protocol is secure against an adversary who can run for t steps, for the following value of t." This enables a protocol designer to know exactly how much security he/she gets. And it brings a new dimension to protocols: rather than just being secure or non-secure, one can be "more" secure than another.

For example, the theorem of [6] characterizing the security of the CBC MAC says that an adversary who runs for time t and sees q correctly MACed messages has chance at most $\epsilon + (3q^2n^2 + 1)/2^l$ of correctly forging the MAC of a new message, where l is the block length of the underlying cipher, n is the number of blocks in any message to which the MAC applies, and ϵ captures the security of the cipher, specifically being the chance of detecting a deviation of the cipher from random behavior in time $t + O(nql)$ given nq input-output examples of the cipher under the same key. (This ϵ is of course a function of the key length of the underlying cipher, but the latter does not need to appear explicitly.) Thus, a user sees exactly how the chance of forgery increases with the number of messages MACed.

Another aspect of the concrete security treatment is to try to preserve as much as possible of the strength of the underlying atomic primitive in transforming it to the protocol. This means we aim for reductions as *strong* as possible. This is important because reduction strength translates directly to protocol efficiency in practice. A weak reduction means that to get the same level of security in our protocol we must use larger keys for the underlying atomic primitive, and this means slower protocols. If the reduction is strong, shorter keys will suffice and the protocol is more efficient. Reduction quality plays a significant role in [6,5,9,11,3,4] all of which achieve tight or close to tight reductions.

We found that *improving* the concrete security was a rich and rewarding line of work, and thinking about it greatly increases understanding of the problem.

In [4] we also concern ourselves with how different formalizations of a notion (in this case, secure encryption) are affected when concrete security is an issue.

3.3 Security versus attacks

Practitioners typically think only about concrete attacks; theoreticians ignore them, since they prove the security. Under the practice oriented provable security approach, attacks and security emerge as opposite sides of the same coin, and complement each other. Attacks measure the degree of insecurity; our quantitative bounds measure the degree of security. When the two meet, we have completely characterized the security of the protocol.

For example, the security of the CBC MAC shown in [6] is the flip-side of attacks like those of Preneel and Van Oorschot [25]. (The latter say that the CBC MAC can be broken once $2^{l/2}$ messages have been MACed, where l is the block length of the underlying cipher. We say, roughly, that it *can't* be broken when *fewer* than this many messages are MACed.) Thus the results of [6,25] complement each other very well. Yet, the literature on these subjects does not reflect this duality appropriately.

We found that even when proofs are provided, much is to be gained by finding the best possible attacks. We find *new kinds* of attacks, which break the system as measured by our more stringent notions of security: an encryption scheme is broken of you can tell whether the message encrypted was 0 or 1, not just if you find the key. This is actually important in practice. Meanwhile, these attacks provide, effectively, the lower bounds to our concrete security analyses, telling us whether the proven security is optimal or not. Publications in which we assess the optimality of our reductions via attacks include [5,3,4].

3.4 The random oracle model

Sometimes, using pseudorandom function families or one-way functions alone, we are not able to find schemes efficient enough for practice. This is true for example in the case of public key encryption or signatures. In such cases, we turn to the random oracle paradigm.

The random oracle paradigm was introduced in [8] as a bridge between theory and practice. The idea is a simple one: namely, provide all parties —good and bad alike— with access to a (public) function h; prove correct a protocol assuming h is truly random, ie. a random oracle; later, in practice, set h to some specific function derived in some way from a standard cryptographic hash function like SHA-1 [22] or RIPEMD-160 [14].

We used the random oracle paradigm most importantly to design OAEP [9] and PSS [11]. These are schemes for (public key) encryption and signature (respectively) based on RSA. They are as efficient as previously used or standardized schemes, but, unlike them, provably achieve strong notions of security in the random oracle model, assuming RSA is a one-way function. These schemes have been quite popular from the point of view of adoption in practice: OAEP is a included in SET, the electronic payment protocol of MasterCard and Visa, where it is used to encrypt credit card numbers, and both OAEP and PSS are being considered for the IEEE P1363 standard.

What's the point of the random oracle paradigm, and what does it buy you? It buys efficiency, plus, we claim, security guarantees which, although not at the same level as those of the standard provable security approach, are arguably superior to those provided by totally ad hoc protocol design. The last point merits some more discussion.

The random oracle paradigm should be used with care and understanding. It is important to neither over-estimate nor under-estimate what this paradigm buys you in terms of security guarantees. First, one must be clear that this is not standard provable security. The function h that we actually use in the final scheme is not random. Thus the question is: what has it bought us to have done the proof in the first place?

The overly skeptical might say the answer is "nothing." This is not quite true. Here is one way to see what it buys. In practice, attacks on schemes involving a SHA-1 derived h and number theory will often *themselves treat h as random*. We call such attacks *generic attacks*. In other words, cryptanalysis of these "mixed" schemes is usually done by assuming h is random. But then the proofs apply, and indeed show that such generic attacks will fail unless the underlying number-theoretic problems are easy. In other words, the analysis at least provably excludes a certain common class of attacks, namely generic ones.

Of course this doesn't include all attacks. But what it tells us is that to successfully attack schemes proven secure in a random oracle model, the cryptanalyst *must* exploit the structure of a specific hash function h. But when both number-theory and hashing are involved (as they are in the schemes like OAEP or PSS), getting profitable cryptanalytic interaction between h and the number-theory is very hard, because the two problems are so "independent" in structure. However this feeling, although it seems to be true, is heuristic. Certainly it relies very much on the idea that the problems are independent.

In comparison with totally ad hoc design, a proof in the random oracle model has the benefit of viewing the scheme with regard to its meeting a strong and formal notion of security, even if this is assuming some underlying primitive is very strong. This is better than not formally modeling the security of the scheme in any way.

This explains why the random oracle model is viewed in [8] as a "bridge between theory and practice."

Since we introduced this model, it has been used in other places, for example in the design and analysis of signature schemes [23,24] and hash functions [12].

3.5 New notions: session key distribution

"Entity authentication" is the process by which a party gains confidence in the identity of a communication partner. It is usually coupled with the distribution of a "session key." These are arguably the most basic problems for secure distributed computation— without a correct solution there can be no meaningful access control or accountability; there cannot even be reliable distribution of work across network resources. Despite a long history and a large literature, this problem rested on no meaningful formal foundation. This is more than an academic complaint: it is an area in which an informal approach has often lead to work which has subsequently been found to be wrong, and in some cases the flaws have taken years to discover.

In [7] we address the two party setting of the problem. It achieves provable security by providing a model, definitions, protocols, and proofs of correctness for these protocols under standard assumptions.

The three party case of this problem may be the most well-known. It was first addressed by Needham and Schroeder in 1978. Its most popular incarnation is the *Kerberos* system. However this system, and existing solutions, suffer from the same problems discussed above. In [10] we provide provably secure protocols for the three party session key distribution problem.

All our protocols are efficient and practical, viable alternatives to current systems. Some have been implemented. Our models have been used to study related key distribution problems, for example in [26].

4 Symmetric encryption

The above has discussed provable security and its practice oriented variant in a general way. Next I would like to illustrate the ideas by looking in more depth at a central problem: encryption. The goal is to motivate the need for strong and formal notions of security and then show how to to adapt the seminal notions of [17] (given in the asymmetric setting) to the symmetric setting. With concrete security definitions in hand, we will turn to analyzing popular encryption modes like CBC or CTR and gauge their merits. We want to answer questions like: are the secure? Which is "better"?

I did this in my talk, for the most part following [4], and refer the reader there for this materiel. Some day, I hope to extend this article by the inclusion of this and other materiel.

Acknowledgments

This presentation is based on ideas developed jointly with Phillip Rogaway.

This work is supported in part by NSF CAREER Award CCR-9624439 and a 1996 Packard Foundation Fellowship in Science and Engineering.

References[5]

1. ANSI X9.9, "American National Standard for Financial Institution Message Authentication (Wholesale)," American Bankers Association, 1981. Revised 1986.
2. ANSI X3.106, "American National Standard for Information Systems – Data Encryption Algorithm – Modes of Operation," American National Standards Institute, 1983.

---

[5] The best place to obtain any of my papers listed below is via http://www-cse.ucsd.edu/users/mihir. Here you will find the full, and most recent, versions.

3. M. BELLARE, R. CANETTI AND H. KRAWCZYK, "Psuedorandom functions revisited: The cascade construction and its concrete security," *Proceedings of the 37th Symposium on Foundations of Computer Science*, IEEE, 1996.

4. M. BELLARE, A. DESAI, E. JOKIPII AND P. ROGAWAY, "A concrete security treatment of symmetric encryption," *Proceedings of the 38th Symposium on Foundations of Computer Science*, IEEE, 1997.

5. M. BELLARE, R. GUÉRIN AND P. ROGAWAY, "XOR MACs: New methods for message authentication using finite pseudorandom functions," *Advances in Cryptology – Crypto 95 Proceedings*, Lecture Notes in Computer Science Vol. 963, D. Coppersmith ed., Springer-Verlag, 1995.

6. M. BELLARE, J. KILIAN AND P. ROGAWAY, "The security of cipher block chaining," *Advances in Cryptology – Crypto 94 Proceedings*, Lecture Notes in Computer Science Vol. 839, Y. Desmedt ed., Springer-Verlag, 1994.

7. M. BELLARE AND P. ROGAWAY, "Entity authentication and key distribution," *Advances in Cryptology – Crypto 93 Proceedings*, Lecture Notes in Computer Science Vol. 773, D. Stinson ed., Springer-Verlag, 1993.

8. M. BELLARE AND P. ROGAWAY, "Random oracles are practical: a paradigm for designing efficient protocols," *Proceedings of the First Annual Conference on Computer and Communications Security*, ACM, 1993.

9. M. BELLARE AND P. ROGAWAY, "Optimal asymmetric encryption – How to encrypt with RSA," *Advances in Cryptology – Eurocrypt 95 Proceedings*, Lecture Notes in Computer Science Vol. 921, L. Guillou and J. Quisquater ed., Springer-Verlag, 1995.

10. M. BELLARE AND P. ROGAWAY, "Provably secure session key distribution– the three party case," *Proceedings of the 27th Annual Symposium on the Theory of Computing*, ACM, 1995.

11. M. BELLARE AND P. ROGAWAY, "The exact security of digital signatures: How to sign with RSA and Rabin," *Advances in Cryptology – Eurocrypt 96 Proceedings*, Lecture Notes in Computer Science Vol. 1070, U. Maurer ed., Springer-Verlag, 1996.

12. M. BELLARE AND D. MICCIANCIO, "A new paradigm for collision-free hashing: Incrementality at reduced cost," *Advances in Cryptology – Eurocrypt 97 Proceedings*, Lecture Notes in Computer Science Vol. 1233, W. Fumy ed., Springer-Verlag, 1997.

13. M. BLUM AND S. MICALI, "How to generate cryptographically strong sequences of pseudo-random bits," *SIAM Journal on Computing*, Vol. 13, No. 4, November 1984, pp. 850–864.

14. H. DOBBERTIN, A. BOSSELAERS AND B. PRENEEL, "RIPEMD-160: A strengthened version of RIPEMD," *Fast Software Encryption*, Lecture Notes in Computer Science 1039, D. Gollmann, ed., Springer-Verlag, 1996.

15. O. GOLDREICH, "On the foundations of modern cryptography," *Advances in Cryptology – Crypto 97 Proceedings*, Lecture Notes in Computer Science Vol. 1294, B. Kaliski ed., Springer-Verlag, 1997.

16. O. GOLDREICH, S. GOLDWASSER AND S. MICALI, "How to construct random functions," *Journal of the ACM*, Vol. 33, No. 4, October 1986, pp. 792–807.

17. S. GOLDWASSER AND S. MICALI, "Probabilistic encryption," *J. of Computer and System Sciences*, Vol. 28, April 1984, pp. 270–299.

18. S. GOLDWASSER, S. MICALI AND R. RIVEST, "A digital signature scheme secure against adaptive chosen-message attacks," *SIAM Journal of Computing*, Vol. 17, No. 2, April 1988, pp. 281–308.

19. ISO 8372, "Information processing – Modes of operation for a 64-bit block cipher algorithm," International Organization for Standardization, Geneva, Switzerland, 1987.

20. M. LUBY AND C. RACKOFF, "How to construct pseudorandom permutations from pseudorandom functions," *SIAM J. Computation*, Vol. 17, No. 2, April 1988.

21. National Bureau of Standards, NBS FIPS PUB 81, "DES modes of operation," U.S Department of Commerce, 1980.

22. National Institute of Standards, FIPS 180-1, "Secure hash standard," April 1995.

23. D. POINTCHEVAL AND J. STERN, "Security proofs for signatures," *Advances in Cryptology – Eurocrypt 96 Proceedings*, Lecture Notes in Computer Science Vol. 1070, U. Maurer ed., Springer-Verlag, 1996.

24. D. POINTCHEVAL AND J. STERN, "Provably secure blind signature schemes," *Advances in Cryptology – ASIACRYPT 96 Proceedings*, Lecture Notes in Computer Science Vol. 1163, M. Y. Rhee and K. Kim ed., Springer-Verlag, 1996.

25. B. PRENEEL AND P. VAN OORSCHOT, "MD-x MAC and building fast MACs from hash functions," *Advances in Cryptology – Crypto 95 Proceedings*, Lecture Notes in Computer Science Vol. 963, D. Coppersmith ed., Springer-Verlag, 1995.

26. V. SHOUP AND A. RUBIN, "Session key distribution using smart cards," *Advances in Cryptology – Eurocrypt 96 Proceedings*, Lecture Notes in Computer Science Vol. 1070, U. Maurer ed., Springer-Verlag, 1996.

27. A. C. YAO, "Theory and applications of trapdoor functions," *Proceedings of the 23rd Symposium on Foundations of Computer Science*, IEEE, 1982.

A Framework for the Management of Information Security

Jussipekka Leiwo and Yuliang Zheng

Peninsula School of Computing and Information Technology
Monash University
McMahons Road, Frankston, Vic 3199, Australia
Phone +61-(0)3-9904 4287, Fax +61-(0)3-9904 4124
E-mail: {skylark,yuliang}@fcit.monash.edu.au

Abstract. Information security is strongly dependent on access control models and cryptographic techniques. These are well established areas of research and practice in the enforcement of technical information security policies but are not capable of supporting development of comprehensive information security within organizations. Therefore, there is a need to study upper level issues to establish organizational models for specifying security enforcement mechanisms and coordinating policies. This paper proposes a model for dealing with high level information security policies. The core is to enforce a continuous refinement of information security requirements aiming at formally deriving technical security policies from high level security objectives. This refinement is carried out by information security harmonization functions. Contribution of this paper is on the specification of a notation for expressing information security requirements and on the specification of a mechanism to formulate harmonization functions.

1 Introduction

Computer security is strongly dependent on access control models and modern cryptography. The well known Bell-LaPadula model for confidentiality [4] triggered significant amount of research leading also to other similar models such as Biba model for integrity [5]. Also, several other lattice based security models were established [20]. These models originated from the military environment where security was prevention of leakage of sensitive information to lower clearance levels. Other models, such as [8], were developed with commercial rather than military environments in mind. Frameworks were also developed to support specification of more flexible authorization rules using formal languages such as [25] and [13] or formal logics [2]. Recently, significant research has been carried out in the area of role based access control models [21]. Well established research in access control models has also led to the evaluation of secure systems according to different criteria, the most significant being the TCSEC by U.S. DoD [1].

Public key cryptography [9] together with an increasing scientific and commercial interest in secure communications led to a rapidly expanding area of research in cryptology. As access control models in centralized systems, cryptography is the foundation of security in distributed systems. Research has led to several private key cryptosystems, such as DES [11] and SPEED [27], and public key cryptosystems such as RSA [19] and ElGamal cryptosystem [10]. Also, several tools have been developed for applications of cryptography. Examples include digital signatures, authentication codes, non-repudiation mechanisms and advanced authentication methods [22]. Integrated security services have been developed to support fundamental objective of information security, provision of cost-effective protection of data and information. Digital signcryption [26] combines encryption and generation of digital signatures to reduce the number of calculations needed and the size of messaged need to be transmitted compared to traditional paradigm with separate encryption and generation of digital signatures.

Access control and cryptographic models provide secure operation of a system based on a well-defined operational criteria, security policy. Access control models enforce a formal access control policy and cryptographic models enforce network security policy. Even though well established and understood, both access control models and cryptographic techniques focus on lower layer activities and do not address critical issues in the organizational coordination of the security of information systems, management of information security. There are several layers of security policies [24] and it is essential that all layers from organizational to technical security policies are addressed. Furthermore, Access control and cryptographic models provide security at low and mid layers in the elaboration stack of the development of secure systems but do not address upper layer issues that are essential in the development of secure systems [14].

This paper provides a comprehensive framework and a systematic approach towards management of information security by studying issues at higher layers in the elaboration stack. The major objective is to provide organizational coordination for the application of security models and to guarantee that specification and implementation of security enforcement measures are cost-effective, consistent and free of conflict, hence, to provide adequate security. Even though specific solutions are introduced, this paper is not intended on being a detailed analysis of related issues, but an introduction of the framework and brief review of preliminary solutions for key issues. Some of the results of Sect. 3.1 and the abstract concept of requirement harmonization has been proposed by authors in [16], and the fundamental contribution of this paper is to show how several abstract issues discussed in that work can be implemented in practice. Section 2 provides an overview of the assumed management architecture for information security. Key issues of the architecture shall be analyzed in detail in Sect. 3. The approach shall be evaluated in Sect. 4, and conclusions drawn in Sect. 5.

2 Management Architecture

From a wide point of view, information security can be seen as a provision of layers of technical and non-technical protection measures up to ecological and social facets of information systems [12]. From a practical and technical research point of view, the scope needs to be narrowed. Within this paper, management of information security refers to the specification and enforcement of information security meta policies that coordinate actual information security policies. Information security meta policy is an abstraction of a policy coordinating specification and enforcement of actual information security policies [15]. These policies then provide actual protection specifications. For the purposes of this paper, boundaries of the duties of managerial information security personnel are specified as follows:

Upper boundary is the formulation of information security requirements based on information security objectives. Information security objectives are informal statements regarding desired security of operations and are usually based on different national and international laws, agreements, standards and organizational business objectives. They are typically set by top management of the organization. Formulation refers to the presentation of these objectives formally in an unambiguous way.

Lower boundary is in the specification of technical security policies based on the upper layer security requirements. From a managerial point of view, it can be assumed that once identified and specified, security enforcement mechanisms can be implemented in a secure manner by technical personnel.

It should be noted that managerial personnel for information security does not necessarily have the competence of dealing with highly formal notations. Their duty is to coordinate this formulation that can be actually carried out by technical security personnel. This means, that the approach towards harmonization and layering of the organization assumed in the framework must be relaxed. The processes described in this paper represent an ideal organization, and need to be adapted to each actual development situation. Internal hierarchies, such as the issue of supervision and actual implementation of tasks such as formulation of security objectives into security requirements, are not considered. Each task and duty requires an internal control structure to provide assurance of correctness but this presentation is mostly concerned with an external view. From an external view, the process can be carried out by a waterfall approach. The theoretical framework is presented as a continuous refinement of requirements with fully specified interfaces. In practical development situations, different feedback mechanisms need to be implemented to coordinate the harmonization. Detailed analysis of these mechanisms is left for future research.

Management architecture for information security refers to a generic framework describing major parties involved in the management of information security, different tasks, and outputs of these tasks. The architecture assumed in this paper is illustrated in Fig. 1. Managerial duties include formulation of security requirements based on organizational security objectives, and harmonization of them reduce level of abstraction step by step and to assure from cost-efficiency of protection. This includes specification of different harmonization, optimization, consistency and correctness criteria for information security requirements. Typically, security requirements originate from more than one source, and therefore it is essential to specify routines and procedures for resolving potential conflicts that may occur among different requirements. These operations lead to the specified technical protection measures that can be then implemented by security enforcement mechanisms, such as access control and cryptographic models.

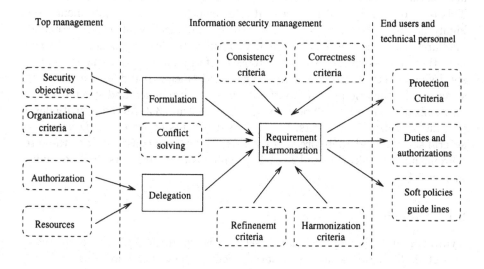

Fig. 1. An architecture for the management of information security

Another track of duties of the management of information security is the specification of duties and authorities for the secure processing of information. Some sources suggest that information security is mostly concerned with the specification of structures of responsibilities within organization [3] and therefore the importance of delegation of duties and authorities should not be underestimated. The top management is in charge of secure business operations and has an authority to set policies that govern entire organization. This authority and responsibility is then delegated to the information security personnel that further designs different structures of responsibilities and different non-technical security enforcement functions, such as user education, to support technical protection measures. Even though essential, the issue shall not be further considered within this paper but the focus shall be on technical policies and mechanisms for transformation of high level security objectives into technical specifications. This is not seen as a significant draw back in the application of the proposed model, since user education, authorizations and duties regarding secure operations are strongly dependent on underlying security solutions, and hence can be specified only after actual technical protection measures have been identified and implemented.

3   Areas of Modeling

Issues identified in the previous section shall be considered with the harmonization of information security requirements. As stated, focus shall be on the specification of technical policies and mechanisms, questions of authority and "soft policies" such as user education shall not be considered. First essential facet is the specification a model for the security development organization [14]. This is studied in Sect. 3.1. Flow and refinement of security requirements from highly descriptive security objectives into concrete specifications of protection measures shall then be considered with respect to this organization. To support this, it is essential to provide tools for formulating requirements and for specifying criteria to process and analyze requirements at different levels of abstraction. Formulation of information security requirements and specification of harmonization criteria shall be studied in Sect. 3.2 and 3.3. As the security development organization suggests, security requirements of systems originate from several sources, and therefore it is essential to evaluate consistency of these requirements. Identification and resolving conflicts of requirements shall be studied in Sect.3.4.

3.1   Modeling the Organization

Typical organization for information security is hierarchical [7]. The architecture of Sect. 2 also assumes that information security personnel is working under top management and structures and responsibilities within the organization can be clearly specified. A formal specification for the security development organization to support this approach has been given in [16], and is based on *Child* and *Parent* relationships. These relationships are determined by the flow of information security requirements within an organization. A flow refers to the refinement path from a high level objective to the actual technical security policy. Let U_1 and U_2 be organizational units. Unit refers to an abstraction of a system component and can be any organizational division, business unit within a division, logical system or a particular component of an information systems. If there is a requirement flow from U_1 to U_2, that is U_1 sets a requirement primitive for U_2 to process, we say that $(U_1, U_2) \in Parent$ and $(U_2, U_1) \in Child$ (alternatively, $U_1 \in Parent(U_2)$ and $U_2 \in Child(U_1)$).

Let $U_1, U_2, \ldots U_n$ represent units so that $(U_i, U_j) \in Parent$, for each $i < j \leq n$. We say that there exists a flow of requirements $F = (U_1, U_2, \ldots, U_n)$. Let $\mathcal{F}$ be a set of flows of requirements within an organization. In each flow $F \in \mathcal{F}$ each U_i represents lower level of abstraction than U_j if $i < j$. This approach helps in dealing with complexity of the management of information security. Requirements can be studied separately at each level of abstraction and managerial decisions regarding protection at each organizational layer can be made based on the most suitable level of abstraction. Due to layered security policies, this is an essential characteristic. Therefore a hierarchy is a logical model for representation of a security organization. Hierarchy is also needed to prevent loops in the flow of requirements. A loop occurs when there exists a $F \in \mathcal{F}$ so that

$F = (U_1, U_2, \ldots, U_k, U_l, \ldots, U_n)$ where k belongs to a lower organizational layer than l, hence representing lower level of abstraction of requirements. Loops in requirement flows must be prohibited to prevent unsolvable circular reductions of abstraction of requirements. An additional benefit of the approach is that it provides flexibility to adapt the security development model into changing environments, where non-traditional organizational structures may occur, such as matrix organizations and virtual organizations where hierarchies are flat and rapidly changing. Full discussion of the organizational modeling is given in [16]. Therefore, it shall not be repeated herein. The specification is concerned with exact notations for different components in the organization, such as units, layers and requirement primitives. It also gives a set of criteria that the organizational model needs to satisfy to be correctly formulated.

3.2 Specification of Information Security Requirements

Several models for the development of secure systems, such as [16] and [6], assume that high level security requirements can be clearly identified and formulated. There are several models for formally specifying either access control or cryptographic requirements, but these deal with lower layers in the elaboration stack. Therefore, it is essential to specify a formal model for expressing information security requirements. These requirements can be roughly classified into three [18]: specific, pervasive and non-technical requirements. With respect to this paper, specific requirements are interpreted as requirements that can be assigned to any specific unit within the organization or to an association connecting two units. Pervasive and non-technical requirements set, for example, requirements regarding to the trusted implementation of security mechanisms or non-technical issues such as user education, and shall therefore not be further studied within this paper. To support the refinement approach by requirement flows, as studied in the previous section, it is essential that these requirements are formulated in a partial manner. This is, the notation must be capable of dealing with requirements that are not fully specified. This requires two properties. First, a mechanism is needed for dealing with classes of security enforcement mechanisms instead of specific enforcement technologies. For example, there is a need to allow protection statements such as "Public Key Cryptography" instead of any specific cryptographic technique. Second, there is a need to deal with some information, such as parameters for security enforcement algorithms, as unspecified.

Communications security is usually seen as a specification of secure association within the system [23]. Within this paper, organizational units (distributed processes) share data over an association, that is an abstraction of a communication channel representing information flow between units. Specification of security requirements is concerned with statements governing provision of security for this association. These statements are based on characteristics of the associations and processes. Association characteristics are expressed as association attributes, and process characteristics as process attributes. Attributes can be further classified into possession attributes or criteria attributes. Possession attributes are those directly related to the association security specification, for example encryption keys, and criteria attributes set properties of possession attributes, such as key length. Further, it should be kept in mind that it is not enough only to specify required protection of information flows, but also the acceptable content of those flows. As some communication mechanisms can not be adequately protected, there is a need to restrict applications of these mechanisms to prevent violations of security. Also, some mechanisms may be banned from some particular associations.

Let P be a process. Notation P_α can be used to represent possession attributes and P_β criteria attributes. Let P and Q be processes, and A an association so that $(P,Q) \in A$. Let A_γ be the security specification of the association. Each γ can be seen as a tuple (c, p, ρ) where c refers to the acceptable content of the association expressed as a well defined communication protocol, p to the required protection measure expressed as a well defined algorithm, and ρ to the parameter coordinating execution of p. Let R be a requirement of form (A, P, Q, c, p, ρ) where A, P, Q, c, p and ρ are as above. Let $\mathcal{R}_S$ be a set of requirements of system S, seen as a collection of tuples $S = \{(P, Q, A)\}$ representing all different associations in the system. Requirement set $\mathcal{R}_S$ can be further analyzed according to criteria as studied in the following section.

As stated before, it is not essential for each component to be specified at high levels of abstractions. Any component of R can be specified either an empty string $\emptyset$ or a generic term describing the type of algorithm or type of protocol to be used. These partially defined requirements are then to be refined at lower layers of abstraction. For example, let P, Q and A be such as $(P,Q) \in A$, and R be of form $R = (A, P, Q, EMAIL, PK - ENC, \emptyset)$. This R can be interpreted as a formulation of a high level statement that all e-mail communication must be encrypted using public key cryptographic algorithm. Parameters, exact e-mail protocols and encryption algorithms are then to be defined at lower layers of abstraction. This is an essential characteristics to enable participation of several organizational layers in the information security process. Comprehensive security requires participation of managerial as well as technical personnel. Therefore, there is a need for intuitive notations for dealing with abstractions of systems. The above example can be made more intuitive describing the units and association according to functionality. For example, renaming association A as "Internet", Process P as "Site 1" and Q as "Site 2". This leads to a requirement description (*Internet, Site 1, Site 2, EMAIL, Public Key Cryptography, $\emptyset$*). Descriptive names simplify understanding of different components and can be further refined to be more formal to support formal security policies.

3.3 Specification of Harmonization Criteria

The major duty of the managerial information security personnel is evaluation and refinement of security requirements to harmonize and optimize them. This is needed for the provision of assurance of correctness, consistency and other properties of the requirement base. Requirement processing, i.e. enforcement of harmonization functions, can be implemented by requirement criteria. The major types of harmonization are requirement refining harmonization, requirement generating harmonization and requirement removing harmonization.

Requirement refining harmonization is refining of individual requirements to optimize them by changing the security specification or by adding detail into incomplete requirement primitives. Requirement refining harmonization is the most common type of harmonization. Since major motivation behind harmonization is optimization of a requirement base, it is mostly concerned with identification of similar protection needs throughout the organization and altering them to meet an organizationally approved criteria.

Requirement generating harmonization uses criteria to generate new requirements into the requirement base. This is mostly used to specify dependencies of requirements, and to specify dependent requirements that can then be further processed by other rules. There are several cases where a dependency of requirements is an essential success factor of information security. For example, assume a high level requirement stating the need for cryptographic protection of communications. Refinement of this requirement to apply public key cryptography also indicates the need for strong authentication, hence there must be a mechanism for generating a new requirement describing the authentication need.

Requirement removing harmonization uses criteria to remove certain requirements from a requirement base. Consider, for example, new technologies such as digital Signcryption [26], that combines encryption and digital signatures to reduce the cost of protection. Combining these types of requirements consists of two phases: refining the encryption to apply signcryption instead, and removing of the requirement stating signature scheme only.

Criteria should be specified conditionally depending on other protection specifications or system attributes, the basic form being of $[f : g]$. Intuitively, for each requirement R, where f is true, modifications should be made such that g becomes true. As the simplest, f and g should be expressed by first order logic statements concerning process or association attributes or security properties. Let H be a harmonization function and $C \in \mathcal{C}$ be a criteria. Harmonization function H should harmonize requirements to provide transformation in the requirement base $\mathcal{R}$ so that $H_C(\mathcal{R}) \Rightarrow \mathcal{R}'$, where $\mathcal{R}'$ is a modified requirement base. For each $R \in \mathcal{R}$ where f is true, should exist a corresponding requirement $S \in \mathcal{R}'$ where g is true, and must exist a harmonization function $H_C(\mathcal{R}) = \mathcal{R}'$.

For example, to refine requirement $R = (A, P, Q, EMAIL, PK - ENC, \emptyset)$ to use SMTP mail protocol and PGP protection, with still undefined set of parameters, the criteria of form $[(r.c = EMAIL) \wedge (r.p = PK - ENC) : (r.c = SMTP) \wedge (r.p = PGP - E)]$ where PGP-E refers to the encryption with PGP. Additional criteria can be set to state that with PGP, also digital signatures, generated using PGP are required. An example of a criteria triggering an addition of a requirement can be of form $[r.p = PGP - e : (p'.c = SMTP) \wedge (p'.p = PGP - S) \wedge p'.\rho = \emptyset]$. Removal of a requirement can be triggered as declaring all the fields to $\emptyset$. Assume, for example, a requirement base $\mathcal{R} = (A, P, Q, EMAIL, PK - ENC, \emptyset), (A, P, Q, EMAIL, SIG, \emptyset)$ stating that Email communication must be both encrypted and signed. Now, let the criteria be specified to enforce application of digital signcryption (SIGNCR) to protect E-mail communications:

$$[(r.c = EMAIL) \land (r.p = PK - ENC) : r.p = SIGNCR]$$
$$[(r.c = EMAIL) \land (r.p = SIG) : (r.c = \emptyset) \land (r.p = \emptyset) \land (r.\rho = \emptyset)]$$

where first criteria refines the protection to be Digital Signcryption instead of Public Key Encryption hence making the digital signature protection obsolete. Second criteria then removes that requirement by declaring all essential fields to be empty.

3.4   Resolving Conflicts of Requirements

Information security requirements typically originate from several sources. Also, different requirements may have different priorities. For example, requirements set by national laws regarding security enforcement should override any organizational requirements. Laws and regulations may set minimum or maximum levels of security for certain security enforcement mechanisms, and no system within the organization should violate these requirements. Organizational structure may also lead one unit to get requirements from more than one upper layer unit. Let $F \in \mathcal{F}$ and $G \in \mathcal{F}$ be requirement flows. Formally, a unit with several parents refers to a case where exists a unit U_i so that $F = (U_1, \ldots, U_i, \ldots, U_n)$ and $G = (U_1', \ldots, U_i', \ldots, U_n')$. As there may be different criteria providing harmonization of requirement primitives to U_i, and as different order of enforcement of this harmonization may lead to different security specifications, it is essential to develop mechanisms to analyze the security enforcement level of a requirement and to solve potential conflicts in the level enforced by different requirements.

First phase is identification of requirements that are in conflict, and once identified, a strategy must be specified to solve this conflict. Let $R \in \mathcal{R}$ be a requirement. An interpretation function $\mathcal{I}_R \to L$ where L is a set of security levels within the organization should be specified for each R. Interpretation function maps each requirement to a predefined security level. Let A be an association. Conflicts can be identified by comparing interpretations of each requirement dealing with A. Let R and S be requirements dealing with association A. If $\mathcal{I}_R < \mathcal{I}_S$ we say that level of requirement R dominates level of requirement S.

Based on these security levels, a conflict solving strategies can be specified and criteria set to modify one or both of conflicting requirements to be consistent. Three fundamental conflict solving strategies can be identified: lower level wins, higher level wins, or hybrid strategies. Lower level wins -strategy can be used, for example, to meet the requirements set by different laws to restrict applications of cryptography. Each requirement dealing with the restricted security enforcement mechanism is analyzed with a requirement that sets the maximum key length, and if higher key length is identified, the conflicting requirement is reduced to the maximum key length allowed by law.

Maximum level enforcement can be used, for example, in the opposite case. Assume that there is a minimum level of security by encryption, set by key length, that each association must satisfy. This can be set as a basic requirement, and each requirement where an association is protected by that mechanism is compared to the basic requirement and if shorter keys are found, the attributes specifying the minimum key length are updated to meet the minimum requirement. To provide flexibility, different hybrid criteria can be based on different logics to set processing principles.

Assume that our example requirement regarding protection of e-mail has been refined by two criteria: $[r.p = PGP - E : r.\rho_{kl} = 512]$ and $[r.p = PGP - E : r.\rho_{kl} = 768]$. The previous one requires key length $(r.\rho_{kl})$ to be 512 bits and the latter to be 768 bits. Obviously, this is a conflict. A simple interpretation function such as

$$
\mathcal{I}_{PGP-E}(kl) = \begin{cases} P & if\ kl = 0 \\ C & if\ kl = 512 \\ S & if\ kl = 768 \\ TS\ if\ kl = 1024 \end{cases} \tag{1}
$$

to map the key length into security class can be specified and depending on the priority of conflicting criteria and the current conflict solving strategy, one of them can be discarded.

4 Analysis of the Approach

If successfully implemented, the framework presented in this paper has applications in several areas of information security. The direct applications are in the development of comprehensive information security in organizations, and due to formal approach taken in [16] the requirement processing can be at least partially automated. Further applications are in the comparison of a given organization to a predefined security criteria. Typically, management of information security has been based on mechanistic risk analysis, but the approach taken in this paper would enable evaluation of the security of complete information systems, hence improving the level of security management. This might also be of interest of organizations that are analyzing security of different providers of, for example, outsourcing services, or by insurance companies willing to estimate whether the security level of their client is acceptable for insurance purposes.

Theoretically, the model deals with information security as a process leading from security objectives to actual technical security policies. The layered nature of the model provides a flexible for feed back mechanism from lower to upper layers. This feed back typically causes changes in high level security requirements. Theoretically, feed back from lower layers can be considered like any other requirement being harmonized. It is important to give high priority to the feed back. Other reasons that trigger such changes are changes in the operational environment, changes on security objectives and periodical checks of information security. It should be noted that the severity of alterations varies. Therefore, the feed back is returned to various layers in the organization. The more severe the alteration, the higher layers are involved. All changes then cause changes in the entire harmonization flow from the highest layer unit involved to the lowest layers of that harmonization flow. This mechanism allows efficient reactions to new requirements. The scope of change can be reduced only to those organizational units involved, and with the support of potential partial automation, rapid adaption can be achieved in the changing information security requirements. This makes the system vulnerable to an unauthorized modification of requirements. Further automation of requirement harmonization may lead to a potential violation of a hostile party by modifying requirement primitives. This would have the advantage of reducing the level of security making it more vulnerable for future attacks. It has been shown by [17] that a mandatory access control model can be established for information security requirements to prevent these violations.

There are several critical success factors for the framework that need to be considered before extensive applications are possible. First key issue is flexibility. Typically, organizations vary from structure and from the nature of information security requirements. Therefore, it is essential the organizational security models based on this framework can reach the adequate flexibility to meet different needs. The formulation of requirement harmonization in [16] sets only minimum restrictions for the organizational structure and results of further research, such as those reported in this paper, suggest that requirements and requirement processing criteria can be set to be flexible enough to meet needs of different organizations.

Another essential success factor is the feasibility of the model. As any formal approach, this also restricts the scope of setting and processing information security requirements. As analyzed earlier, the focus is mostly on specific requirements and different tools are needed for analysis of pervasive and non-technical requirements. Such requirements can be set as attributes of processes and hence included in the framework, but automated analysis of their properties may not be easily applicable. As these requirements are supporting requirements for specific security requirements, it is believed that this restriction is not too strongly limiting potential for the application of the framework.

Another restriction set by the current approach is that the criteria as suggested in this paper are only capable of providing assurance from internal properties of a requirement base, such as correctness, freedom of conflicts, and consistency. External properties such as comprehensiveness, that is weather all relevant requirements are included in the requirement base, are not within the scope of the proposed approach. Based on this work, it is assumed that personnel on the management of information security are competitive and capable of identifying all relevant requirements and their dependencies. Hence, the responsibility of comprehensiveness is left on the personnel.

Third success factor is the development of top-down tools to support application of the framework. Development of information security is typically a top-down process, and not fully carried out by information security specialists, but communication among different personnel groups is needed. Therefore, success application of the framework presented here need supporting graphical top-down tools. Similarly than in system engineering, there is a need for tools that can be used and understood by different technical and non-technical personnel groups, and that support the framework presented herein. Also, it is essential to identify the parts that can be automated, and develop tools that support automated analysis of requirements. As the process-association -model for formulating security requirements suggests, traditional structured, data-flow based system development tools might be applicable also in the development of secure systems. Further, recent trends suggest that object oriented modeling tools are taking over structured analysis tools, and should also be considered in the security context.

5 Conclusions and Future Work

A framework has been proposed for the development of comprehensive information security in organizations. The focus has been on the formulation and processing of information security requirements, based on high level security objectives, to reduce abstraction of requirements, improve cost-efficiency of protection, to assure from consistency and other properties of the requirement base, and to solve conflicts of different requirements. This framework consists of several major areas that each need to be considered. The success of the approach is based on the several issues analyzed within this paper. Development of a generally applicable model for comprehensive information security is a significantly large task. Therefore, the focus of this paper has been on a generic framework and identification of major areas of modeling that need to be further analyzed. The scope of concept "management of information security" has been reduced to a systematic processing of information security requirements. This processing should lead to the specification of technical security policies to be enforced by security enforcement technologies.

Each component of the model introduced herein and preliminary solutions provided can be further developed and interfaces between different components can be analyzed in detail. The view towards the framework has been external. Internal structure of hierarchies and feed back mechanisms of different components of the model has not been considered. Externally, feed back of lower layers can be considered as any other requirement of harmonization. Management of information security as a whole is a large subject, and models such as [12] suggest a very wide point of view, where the areas of research expand widely also to non-traditional areas of research in computer science. Therefore, it has been an intentional choice within this paper to restrict on issues that have direct relationship to the specification of meta policies that coordinate actual technical security policies. From the layered security policy model [24] point of view, this means that focus is on administrative security policies, and in their relationships to upper and lower layer policies. Participation of several organizational layers in the design of information security sets important requirements for tools supporting the design. As managerial personnel needs to be involved, it is imperative that tools are developed to support their participation by providing intuitive, preferably diagrammatic, tools for dealing with information security requirements. This requires a high level informal notation for requirements and harmonization functions.

Of course, the nature of different levels of security policies is a controversial issue. It is clear that the security policy objective is of very informal nature, and technical security policies need to be formal to automate their enforcement, and to enable analysis of security. The major contribution of this paper has been identification of components that have a major impact on the formulation of security requirements to satisfy security policy objectives, and to identify components needed in the potentially automated analysis of security at the organizational level.

Acknowledgments

Authors would like to express their gratitude to the organizing committee of 1997 Information Security Workshop regarding generous funding towards presentation of this paper. We are also grateful to Dr. Jun Han and anonymous referees for constructive comments regarding early drafts of this paper. Part of the work has been completed while second author was on sabbatical at the University of Tokyo. He would like to extend his thanks to Professor Hideki Imai for hospitality.

References

1. Trusted computer systems evaluation criteria. U.S. Department of Defence, 1983.
2. M. Adabi, M. Burrows, B. Lampson, and G. Plotkin. A calculus for access control in distributed systems. In *Advances in Cryptology - Crypto'91*, 1991.
3. J. Backhouse and G. Dhillon. Structures of responsibility and security of information systems. *European Journal of Information Systems*, 5:2–9, 1996.
4. D. E. Bell and L. J. LaPadula. Secure computer systems: Mathematical foundations and model. Technical Report M74-244, MITRE Corporation, Bedford, MA,USA, 1975.
5. K. Biba. Integrity considerations for secure computer systems. Technical Report TR-3153, MITRE Corporation, Bedford, Massachusetts, USA, 1977.
6. H. Booysen and J. Eloff. A methodology for the development of secure application systems. In *Proceedings of the IFIP TC11 11th International Conference on Information Security*, 1995.
7. E. R. Buck. *Introduction to Data Security and Controls*. QED Technical Publishing Group, Wellesley, MA, USA, second edition, 1991.
8. D. D. Clark and D. R. Wilson. A comparison of commercial and military security policies. In *1987 IEEE Symposium on Security and Privacy*, 1987.
9. W. Diffie and M. E. Hellman. New Directions in Cryptography. *IEEE Transactions on Information Theory*, IT–22(6):644–654, Nov. 1976.
10. T. ElGamal. A public key cryptosystem and a signature scheme based on discrete logarithms. *IEEE Transactions on Information Theory*, 31(4):469–472, 1985.
11. Federal Information Processing Standards Publications (FIPS PUB) 46. *Data Encryption Standard*. National Bureau of Standards, Jan. 1977.

12. A. Hartmann. Comprehensive information technology security: A new approach to respond ethical and social issues surrounding information security in the 21st century. In *Proceedings of the IFIP TC11 11th international conference of Information Security*, Cape Town, South Africa, May 1995.

13. S. Jajodia, P. Samarati, and V. S. Subrahmanian. A logical language for expressing authorizations. In *Proceedings of the IEEE Symposium on Security and Privacy*, 1997.

14. L. J. LaPadula. Foreword for republishing of the Bell-LaPadula model. *Journal of Computer Security*, 4:233–238, 1996.

15. J. Leiwo and S. Heikkuri. Clarifying concepts of information security management. In *Proceedings of the 2nd International Baltic Workshop on DB and IS*, Tallinn, Estonia, June 1996.

16. J. Leiwo and Y. Zheng. A formal model to aid in documenting and harmonization of information security requirements. In *Proceedings of the IFIP TC11 13th International Conference on Information Systems Security*, 1997.

17. J. Leiwo and Y. Zheng. A mandatory access control policy model for information security requirements. In *Proceedings of the 21st Australasian Computer Science Conference (ACSC'98)*, 1998.

18. S. Muftic, A. Patel, P. Sanders, R. Colon, J. Heijnsdijk, and U. Pulkkinen. *Security Architecture for Open Distributed Systems*. John Wiley & Sons, 1994.

19. R. L. Rivest, A. Shamir, and L. M. Adleman. A Method for Obtaining Digital Signatures and Public–Key Cryptosystems. *Commun. ACM*, 21(2):120–126, Feb. 1978.

20. R. S. Sandhu. Lattice-based access control models. *IEEE Computer*, pages 9–19, Nov. 1993.

21. R. S. Sandhu, E. J. Coyne, H. J. Feinstein, and C. E. Youman. Role-based access control models. *IEEE Computer*, 29(2):38–47, Feb. 1996.

22. B. Schneier. *Applied Cryptography*. John Wiley & Sons, New York, second edition, 1996.

23. W. Stallings. *Network and Internetwork Security: Principles and Practise*. Prentice Hall, Inc., Englewood Cliffs, NJ, USA, 1995.

24. D. F. Sterne. On the buzzword Security Policy. In *IEEE Symposium on Security and Privacy*, 1991.

25. T. Y. Woo and S. S. Lam. Authorization in distributed systems: A formal approach. In *Proceedings of 1992 IEEE Symposium on Research in Security and Privacy*, 1992.

26. Y. Zheng. Digital signcryption or how to achieve cost(signature & encryption) $\leq$ cost (signature) + cost(encryption). In *Advances in Cryptology - Crypto'97*, number 1294 in Lecture Notes in Computer Science. Springer-Verlag, 1997.

27. Y. Zheng. The SPEED cipher. In *Proceedings of the Financial Cryptography'97*, 1997.

Specifying Security in a Composite System

J.-M. Kabasele-Tenday

Unité Informatique - Université catholique de Louvain
Place Ste-Barbe 2,
1348 Louvain-la-Neuve, Belgium
Email : jmk@info.ucl.ac.be

Abstract. This paper proposes a formal definition of " security " in a composite system . By composite system, we mean a system which is composed of an automated and a human part. This split of systems in two parts characterizes the computer environment where human presence is unavoidable. Our results are a generalization of [6]. The scope of [6] was limited to three access modes, that is read, write, execute. In this paper, we extend this scope by addressing all possible operations. We also provide a syntactic way, based on the proposed security formal definition, of describing threats during the requirement analysis process. To handle the security problem when designing a system, it is important to integrate threats in the requirements document. Up to now, there were only " methods " to derive threats [arbitrary or threat trees method], not to express them unambiguously.

Keywords : security, security specification, composite system, threats, secure system.

1 Introduction

People dealing with security in computing systems have been proposing methods, tools, theories, etc. to support integration of security in the design process. Several algorithms, cryptographic protocols, encryption techniques, disclosure models, integrity models, etc., have been designed for some specific security problems. But a main problem remains : what is " security " for an automated-system and how to present security threats in requirements documents (Contract) both for customer and designer? Commonly, security is specified as a set of constraints ensuring integrity, secrecy, etc. This definition seems right in an information system but fails in other systems such as a stock management system, where one possible threat is " stealing of resources " for example.

The response to this question is a key issue in order to choose adequate models or protocols and/or to improve existing ones to fix the real threats. Furthermore, a correct specification of system security features in requirements documents is a good way to mitigate vulnerabilities and prevent systems from attacks.

The goal of this paper is to provide a rigorous definition of security in a composite system and to propose a general syntactic way of expressing threats in a system. Our results rely both on relevant research results in Software Engineering theory [7] [3] and on a mathematical background. In the second section, we shall present some relevant results of Software Engineering as well as some classical results in security theory. Software Engineering, particularly Requirements Engineering, allows to describe " computing systems " in general. Thanks to those results, it is possible to understand " what " security is in a computing environment. The third section will be introduced by some security features and a formal definition of security will be deduced according to the previous discussions. As consequence, the fourth section will be assigned to the syntax of threats in requirements documents. This syntax will be based on the characteristics issued from the formal definition. Finally, other issues and future works are discussed in the concluding section.

2 Background

2.1 System specification

A lot of methodologies are available for specifying computing systems in software engineering. Many abstractions have been used to model system behaviors [5].

The Object-oriented paradigm is currently one of the most used modeling processes for describing a system during the software life-cycle [7]. In this paradigm, the system is described as a collection of discrete objects. An object is an abstraction of interest in the problem to solve. It incorporates data structures which denote both its characteristics, and its behavior. Characteristics are called " attributes " and behaviors are called methods, operations or actions.

In this context, we define a system as a collection of objects inter-acting for fixed goals. A goal of the system is an objective that the system is assumed to achieve in its life-cycle. It denotes a state or a collection of states that users expect the system to reach.

It is easy to see that this definition covers as well the three models, object, functional and dynamic models presented in [7] as the view of a system in [3]. In [7], the object model describes the structure of objects in the system without care to changes that are captured by the dynamic model by the way of system scenarios. The functional model describes the data flow. Functions are invoked as actions in the dynamic model and are shown as operations on object in the object model.

In addition to interesting objects, [3] extends the view of the system with specific features such as Goals, Constraints, Scenarios, etc. and provides a syntax that outlines the characteristics of each item. An object can be specialized as an Entity or an Agent. An Agent denotes an object that can control the transition of the system whereas an Entity is a passive object, that is an object which can not manipulate other objects in the system. In other words, an Entity can not be the performer of an operation.

This result is very useful in the security view of the system as argued next. We need this distinction between Entity and Agent to be able to control or to capture the behavior of Agents and thus the system behavior.

Notation: In the following, the term Object will denote passive object and Agent remains the active object. It is clear that an Agent can sometimes behave as passive Object.

Some relevant specific characteristics of agents are detailed in [3]. They are: *CapableOf, Execute, motivation, cost,* and *reliability.* These features will be encapsulated as attributes in the Agent definition and their values will be critical for security matters.

CapableOf is an Agent attribute that denotes the list of operations he has the skill to perform in the system.

Execute is an attribute denoting the operations the agent is assigned to. It is important to note here that an agent is not necessarily assigned to all operations he is capable of.

Motivation, cost and reliability are features of the relationship between the agent and the operations he is able to perform. Those characteristics can help to assign operations to Agents according to the objectives of the system [3].

Notation : Let x be a object, we will note $x.\langle attribute \rangle$ to address a specific attribute. For example, if a system has an Agent called " client ", we can have

$$client.capableof = \{buy, pay, \dots\}$$

Definition 1. A system state is its snapshot at a precise moment of its lifecycle. It is a function that corresponds to all current values of all objects attributes and operations status in the system at this time. A system has an initial state. When it is running, since objects inter-act, states change. A system state can be represented as a first-order logical assertion. Later in this paper, we shall define it as a collection of sets.

We assume our system to be closed, that is all agents and objects are considered parts of the system. Normally, no stimulus does come from outside. In this context, if an " external " agent attempts to perform any system operation, it is considered as an attack.

Property: All system states are not desired by the client when the system is set up. Restrictions must be defined on a system to avoid " unwished " states. However, it is always technically possible that an implemented system achieves an unexpected state or goal.

This can be possible for many reasons, mainly either the system or its environment has design or accidental faults, or an Agent executes an operation he is not assigned to.

2.2 Informal discussion on security

Security is a set of constraints and techniques that restrict objects and agents behaviors in order to confine the system in the expected states, even if a *malicious* agent wants either to block an occurrence of a wished state or to bring the system into an unwanted state. When no malicious agent is considered, constraints concern reliability and not security.

Definition 2. - threat - vulnerability - attack

- A *threat* is any potential occurrence of behavior that can move the system in an unwanted state.
- A *vulnerability* is some unfortunate characteristics or faults that make a threat possible.
- An *attack* is an action using a vulnerability by a malicious agent to perform a threat.

Note and comments : Since the system has many steps in its life-cycle and will be running in an environment, it is clear that vulnerabilities can be caused by bad specifications in early stages of requirements analysis and not only by flaws in protocols design or in the implementation environment.

There are a lot of other concepts used in security theory to describe some classical models. Those are security level, security label, security clearance function, reference monitor, " own " function, " dominates " relation, the lattice structure, and so on. The Reference monitor is the " black box " that receives each request to perform an action from an agent and either grants or denies the execution. More details on these concepts can be found in [Amo94]. We can just outline that level and label can be encapsulated in the object as attributes.

3 Formal definition of a secure system

The results presented in this section are a generalization of [6] specification of security. The scope of [6] was limited to that of the Bell-LaPadula model [2], that is to three access modes: read, write, execute and the " *file* " as the unique relevant object type of the system. We extend this scope by addressing all possible operations or actions, and all type of objects.

3.1 Framework and system model

Let S be the set of all agents in the system, O the set of all objects and A the set of all operations in the system.

System state : Informally, a state is a snapshot of a running system. The state transitions are caused by agents processing operations that modify object attributes and behaviors, it makes sense to represent the system snapshot as set of triplets " S x O x A ". We call respectively B and V the set of all states and the set of acceptable states. Formally, a state v of the system is an element such that

$$v \in V \subseteq B$$

where $B \subseteq P(S \ X \ O \ X \ A)$. [1]

Since v is a set of triplets, it has the form { (s1,o1,op1), ... (sn,on,opn)}. *In each triplet (s,o,op), " s " is an agent performing operation " op " that modifies object " o ".*

Composite System: Let R be the set of all requests to the reference monitor and V the set of acceptable states. At a moment, if the system is in a state v and agent s applies for a set of operations [scenario], if the application is granted, then the system will move from the actual state v to an other state v*. The system transition function T will be formally defined as a function

$$T : S \ x \ R \ x \ V \longrightarrow V$$

Composite system model :A composite system is a state machine $\Sigma(V, R, T, V_{init})$, where V, R, and T are defined above. V_{init} is the set of initial states.

State reachability: A state v is reachable if and only if either v is an initial state or there exists a sequence of states such that v is its final states. Formally, a state v is reachable when

i) $v \in V_{init}$ or
ii) $\exists$ sequence $\langle (s_0, r_0, v_0), ..., (s_n, r_n, v_n) \rangle$ such that
$v0 \in v_{init}$, $T(s_n, r_n, v_n) = v$, and $\forall i, 0 \leq i < n$, $T(s_i, r_i, v_i) = v_{i+1}$.

3.2 Security-related Concepts

Trusted Agent: An agent is said to be trusted in a system if his motivation to execute any operation is always assumed to be good, in opposition to malicious. Operations requested by trusted agents are always accepted unconditionally by the system. [2]

---

[1] If A is a set, P(A) denotes the set of sub sets of A.

[2] We can formally redefine this notion according to security techniques defined in [1].
  If we consider the join relation on the lattice (Label, dominate, join, meet),
  an agent X such that $\forall$ X, x1, x2, ...xn $\in$ Label
  join(x1,x2,...,xn) = X [iff X dominates x1 AND X dominates x2 AND ...AND X dominates xn.] is trusted agent

Maintainer Agent For the sake of simplicity, let us assume that security is controlled by means of security levels. It is clear that security can not be maintained when any agent is able to change his security level. This is clearly expressed in BLP model [2] where the responsibility of an operation depends on security level. For example, an agent with low security level can not read a document of the high security level.

Definition: A Maintainer agent is an agent assigned to change security levels of other agents in the system. Formally, Let us define functions Cs and Co on sets S and O where Cs(s) and Co(o) refer respectively to the sets of agents assigned to change security level of agent s and object o.

$$Cs : S \longrightarrow P(S)$$

$$Co : O \longrightarrow P(S)$$

We designate agents in Cs(s) and Co(o) as the sets of maintainer agents.

Precedence relation A lot of constraints may be expressed in the system requirement. Constraints refer to general conditions that must be satisfied by the composite system. This paragraph concerns one of the most regular constraints in system specifications. We call it *precedence relation*.

Definition and notation: Let p and q be two system states. We say that p precede q if and only if state q never occurs if state p has not been occurred before. We will note this relation

precede(p,q) or $p \lhd q$

Examples :

i) In an Educational exam system, it is stipulated that a student can not read the exam before the scheduled date for this exam.

ii) In a Bank system, a customer can not withdraw money before he has made a deposit.

Those examples are explicit enough to highlight the importance of this precedence constraint in system requirements in general and in security concerns especially.

3.3   Security in the system

Secure state: A state v is secure if and only if

$\forall(x, y, op) \in v$, $op \in x.execute$ AND x *dominates* y for op at that moment. (1)

Let us recall that x is an agent, y is an object , op is an operation, and a state v is a set of triplets (agent, object, operation). The intuition behind this statement is that for each triplet (x,y,op) in the state v, the agent " x " is allowed to execute the operation " op " defined to act on object " y " during the system running.

Moreover, at this moment, the security label of the subject x is greater than the security label of y for operation op. Let us note that security label depends on operation and is assumed to be set up by the maintainer agent according to the system specification.

If the agent x is allowed to execute the operation " op " and the maintainer agent decides to change its security label for op such that he does not dominate y, then if x run op at this moment, the resulting state is " insecure ". In the other hand, a malicious agent 'ag' within a security label is limited to his ag.execute list of operations.

This definition integrates, from the *dominate* relation, both the lattice-based view of security and the requirement-based models such that of Clark-Wilson [1].

Secure transition: a transition function T is secure in normal conditions if :

i) The precedence relation is invariant : this means, it is not possible to get, by transition function T, a sequence $\langle ...,(s_i, r_i, w),...,(s_j, r_j, v),...\rangle$ whereas constraint *precede(v,w)* is specified on the system.

ii) Non-maintenance is stable, in other words a non maintainer agent can not move to maintainer agent status by the application of the transition function T. Formally,
   if $T(s,r,v) = v^*$, where v* is the new state after transition T,
   1. $\forall x \in S$, $x.security\_level$ in $v \neq x.security\_level$ in $v^* \implies s \in$ Cs(x).
   2. $\forall y \in O$, $y.security\_level$ in $v \neq y.security\_level$ in $v^* \implies s \in Co(y)$.

iii) Distrust is stable, that is a non trusted agent in v can not become a trusted agent in v*.

Secure system definition: A necessary condition that a composite system is secure is :

(1) All reachable states are secure,
(2) its transition function is secure and
(3) responsiveness is ensured.

The third sub condition means that when a request is made, a response will follow within an acceptable delay. This later case is to ensure that the reference monitor is not blocked by a malicious agent.

4 Threat description

4.1 Definition

We understood earlier that a threat is a conceivable sequence of transitions that can move the system from an acceptable system state to an unacceptable state. According to the previous discussion, we can deduce the following statements.

Statement : Let $\Sigma(S, R, T, v_{init})$ be the composite system. A conceivable sequence $\langle (s_1, r_1, v_1)...(s_k, r_k, v_k) \rangle where (s_i, r_i, v_i) = T(s_{i-1}, r_{i-1}, v_{i-1})$ is a threat if at least one of the following conditions is satisfied:

   i) $\exists$ s $\in \{s_1, ..., s_k\}$ such that $s \in S$. In other words, an outsider agent applied an operation, i.e. caused a states transition.

   ii) $\exists$ a state $v_j \ni (X, y, op)$ such that X.op not $\in$ X.execute or X not dominates y for op, $1 \leq j \leq k$.

   iii) The Transition function is vulnerable. That is, its implementation or specification does not ensure Distrust stability, non-maintenance invariance or precedence stability, as specified in the definition of " secure transition".

   iv) Responsiveness is not ensured for operations concerned by this property.

From this definition, we can outline that a threat is characterized by agents, objects and operations.

4.2 Threats types examples and potential threats identification

In a distributed information system where read, write, execute, send, receive, etc. are the bulk of system operations, the most known threats are disclosure or secrecy and data integrity. The disclosure refers to the possibility of an non authorized agent reading a document file. The integrity threats concerns any unauthorized change to files stored or in transit. A Taxonomy of threats is available in the literature [1]. Cryptographic theories and protocols are dealing with disclosure and integrity threats.

To identify potential threats during the specification process, it has been proposed to use a structured way called threat trees [1] rather than the arbitrary threat lists that had been used before. The root of the threats tree represents the complete set of potential threats to the system. This set is then iterative divided in subsets represented by the intermediary nodes in the tree. The leaves are individual threats. For further information, one can consult [1] or other literature.

4.3   A syntax of threats

A Syntax of threats must allow potential threats to be specified in the system requirements document, so that all people involved in the system life-cycle can unambiguously identify the security problem and solve it in a reliable way. We have outlined that threats are concerned by Agents, objects and operations.

The syntax presented below [Fig.1] covers relevant threats characteristics discussed above according to the object-oriented modeling. Commentaries in curly brackets follow each attribute. It is possible to add others attributes discussed in the threat trees method ; for example risk, criticality, effort.

```
Begin_threat
Threat_Identifier :{ Identifier used to handle the threat }
Type: { class or category of threat, e.g. disclosure, integrity, ... }
Objects : { set of threatened objects concerned by the current threat }
Agents : { agents involved in the potential occurrence of an attack}
Description : {formal and/or informal definition of threat }
Operations : { Set of critical operations in the threat sequence }
End_Threat.
```

Fig.1 Threat syntax

The threats part in a system specification document will be a list of such modules. An example of three threats of an Exam environment in a Distance learning system [4] is given below :

```
Threat_Identifier : Discl01
Type: disclosure
Objects : exam
Agents : students
Description : a student read the exam content before the fixed date
Operations : login , read, copy, receive
End_Threat.
Threat_Identifier : Discl02
Type: disclosure
Objects : answer { of exam }
Agents : students
Description: student reads answers of other student during the exam test.
Operations : login , read, copy, receive, send, transfer file, ...
End_Threat.
Threat_Identifier : Integ01
Type: Integrity
Objects : exam answers
Agents : students
Description : a student modifies his exam answers after the session.
Operations : login , write
End_Threat.
```

5 Conclusions

We have formally stated necessary conditions for a system to be secure[3.3]. From this definition, we have deduced a threat definition and syntax.

The scope of those results is not only the known threats such as disclosure, integrity, denial of service, etc. It concerns any threat to a composite system in general. This can be a transportation system where main operations are get in , get out , move, etc. or a stock management system where threat such as "stealing resource " can be expressed in the syntax[4.3]. But mainly, thanks to this syntax, it is possible to include a threat paragraph in a requirement specification document. Thus, all people involved in the design and analysis process can identify security problems and handle these together with the global design model.

In the future, it will be interesting to deduce the threats taxonomy by means of the threat definition proposed in this paper.

Acknowledgments I gratefully acknowledge financial support of the Commission of the European Communities (D.G. XIII, INCO 950363) that has been sponsoring the TELESUN project and, within it, our research. The organizing committee of the 1997 Information Security Workshop financed the presentation of this paper, I am thankful for their generosity. I would also like to deeply thank Professor Marc Lobelle for his time passed in reviewing the draft of this document. Discussions with Professor Jean-Jacques Quisquater clarified some ideas of this paper. We are really grateful.

References

1. Amoroso,E. : Fundamentals of Computer security technology. Prentice Hall, New Jersey (1994)
2. Bell, D.,LaPadula, L.: Secure Computer System : Unified Exposition and Multics Interpretation. MTR**2997**, MITRE Corp. (1976)
3. Dardenne, A.; et al: Goal-directed Requirements Acquisition. Science of Comp. Progr., vol. **20** (1993), 3–50.
4. Kabasele-Tenday,J.M.: Threats in Tele-teaching. To be presented at 7th WCCEE, Torino, Italy, (1998)
5. Jacobson, I., et al.: Object-Oriented Software Engineering, A Use case driven approach. Addison-Wesley. (1992)
6. McLean, J. : The Algebra of Security. IEEE Symposium on security and privacy, Oakland, CA,(1988)
7. Rumbaugh, J. et al : Object-oriented modeling and design. Prentice-Hall,New Jersey, (1991)

On Rough Sets and Inference Analysis

Kan Zhang

Cambridge University Computer Laboratory
Pembroke Street, Cambridge CB2 3QG, UK
Email: kz200@cl.cam.ac.uk

Abstract. In this paper, we give an overview of a promising approach to inference detection and analysis in relational databases, first introduced in [25]. The approach employs techniques from rough sets theory and is able to take into account of all *certain* and *possible* material implications in the data, including functional dependencies. It can also be used to address inference threats posed by rule-induction techniques from data mining. A major advantage of this approach is that the quantitative measure IRI is computed directly from data without knowledge input from System Security Officer. By comparing with other techniques, we attempt to convey the merits of rough sets based approach.

1 Introduction

In multilevel databases, inference problem has long been identified as a major threat to security. An inference problem in a multilevel database arises when a user with a low-level clearance, accessing information of low classification, is able to draw conclusions about information at higher classifications [18].

There is often no immediate or obvious connection between the low data and the inferred high data; however, an inferential chain may link the low and high data through low relations, constraints, and rules, some of which may not be explicitly stored in the database. The inference problem is especially difficult when it often involves information that is not explicitly represented in the database and thus not easily considered by automatic tools.

Preventing all inference of sensitive information by uncleared individuals has been seen as a problem of overwhelming difficulty [5]. Most of available approaches try to achieve, in principle, a complete model of all knowledge and information that might be used to infer the sensitive data, which is generally impractical, as well as the ability to recognize all sensitive implications of that information, which is generally impossible.

To some extent, all knowledge-based approaches, e.g. [16, 11, 6, 23, 5, 10, 4, 19], need help from System Security Officer (SSO) to generate related structures. The knowledge input from SSO represents the semantics of application. The fact that SSO can never be sure he knows all the dependencies among data means that available approaches only provide partial solutions. At most, they can claim that *to the best of our knowledge* there is no inference channel. There might well be data dependencies that the SSO is unaware of or are introduced into the database during its lifetime, which were not envisioned at database design time.

A particularly difficult and important problem involves the ability to draw partial conclusions about sensitive information, even when the information may not be directly inferable. This problem argues for a more quantitative model of inferability.

Sometimes inference is *certain*, such as through functional dependency. However, more frequently we have cases in which inference is partial or with certain probability. Several previous works have addressed this situation, e.g. [16,6,1]. However, in existing approaches the probabilities are either assumed (e.g. [1]) or computed with the knowledge from SSO (e.g. [16,6]). This is not satisfactory due to the limits of SSO's understanding of the semantics of application.

More recently, knowledge discovery in databases (KDD) or data mining (DM) techniques raise new security concerns for databases [14]. One of the primary approaches in KDD is *rule induction*, or learning from examples (see, for example, [12,20]). The derived generalized rules from KDD may open up new inference channels. Since the SSO may not be aware of such generalized rules, previous approaches are inadequate in addressing threats posed by KDD or DM.

In [25], we introduced a new approach to inference analysis in relational databases. The approach employs techniques from rough sets theory. Instead of trying to capture the semantics of application through various structures as used in previous approaches, we try to analyse inference risks through material implications that actually exist in the data.

In [15], Marks insightfully formalises general inference as material implication. He goes on using *Patterns* to detect all *certain* material implications reflected in the data. Our rough sets based approach proposed in [25] is able to capture both *certain* and *possible* material implications reflected in the data. In addition, rough sets based approach has other desirable properties, such as addressing generalized rules.

In this paper, we give an overview of the applicability of rough sets theory to inference detection and analysis problem. By comparing with other techniques, we attempt to convey the merits of rough sets based approach. The paper is organised as follows. The underlying idea of our approach is given in section 3. In section 4, we give necessary concepts of rough sets theory. Details of our approach is presented in section 5. Discussions of the approach follows in section 6. We draw our conclusions in section 7.

2 A Different Approach

Inference in a database is said to occur if, by retrieving a set of tuples $\{T\}$ having attributes $\{A\}$ from the database, it is possible to specify a set of tuples $\{T'\}$, having attributes $\{A'\}$, where $\{T'\} \not\subset \{T\}$ or $\{A'\} \neq \{A\}$ [15]. In logic settings, we say there exists a *material implication*, denoted $(T, A) \Rightarrow (T', A')$, that relates the two sets. In other studies, material implications are sometimes referred to as *secondary paths* [1] or *inference channels* [18].

In classical terms, inference in relational databases is used to refer to logical process of proving or deriving some classified attribute values for some tuples from some unclassified attribute values. In this sense, inference is associated with some type of causal relationship, such as functional dependencies. As has been pointed out by Marks in [15], material implication is more general than functional dependency. Material implications only require that sets of data and attributes occur together, regardless of whether one causes the other, both are caused by a third activity, or they occur by coincidence.

We assume the *closed world assumption* (CWA). By CWA we mean that the data instances are complete and domain definitions are fully instantiated. Under CWA, all the material implications corresponding to possible inferences can be derived from data. This does not mean all the knowledge needed to complete an inference chain has to reside in the database, i.e. the database doesn't have to contain all the semantics of an application. A chain of inference can be completed using outside knowledge. However, since the start and the end attribute values of an inference chain are in the database, a material implication corresponding to that inference chain must exist in the data and we should be able to discover that material implication from data under CWA. For detailed discussion of material implication and inference chain, please see [15].

Unlike previous approaches, here we are not trying to discover the semantics of application or the knowledge that can be used for possible logical inferences. As we have pointed out before, knowledge-based approaches may be incomplete since neither the database nor SSO may have/know all the semantics of application. Instead we use rough set theory as our tool to capture the *semantics of data* [1] and quantify the inference risks through material implications. Since all logical inferences have corresponding material implications in the database, we are able to address all the possible inferences through material implications. Meanwhile, not all material implications have the corresponding logical inference paths, i.e. there may not be any apparent causal reason for a particular material implication. However, we think such material implications are still a legitimate concern for the current state of data in the database.

In this study, we take a different view of inference threats from that of Marks [15]. We think that if a material implication is valid for the data in a database, it should be considered as a possible inference path and should be taken into account by SSO. There might not be logical reasons for a particular material implication. However, the lack of causal reasons may due to the limits of SSO's understanding of the semantics of application. For example, in the case of scientific data, causality is what scientists are trying to discover in the research process. On the other hand, even if a material implication is just a coincidence, the very fact that this coincident is valid in the current state of data means that it is a legitimate concern. The material implication may be picked up by an attacker's data mining tools and used to derive a valid classified association

---

[1] In our study, we use the term *semantics of data* to mean the properties of data in KRS context, which is independent from the semantics of application represented by the relational database.

unexpectedly. The attacker may not necessarily believe the results, but, at least, the validity of the material implication alarms the attacker that this could be true.

3 Concepts of Rough Sets

Rough sets theory was first introduced by Pawlak [17]. The primary problem addressed by the technique of rough sets is the discovery, representation and analysis of data regularities.

In rough sets theory, a *Knowledge Representation System*(KRS) is a quadruple

$$S = (U, A, V, f),$$

where U is a non-empty, finite set called universe, A is a finite set of attributes, $V = \cup V_a$ is a union of domains V_a of attributes a belonging to A, and $f :$ $U \times A \to V$ is an information function such that $f(x, a) \in V_a$ for every $a \in A$ and $x \in U$.

The information function assigns attribute values to objects belonging to U. The Knowledge representation System allows for convenient tabular representation of data, which is similar to a relational table in the relational data base model (cf. Codd [3]). However, the relational model is not interested in the meaning of the information stored in the table. The emphasis is placed on efficient data structuring and manipulation. In the Knowledge Representation System the attribute values, i.e., the table entries, have associated explicit meaning as features or properties of the objects.

The key idea in the rough sets approach stems from the observation that imprecise representation of data helps uncover data regularities. The question is how much imprecision should be allowed without loss of essential information which is understood here as an ability to discern, fully or partially, a concept or a class of concepts. The quality of the information is measured in the framework of rough sets by using the notions of lower and upper set approximation [17].

To maximally reduce the degree of precision, the idea of *reduct* is used which allows for discernibility-preserving elimination of irrelevant information. After finding reducts for each concept, the maximally imprecise, that is with easily determinable patterns, representation of data is obtained. Based on such a representation, general rules characterizing each concept can be computed. The computation of rules can be reduced to the problem of finding prime implicants of a Boolean function called indiscernibility function. Also, the degree of functional dependency between attributes can be computed by using the idea of set lower bound. The subsequent computation of relative reducts allows one to find all alternative groups of attributes which are non-redundant and preserve the dependency level. This kind of a feature is particularly useful for knowledge discovery applications [27].

4 Inference Risk Index

In this work, we assume that data is stored in a relational database consisting of a series of tables and sensitive data items are protected by element-level labelling. We will further assume the universal relation paradigm [24] and view a relational database as a single table containing all the attributes from the entire database. We are not concerned about the actual mechanics of forming the view of a universal relation. We are only interested in evaluating the inference risks for those classified data items in the universal relation.

A relational table can be viewed as a Knowledge Representation System in which columns are labelled by attributes, rows are labelled by the objects and the entry in column p and row x has the value $p(x)$. Each row in the relational table represents *information* about some object in universe U. However, the relational model is not interested in the meaning of the information stored in the table. Consequently the objects about which information is contained in the table may not be represented in the table. Whereas in the KRS all objects are explicitly represented and the attribute values, i.e., the table entries, have associated explicit meaning as features or properties of the objects.

One way to conciliate the two models is to take the primary key K in the relational table as object identifier and all other attributes in the relational table as attributes in KRS. In doing so, we may lost some information contained in the primary key attributes which is relevant to the semantics of application.

Another way to get around this is to add another attribute which assigns a unique identifier to each row of the relational table. In this case, all the attributes in the original relational table become attributes in the corresponding KRS and there is no information loss. However, in the relational data model there is always a primary key which identifies every object in the table, which means the derived KRS is selective. This situation may still happen even if we use primary key as object identifier. Selective KRS is not itself difficult to analyse, but we might have to lower the degree of precision in order to derive generalized rules.

For simplicity, we assume a two-level labelling system, Classified and Unclassified. Given a universal relation R and its set of attributes A', we view the relational table as a KRS in which every tuple of R is an object of universe U with the value x of primary key K as object identifier. The corresponding KRS has attribute set $A = A' - K$. The quantitative measure Inference Risk Index (IRI) for each subset of classified attribute values belonging to the same object is defined by [25]:

Definition For a classified data element set (x, P) in column set P and row x with value set P_x, let attribute set B denote the set of attributes whose values are classified for object x ($P \subseteq B$). Let attribute sets $C = A - B$ and $D = P$. The associated **Inference Risk Index** $IRI(x, P)$ for data element set (x, P) is defined as

$$IRI(x, P) = \frac{card([x]_{IND(C)} \cap [x]_{IND(D)})}{card([x]_{IND(C)})}$$

where $card$ is the cardinality of a set, $[x]_{IND(C)}$ and $[x]_{IND(D)}$ are the equivalent classes of $IND(C)$ and $IND(D)$ containing x, respectively.

Intuitively, IRI gives us a quantitative measure of inference risks due to possible material implications existing in the database. It is computed from data directly.

From the definition of IRI, it is easy to see for any classified data element set (x, P), $0 < IRI(x, P) \leq 1$. If $IRI(x, P) = 1$, we have $[x]_{IND(C)} \subseteq [x]_{IND(D)}$ which means there is a *certain* rule that can be induced from C to D for all the objects/tuples in $[x]_{IND(C)}$, i.e. there is a *certain* material implication $([x]_{IND(C)}, C) \Rightarrow ([x]_{IND(C)}, D)$.

Since it is always true that $x \in ([x]_{IND(C)} \cap [x]_{IND(D)})$, there is always a *possible* rule that can be induced from C to D for all the objects/tuples in $[x]_{IND(C)}$, i.e. there is a *possible* material implication $([x]_{IND(C)}, C) \Rightarrow ([x]_{IND(C)}, D)$. Therefore, $IRI(x, P)$ is always greater than 0. This is obvious since object/tuple x itself is a valid instance for the *possible* material implication.

Specifically, if $IND(C) \subseteq IND(D)$, i.e. D is functionally dependent on C, $IRI(x, P) = 1$ for any value of P_x. This conforms to our intuitive notion of functional dependency. Since attribute set C functionally determines attribute set D, given values of C the attacker should be able to infer values for D. Please note that there are cases where there is no functional dependency between C and D, but IRI still equal to 1. In these cases, there are *certain* rules between C and D that are valid only for the specific value of P_x, not for all the possible values of C and D in terms of the classical definition of functional dependency.

5 Applicability of Rough Sets

From the definition of IRI, we are able to address all the material implications existing in the data. However, in real applications, not all these material implications accurately capture the dependencies of data. Some irrelevant attributes may contribute, even though in a negligible way under CWA, to the discernibility of knowledge C, therefore, disturb the real dependency we are trying to express using IRI.

Techniques from rough sets are well suited for removing these noises that may disguise true dependencies in the data, i.e. by computing the most significant attribute sets through the concept of relative reducts. In fact, the main problems that can be approached using rough sets theory include data reduction (i.e. elimination of superfluous data), discovery of data dependencies, estimation of data significance and discovery of cause-effect relationships.

Sometimes, the discernibility of the derived KRS is very high. We may find a large amount of material implications, but each of them may just have a small number of valid instances in the database. This might not be interesting since we might want to know the inference risks due to qualitative rules. In this case, we can try to generalize some of the attributes in order to discover and evaluate qualitative rules.

The rough sets approach that underlies the whole technique is based on the intuitive observation that lowing the degree of precision in the representation of objects, for example, by replacing the numeric temperature measurements by qualitative ranges of HIGH, NORMAL, or LOW, makes the data regularities more visible and easier to characterise in terms of rules. Lowering the representation accuracy, however, might lead to the undesired loss of information expressed in the reduced ability to discern among different concepts. To analyse and evaluate the effect of different representation accuracies on concept discernibility levels, a number of analytic tools have been developed [26]. By using these tools, one can attempt to find a representation method that would compromise between sufficient concept discernibility and the ability to reveal essential data regularities. It is, in fact, the ability of rough sets based approach to generalise the concepts that enables it to deter attempts to use generalized rules discovered by data mining for inference [12, 20].

In real applications, some data values of a relational table may be missing or imprecise. Consequently, the derived KRS is incomplete. The rough sets based methods are particularly useful for reasoning from qualitative, imprecise or incomplete data. For simplicity, in [25] we assume that all data items are precisely defined. Interested readers are referred to [21, 22] for dealing with uncertain data in rough sets context.

Another advantage of rough sets based approach is that programs implementing its methods can easily run on parallel computers, which allows for fast and efficient evaluation of IRI.

6 Discussion

6.1 Probabilistic Data Analysis

Rough sets theory is a mathematical tool to deal with vagueness and uncertainty. This technique, which is complementary to statistical methods of inference, provides a new insight into properties of data. The main focus of this technique is on the investigation of structural relationships in data rather than probability distributions, as is the case in statistical theory.

One of the main advantages of rough sets theory is that it does not need any preliminary or additional information about data, such as probability distribution in statistics, basic probability assignment in the Dempster-Shafer theory, or grade of membership or the value of possibility in fuzzy set theory [7].

Moreover, the rough sets approach makes no assumption about data as probabilistic methods do, e.g. normality of distributions, similar cardinality or large sizes of classes, and it does not use their typical operators of data aggregation (e.g. mean value) in the course of the analysis.

Another advantage of rough sets approach over probabilistic methods is that the rough sets approach is dealing particularly well with analysis of information systems coming from human experience, where qualitative attributes exists naturally [13].

6.2 KDD

Rough sets theory concerns the classificatory analysis of imprecise, uncertain or incomplete information. It is a very effective methodology for data analysis and discovering rules in the attribute-value based domains. It is also an efficient tool for database mining in relational databases [14].

On the other hand, techniques used in KDD can be readily used in our inference risk analysis approach. For example, in large databases, we can first generalize the data by performing attribute-oriented induction and then applies the rough sets techniques to the generalized relation to find data dependency among the generalized attributes and choose the best minimal attribute set to represent the final generalized relation. The final generalized relation can also be transformed into logical rule form [8, 9].

6.3 Future Work

In computing IRI, deciding the most significant subset of C is a tricky part. Further work are needed to find optimal algorithms.

Various database dependencies can be defined using indiscernibility relations, such as functional dependency, multivalued dependency, embedded multivalued dependency, decomposition, join dependency, Boolean dependency [2]. We have considered functional dependency in relational databases through material implication in [25]. How to extend our model to cover other dependencies is an interesting topic.

Finally, we should point out that the definition of IRI in [25] is conservative since $IND(C)$ and $IND(D)$ are calculated with full knowledge of relevant data in the database. In reality, an attack can only see part of the data needed. It is interesting to see how one can estimate the inference risks more accurately.

7 Conclusion

In this paper, we give an overview of a promising approach to inference detection and analysis in relational databases, first introduced in [25]. The approach employs techniques from rough sets theory and is able to take into account of all *certain* and *possible* material implications in the data, including functional dependencies. It can also be used to address inference threats posed by rule-induction techniques from data mining. A major advantage of this approach is that the quantitative measure IRI is computed directly from data without knowledge input from System Security Officer. By comparing with other techniques, we attempt to convey the merits of rough sets based approach.

Acknowledgements

I would like to thank Roger Needham and anonymous reviewers for helpful comments.

References

1. L. Binns, Inference through secondary path analysis, *Proc. Sixth IFIP Working Conf. Database Security*, Vancouver, B.C., Canada, Aug. 1992.
2. W. Buszkowski and E. Orlowska, On the Logic of Database Dependencies, *Bulletin of Polish Academy of Sciences, Mathematics*, Vol. 34, No. 5-6, 1986.
3. E.F. Codd, A Relational Model of Data for Large Shared Data Banks, *Comm. ACM*, Vol. 13, pp. 377-387, 1970.
4. H.S. Delugach and T.H. Hinke, Wizard: A Database Inference Analysis and Detection System, *IEEE Trans. on Knowledge and Data Engineering*, Vol. 8, No. 1, Feb 1996.
5. T.D. Garvey, T.F. Lunt, X. Qian, and M. Stickel, Toward a tool to detect and eliminate inference problems in the design of multilevel databases, *Proc. Sixth IFIP Working Conf. Database Security*, Vancouver, B.C., Canada, Aug. 1992.
6. T.D. Garvey, T.F. Lunt and M.E. Stickel, Abductive and Approximate Reasoning Models for Characterising Inference Channels, *Proc. of the Computer Security Foundations Workshop IV*, 1991.
7. J.W. Grzymala-Busse, Knowledge acquisition under uncertainty – A rough set approach, *J. Intel. Rob. Syst.*, 1(1), pp 3-16, 1988.
8. J. Han, Y. Cai and N. Cercone, Knowledge Discovery in Databases: An Attribute-Oriented Approach, *Proc. 18th VLDB Conf.*, Vancouver, B.C., Canada, pp. 340-355, 1992.
9. X. Hu, N. Cercone and J. Han, An Attribute-Oriented Rough Set Approach for Knowledge Discovery in Databases, *Proc. International Workshop on Rough Sets, Fuzzy Sets and Knowledge Discovery*, Banff, Alberta, Canada, Oct., 1993.
10. T.H. Hinke and H.S. Delugach, AERIE: An Inference Modelling and Detection Approach for Databases, *Proc. Sixth IFIP Working Conf. Database Security*, Vancouver, B.C., Canada, Aug. 1992.
11. T.H. Hinke, Inference Aggregation Detection in Database Management Systems, *Proc. 1988 IEEE Symposium on Security and Privacy*, April 1988.
12. X. Hu, N. Shan, N. Cercone and W. Ziarko, DBROUGH: A Rough Set Based Knowledge Discovery System, *Proc. 8th Int'l Symp. on Methodologies for Intelligent Systems*, Charlotte, NC., USA, 1994. (LNCS 869)
13. E. Krusinska, A Babic, R. Slowinski and J. Stefanowski, Comparison of the rough sets approach and probabilistic data analysis techniques on a common set of medical data, in *Intelligent Decision Support*, R. Slowinski, (ed.), Kluwer Academic Publishers, 1992.
14. T.Y. Lin, T.H. Hinke, D.G. Marks, and B. Thuraisingham, Security and Data Mining, *Proc. Ninth IFIP Working Conf. Database Security*, Aug. 1995.
15. D.G. Marks, Inference in MLS Database Systems, *IEEE Trans. on Knowledge and Data Engineering*, Vol. 8, No. 1, Feb 1996.
16. M. Morgenstern, Controlling Logical Inference in Multilevel Database Systems, *Proc. 1988 IEEE Symposium on Security and Privacy*, 1988.
17. Z. Pawlak, Rough Sets, In *Theoretical Aspects of Reasoning About Data*. Kluwer, Netherlands, 1991.
18. X. Qian, M.E. Stickel, P.D. Karp, T.F. Lunt, T.D. Garvey, Detection and Elimination of Inference Channels in Multilevel Relational Database Systems, *Proc. 1993 IEEE Symposium on Security and Privacy*, 1993.
19. S. Rath, D. Jones, J. Hale and S. Shenoi, A Tool for Inference Detection and Knowledge Discovery in Databases, *Proc. Ninth IFIP Working Conf. Database Security*, Aug. 1995.

20. R. Srikant and R. Agrawal, Mining Generalized Association Rules, *Proc. of the 21st Int'l Conference on Very Large Databases*, 1995.

21. R. Slowinski, J. Stefanowski: Rough classification in incomplete information systems, *Mathematical and Computer Modelling* 12 (1989) no.10/11, 1347-1357.

22. R. Slowinski, J. Stefanowski: Rough-Set Reasoning about Uncertain Data, *Fundamenta Informaticae*, 27(2/3): 229-243 (1996)

23. B. Thuraisingham, The Use of Conceptual Structures for Handling the Inference Problem, *Proc. fifth IFIP Working Conf. Database Security*, Shepherdstown, WV, November 1991.

24. J.D. Ullman, *Principles of Database and Knowledge-Base Systems*, vols. I and II, Rockville, MD.: Computer Science Press, 1988, 1989.

25. K. Zhang, IRI: A Quantitative Approach to Inference Analysis in Relational Databases, *Proc. 11th IFIP Working Conf. Database Security*, Lake Tahoe, CA, August 1997.

26. W. Ziarko, The Discovery, Analysis, and Representation of Data Dependencies in Databases, in *Knowledge Discovery in Databases*, G. Piatetsky-Shapiro and W.J. Frawley, (eds) Menlo Park, CA: AAAI/MIT, 1991, 195-209.

27. W. Ziarko, Rough Sets and Knowledge Discovery: An Overview, *Proc. International Workshop on Rough Sets, Fuzzy Sets and Knowledge Discovery*, Banff, Alberta, Canada, Oct., 1993.

Arbitrated Unconditionally Secure Authentication Scheme with Multi-senders

Tzonelih Hwang and Chih-Hung Wang

Institute of Information Engineering, National Cheng-Kung University
No.1, University Road, Tainan, Taiwan, R.O.C.
Fax: +886-6-2747076
E-mail: hwangtl@server2.iie.ncku.edu.tw

Abstract. Previously, Desmedt and Seberry developed a practical proven secure authentication scheme with arbitration. Their scheme, however, only provides an environment for a single sender. Nevertheless, in real applications, many senders may collaboratively send a message to the receiver and convince the receiver that the message is actually transmitted by them. In this paper, we present an efficient scheme which (a) is unconditionally secure against denial by the senders having sent a message and (b) reduces the size of evidence for the authentic message in a multi-senders environment.

Keywords: Authentication Scheme, Unconditionally Secure, Message Authentication Code

1 Introduction

The first Simmons [11] introduced an unconditionally secure authentication scheme with an arbiter. Although capable of resolving the disputes between the sender and receiver, that scheme cannot prevent the arbiter from attacking. To overcome this problem, Desmedt and Yung [3] improved the Simmons' scheme. Unfortunately, both schemes are infeasible because the keys used in their scheme can be used only once. If the distributed keys are re-used, security would be compromised.

A practical proven secure authentication scheme with arbitration has been proposed by Desmedt and Seberry [4]. In this scheme, the distributed keys can be reused and the arbiter need not be active when messages are transmitted. This scheme provides an environment for a single sender to convince the receiver having sent a message. However, if a group of senders cooperatively send a message to the receiver, then the receiver should be able to ascertain that the message is authentic.

A good multi-senders authentication scheme should reduce the size of the evidence of the authentic message (this evidence is necessary to resolve a dispute between the senders and the receiver). However, achieving such reduction is really difficult if directly iterate the scheme of [4]. Therefore, we propose a new scheme that, by means of our key distribution/management strategy, will reduce the size of evidence and the number of enciphering keys to be held by the senders. In addition, the proposed scheme does not degrade the security level claimed in [4], which is unconditionally secure against denial by the sender of having sent a message, and conditionally secure against the frauds of impersonating the senders or substituting a message by the receiver or arbiter.

2 The Multi-senders Scheme

Our scheme involves three parties. Let us call S_i, for $i = 1, 2, \cdots, m$, the senders, R the receiver, and A the arbiter. Now, the situation is that all of the senders want to cooperatively send a message M to the receiver. We mention here that the keys required in our scheme need not be strictly defined because they would be chosen according to a prescribed authentication algorithm.

2.1 Distribution Phase

The arbiter A selects an $m \times n$ key matrix

$$K = \begin{pmatrix} k_{1,1} & k_{1,2} & \ldots & k_{1,n} \\ k_{2,1} & k_{2,2} & \ldots & k_{2,n} \\ \cdots\cdots\cdots\cdots\cdots \\ k_{m,1} & k_{m,2} & \ldots & k_{m,n} \end{pmatrix}$$

and sends ith row of matrix K to S_i. Then A sends $\lfloor \frac{n}{2} \rfloor$ columns to R randomly chosen from the matrix K with uniform probability distribution. The indices of these columns form a subset I $(= \{i_1, i_2, \cdots, i_{\lfloor \frac{n}{2} \rfloor}\})$ of the set $\{1, 2, \cdots, n\}$. These $\lfloor \frac{n}{2} \rfloor$ columns of the matrix K are defined as another matrix

$$K' = \begin{pmatrix} k_{1,i_1} & k_{1,i_2} & \ldots & k_{1,i_{\lfloor \frac{n}{2} \rfloor}} \\ k_{2,i_1} & k_{2,i_2} & \ldots & k_{2,i_{\lfloor \frac{n}{2} \rfloor}} \\ \cdots\cdots\cdots\cdots\cdots \\ k_{m,i_1} & k_{m,i_2} & \ldots & k_{m,i_{\lfloor \frac{n}{2} \rfloor}} \end{pmatrix}$$

, which is the verification key matrix of R.

To prevent the arbiter's attack, each sender S_i sends R a key $k_{i,n+1}$ through a private channel.

2.2 Authentication Phase

Sequential Model. To send the message M to the receiver R, all senders first cooperatively determine an order list L. Without losing the generality, assume this order list L is $\{S_1, S_2, \cdots, S_m\}$. Initially, S_1 sends $(M, C_{k_{1,1}}, C_{k_{1,2}}, \cdots, C_{k_{1,n+1}})$ to S_2, where $C_{k_{1,j}}$ $(j = 1, 2, \cdots, n+1)$ denotes the message authentication code (MAC) of the message $[M \parallel ID_1]$ (ID_1 is the identity of S_1 and "$\parallel$" denotes "concatenate") related to the key $k_{1,j}$. When S_i $(2 \leq i \leq m)$

receives the ordered tuple $(M, C_{k_{i-1,1}}, C_{k_{i-1,2}}, \cdots, C_{k_{i-1,n+1}})$ from S_{i-1}, he computes an ordered tuple $(M, C_{k_{i,1}}, C_{k_{i,2}}, \cdots, C_{k_{i,n+1}})$, and sends it to S_{i+1}, where $C_{k_{i,j}}$ $(j = 1, 2, \cdots, n+1)$ denotes the MAC of the message $[M \parallel C_{k_{i-1,j}} \parallel ID_i]$ (ID_i is the identity of S_i) related to the key $k_{i,j}$. Finally, S_m sends the ordered tuple $(M, C_{k_{m,1}}, C_{k_{m,2}}, \cdots, C_{k_{m,n+1}})$ and the list L to R.

The receiver R verifies the ordered tuple $(M, C_{k_{m,1}}, C_{k_{m,2}}, \cdots, C_{k_{m,n+1}})$ by using the verification key matrix K'. We describe the verification steps of R as follows:

Step 1: R computes the $C_{k_{1,j}}$ from the message $[M \parallel ID_1]$ by using the key $k_{1,j}$, where $j \in I \cup \{n+1\}$.
Step 2: R computes the $C_{k_{i,j}}$, $2 \leq i \leq m$, from the mesage $[M \parallel C_{k_{i-1,j}} \parallel ID_i]$ by using the key $k_{i,j}$, where $j \in I \cup \{n+1\}$.
Step 3: R verifies $C_{k_{m,j}}$: if all $C_{k_{m,j}}$'s $(j \in I \cup \{n+1\})$ are consistent with that the S_m sends, then R accepts M as authentic; otherwise, R rejects.

Simultaneous Model. Assume that S_d is a dealer in $\{S_1, S_2, \cdots, S_m\}$. To send the message M to R, each sender S_i computes a ordered tuple $(M, C_{k_{i,1}}, C_{k_{i,2}}, \cdots, C_{k_{i,n+1}})$ and sends it to S_d, where $C_{k_{i,j}}$ $(j = 1, 2, \cdots, n+1)$ denotes the MAC of $[M \parallel ID_i]$. Upon receiving all S_is' ordered tuples, S_d computes $(M, C_1^*, C_2^*, \cdots, C_{n+1}^*)$ and sends it to R, where $C_j^* = \bigoplus_{i=1}^{m} C_{k_{i,j}}$.

The receiver R verifies $(M, C_1^*, C_2^*, \cdots, C_{n+1}^*)$ by using the verification key matrix K'. He computes $C_{k_{i,j}}$ from the message $[M \parallel ID_i]$ by using the key $k_{i,j}$, where $j \in I \cup \{n+1\}$. Then R verifies $\bigoplus_{i=1}^{m} C_{k_{i,j}}$, $j \in I \cup \{n+1\}$: if they are consistent with C_j^*'s sent by S_d, R accepts M as authentic; otherwise, R rejects.

Remark: Re-distributing the keys. If R rejects M, then R should request A distributing new keys between all senders and R unless all $C_{k_{m,j}}$'s (or C_j^*'s) were incorrect.

2.3 Dispute Phase

When a dispute occurs, the receiver R presents the evidence $(M, C_{k_{m,1}}, C_{k_{m,2}}, \cdots, C_{k_{m,n}})$ (or $(M, C_1^*, C_2^*, \cdots, C_{n+1}^*)$ in simultaneous model) to the arbiter. The arbiter will accepts that M is authentic and should be sent by $\{S_1, S_2, \cdots, S_m\}$ if he find that all $C_{k_{m,j}}$'s(or C_j^*'s), $j \in I$, are correct and at least one more $C_{k_{m,j}}$(or C_j^*), $j \notin I$, is also correct.

3 Security Analysis

As our scheme easily proves, the success probability of a single malicious sender $\bar{S}_i$ to execute a denial attack is given by $\frac{1}{\binom{n}{\lfloor \frac{n}{2} \rfloor}}$ [4]. If $\bar{S}_i$ guesses exactly the indices of $\lfloor \frac{n}{2} \rfloor$ keys which R owns from the indices set $\{1, 2, \cdots, n\}$, then he can send R wrong evidence (it will be rejected by A) but R accepts it. However, this success probability would be negligible if n is sufficiently large. As long as one more $C_{k_{m,j}}$ (or C_j^*), $j \notin I$ is correct ($\bar{S}_i$ does not guess it), then A will accept this evidence and $\bar{S}_i$ will fail to perform a denial attack.

Assume that t $(2 \leq t \leq m)$ senders $(\bar{S}_1, \cdots, \bar{S}_t)$ conspire to execute a denial attack. Each $\bar{S}_i$ may only guess a part of indices of $\lfloor \frac{n}{2} \rfloor$ keys (i.e., $\{j_{\bar{S}_i}^* \in [1, n]\}$; number of $\{j_{\bar{S}_i}^*\}$ is less than or equal to $\lfloor \frac{n}{2} \rfloor$). If $\bigcup_{i=1}^{t} \{j_{\bar{S}_i}^*\}$ are exactly equal to the indices of $\lfloor \frac{n}{2} \rfloor$ keys which R owns, then these t senders can successfully send R wrong evidence. However, the success probability of this case is also given by

$$\frac{1}{\binom{n}{\lfloor \frac{n}{2} \rfloor}}$$

For the arbiter A, he cannot send a message to R such that R accepts it as authentic because A doesn't know the key $k_{i,n+1}$ shared between S_i and R. In addition, the outsider or receiver cannot impersonate the senders to send the messages or substitute the messages transmitted from the senders unless he breaks the MAC algorithm used in our scheme. We mention here that the MAC algorithm used in our scheme should be (proven) secure enough to prevent the attacks of outsider or receiver. The secure MAC algorithm can be constructed by using the block cipher [1,6,7], or "keying" a cryptographic hash function (e.g., MD5 [10] or SHA [5]) [2,9,12]. Thus, the proposed scheme is conditionally secure against the impersonating attack of the arbiter, a receiver or an outsider.

4   Key Management Issue

Assume there are v members in the system. We propose a key distribution/ management strategy such that any set of ω $(1 \leq \omega \leq v - 1)$ senders can send the message to any other member in the system and convince the receiver that the message is actually transmitted by them. Our key distribution strategy is described as follows.

Let $u_1, u_2, \cdots, u_v$ be all members in the system. Initially, the arbiter (or key distribution center) distributes the keys to u_l $(1 \leq l \leq v)$ such as

$$EK_l = \begin{pmatrix} k_{l_1,1} & k_{l_1,2} & \cdots & k_{l_1,n} \\ k_{l_2,1} & k_{l_2,2} & \cdots & k_{l_2,n} \\ \cdots\cdots\cdots\cdots\cdots\cdots\cdots \\ k_{l_{l-1},1} & k_{l_{l-1},2} & \cdots & k_{l_{l-1},n} \\ k_{l_{l+1},1} & k_{l_{l+1},2} & \cdots & k_{l_{l+1},n} \\ \cdots\cdots\cdots\cdots\cdots\cdots\cdots \\ k_{l_v,1} & k_{l_v,2} & \cdots & k_{l_v,n} \end{pmatrix}$$

for enciphering and

$$VK_l = \left(\begin{array}{cccc} k_{1_l,i_1} & k_{1_l,i_2} & \cdots & k_{1_l,i_{\lfloor \frac{n}{2} \rfloor}} \\ k_{2_l,i_1} & k_{2_l,i_2} & \cdots & k_{2_l,i_{\lfloor \frac{n}{2} \rfloor}} \\ \hdotsfor{4} \\ k_{l-1_l,i_1} & k_{l-1_l,i_2} & \cdots & k_{l-1_l,i_{\lfloor \frac{n}{2} \rfloor}} \\ k_{l+1_l,i_1} & k_{l+1_l,i_2} & \cdots & k_{l+1_l,i_{\lfloor \frac{n}{2} \rfloor}} \\ \hdotsfor{4} \\ k_{v_l,i_1} & k_{v_l,i_2} & \cdots & k_{v_l,i_{\lfloor \frac{n}{2} \rfloor}} \end{array} \right)$$

for verification ($i_z \in I$, $z = 1, 2, \cdots, \lfloor \frac{n}{2} \rfloor$), where the jth row of EK_l denotes the u_l's enciphering keys used for sending a message to u_j, and jth row of VK_l denotes the u_l's verification keys used for verifying the message sent by u_j. Thus, u_l has sufficient ability to send messages to any others and verify the messages sent by any set of senders in the system.

We can publish n public values to reduce the number of enciphering keys. **Figure 1** depicts the method. Assume that $p_1, p_2, \cdots, p_n$ are n public values. The arbiter generates $(k_{l_1}, k_{l_2}, \cdots, k_{l_{l-1}}, k_{l_{l+1}}, \cdots, k_{l_v})$ for u_l and distributes them to u_l. The keys of EK_l (i.e., $(k_{l_i,1}, k_{l_i,2}, \cdots, k_{l_i,n})$, $1 \le i \le u; i \ne l$), is computed by enciphering $p_1, p_2, \cdots, p_n$ with the key k_{l_i} (i.e., $k_{l_i,j} = E_{k_{l_i}}(p_j)$, $1 \le j \le n$). Note that E can be any secure symmetric encryption algorithm (e.g., DES [7] or IDEA [6]) or a strong keyed one-way (hash) algorithm [2]. Therefore, u_l only needs to keep $(k_{l_1}, k_{l_2}, \cdots, k_{l_{l-1}}, k_{l_{l+1}}, \cdots, k_{l_v})$ and then he can follow the arbiter's procedure to derive the jth row of enciphering key matrix when he wants to send a message to u_j. However, in this case, the number of verification keys cannot be reduced.

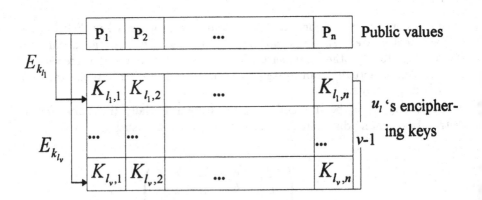

Fig. 1. The key distribution/management strategy

Re-distributing the keys. If the receiver R $(= u_j)$ rejects the message sent by a few senders, then u_j will ask the arbiter to re-distribute new keys for all members in the system. The arbiter changes k_{l_j} of u_l, where $l \neq j$, and all verification keys of u_j. Though re-distributing keys needs large overheads, it is unfrequently performed. Since the sender finds it difficult to successfully execute a denial attack, he cannot be entrapped to send R wrong evidence.

5   Comparisons

Table 1 compares the proposed scheme and the scheme of directly iterating of [4]. Assume that there are v members in the system and ω senders cooperately send a message to the receiver.

Table 1. The comparisons of keys and evidence

	Size of evidence	Number of en-ciphering keys	Number of verification keys	Number of public values
*The proposed scheme	n	$v(v-1)$	$\lfloor \frac{n}{2} \rfloor \times v(v-1)$	n
The scheme of directly iterating of [4]	ωn	$v(v-1) \times n$	$\lfloor \frac{n}{2} \rfloor \times v(v-1)$	0

6   Conclusions

Our multi-senders authentication scheme is unconditionally secure against the denial attack. The scheme reduces the size of evidence for multi-senders. The scheme proposed herein also contains a key distribution/management strategy to reduce the number of enciphering keys in the environment of multi-senders.

References

1. Bellare, M., Guerin, R. and Rogaway, P.: XOR MACs: new methods for message authentication using finite pseudorandom functions. In Advances in Cryptology-Crypto'95 proceedings, pages 15-28, Springer-Verlag, 1995.
2. Bellare, M., Canetti, R. and Krawczyk, H.: Keying hash functions for message authentication. In Advances in Cryptology-Crypto'96 proceedings, pages 1-15, Springer-Verlag, 1996.
3. Desmedt, Y., Yung, M.: Arbitrated unconditionally secure authentication can be unconditionally protected against arbiter's attacks. In Advances in Cryptology-Crypto '90 proceedings, pages 177-188, Springer-Verlag, 1991.

4. Desmedt, Y., Seberry, J.: Practical proven secure authentication with arbitration. In Advances in Cryptology-Auscrypt '92 proceedings, pages 27-32, Springer-Verlag, 1992.

5. FIPS 180-1, Secure hash standard, NIST, US Department of Commerce, Washington D.C., April 1995.

6. Lai, X. and Massey, J.: A proposal for a new block encryption standard. In Advances in Eurocrypt'90 proceedings, pages 389-404, Springer-Verlag, 1991.

7. National Bureau of Standards. Data encryption standard. Federal Information Proceedings Standards Publication FIPS PUB 46, U.S. Department of Commerce, January 1977.

8. Needham, R., Schroeder, M.: Using Encryption for Authentication in Large Networks of Computers. Comm. ACM, 21(12):993-999, 1978.

9. Preneel, B. and Oorschot, V.: MDx-MAC and building fast MACs from hash function. In Advances in Cryptology-Crypto'95 proceedings, pages 1-14, Springer-Verlag, 1995.

10. Rivest, R. L.: The MD5 message-digest algorithm. Request for comments (RFC) 1321. Internet activities board, Internet Privacy Task Force, April, 1992.

11. Simmons, G.: A Cartesian Product Construction for Unconditionally Secure Authentication Codes that Permit Arbitration. Journal of Cryptology, 2:77-104, 1990.

12. Tsudik, G.: Message authentication with one-way hash functions. In Proceedings of Infocom 92, vol.3, pages 2055-2059, IEEE Press, 1992.

Group Signatures for Hierarchical Multigroups

Seungjoo Kim[1] Sangjoon Park[2] and Dongho Won[1]

[1] Dept. of Inform. Engineering, Sung-Kyun-Kwan Univ.,
300 Chunchun-dong, Suwon, Kyunggi-do, 440-746, Korea
E-mail : {sjkim, dhwon}@simsan.skku.ac.kr
URL : http://dosan.skku.ac.kr/
[2] #0710, ETRI, Yusong P.O.BOX 106, Taejon, 305-600, Korea
E-mail : sjpark@dingo.etri.re.kr

Abstract. At Eurocrypt'91, D. Chaum and E. Heyst introduced the notion of group signatures, which allow members of a group to make signatures on behalf of the group while remaining anonymous. This paper first presents a new type of group signatures for hierarchical multigroups. In group signatures for hierarchical multigroups, a user who is a member of a higher group is not only able to make a group signature of his higher group, but also able to make a group signature of lower affiliated group without disclosing his higher membership, while the size of the secret data is independent of the number of the groups in which the user participates. Furthermore, if necessary, the group authority identifies a signer from the given group signature.

1 Introduction

Group signatures, introduced by D. Chaum and E. Heyst at Eurocrypt'91, allow individual members of a group to sign messages on behalf of the group while remaining anonymous. Furthermore, in case of disputes later a trusted authority, who is given some auxiliary information, can identify the signer. So far, Many group signature schemes have been presented, and have tried to construct an efficient and secure signature scheme.

However, all previously proposed solutions consider the case that a user join only one group so, when a user participates in many groups, he must keep one secret information for each group. This is very inefficient. Actually, there are many situations in which a user participates in more than one group. In this paper, we present the first group signature for hierarchical multigroups. When the set of groups is hierarchical, a signer, who is a member of a certain set of groups GN, can generate secret information corresponding to the lower affiliated groups $GN' \subset GN$ from a master secret information (called "master secret key"). And then he can generate a valid group signature of GN' without revealing nothing but membership to GN'.

1.1 Related Work

Group signatures have been proposed by Chaum and Heyst [1]. Their schemes have been improved by L. Chen and T.P. Pedersen, who first use a Schoenmaker's protocol to hide a signer's identity [2]. Also, H. Petersen suggested a general method to convert any ordinary digital signature into a group signature scheme [3]. Petersen's method combines the Stadler's verifiable encryption of discrete logarithm[4] and the Schoenmaker's protocol. [3] Recently, J. Camenisch and M. Stadler presented the first group signature scheme whose public key and signatures have length independent of the number of group members of one group [8]. But this isn't independent of the number of groups. [4]

And, at Eurocrypt'90, K. Ohta, T. Okamoto and K. Koyama proposed two schemes for membership proof in hierarchical multigroups, in which a method of combining many secret witness for memberships in several groups into one, is suggested [11]. Ohta also referred to membership signature schemes based on their membership proof in hierarchical multigroups. The main difference between Ohta's and ours is that, in Ohta's scheme, the signature cannot be opened.

Furthermore, C. Shu, T. Matsumoto and H. Imai proposed multi-purpose proof system, in which a user can execute various proof protocols (identity proof, membership proof without revealing identity, and identity & membership proof) with one secret data [12]. Shu also presented secret hiding participation method, where a user, who participates in a group, must take a procedure only with the group administrator, and the secrets of the users and the group administrators are isolated each other.

In our system, user's master secret key for membership is generated by the method in [11] and [12]. And, with the master secret key, a user generates a group signature[5] by using Stadler's verifiable encryption of e-th root[4] and Schoenmaker's method[2].

2 Requirements and Models

The main aim of our group signatures for hierarchical multigroups is to enable a user keep only one secret information to execute various group signatures as convenient as possible. There are five basic requirements for our group signatures for hierarchical multigroups [1][11].

1. (*Unforgeability*) only members of the group can sign messages.
2. (*Anonymity & Unlinkability*) the recipient of the signature can verify that it is a valid signature of that group, but cannot discover which group member made it, also cannot decide whether two signatures have been issued by the same group member.
3. (*Open*) in case of dispute later, the signature can be opened by either the group members together or a group authority(trustworthy center/group administrator), so that the person who signed the message is revealed.

---

[3] At the same time, authors proposed the similar notion to [3], which is based on [6], independently [5].

[4] Also, [9] previously proposed schemes with fixed size public keys, but this was firstly broken by [10].

4. (*Group hierarchy*) if the center sets up some group hierarchically, a user, who is a member of a higher group, is not only able to generate a group signature of his higher group, but also able to generate a group signature of lower affiliated group without disclosing his higher membership to the verifier.

5. (*Efficiency of user*) the size of the secret information used by a user is independent of the number of the groups to which the user belongs.

Our model consists of three parties such as a trustworthy center (TC) established through the cooperation of various groups, a number of group administrators (GA), and a set of users (U) each of which may belong to several groups. The duty of TC is to manage the registration of the user's name and the group's name. GA is a manager who can accept users to be the members of a particular group. GA(or TC) can open his member's group signature, if necessary. U is a person who must at first register his name in the center and may participate in any group if the administrator of the group accepts him. So, besides above five basic requirements, our scheme meets the following additional conditions [12].

6. (*Autonomy*) When a user participates in a group, it is sufficient that he performs a protocol only with the group administrator.

7. (*Secret isolation*) The secrets of center cannot be derived from the public information by the group administrators and the users. The secrets of the group administrators and the users cannot be derived by each other. The user's secret witness for a group signature is not known even to the group administrator of the same group.

3 Registration and Participation

The center chooses a RSA modulus[13] $n = p_1 \cdot p_2$, where p_1 and p_2 are large prime numbers and $p_1 - 1$ and $p_2 - 1$ have common large(160 bits) prime factor q and selects $g \in Z_n$ with the order of q, where $Z_n = \{0, 1, \cdots, n - 1\}$. Now, a trustworthy center generates his key pair (x, y) with $y = g^x \bmod n$ and publishes the public key y. The trustworthy center also selects the security parameter t, such that the maximum number of the groups that the center can manage should be selected as quite less than t, and a secret random polynomial f of degree $t - 1$ such that $f(i) = a_0 + a_1 i + \cdots + a_{t-1} i^{t-1}$.

3.1 Registration

Registration part consists of two phases as follows.

1. (*Group Registration*) A group administrator registers his group to the center, and then the center gives the group administrator a secret information corresponding to the name of the group.

2. (*User Registration*) A user registers his name to the center, who gives the user some secrets originated from the user's identity.

We assume that a center is trustworthy.

Group Registration

1. When a new group administrator GA_i wants to register in center, he should describe his group name GN_i to the center.
2. Given GN_i, the center randomly selects C_i such that $1 \leq C_i \leq \phi(n)$, and computes a G_i, where

$$f(C_i) = a_0 + a_1 C_i + \cdots + a_{t-1} C_i^{t-1} \bmod \phi(n),$$

$$\gcd(f(C_i), \phi(n)) = 1,$$

$$G_i = \frac{1}{f(C_i)} \bmod \phi(n),$$

$$\gcd(G_i, G_j) = 1, \text{ for } i \neq j.$$

3. Finally, the center publishes (GN_i, G_i), and gives C_i to the group administrator GA_i in a secure way. $f(C_i)$ is kept as a secret by the center.

User Registration

1. When a user l wants to register his name in center, he describes his identity information ID_l to the center.
2. After checking the user's physical identity, the center computes

$$S_l = (ID_l^{a_0} \bmod n, \cdots, ID_l^{a_{t-1}} \bmod n)$$

and give (ID_l, S_l) to user l secretly. The center publishes user l's identity information ID_l.

3.2 Participation

When a user l wishes to participate in a group GN_i, he must conduct a protocol with group administrator GA_i as follows. Through this protocol, GA_i helps user l to compute a secret witness

$$u_{il} = ID_l^{\frac{1}{G_i}} \bmod n$$

of GN_i, but GA_i cannot know the secret witness.

User Participation

1. User l selects $2m$ random numbers $(r_{1k}, r_{2k}) \in_R Z_n^*$ for $1 \leq k \leq m$ such that $\gcd(r_{1k}, r_{2k}) = 1$, and computes

$$T_{1k} = ID_l^{r_{1k}} \bmod n \text{ and } T_{2k} = ID_l^{r_{2k}} \bmod n.$$

User l gives group administrator GA_i

$$(T_{11}, T_{21}, \cdots, T_{1m}, T_{2m}).$$

2. GA_i sends user l a random binary vector $e = \{e_1, \cdots, e_m\} \in_R \{0,1\}^m$
3. User l gives Y_k to GA_i such that for $k = 1, \cdots, m$,

$$Y_k = (r_{1k}, r_{2k}), \text{ if } e_k = 0,$$
$$Y_k = (S_l^{r_1 k}, S_l^{r_2 k}), \text{ if } e_k = 1,$$

where

$$S_l^{r_{1k}} = (ID_l^{a_0 r_{1k}} \bmod n, \cdots, ID_l^{a_{t-1} r_{1k}} \bmod n),$$
$$S_l^{r_{2k}} = (ID_l^{a_0 r_{2k}} \bmod n, \cdots, ID_l^{a_{t-1} r_{2k}} \bmod n).$$

4. GA_i confirms if $(Y_1, \cdots, Y_m)$ is correct as follows. If $e_k = 0$ for $1 \leq k \leq m$, GA_i checks

$$T_{1k} \overset{?}{=} ID_l^{r_{1k}} \bmod n, T_{2k} \overset{?}{=} ID_l^{r_{2k}} \bmod n \text{ and } \gcd(r_{1k}, r_{2k}) \overset{?}{=} 1.$$

If $e_k = 1$, GA_i computes

$$u_{il}^{r_{1k}} = \prod_{j=0}^{t-1} (ID_l^{a_j r_{1k}})^{C_i^j} \bmod n = ID_l^{f(C_i) r_{1k}} \bmod n = ID_l^{\frac{1}{G_i} r_{1k}} \bmod n,$$

$$u_{il}^{r_{2k}} = \prod_{j=0}^{t-1} (ID_l^{a_j r_{2k}})^{C_i^j} \bmod n = ID_l^{f(C_i) r_{2k}} \bmod n = ID_l^{\frac{1}{G_i} r_{2k}} \bmod n.$$

Furthermore, GA_i checks whether

$$(u_{il}^{r_{1k}})^{G_i} \overset{?}{=} T_{1k} \bmod n \text{ and } (u_{il}^{r_{2k}})^{G_i} \overset{?}{=} T_{2k} \bmod n.$$

Step 1.– step 4. should be repeated λ times for a suitable number λ. If each iteration is successful, GA_i judges that user l does not cheat and continues to do step 5, otherwise, halts.

5. GA_i chooses a $(S_l^{r_{1k}}, S_l^{r_{2k}})$ for some k, and gives $(u_{il}^{r_{1k}}, u_{il}^{r_{2k}})$ and corresponding (T_{1k}, T_{2k}) to user l.
6. User l checks whether

$$(u_{il}^{r_{1k}})^{G_i} = ID_l^{r_{1k}} \text{ and } (u_{il}^{r_{2k}})^{G_i} = ID_l^{r_{2k}}$$

Then, l computes u_{il} from $u_{il}^{r_{1k}}$ and $u_{il}^{r_{2k}}$ with the Euclid's algorithm. He calculates α and β satisfying

$$\alpha \cdot r_{1k} + \beta \cdot r_{2k} = 1$$

using Euclid's algorithm. Note that $\gcd(r_{1k}, r_{2k}) = 1$. Then

$$(u_{il}^{r_{1k}})^\alpha \cdot (u_{il}^{r_{2k}})^\beta = u_{il} \bmod n$$

holds. If this step is successful, the participation is finished.

Master Secret Witness Generation

If a user l is participated in groups $GN = \{GN_1, \cdots, GN_w\}$, for some integer w, he holds secret witnesses $ID_l^{\frac{1}{\sigma_1}}, \cdots, ID_l^{\frac{1}{\sigma_w}}$. By using the method of [11], he can compute the master secret witness

$$u_l = ID_l^{\prod_{GN_i \in GN} \frac{1}{\sigma_i}} \bmod n.$$

¿From the master secret witness and $\{G_1, \cdots G_w\}$, user l can compute a secret witness for group signature of any group in which he is participated.

4 Group Signatures for Hierarchical Multigroups

Our method combines the Stadler's verifiable encryption of e-th root and Schoenmaker's method [5][6]. A signer uses verifiable encryption of e-th root to prove that a group administrator can identify himself later, and by Schoenmaker's method, he proves that he knows a secret key corresponding to at least one identity of a group member, which is used for signing.

Let $\{ID_1, \cdots, ID_k\}$ be a set of identities of members registered in center and $h(\cdot)$ be a secure hash function. For simplicity, a member ID_1 is to generate a group signature on message M for the groups $GN' \subset GN$ without revealing his identity and his other membership.

Signing Phase

1. User ID_1 should firstly calculate u_1' from u_1 as follows :

$$u_1' = u_1^{\prod_{GN_i \in GN-GN'} G_i} \bmod n = ID_1^{\prod_{GN_i \in GN'} \frac{1}{\sigma_i}} \bmod n.$$

2. He picks a random number $r \in_R Z_n$, and computes

$$R = r^{\prod_{GN_i \in GN'} G_i} \bmod n \text{ and } c = u_1'^{h(M,R)} \cdot r \bmod n.$$

3. With c and the center's public key y, compute the ciphertext (A, B) such that
$$A = g^\alpha \bmod n \text{ and } B = c \cdot y^\alpha \bmod n,$$
   where α is random in Z_n (If we use group administrator's public key instead of center's public key, then the group authority can identify the signer later).

4. Calculate $C_j = ID_j^{h(M,R)} \cdot R \bmod n$ for $j = 1, \cdots, k$.

5. $w_1, \cdots, w_k$ and $d_2, \cdots, d_k$ are randomly chosen in Z_q and compute t_{g_1}, t_{y_2}, t_{g_j} and t_{y_j} $(j = 2, \cdots, k)$, where

$$t_{g_1} = g^{w_1} \bmod n,$$

$$t_{y_1} = y^{(\prod_{GN_i \in GN'} G_i) \cdot w_1} \bmod n,$$

$$t_{g_j} = g^{w_j} \cdot A^{d_j} \bmod n,$$

$$t_{y_j} = y^{(\prod_{GN_i \in GN'} G_i) \cdot w_j} \cdot (B^{\prod_{GN_i \in GN'} G_i} / C_j)^{d_j} \bmod n.$$

6. With $d_1 = d - \sum_{j=2}^{k} d_j \bmod q$, where $d = h(t_{g_1}, \cdots, t_{g_k}, t_{y_1}, \cdots, t_{y_k}, A, B, h(M, R))$, compute $r_1, \cdots, r_k$ as follows :

$$r_1 = w_1 - d_1 \cdot \alpha \bmod q \text{ and } r_j = w_j \ (2 \leq j \leq k).$$

7. Then the group signature GS for GN' is

$$GS = (M, R, A, B, d, d_1, \cdots, d_k, r_1, \cdots, r_k).$$

Verification Phase

1. A receiver firstly checks whether $d \overset{?}{=} \sum_{j=1}^{k} d_j \bmod q$.
2. And then he computes $C_j = ID_j^{h(M,R)} \cdot R \bmod n$ for $j = 1, \cdots, n$, and also calculates t_{g_j} and t_{y_j} $(j = 1, \cdots, k)$, where

$$t_{g_j} = g^{r_j} \cdot A^{d_j},$$

$$t_{y_j} = y^{(\prod_{GN_i \in GN'} G_i) \cdot r_j} \cdot (B^{\prod_{GN_i \in GN'} G_i} / C_j)^{d_j} \bmod n.$$

3. If the equation $d = h(t_{g_1}, \cdots, t_{g_k}, t_{y_1}, \cdots, t_{y_k}, A, B, h(M, R))$ holds, he accepts the signature GS for the groups GN'.

Open Phase

A trustworthy center can identify the signer without any assistance of group members.

1. A center firstly obtains $c = B/A^x \bmod n$ by deciphering the ciphertext (A, B).
2. Find ID_j satisfying the equation,

$$c^{\prod_{GN_i \in GN'} G_i} \overset{?}{=} ID_j^{h(M,R)} \cdot R = C_j \bmod n \ (j = 1, \cdots, k).$$

Security & Improvement : A receiver and a group administrator GA, who have no secret keys u_i $(i = 1, \cdots, k)$ of the group GN, cannot generate a group signature. If $d = h(t_{g_1}, \cdots, t_{g_k}, t_{y_1}, \cdots, t_{y_k}, A, B, h(M, R))$ is given, then it is hard to get another A, B, t_{g_i}'s and t_{y_i}'s because $h(\cdot)$ is a secure hash function. Assume GS is a group signature of a group member with the identity ID_1 and $S = \{z | z = g^i \bmod n\}$. Then, t_{g_i} and t_{y_1} are randomly distributed in S. On the other hand, the possibility of $t_{y_i} \notin S$ is very high. However, they cannot determine whether t_{y_i} is an element of S or not. Moreover, since they do not know x, they cannot derive the ordinary signature c from (A, B).

We can improve our scheme by combining our results and Camenisch's [8]. Improved solution may have the following desirable properties :

- the length of the group's public key and of the signatures are, as well as the computational effort for signing and verifying, independent of the number of group members.
- the size of the group member's secret key is independent of the number of groups.

Our improved version will be presented in the full paper, soon.

5 Conclusion

This paper has presented the concept of "group signatures for hierarchical multigroups". In our system a user only needs to remember one secret data to be able to generate group signatures of many groups. It may be quite convenient that a user need not keep many secrets to generate various group signatures. The detailed security analysis for the whole system is still left to further study.

References

1. D. Chaum and E. van Heyst, "Group signatures," *Advances in Cryptology – Eurocrypt'91*, Springer–Verlag, *Lecture Notes in Computer Science* Vol. 547, 1992, pp.257-265.
2. L. Chen and T.P. Pedersen, "New group signature schemes," *Advances in Cryptology – Eurocrypt'94*, Springer–Verlag, *Lecture Notes in Computer Science* Vol. 950, 1995, pp.163-173.
3. H. Petersen, "How to convert any digital signature scheme into a group signature scheme," *The Proceedings of Security Protocols Workshop'97*, 1997.
4. M. Stadler, "Publicly verifiable secret sharing," *Advances in Cryptology – Eurocrypt'96*, Springer–Verlag, *Lecture Notes in Computer Science* Vol. 1070, 1996, pp.190-199.
5. S.J. Park, S.J. Kim and D.H. Won, "ID-based group signature," *Electronics Letters*, 1997, pp.1616-1617.
6. S.J. Kim, S.J. Park and D.H. Won, "Equivocally verifiable encryption and its applications," *manuscript*, 1997.
7. J. Camenisch, "Efficient and generalized group signatures," *Advances in Cryptology – Eurocrypt'97*, Springer–Verlag, *Lecture Notes in Computer Science* Vol. 1233, 1997, pp.465-479.
8. J. Camenisch and M. Stadler, "Efficient group signature schemes for large groups," *Advances in Cryptology – Crypto'97*, Springer–Verlag, *Lecture Notes in Computer Science* Vol. 1294, 1997, pp.410-424.
9. S.J. Park, I.S. Lee and D.H. Won, "A practical group signature," *Proceedings of the 1995 Japan-Korea Joint Workshop on Information Security and Cryptography*, 1995, pp.127-133.
10. S.J. Park and D.H. Won, "Remarks on practical group signature," *manuscript*, 1996.
11. K. Ohta, T. Okamoto, and K. Koyama, "Membership authentication for hierarchical multigroups using the extended Fiat–Shamir scheme," *Advances in Cryptology – Eurocrypt'90*, Springer–Verlag, *Lecture Notes in Computer Science* Vol. 473, 1991, pp.446-458.
12. C. Shu, T. Matsumoto, and H. Imai, "A multi-purpose proof system," *IEICE Trans. Fundamentals*, Vol.E75-A, No.6, 1992, pp.735-743.
13. R. Rivest, A. Shamir, and L. Adleman, "A method for obtaining digital signatures and public-key cryptosystems," *Communications of the ACM*, 21(2):120-126, Feb, 1978.
14. S. Kim and B.S. Um, "A multipurpose membership proof system based on discrete logarithms," *The Proceedings of Korea-Japan Joint Workshop on Information Security and Cryptology'93*, 1993, pp.177-183.

15. L.C. Guillou and J.J. Quisquater, "A paradoxical identity-based signature scheme resulting from zero–knowledge," *Advances in Cryptology – Crypto'88*, Springer–Verlag, *Lecture Notes in Computer Science* Vol. 403, 1990, pp.216-231.

16. K. Ohta and T. Okamoto, "Practical extension on Fiat–Shamir scheme," *Electron. Lett.*, 1988, **24**, (15), pp.955-956.

Threshold Proxy Signature Schemes

Kan Zhang

Cambridge University Computer Laboratory
Pembroke Street, Cambridge CB2 3QG, UK
Email: kz200@cl.cam.ac.uk

Abstract. Delegation of rights is a common practice in the real world. Proxy signature schemes have been invented to delegate signing capability efficiently and transparently. In this paper, we present a new nonrepudiable proxy signature scheme. Nonrepudiation means the signature signers, both original and proxy signers, cannot falsely deny later that he generated a signature. In practice, it is important and, sometimes, necessary to have the ability to know who is the actual signer of a proxy signature for internal auditing purpose or when there is abuse of signing capability. The new nonrepudiable proxy signature scheme also has other desirable properties, such as proxy signature key generation and updating using insecure channels. We also show how to construct threshold proxy signature schemes with an example. Threshold signatures are motivated both by the need that arises in some organizations to have a group of employees agree on a given message (or a document) before signing it, as well as by the need to protect signature keys from the attack of internal and external adversaries. Our approach can also be applied to other ElGamal-like proxy signature schemes.

1 Introduction

Delegations of various kinds are common practice in society. One of them is delegation of signing capabilities within organizations. If a manager of a company goes on holiday, he has to delegate to his deputy the capability to sign on behalf of the company. A solution in the paper based world is to have a corporate seal. A corporate seal represents the organization, not the person who has authority to use the seal. A major difference between signing by hand and signing by seal is that seal is transferable. This transferability allows efficient and flexible delegation of signing capability, and therefore reduces costs.

The requirement here is transparent delegation, which means the customers of the company are not affected. The signatures presented to them are the same as before and they can verify the signatures using the same process. It will be economically infeasible for a big company to notify all its customers each time there is a personnel change in the company. Unfortunately, basic digital signature schemes, like signing by hand, are not transferable. Digital signature schemes rely on a secret signature key which only the certified person knows. If this secret key is delegated to another person, it can no longer be identified with that person and, hence, the underlying assumption of digital signature schemes is broken. What we need is a way to delegate the signing capability without revealing the secret key such that the recipients can verify the proxy signatures from a proxy signer using the original signature key with minimum changes to the verification process.

To facilitate delegation of signing capability in the electronic world, proxy signature schemes has been proposed. Mambo, Usuda and Okamoto proposed a proxy signature scheme, hereafter referred to as MUO scheme, based on discrete logarithm for partial delegation of signing capability [13]. In a partial delegation, a proxy signature key s created from the original signature key x is given to a proxy signer. Signatures created using the proxy signature key can be verified using a modified verification equation in such a way that the verifier can be convinced that the signature is from an authorised party of the original signer. Signatures created by a proxy signer are distinguishable from those by the original signer. The verifier needs to verify one signature only and only the public key of the original signer is required. Therefore, compared with delegation by warrant, partial delegation is more efficient and transparent requiring less changes to the original verification process.

However, MUO scheme doesn't provide nonrepudiation of proxy signatures. In MUO scheme, while a valid proxy signature cannot be disavowed by the original or the proxy signer, it is impossible to decide who is the actual signer of a proxy signature since both the original signer and the proxy signer know the proxy signature key. In practice, it is important, and sometimes necessary, to have the capability to know who is the actual signer of a proxy signature for internal auditing purpose or when there is abuse of signing capability. We call this property *Nonrepudiation*. Another drawback of MUO scheme is that it requires a secure channel to pass the proxy signature key from the original signer to the proxy signer. Anyone who can intercept this proxy signature key can impersonate the proxy signer.

In [18], we proposed a nonrepudiable proxy signature scheme which overcomes these shortcomings. The nonrepudiation property is achieved through a partially blind proxy signature key generation protocol adapted from blind Nyberg-Rueppel signature scheme by Camenisch et al. [3]. In this paper, we present another variant of the nonrepudiable proxy signature scheme. It has similar properties to the previous one. We also show how to convert regular proxy signature schemes into threshold proxy signature schemes.

In threshold proxy signature schemes, the secret proxy signature key is shared by a group of n proxy signers. In order to produce a valid proxy signature on a given message m, individual proxy signers produce their *partial signatures* on message m, and then combine them into a full proxy signature on m. Threshold signatures are motivated both by the need that arises in some organizations to have a group of employees agree on a given message (or a document) before signing it, as well as by the need to protect signature keys from the attack of internal and external adversaries.

The paper is organized as follows. In section 2, we give a short description of previous work on which our work is based. Next, we present a second type of nonrepudiable proxy signature schemes. How to convert regular proxy signature schemes into threshold proxy signature schemes is shown in section 4. We draw our conclusion in section 5.

2 Previous work

2.1 Proxy Signature Scheme by Mambo, Usuda and Okamoto

Recently, Mambo, Usuda and Okamoto proposed a proxy signature scheme for partial delegation of signing capability, which has many desirable properties [13]. In this section, we give a brief description of the MUO scheme. Interested readers are referred to [13] for details.

The system parameters consist of a prime p, a prime factor q of $p-1$, and an element $g \in Z_p^*$ of order q. The original signer's private key is a random element $x \in Z_q$, while the corresponding public key is $y = g^x$ (mod p). MUO scheme uses the following protocol.

- Step 1. (Proxy key generation) An original signer selects $k \in Z_q$ at random and computes $r = g^k \bmod p$. After that, he calculates proxy signature key $s = x + kr \bmod q$.
- Step 2. (Proxy key delivery) The original signer gives (s, r) to a proxy signer in a secure way.
- Step 3. (Proxy key verification) The proxy signer checks that

$$g^s = yr^r (\bmod p) \tag{1}$$

If (s, r) passes this congruence, she accepts it as a valid proxy signature key. Otherwise, she rejects it and requests another one, or she can simply stops the protocol.
- Step 4. (Signing by the proxy signer) When the proxy signer signs a message m on behalf of the original signer, she computes a signature S_p using the original signature scheme and s as the secret signature key. The proxy signature is (S_p, r).
- Step 5. (Verification of the proxy signature) The verification of the proxy signature is carried out by the same checking operation as in the original signature scheme except for replacing y with $y' = yr^r (\bmod p)$.

The following equation can be used as an alternative to equation (1).

$$g^s = y^r r (\bmod p) \tag{2}$$

Equation (1) and (2) correspond to a special case (message m equals 1) of Yen-Laih [17] and Nyberg-Rueppel [14] signature schemes, respectively. The authors of MUO scheme stated the following properties.

- *Unforgeability* Only the original signer and the designated proxy signer can create a valid proxy signature.

- *Proxy signer's deviation* A proxy signer cannot create a valid proxy signature not detected as a proxy signature.
- *Verifiability* From proxy signatures, a verifier can be convinced of the original signer's agreement on the signed message.
- *Distinguishability* Valid proxy signatures are distinguishable from normal self-signing signatures.
- *Identifiability* An original signer can determine the proxy signer's identity from a proxy signature.
- *Undeniability* Once a proxy signer creates a valid proxy signature for an original signer, it is not disavowed even by the proxy signer.

2.2 Nonrepudiable Proxy Signature Scheme (NPS1)

In [18], We have shown how to add nonrepudiation to existing proxy signature schemes. Nonrepudiation means the signature signers, both original and proxy signers, cannot falsely deny later that he generated a signature. This property is achieved through a partially blind signature key generation protocol adapted from fully blind Nyberg-Rueppel signature scheme [3]. The new proxy signature scheme fits in the same general framework as MUO scheme. Therefore, the desirable properties of MUO scheme can also be said about our nonrepudiable scheme. In addition, our scheme has some new properties, such as proxy signature key generation and updating using insecure channels. The protocol goes as follows.

1. Original signer selects $\tilde{k} \in Z_q$, computes $\tilde{r} = g^{\tilde{k}}(\bmod p)$, and sends $\tilde{r}$ to Proxy signer.
2. (a) Proxy signer randomly selects $\alpha \in Z_q$, computes

$$r = g^\alpha \tilde{r}(\bmod p) \qquad (3)$$

   (b) Proxy signer checks whether $r \in Z_q^*$. If this is not the case, he goes back to step (a). Otherwise, he sends r to Original signer.
3. Original signer computes $\tilde{s} = rx + \tilde{k}(\bmod q)$ and forwards $\tilde{s}$ to Proxy signer.
4. Proxy signer computes $s = \tilde{s} + \alpha(\bmod q)$, and check if the following equality holds:

$$g^s = y^r r(\bmod p) \qquad (4)$$

If it holds, Proxy signer accepts s as a valid proxy signature key from Original signer.
5. Proxy signature generation and verification are the same as in MUO scheme.

3 A New Nonrepudiable Proxy Signature Scheme (NPS2)

It is obvious that the above proxy signature key generation process is an adapted version of the blind Nyberg-Rueppel scheme proposed by Camenisch et al. [3]

(see Appendix). In [3], two blinding factors, $\alpha \in Z_q$ and $\beta \in Z_q^*$, are used. It is proved that given a valid signature (r, s) and any view V representing the original signer's complete view of an execution of the protocol, i.e. his random coin tosses and all exchanged values, there exists a unique pair of blinding factors $\alpha \in Z_q$ and $\beta \in Z_q^*$. Since the original signer chooses the blinding factors α and β randomly, the full blindness of the signature scheme follows.

To convert the fully blind signature scheme into a partial one, we can use a fixed public known value for β. For simplicity, we choose $\beta = 1(\bmod q)$. In this case, r, and, therefore mg^α are known to the original signer. To further uniquely decide a α and, therefore, s, we need to let message m publicly known. For simplicity, we choose $m = 1$. This reduces the underlying Nyberg-Rueppel scheme (see Appendix) to the one used in MUO scheme (Eq 2). And the original blind Nyberg-Rueppel scheme becomes the one we use in [18].

Another way to generate a partially blind proxy signature key as in [18] is to let $\alpha = 0$ and use β as the only blinding factor. The protocol goes as follows.

1. Original signer selects $\tilde{k} \in Z_q$, computes $\tilde{r} = g^{\tilde{k}}(\bmod p)$, and sends $\tilde{r}$ to Proxy signer.
2. (a) Proxy signer randomly selects $\beta \in Z_q^*$, computes $r = \tilde{r}^\beta(\bmod p)$ and $\tilde{m} = r\beta^{-1}(\bmod q)$.
   (b) Proxy signer checks whether $\tilde{m} \in Z_q^*$. If this is not the case, he goes back to step (a). Otherwise, he sends $\tilde{m}$ to Original signer.
3. Original signer computes $\tilde{s} = \tilde{m}x + \tilde{k}(\bmod q)$ and forwards $\tilde{s}$ to Proxy signer.
4. Proxy signer computes $s = \tilde{s}\beta(\bmod q)$, and check if the following equality holds:

$$g^s = y^r r(\bmod p) \tag{5}$$

If it holds, Proxy signer accepts s as a valid proxy signature key from Original signer.
5. Proxy signature generation and verification are the same as in MUO scheme.

This new nonrepudiable proxy signature scheme has the same properties as the one given in [18], e.g. proxy key generation and updating using insecure channels. The difficulty of finding the corresponding proxy signature key s by the original signer knowing r is equivalent to solving a discrete logarithm problem. On the other hand, the difficulty of computing x, $\tilde{k}$ or forging another valid signature that satisfies equation (5) by the proxy signer is guaranteed by the underlying signature scheme [14]. Note that message substitution attack is not feasible in our scheme since we require a constant message $m = 1$. For more detailed discussions, interested readers are referred to [18].

We notice that in [9], Horster et al. classified a large number of hidden and weak ElGamal-like signature schemes under a single framework. Our partially blind signature protocols can also be seen as a special form (when $m = 1$) of some of the variants in [9].

4 Threshold Proxy Signature Schemes

Threshold signatures are part of a general approach known as *threshold cryptography* which was introduced by the works of Boyd [2], Desmedt [4], and Desmedt and Frankel [6]. For an overview of the field, the reader is referred to [5]. Particular examples of solutions to threshold ElGamal-like signatures can be found in [8, 12, 10, 7].

Generally speaking, threshold signature schemes can be classified into the following two categories: (1) schemes with the assistance of a mutually trusted party to decide the group secret signature key s and generate individual shares for all group members [16, 1, 8]; and (2) schemes without the assistance of a mutually trusted party. In schemes without a mutually trusted party, all group members *collectively* choose and distribute the group secret signature key s [8, 12, 10, 7].

A threshold proxy signature scheme is a threshold signature scheme with the additional requirement that the group secret s, i.e. proxy signature key, should have a special form satisfying Eq (4). In this paper, we will focus on how to generate the individual shares for every group member such that Eq (4) is satisfied. Once individual shares are in place, the signing and verification of threshold proxy signatures are the same as existing threshold schemes [8, 7].

In MUO scheme, since the original signer is trusted to choose the secret proxy signature key, naturally he can serve as a trusted party to generate and deliver the shares to a group of proxy signers. It turns out to be direct applications of some (verifiable) secret sharing schemes [16, 1, 15], which we will not discuss any more. In the following, we will present a threshold proxy share generation scheme based on nonrepudiable proxy signature schemes. The shares have to be generated in such a way that nonrepudiation between the original signer and the proxy group is preserved, i.e. without a trusted party.

We assume there is a group of n proxy signers p_i, $i = 1, ..., n$, where $n \in Z_q^*$. We further assume that all the participants have access to a dedicated broadcast channel; by dedicated we mean that if a participant broadcasts a message, it will be recognized by the other participants as coming from him.

4.1 (n, n) proxy share generation based on NPS1

1. The original signer selects $\tilde{k} \in Z_q$, computes $\tilde{r} = g^{\tilde{k}} \pmod{p}$, and broadcasts $\tilde{r}$.

2. (a) Each proxy signer p_i randomly selects $\alpha_i \in Z_q$, computes

$$r_i = g^{\alpha_i} \tilde{r} \pmod{p} \tag{6}$$

   (b) Each proxy signer p_i checks whether $r_i \in Z_q^*$. If this is not the case, he goes back to step (a). Otherwise, he broadcasts r_i.

3. The original signer computes $r = \prod_{i=1}^{n} r_i$ and $\tilde{s} = n^{-1} r x + \tilde{k} \pmod{q}$ and broadcasts $\tilde{s}$.

4. Each proxy signer computes $r = \prod_{i=1}^{n} r_i$, $s_i = \tilde{s} + \alpha_i \pmod{q}$, and check if the following equality holds:

$$g^{\tilde{s}} = y^{n^{-1}r} \tilde{r} \pmod{p} \tag{7}$$

If it holds, proxy signer p_i accepts s_i as a valid proxy share from the original signer. Otherwise, p_i broadcasts an error and stops.

Theorem If the above protocol completes successfully, the n proxy signers share a valid proxy signature key, i.e. the following equality holds:

$$g^{\Sigma s_i} = y^r r \pmod{p} \tag{8}$$

(Proof will be given in the full paper.)

4.2   (t, n) threshold proxy share generation

A (t, n) threshold secret sharing scheme is a protocol in which partial information, i.e. *shares*, about a *secret* are distributed to n participants such that

- Any group of fewer than t participants cannot obtain any information about the secret.
- Any group of at least t participants can compute the secret in polynomial time.

Having a (n, n) proxy signature key sharing from the above protocol, a (t, n) threshold proxy signature key sharing can be obtained by directly applying the verifiable secret sharing protocol by Pedersen [15], since the public information about each secret share, i.e. g^{s_i}, are publicly known. In doing so, we avoid Langford's attack [11].

4.3   Discussions

The security analysis and properties (apart from the threshold property) of the threshold NPS1 scheme presented above are very similar to those of NPS1 itself. Interested readers are referred to [18] for detailed discussions.

5   Conclusions

In this paper, we present another nonrepudiable proxy signature scheme which has similar properties as a previous one. The general approach to construct threshold proxy signature schemes is shown with an example. Generalizations to other ElGamal-like proxy signature schemes will be given in the full paper.

Acknowledgements I am grateful to Roger Needham, Ross Anderson, Yacov Yacobi and anonymous referees for helpful comments.

References

1. G.R. Blakley, Safeguarding Cryptographic Keys, *Proc. AFIPS 1979 Nat. Computer Conf.*, 48 (1979), pp 313-317.
2. C. Boyd, Digital Multisignatures, In H. Baker and F. Piper, editors, *Cryptography and Coding*, pages 241-246, Claredon Press, 1986.
3. J.L. Camenisch, J-M. Piveteau, and M.A. Stadler, Blind Signatures Based on the Discrete Logarithm Problem, *Proc. EUROCRYPT'94*, Springer Verlag, 1994, pp. 428-432.
4. Y. Desmedt, Society and group oriented cryptography: A new concept. In Carl Pomerance, editor, *Proc. CRYPTO'87*, LNCS 293, Springer-Verlag, 1988.
5. Y. Desmedt, Threshold Cryptography, *European Transaction on Telecommunications and Related Technologies*, Vol. 5, No. 4, 1994, pp 35-43.
6. Y. Desmedt and Y. Frankel, Threshold cryptosystems. In G. Brassard, editor, *Proc. CRYPTO'89*, LNCS 435, Springer-Verlag, 1990.
7. R. Gennaro, S. Jarecki, H. Krawczyk and T. Rabin, Robust Threshold DSS Signatures, *Proc. EUROCRYPT'96*, LNCS 1070, Springer-Verlag, 1996.
8. L. Harn, Group oriented (t, n) digital signature scheme and digital multisignature, *IEE Proc.-Comp. Digit. Tech.*, 141(5), Sept 1994.
9. P. Horster, M. Michels, H. Petersen, Hidden signature schemes based on the discrete logarithm problem and related concepts, *Proc. Communications and Multimedia Security*, Chapman & Hall, 1995, pp 162-177.
10. S. Langford, Threshold DSS Signatures without a Trusted Party, *Proc. CRYPTO'95*, LNCS 963, Springer-Verlag, 1995.
11. S. Langford, Weaknesses in Some Threshold Cryptosystems, *Proc. CRYPTO'96*, Springer-Verlag, 1996.
12. C. Li, T. Hwang and N. Lee, *(t, n)*-threshold signature scheme based on discrete logarithm, *Proc. EUROCRYPT'94*, Springer-Verlag, 1995.
13. M. Mambo, K. Usuda and E. Okamoto, Proxy Signatures for Delegating Signing Operation, *Proc. 3rd ACM Conference on Computer and Communications Security*, 1996.
14. K. Nyberg and R.A. Rueppel, A New Signature Scheme Based on the DSA Giving Message Recovery, *Proc. 1st ACM Conference on Computer and Communications Security*, 1993.
15. T. Pedersen, Distributed provers with applications to undeniable signatures, *Proc. EUROCRYPT'91*, Springer-Verlag, 1991.
16. A. Shamir, How to Share a Secret, *Communications of the ACM*, 22:612-613, 1979.
17. S.M. Yen and C.S. Laih, New Digital Signature Scheme Based on Discrete Logarithm, *Electronics Letters*, Vol. 29, No. 12, pp. 1120-1121, 1993.
18. K. Zhang, Nonrepudiable Proxy Signature Schemes, manuscript, 1997.

A Nyberg-Rueppel Scheme

Nyberg-Rueppel scheme [14] is briefly described here. The system parameters consist of a prime p, a prime factor q of $p - 1$, and an element $g \in Z_p^*$ of order q. The signer's private key is a random element $x \in Z_q$, while the corresponding public key is $y = g^x$ (mod p). To sign a message m, which is an integer relatively prime to q, the signer selects $k \in Z_q$ at random and computes r and s as follows:

$$r = mg^k \pmod{p}$$

$$s = xr + k \pmod{q}$$

The pair (r, s) is the signature of the message m. To verify the validity of a signature, one checks that the following equality holds:

$$m = g^{-s} y^r r \pmod{p}.$$

B Blind Nyberg-Rueppel Scheme by Camenisch, Piveteau and Stadler

1. Alice selects $\tilde{k} \in Z_q$, computes $\tilde{r} = g^{\tilde{k}} \pmod{p}$, and sends $\tilde{r}$ to Bob.
2. (a) Bob randomly selects $\alpha \in Z_q$ and $\beta \in Z_q^*$, computes $r = m g^\alpha \tilde{r}^\beta \pmod{p}$ and $\tilde{m} = r\beta^{-1} \pmod{q}$.
   (b) Bob checks whether $\tilde{m} \in Z_q^*$. If this is not the case, he goes back to step a). Otherwise, he sends $\tilde{m}$ to Alice.
3. Alice computes $\tilde{s} = \tilde{m}x + \tilde{k} \pmod{q}$ and forwards $\tilde{s}$ to Bob.
4. Bob computes $s = \tilde{s}\beta + \alpha \pmod{q}$.

The pair (r, s) is a Nyberg-Rueppel signature of the message m and the above protocol is a blind signature scheme.

Signcryption and Its Applications in Efficient Public Key Solutions

Yuliang Zheng

Monash University, McMahons Road, Frankston, Melbourne, VIC 3199, Australia
Email: yuliang@mars.fcit.monash.edu.au
URL: http://www-pscit.fcit.monash.edu.au/~yuliang/

Abstract. Signcryption is a new paradigm in public key cryptography that *simultaneously* fulfills both the functions of digital signature and public key encryption in a logically single step, and with a cost *significantly* lower than that required by the traditional "signature followed by encryption" approach. This paper summarizes currently known construction methods for signcryption, carries out a comprehensive comparison between signcryption and "signature followed by encryption", and suggests a number of applications of signcryption in the search of efficient security solutions based on public key cryptography.

Keywords

Authentication, Digital Signature, Encryption, Key Distribution, Secure Message Delivery/Storage, Public Key Cryptography, Security, Signcryption.

1 Introduction

To avoid forgery and ensure confidentiality of the contents of a letter, for centuries it has been a common practice for the originator of the letter to sign his/her name on it and then seal it in an envelope, before handing it over to a deliverer.

Public key cryptography discovered nearly two decades ago [9] has revolutionized the way for people to conduct secure and authenticated communications. It is now possible for people who have never met before to communicate with one another in a secure and authenticated way over an open and insecure network such as the Internet. In doing so the same two-step approach has been followed. Namely before a message is sent out, the sender of the message would sign it using a digital signature scheme, and then encrypt the message (and the signature) using a private key encryption algorithm under a randomly chosen message encryption key. The random message encryption key would then be encrypted using the recipient's public key. We call this two-step approach signature-then-encryption.

Signature generation and encryption consume machine cycles, and also introduce "expanded" bits to an original message. Symmetrically, a comparable amount of computation time is generally required for signature verification and decryption. Hence the cost of a cryptographic operation on a message is typically measured in the message expansion rate and the computational time invested by both the sender and the recipient. With the current standard signature-then-encryption approach, the cost for delivering a message in a secure and authenticated way is essentially the sum of the cost for digital signature and that for encryption.

In [30], we addressed a question on the cost of secure and authenticated message delivery, namely, *whether it is possible to transfer a message of arbitrary length in a secure and authenticated way with an expense less than that required by signature-then-encryption.* In the same paper, we also presented a positive answer to the question. In particular, we discovered a new cryptographic primitive termed as "signcryption" which *simultaneously* fulfills both the functions of digital signature and public key encryption in a logically single step, and with a cost *significantly* smaller than that required by signature-then-encryption. More specifically, it has been shown in [30] that for the minimum security parameters recommended for the current practice (size of public moduli = 512 bits), signcryption costs 58% less in average computation time and 70% less in message expansion than does signature-then-encryption based on the discrete logarithm problem, while for security parameters recommended for long term security (size of public moduli = 1536 bits), it costs on average 50% less in computation time and 91% less in message expansion than does signature-then-encryption using the RSA cryptosystem. The saving in cost grows proportionally to the size of security parameters. Hence it will be more significant in the future when larger parameters are required to compensate theoretical and technological advances in cryptanalysis.

The following section is an exposition on how signcryption can be implemented by the use of so-called shortened ElGamal based digital signature schemes.

2 Digital Signcryption — A More Economical Approach

Intuitively, a digital *signcryption* scheme is a cryptographic method that fulfills both the functions of secure encryption and digital signature, but *with a cost smaller than that required by signature-then-encryption.* Using the terminology in cryptography, it consists of a pair of (polynomial time) algorithms (S, U), where S is called the *signcryption algorithm*, while U the *unsigncryption algorithm*. S in general is probabilistic, while U is most likely to be deterministic. (S, U) satisfy the following conditions:

1. *Unique unsigncryptability* — Given a message m of arbitrary length, the algorithm S *signcrypts* m and outputs a *signcrypted text* c. On input c, the algorithm U *unsigncrypts* c and recovers the original message un-ambiguously.
2. *Security* — (S, U) fulfill, simultaneously, the properties of a secure encryption scheme and those of a secure digital signature scheme. These properties mainly include: confidentiality of message contents, unforgeability, and non-repudiation.

3. *Efficiency* — The computational cost, which includes the computational time involved both in signcryption and unsigncryption, and the communication overhead or added redundant bits, of the scheme is *smaller* than that required by the best currently known signature-then-encryption scheme with comparable parameters.

The rest of this section is devoted to seeking for concrete implementations of signcryption.

Since its publication in 1985, ElGamal digital signature scheme [11] has received extensive scrutiny by the research community. In addition, it has been generalized and adapted to numerous different forms (see for instance [26, 4, 23, 25] and especially [14] where an exhaustive survey of some 13000 ElGamal based signatures has been carried out.)

In [30], a method for shortening an ElGamal based signature is shown. Applying the shortening method to Digital Signature Standard (DSS) yields two different shortened signature schemes. These two schemes are summarized in Table 1, and are denoted by SDSS1 and SDSS2 respectively. As a side note, both SDSS1 and SDSS2 are preferable to DSS in the sense that they admit a shorter signature and provable security (albeit under a strong assumption).

Shortened schemes	Signature (r, s) on a message m	Verification of signature	Length of signature
SDSS1	$r = hash(g^x \bmod p, m)$ $s = x/(r + x_a) \bmod q$	$k = (y_a \cdot g^r)^s \bmod p$ check whether $hash(k, m) = r$	$\lvert hash(\cdot) \rvert + \lvert q \rvert$
SDSS2	$r = hash(g^x \bmod p, m)$ $s = x/(1 + x_a \cdot r) \bmod q$	$k = (g \cdot y_a^r)^s \bmod p$ check whether $hash(k, m) = r$	$\lvert hash(\cdot) \rvert + \lvert q \rvert$

p: a large prime (public to all),
q: a large prime factor of $p - 1$ (public to all),
g: an integer with order q modulo p chosen randomly from $[1, \ldots, p-1]$ (public to all),
$hash$: a one-way hash function (public to all),
x: a number chosen uniformly at random from $[1, \ldots, q - 1]$,
x_a: Alice's private key, chosen uniformly at random from $[1, \ldots, q - 1]$,
y_a: Alice's public key ($y_a = g^{x_a} \bmod p$).

Table 1. Examples of Shortened and Efficient Signature Schemes

2.1 Implementing Signcryption with Shortened Signature

An interesting characteristic of a shortened ElGamal based signature scheme obtained in the method described above is that although $g^x \bmod p$ is not explicitly contained in a signature (r, s), it can be recovered from r, s and other

Parameters public to all:
p — a large prime
q — a large prime factor of $p-1$
g — an integer with order q modulo p chosen randomly from $[1, \ldots, p-1]$
hash — a one-way hash function whose output has, say, at least 128 bits
KH — a keyed one-way hash function
(E, D) — the encryption and decryption algorithms of a private key cipher
Alice's keys:
x_a — Alice's private key, chosen uniformly at random from $[1, \ldots, q-1]$
y_a — Alice's public key ($y_a = g^{x_a} \bmod p$)
Bob's keys:
x_b — Bob's private key, chosen uniformly at random from $[1, \ldots, q-1]$
y_b — Bob's public key ($y_b = g^{x_b} \bmod p$)

Table 2. Parameters for Signcryption

public parameters. This motivates us to construct a signcryption scheme from a shortened signature scheme.

We exemplify our construction method using the two shortened signatures in Table 1. The same construction method is applicable to other shortened signature schemes based on ElGamal. As a side note, Schnorr's signature scheme, without being further shortened, can be used to construct a signcryption scheme which is slightly more advantageous in computation than other signcryption schemes from the view point of a message originator.

In describing our method, we will use E and D to denote the encryption and decryption algorithms of a private key cipher such as DES [22] and SPEED [31]. Encrypting a message m with a key k, typically in the cipher block chaining or CBC mode, is indicated by $E_k(m)$, while decrypting a ciphertext c with k is denoted by $D_k(c)$. In addition we use $KH_k(m)$ to denote hashing a message m with a keyed hash algorithm KH under a key k. An important property of a keyed hash function is that, just like a one-way hash function, it is computationally infeasible to find a pair of messages that are hashed to the same value (or collide with each other). This implies a weaker property that is sufficient for signcryption: given a message m_1, it is computationally intractable to find another message m_2 that collides with m_1. In [1] two methods for constructing a cryptographically strong keyed hash algorithm from a one-way hash algorithm have been demonstrated. For most practical applications, it suffices to define $KH_k(m) = hash(k, m)$, where *hash* is a one-way hash algorithm.

Assume that Alice has chosen a private key x_a from $[1, \ldots, q-1]$, and made public her matching public key $y_a = g^{x_a} \bmod p$. Similarly, Bob's private key is x_b and his matching public key is $y_b = g^{x_b} \bmod p$. Relevant public and private parameters are summarized in Table 2.

As shown in Table 3, the signcryption and unsigncryption algorithms are remarkably simple. The signcrypted version of a message m is composed of three parts c, r and s from which the recipient can recover the original message. Note that in the table, $\in_R$ indicates an operation that chooses an element uniformly at random from among a set of elements.

Signcryption of m by Alice the Sender		Unsigncryption of (c, r, s) by Bob the Recipient
$x \in_R [1, \ldots, q-1]$ $(k_1, k_2) = hash(y_b^x \bmod p)$ $c = E_{k_1}(m)$ $r = KH_{k_2}(m)$ $s = x/(r + x_a) \bmod q$ $\quad$ if SDSS1 is used, or $s = x/(1 + x_a \cdot r) \bmod q$ $\quad$ if SDSS2 is used.	$\Rightarrow c, r, s \Rightarrow$	$(k_1, k_2) = hash((y_a \cdot g^r)^{s \cdot x_b} \bmod p)$ $\quad$ if SDSS1 is used, or $(k_1, k_2) = hash((g \cdot y_a^r)^{s \cdot x_b} \bmod p)$ $\quad$ if SDSS2 is used. $m = D_{k_1}(c)$ Accept m only if $KH_{k_2}(m) = r$

Table 3. Example Implementations of Signcryption

With the signcryption algorithm described in the left column of the table, the output of the one-way hash function $hash$ used in defining $(k_1, k_2) = hash(y_b^x \bmod p)$ should be sufficiently long, say of at least 128 bits, which guarantees that both k_1 and k_2 have at least 64 bits. Also note that in practice, (k_1, k_2) can be defined in a more liberal way, such as $(k_1, k_2) = y_b^x \bmod p$ and $(k_1, k_2) = fd(y_b^x \bmod p)$, where fd denotes a folding operation.

The unsigncryption algorithm works by taking advantages of the property that $g^x \bmod p$ can be recovered from r, s, g, p and y_a by Bob.

In the following we use SCS1 and SCS2 to denote the two signcryption schemes constructed from SDSS1 and SDSS2 respectively.

2.2 Name Binding

In some applications such as electronic cash payment protocols, the names/identifiers of participants involved may need to be tightly bound to messages exchanged. This can be achieved by explicitly including their names into the contents of a message. Alternatively, data related to participants' names, such as public keys and their certificates, may be included in the computation of r in the signcryption algorithm. Namely, we may define

$$r = KH_{k_2}(m, bind\_info)$$

where $bind\_info$ may contain, among other data, the public keys or public key certificates of both Alice the sender and Bob the recipient. The corresponding unsigncryption algorithm can be modified accordingly. Compared with an exponentiation modulo a large integer, the extra computational cost invested in hashing $bind\_info$ is negligible.

Involving the recipient's public key y_b or his public key certificate in the computation of r is particularly important. To see this point, let (c, r, s) be a signcrypted text of m (from Alice to Bob) where the computation of r does not involve identification information on Bob the recipient, and consider a situation where m represents a committment/statement for Alice to transfer a certain amount of money (or valuable goods) to the recipient of the message. Assume that a third participant Cathy has x_c as her private key and $y_c = g^{x_c} \bmod p$ as her matching public key. Furthermore, assume that Bob and Cathy are a pair of collusive and dishonest friends, and that their private keys are related by $x_b = w \cdot x_c \bmod q$. Then a modified text (c, r, s^*), where $s^* = w \cdot s \bmod q$, may represent a perfectly *valid* message from Alice to Cathy, and hence it might be obligatory for Alice to pay the same of amount money to both Bob and Cathy ! Clearly, such a collusive attack can be easily thwarted by defining $r = KH_{k_2}(m, y_b, etc)$.

2.3 Extensions

Signcryption schemes can also be derived from ElGamal-based signature schemes built on other versions of the discrete logarithm problem such as that on elliptic curves [16]. In addition, Lenstra's new method for constructing sub-groups based on cyclotomic polynomials [17] can also be used to implement signcryption even more efficiently.

There is also a marginally less efficient version of signcryption schemes in which Alice's private key x_a participates in the computation of k. Taking SCS1 as an example, we can re-define the computation of k by Alice in the signcryption algorithm as $k = hash(y_b^{x+x_a} \bmod p)$, and correspondingly, the computation of k by Bob in the unsigncryption algorithm as $k = hash((y_a^{(s+1) \cdot x_b}) \cdot (g^{r \cdot s \cdot x_b}) \bmod p)$.

3   Cost of Signcryption v.s. Cost of Signature-Then-Encryption

The most significant advantage of signcryption over signature-then-encryption lies in the dramatic reduction of computational cost and communication overhead which can be symbolized by the following inequality:

$$\text{Cost(signcryption)} < \text{Cost(signature)} + \text{Cost(encryption)}.$$

The purpose of this section is to examine the advantage in more detail. The necessity of such an examination is justified by the facts that the computational cost of modular exponentiation is mainly determined by the size of an exponent, and that RSA and discrete logarithm based public key cryptosystems normally employ exponents that are quite different in size.

For readers who are not interested in technical details in the comparison, Table 4 summarizes the advantage of SCS1 and SCS2 over discrete logarithm based signature-then-encryption, while Table 5 summarizes that over RSA based signature-then-encryption.

security parameters			saving	saving in
$\|p\|$	$\|q\|$	$\|KH.(\cdot)\|$	average comp. cost	comm. overhead
512	144	72	58%	70.3%
1024	160	80	58%	81.0%
1536	176	88	58%	85.3%
2048	192	96	58%	87.7%
4096	256	128	58%	91.0%
8192	320	160	58%	94.0%
10240	320	160	58%	96.0%

$$\text{saving in average comp. cost} = \frac{(5.17-2.17)\ \text{modular exponentiations}}{5.17\ \text{modular exponentiations}} = 58\%$$

$$\text{saving in comm. cost} = \frac{|hash(\cdot)|+|q|+|p|-(|KH.(\cdot)|+|q|)}{|hash(\cdot)|+|q|+|p|}$$

Table 4. Saving of Signcryption over Signature-Then-Encryption Using Schnorr Signature and ElGamal Encryption

security parameters			advantage in	advantage in
$\|p\|(=\|n_a\|=\|n_b\|)$	$\|q\|$	$\|KH.(\cdot)\|$	average comp. cost	comm. overhead
512	144	72	0%	78.9%
1024	160	80	32.3%	88.3%
1536	176	88	50.3%	91.4%
2048	192	96	59.4%	93.0%
4096	256	128	72.9%	95.0%
8192	320	160	83.1%	97.0%
10240	320	160	86.5%	98.0%

$$\text{advantage in average comp. cost} = \frac{0.375(|n_a|+|n_b|)-3.25|q|}{0.375(|n_a|+|n_b|)}$$

$$\text{advantage in comm. cost} = \frac{|n_a|+|n_b|-(|KH.(\cdot)|+|q|)}{|n_a|+|n_b|}$$

Table 5. Advantage of Signcryption over Signature-Then-Encryption based on RSA with *Small Public Exponents*

3.1 A Comparison with Signature-Then-Encryption Using Schnorr Signature and ElGamal Encryption

Saving in computational cost With the signature-then-encryption based on Schnorr signature and ElGamal encryption, the number of modular exponentiations is three, both for the process of signature-then-encryption and that of decryption-then-verification.

Among the three modular exponentiations for decryption-then-verification, two are used in verifying Schnorr signature. More specifically, these two exponentiations are spent in computing $g^s \cdot y_a^r \bmod p$. Using a technique for fast computation of the product of several exponentials with the same modulo which has been attributed to Shamir (see [11] as well as Algorithm 14.88 on Page 618 of [21]), $g^s \cdot y_a^r \bmod p$ can be computed, on average, in $(1+3/4)|q|$ modular multiplications. Since a modular exponentiation can be completed, on average, in about $1.5|q|$ modular multiplications when using the classical "square-and-multiply" method, $(1 + 3/4)|q|$ modular multiplications is computationally equivalent to 1.17 modular exponentiations. Thus with "square-and-multiply" and Shamir's technique, the number of modular exponentiations involved in decryption-then-verification can be reduced from 3 to 2.17. The same reduction techniques, however, cannot be applied to the sender's computation. Consequently, the combined computational cost of the sender and the recipient is 5.17 modular exponentiations.

In contrast, with SCS1 and SCS2, the number of modular exponentiations is one for the process of signcryption and two for that of unsigncryption respectively. Since Shamir's technique can also be used in unsigncryption, the computational cost of unsigncryption is about 1.17 modular exponentiations. The total average computational cost for signcryption is therefore 2.17 modular exponentiations. This represents a

$$\frac{5.17 - 2.17}{5.17} = 58\%$$

reduction in average computational cost.

Saving in communication overhead The communication overhead measured in bits is $|hash(\cdot)| + |q| + |p|$ for the signature-then-encryption based on Schnorr signature and ElGamal encryption, and $|KH.(\cdot)| + |q|$ for the two signcryption schemes SCS1 and SCS2, where $|x|$ refers to the size of a binary string, $hash$ is a one-way hash function and KH is a keyed hash function. Hence the saving in communication overhead is

$$\frac{|hash(\cdot)| + |q| + |p| - (|KH.(\cdot)| + |q|)}{|hash(\cdot)| + |q| + |p|}$$

Assuming that the one-way hash function $hash$ used in the signature-then-encryption scheme and the keyed hash function KH used in the signcryption scheme share the same output length, the reduction in communication overhead is $|p|$. For the minimum security parameters recommended for use in current practice: $|KH.(\cdot)| = |hash(\cdot)| = 72$, $|q| = 144$ and $|p| = 512$, the numerical value for the saving is 70.3%. One can see that the longer the prime p, the larger the saving.

3.2   A Comparison with Signature-Then-Encryption Using RSA

Advantage in computational cost With RSA, it is a common practice to employ a relatively small public exponent e for encryption or signature verification, although cautions should be taken in light of recent progress in cryptanalysis against RSA with an small exponent (see for example [8, 7]). Therefore the main computational cost is in decryption or signature generation which generally involves a modular exponentiation with a *full size* exponent d, which takes on average 1.5ℓ modular multiplications using the "square-and-multiply" method, where ℓ indicates the size of the RSA composite involved. With the help of the Chinese Remainder Theorem, the computational expense for RSA decryption can be reduced, theoretically, to a quarter of the expense with a full size exponent, although in practice it is more realistic to expect the factor to be between $1/4$ and $1/3$. To simplify our discussion, we assume that the maximum speedup is achievable, namely the average computational cost for RSA decryption is $\frac{1.5}{4}\ell = 0.375\ell$ modular multiplications.

For the signature-then-encryption based on RSA, four (4) modular exponentiations are required (two with public exponents and the other two with private exponents). Assuming small public exponents are employed, the computational cost will be dominated by the two modular exponentiations with full size private exponents. When the Chinese Remainder Theorem is used, this cost is on average $0.375(|n_a| + |n_b|)$ modular multiplications, where n_a and n_b are the RSA composites generated by Alice and Bob respectively.

As discussed earlier, the two signcryption schemes SCS1 and SCS2 both involve, on average, 2.17 modular exponentiations, or equivalently $3.25|q|$ modular multiplications, assuming the "square-and-multiply" method and Shamir's technique for fast computation of the product of exponentials with the same modulo are used. This shows that the signcryption schemes represent an advantage of

$$\frac{0.375(|n_a| + |n_b|) - 3.25|q|}{0.375(|n_a| + |n_b|)}$$

in average computational cost over the RSA based signature-then-encryption. For small security parameters, the advantage is less significant. This situation, however, changes dramatically for large security parameters: consider $|n_a| = |n_b| = |p| = 1536$ and $|q| = 176$ which are recommended to be used for long term (say more than 20 years) security, the signcryption schemes show a 50.3% saving in computation, when compared with the signature-then-encryption based on RSA.

The advantage of the signcryption schemes in computational cost will be more visible, should large public exponents be used in RSA.

Advantage in communication overhead The signature-then-encryption based on RSA expands each message by a factor of $|n_a| + |n_b|$ bits, which is multiple times as large as the communication overhead $|KH.(\cdot)| + |q|$ of the two signcryption schemes SCS1 and SCS2. Numerically, the advantage or saving of the signcryption schemes in communication overhead over the signature-then-encryption based on RSA is as follows:

$$\frac{|n_a| + |n_b| - (|KH.(\cdot)| + |q|)}{|n_a| + |n_b|}$$

For $|n_a| = |n_b| = 1536$, $|q| = 176$ and $|KH.(\cdot)| = 88$, the advantage is 91.4%. The longer the composites n_a and n_b, the larger the saving by signcryption.

Note that we have chosen not to compare the signcryption schemes with unbalanced RSA recently proposed by Shamir [28]. The main reason is that while the new variant of RSA is attractive in terms of its computational efficiency, its security has yet to be further scrutinized by the research community.

4 More on Signcryption v.s. Signature-then-Encryption

In the previous section we concentrated on saving in computation and communication offered by signcryption schemes. A natural question is why signcryption schemes can achieve the savings. To search for a possible answer to the question, we have further compared signcryption with "signature-then-encryption" and "signature-then-encryption-with-a-static-key", in terms of key management, forward secrecy, past recovery, repudiation settlement and users' "community" or world orientation.

We use the following encryption algorithm as an example of "signature-then-encryption-with-a-static-key": (c, r, s) where $c = E_k(m)$, $k = KH_{SV}(r, s)$, SV is a static key shared between Alice and Bob, and (r, s) is Schnorr's signature on m. Typical examples of SV include (a) a pre-shared random string between Alice and Bob, (b) the Diffie-Hellman key $g^{x_a x_b} \bmod p$, and (c) a shared key generated by an identity-based key establishment scheme such as the key pre-distribution scheme [19].

4.1 Static Key Management

We focus narrowly on the way a static key SV between two users is generated and stored. If SV is defined as a pre-shared random string between Alice and Bob, then first of all there is a cost associated with distributing the key before a communication session takes place. In addition, storing it in secure memory incurs a burden to a user, especially when the number of keys to be kept securely is large. (These problems contributed to the motivation for Diffie and Hellman to discover public key cryptography [9].)

On the other hand, if SV is defined as the Diffie-Hellman key $g^{x_a x_b} \bmod p$, then prior to using the value, a modular exponentiation is required on both Alice and Bob's sides. Alice and Bob may save the exponentiation by computing $SV = g^{x_a x_b} \bmod p$ and storing it in secure memory. But then they face the same problem with secure storage as that for a pre-shared random string. Similar discussions apply to the case where SV is defined as a shared key using the key pre-distribution scheme.

Now it becomes clear that static key generation/storage is a problem for "signature-then-encryption-with-a-static-key", but not for signcryption or "signature-then-encryption".

4.2 Forward Secrecy

A cryptographic primitive or protocol provides forward secrecy with respect to a long term private key if compromise of the private key does not result in compromise of security of previously communicated or stored messages.

With "signature-then-encrytpion", since different keys are involved in signature generation and public key encryption, forward secrecy is in general guaranteed with respect to Alice's long term private key. (Nevertheless, loss of Alice's private key renders her signature forgeable.) In contrast, with the signcryption schemes, it is easy to see that knowing Alice's private key alone is sufficient to recover the original message of a signcrypted text. Thus no forward secrecy is provided by the signcryption schemes with respect to Alice's private key. A similar observation applies to "signature-then-encryption-with-a-static-key" with respect to Alice's shared static key.

Forward secrecy has been regarded particularly important for session key establishment [10]. However, to fully understand its implications to practical security solutions, we should identify (1) how one's long term private key may be compromised, (2) how often it may happen, and (3) what can be done to reduce the risks of a long key being compromised. In addition, the cost involved in achieving forward secrecy is also an important factor that should be taken into consideration.

There are mainly three causes for a long term private key being compromised: (1) the underlying computational problems are broken; (2) a user accidentally loses the key; (3) an attacker breaks into the physical or logical location where the key is stored.

As a public key cryptosystem always relies on the (assumed) difficulty of certain computational problems, breaking the underlying problems renders the system insecure and useless. Assuming that solving underlying computational problems is infeasible, an attacker would most likely try to steal a user's long term key through such a means as physical break-in.

To reduce the impact of signcryption schemes' lack of forward secrecy on certain security applications, one may suggest users change their long term private keys regularly. In addition, a user may also use techniques in secret sharing [27] to split a long term private key into a number of shares, and keep each share in a separate logical or physical location. This would significantly reduce the risk of a long term key being compromised, as an attacker now faces a difficult task to penetrate in a larger-than-a-threshold number of locations in a limited period of time.

4.3 Past Recovery

Consider the following scenario: Alice signs and encrypts a message and sends it to Bob. A while later, she finds that she wants to use the contents of the message again.

To satisfy Alice's requirement, her electronic mail system has to store some data related to the message sent. And depending on cryptographic algorithms used, Alice's electronic mail system may either (1) keep a copy of the signed and encrypted message as evidence of transmission, or (2) in addition to the above copy, keep a copy of the original message, either in clear or encrypted form.

A cryptographic algorithm or protocol is said to provide a past recovery ability if Alice can recover the message from the signed and encrypted message alone using her private key.

Obviously a cryptographic algorithm or protocol provides past recovery if and only if it does *not* provide forward secrecy with respect to Alice the sender's long term private key.

Thus both signcryption and "signature-then-encryption-with-a-static-key" provide past recovery, while "signature-then-encrytpion" does not.

In terms of past recovery, one may view "signature-then-encrytpion" as an information "black hole" with respect to Alice the sender: whatsoever Alice drops in the "black hole" will never be retrieval to her, unless a separate copy is properly kept. Therefore signcryption schemes are more economical with regard to secure and authenticated transport of large data files. It is even more so when Alice has to broadcast the same message to a large number of recipients. (See also Section 6 for more discussions on broadcasting).

4.4 Repudiation Settlement

Now we turn to the problem of how to handle repudiation. With signature-then-encryption, if Alice denies the fact that she is the originator of a message, all Bob has to do is to decrypt the ciphertext and present to a judge (say Julie) the message together with its associated signature by Alice, based on which the judge will be able to settle a dispute.

With digital signcryption, however, the verifiability of a signcryption is in normal situations limited to Bob the recipient, as his private key is required for unsigncryption. Now consider a situation where Alice attempts to deny the fact that she has signcrypted and sent to Bob a message m. Similarly to signature-then-encryption, Bob would first unsigncrypt the signcrypted text, and then present the following data items to a judge (Julie): q, p, g, y_a, y_b, m, r, and s. One can immediately see that the judge cannot make a decision using these data alone. To solve this problem, Bob and the judge have to engage in an interactive zero-knowledge proof/argument protocol. Details will be discussed in Section 5.3.

At the first sight, the need for an interactive repudiation settlement procedure between Bob and the judge may be seen as a drawback of signcryption. Here we argue that interactive repudiation settlement will not pose any problem in practice and hence should not be an obstacle to practical applications of signcryption. In the real life, a message sent to Bob in a secure and authenticated way is meant to be readable by Bob only. Thus if there is no dispute between Alice and Bob, direct verifiability by Bob only is precisely what the two users want. In other words, in normal situations where no disputes between Alice and Bob occur, the full power of universal verifiability provided by digital signature is never needed. (For a similar reason, traditionally one uses signature-then-encryption, rather than encryption-then-signature. See also [6] for potential risks of forgeability accompanying encryption-then-signature.) In a situation where repudiation does occur, interactions between Bob and a judge would follow. This is very similar to a dispute on repudiation in the real world, say between a complainant (Bob) and a defendant (Alice), where the process for a judge to resolve the dispute requires in general interactions between the judge and the complainant, and furthermore between the judge and an expert in hand-written signature identification, as the former may rely on advice from the latter in correctly deciding the origin of a message. The interactions among the judge, Bob the recipient and the expert in hand-written signature identification could be time-consuming and also costly.

4.5 "Community" or World Orientation

With the signcryption schemes, both Alice and Bob have to use the same p and g. So they basically belong to the same "community" defined by p and g. Such a restriction does not apply to "signature-then-encryption".

Similar restrictions apply to "signature-then-encryption-with-a-static-key" where the static key is derived from the Diffie-Hellman key $g^{x_a x_b} \bmod p$, or a key pre-distribution scheme [19]. Such restrictions seem to be inherent with cryptographic protocols based on the Diffie-Hellman public key cryptosystem [9]. A recent example of such protocols is an Internet key agreement protocol based on ISAKMP and Oakley [13].

In the case where a static key is a pre-shared random string between Alice and Bob, whether or not Alice and Bob belong to the same "community" will be determined by the underlying protocol for distributing the pre-shared random string.

In theory, the requirement that both Alice and Bob belong to the same "community" does limit the number of users with whom Alice can communicate using a signcryption scheme. In reality, however, all users belong to several "communities", and they tend to communicate more with users in the same group than with outsiders: users (including banks and individuals) of a certain type of digital cash payment system, employees of a company and citizens of a country, to name a few. Therefore the "community" oriented nature of signcryption schemes may not bring much inconvenience to their use in practice.

Table 6 summarizes all the comparisons we have carried out in this section.

4.6 Why Can Signcryption Save ?

Now we come back to the question of why signcryption has a cost similar to that of Schnorr signature. At the first sight, one might think that a possible answer would lie in the fact that with signcryption, forward secrecy is lost with respect to the sender's long term private key. However, signcryption offers past recovery which cannot be achieved by "signature-then-encryption". In other words, past recovery is not something for free. So perhaps loss of forward secrecy does not directly contribute to the low cost of signcryption. Rather, one may consider that the cost for forward secrecy has been somehow transformed to achieve past recovery.

Various Dimensions	Signcryption	Sign-then-Enc with a Static Key	Sign-then-Enc
Cost in Comp. & Comm.	$\approx$ Cost(signature)	$\approx$ Cost(signature)	Cost(signature) + Cost(encryption)
Static key Management	N/A	Distribution, Derivation, Secure storage	N/A
Forward Secrecy	No	No	Yes
Past Recovery	Yes	Yes	No
Repudiation Settlement	Interactive	Non-interactive	Non-interactive
World Orientation	No	Yes & No (see Section 4.5)	Yes

Table 6. Other Aspects of Signcryption v.s. Signature-then-Encryption

It seems more likely that the loss of non-interactive repudiation settlement, together with the fact that users are all confined to the same "community" defined by p and g, has contributed to the low cost of signcryption.

5 Unforgeability, Non-repudiation and Confidentiality of Signcryption

Like any cryptosystem, security of signcryption in general has to address two aspects: (1) to protect what, and (2) against whom. With the first aspect, we wish to prevent the contents of a signcrypted message from being disclosed to a third party other than Alice, the sender, and Bob, the recipient. At the same time, we also wish to prevent Alice, the sender, from being masquerade by other parties, including Bob. With the second aspect, we consider the most powerful attackers one would be able to imagine in practice, namely adaptive attackers who are allowed to have access to Alice's signcryption algorithm and Bob's unsigncryption algorithm.

We say that a signcryption scheme is secure if the following conditions are satisfied:

1. Unforgeability — it is computationally infeasible for an adaptive attacker (who may be a dishonest Bob) to masquerade Alice in creating a signcrypted text.
2. Non-repudiation — it is computationally feasible for a third party to settle a dispute between Alice and Bob in an event where Alice denies the fact that she is the originator of a signcrypted text with Bob as its recipient.
3. Confidentiality — it is computationally infeasible for an adaptive attacker (who may be any party other than Alice and Bob) to gain any partial information on the contents of a signcrypted text.

The following sub-sections are devoted to discussions of the security of the signcryption schemes SCS1 and SCS2.

5.1 Unforgeability

Regarding forging Alice's signcryption, a dishonest Bob is in the best position to do so, as he is the only person who knows x_b which is required to directly verify a signcrypted text from Alice. In other words, the dishonest Bob is the most powerful attacker we should look at. Given the signcrypted text (c, r, s) of a message m from Alice, Bob can use his private key x_b to decrypt c and obtain $m = D_{k_2}(c)$. Thus the original problem is reduced to one in which Bob is in possession of (m, r, s). The latter is identical to the unforgeability of SDSS1 or SDSS2.

SDSS1 and SDSS2 can be shown to be unforgeable. Therefore we conclude that both signcryption schemes SCS1 and SCS2 are unforgeable against adaptive attacks, under the assumption that the keyed hash function behaves like a random function.

5.2 Confidentiality

Next we consider the confidentiality of message contents. We use SCS1 as an example, as discussions for SCS2 are similar. Given the signcrypted text (c, r, s) of a message m from Alice, an attacker can obtain $u = (y_a \cdot g^r)^s = g^x \bmod p$. Thus to the attacker, data related to the signcrypted text of m include: q, p, g, $y_a = g^{x_a} \bmod p$, $y_b = g^{x_b} \bmod p$, $u = g^x \bmod p$, $c = E_{k_1}(m)$, $r = KH_{k_2}(m)$, and $s = x/(r + x_a) \bmod q$.

We wish to show that it is computationally infeasible for the attacker to find out any partial information on the message m from the related data listed above. We will achieve our goal by reduction: we will reduce the confidentiality of another encryption scheme to be defined shortly (called C_{kh} for convenience) to the confidentiality of SCS1.

The encryption scheme C_{kh} is based on ElGamal encryption scheme. With this encryption scheme, the ciphertext of a message m to be sent to Bob is defined as ($c = E_{k_1}(m)$, $u = g^x \bmod p$, $r = KH_{k_2}(m)$) where (1) x is chosen uniformly at random from $[1, \ldots, q-1]$, and (2) $(k_1, k_2) = k = hash(y_b^x \bmod p)$, It turns out C_{kh} is a slightly modified version of a scheme that has received special attention in [29, 3]. (See also earlier work [33].) Using a similar argument as that in [29, 3], we can show in the following that for C_{kh}, it is computationally infeasible for an adaptive attacker to gain any partial information on m.

5.3 Non-repudiation

As discussed in Section 4, signcryption requires a repudiation settlement procedure different from the one for a digital signature scheme is required. In particular, the judge would need Bob's cooperation in order to correctly decide the origin of the message. In what follows we describe three possible repudiation settlement procedures, each requiring a different level of trust on the judge's side.

With a Trusted Tamper-Resistant Device — If a tamper-resistant device is available, a trivial settlement procedure starts with the judge asking Bob to provide the device with q, p, g, y_a, y_b, m, c, r, s and his private key x_b, together with certificates for y_a and y_b. The tamper-resistant device would follow essentially the same steps used by Bob in unsigncrypting (c, r, s). It would output "yes" if it can recover m from (c, r, s), and "no" otherwise. The judge would then take the output of the tamper-resistant device as her decision. Note that in this case, Bob puts his trust completely on the device, rather than on the judge.

By a Less Trusted Judge — Another possible solution would be for Bob to present $v = u^{x_b} \bmod p$, rather than x_b, to the judge. Bob and the judge then engage in a zero-knowledge interactive/non-interactive proof/argument protocol (with Bob as a prover and the judge as a verifier), so that Bob can convince the judge of the fact that v does have the right form. (A possible candidate protocol is a 4-move zero-knowledge proof protocol developed in [5].)

Bob has to be aware of the fact that with this repudiation settlement procedure, the judge can obtain from v, r, s and y_b the Diffie-Hellman shared key between Alice and Bob, namely $k_{DH,ab} = g^{x_a x_b} \bmod p$ ($= v^{1/s} y_b^{-r} \bmod p$ for SCS1). With $k_{DH,ab}$, the judge can find out v^* for other communication sessions between Alice and Bob, and hence recover the corresponding messages ($v^* = k_{DH,ab}^{s^*} y_b^{r^* \cdot s^*} \bmod p$ for SCS1). Therefore Bob may not rely on this repudiation settlement procedure if the judge is not trusted by either Alice or Bob.

By any (Trusted/Untrusted) Judge — Now we describe a repudiation settlement procedure that works even in the case when the judge corrupts and is not trusted. The procedure uses techniques in zero-knowledge proofs/arguments [1] and guarantees that the judge can make a correct decision, with no useful information on Bob's private key x_b being leaked out to the judge.

First Bob presents following data to the judge: q, p, g, y_a, y_b, m, c, r, s and certificates for y_a and y_b. Note that Bob does not hand out x_b, k or $v = u^{x_b} \bmod p$. The judge then verifies the authenticity of y_a and y_b. If satisfied both with y_a and y_b, the judge computes $u = (y_a \cdot g^r)^s \bmod p$ when SCS1 is used, and $u = (g \cdot y_a^r)^s \bmod p$ when SCS2 is used instead. Bob and the judge then engage in a zero-knowledge interactive protocol, with Bob as a prover and the judge as a verifier.

The goal of the protocol is for Bob to convince the judge of the fact that he

---

[1] The main difference between a proof and an argument in the context of zero-knowledge protocols is that, while an argument assumes that a prover runs in polynomial time, a proof works even if a prover has unlimited computational power. A zero-knowledge argument suffices for most cryptographic applications, including repudiation settlement in signcryption.

knows a satisfying assignment $z = x_b$ to the following Boolean formula φ:

$$\varphi(z) = (g^z \bmod p == y_b) \wedge (D_{k_1}(c) == m) \wedge (KH_{k_2}(D_{k_1}(c)) == r)$$

where k_1 and k_2 are defined by $(k_1, k_2) = hash(u^z \bmod p)$, and $==$ denotes equality testing.

φ is clearly a satisfiable Boolean formula in the class of NP. There are a large number of zero-knowledge proof/argument protocols for NP statements in the literature. An example of such protocols is a 4-move protocol recently proposed in [2].

Properties of such a zero-knowledge repudiation settlement procedure include: (1) the judge always correctly announces that (c, r, s) is originated from Alice when it is indeed so; (2) the probability is negligibly small for the judge to declare that (c, r, s) is originated from Alice when in fact it is not; (3) no useful information on Bob's private key x_b is leaked to the judge (or any other parties).

Two remarks on the interactive repudiation settlement procedure follow. First, the message m may be dropped from the data items handed over to the judge, if Bob does not wish to reveal the contents of m to the judge. Second, Bob may include k into the data handed over to the judge if k is defined as $k = hash(y_b^x \bmod p)$ in which a one-way hash function $hash$ is involved. This will reduce the computation and communication load involved in the interactions without compromising the security of x_b, especially when $hash$ is a cryptographically strong function that does not leak information on its input.

Finally we note that if Bob and the judge share a common random bit string, then the number of moves of messages between Bob and the judge can be minimized to 1, by the use of a non-interactive zero-knowledge proof protocol such as the one proposed in [15].

6 Signcryption for Multiple Recipients

So far we have only discussed the case of a single recipient. In practice, broadcasting a message to multiple users in a secure and authenticated manner is an important facility for a group of people who are jointly working on the same project to communicate with one another. In this scenario, a message is broadcast through a so-called multi-cast channel, one of whose properties is that all recipients will receive an identical copy of a broadcast message. Major concerns with broadcasting to multiple recipients include security, unforgeability, non-repudiation and consistency of a message. Here consistency refers to that all recipients recover an identical message from their copies of a broadcast message, and its aim is to prevent a particular recipient from being excluded from the group by a dishonest message originator.

With the traditional signature-then-encryption, the standard practice has been to encrypt the message-encryption key using each recipient's public key and attach the resulting ciphertext to the signed and also encrypted message. RFC1421 [18] details a standard based on RSA. A similar scheme for multiple recipients can be defined using cryptographic schemes based on the discrete logarithm problem, such as "Schnorr signature-then-ElGamal encryption".

Now we show that a signcryption scheme can be easily adapted to one for multiple recipients. We assume that there are t recipients R_1, R_2, ..., R_t. The private key of a recipient R_i is a number x_i chosen uniformly and independently at random from $[1, ..., q-1]$, and his matching public key is $y_i = g^{x_i} \bmod p$.

Table 7 details how to modify SCS1 into a multi-recipient signcryption scheme which we call SCS1M. SCS2M is constructed similarly from SCS2, and hence not shown in the Table. The basic idea is to use two types of keys: the first type consists of only a single randomly chosen key (a message-encryption key) and the second type of keys include a key chosen independently at random for each recipient (called a recipient specific key). The message-encryption key is used to encrypt a message with a private key cipher, while a recipient specific key is used to encrypt the message-encryption key.

Having specified SCS1M, a signcryption for multiple recipients, next we proceed to examining other major issues with the scheme: message consistency, confidentiality, unforgeability, non-repudiation and efficiency.

As we discussed earlier, a message delivery scheme for multiple recipients is said to be consistent if messages recovered by the recipients are identical. Such a requirement is essential in the case of multiple recipients, as otherwise Alice the sender may be able to exclude a particular recipient from the group of recipients by deliberately causing the recipient to recover a message different from the one recovered by other recipients. With a signature-then-encryption scheme for multiple recipients, message consistency is not a problem in general. With SCS1M message consistency is achieved through the use of two techniques: (1) a message m is encrypted *together with the hashed value* $h = KH_k(m)$, namely $c = E_k(m, h)$. (2) m and k are both involved in the formation of r_i and s_i through $r_i = KH_{k_{i,2}}(m, h)$. These two techniques effectively prevent a recipient from being excluded from the group by a dishonest message originator.

Similarly to the case of a single recipient, identification information on each recipient R_i can be tied to a signcrypted text by involving R_i's public key in the computation of r_i (see Section 2.2).

Next we examine the efficiency of the schemes.

Comparison with a Discrete Logarithm Based Scheme — We compare SCS1M and SCS2M with the signature-then-encryption for multiple recipients based on Schnorr signature and ElGamal encryption. Saving by SCS1M (and by SCS2M) in computational cost and communication overhead can be summarized as follow: the number of modular exponentiations is reduced (1) for Alice the sender, from $2t+1$ to t (i.e., by a factor of larger than 50%), and (2) for each recipient, from 2.17 to 1.17 (i.e., by a factor of 45.2% on average, assuming Shamir's fast evleuation of the product of exponentials is used), while the communication overhead measured in bits is reduced from $t \cdot (|k|+|p|)+|hash(\cdot)|+|q|$ to $t \cdot (|k|+|KH.(\cdot)|+|q|)+|KH.(\cdot)|$. As $|p|$ is in general far larger than $|KH.(\cdot)|+|q|$ (compare $|p| = 512$ with $|KH.(\cdot)| = 72$ and $|q| = 144$), the saving in communication overhead is significant. To summarize the above discussion, SCS1M

Signcryption by Alice the Sender for Multi-Recipients

An input to this signcryption algorithm for multi-recipients consists of a message m to be sent to t recipients $R_1, \ldots, R_t$, Alice's private key x_a, R_i's public key y_i for all $1 \le i \le t$, q and p.

1. Pick a random message-encryption key k, calculate $h = KH_k(m)$, and encrypt m by $c = E_k(m, h)$.
2. Create a signcrypted text of k for each recipient $i = 1, \ldots, t$:
   (a) Pick a random number v_i from $[1, \ldots, q-1]$ and calculate $k_i = hash(y_i^{v_i} \bmod p)$. Then split k_i into $k_{i,1}$ and $k_{i,2}$ of appropriate length.
   (b) $c_i = E_{k_{i,1}}(k)$.
   (c) $r_i = KH_{k_{i,2}}(m, h)$.
   (d) $s_i = v_i / (r_i + x_a) \bmod q$.

Alice then broadcasts to all the recipients $(c, c_1, r_1, s_1, \ldots, c_t, r_t, s_t)$.

Unsigncryption by Each Recipient

An input to this unsigncryption algorithm consists of a signcrypted text $(c, c_1, r_1, s_1, \ldots, c_t, r_t, s_t)$ received through a broadcast channel, together with a recipient R_i's private key x_i where $1 \le i \le t$, Alice's public key y_a, g, q and p.

1. Find out (c, c_i, r_i, s_i) in $(c, c_1, r_1, s_1, \ldots, c_t, r_t, s_t)$.
2. $k_i = hash((y_a \cdot g^{r_i})^{s_i \cdot x_i} \bmod p)$. Split k_i into $k_{i,1}$ and $k_{i,2}$.
3. $k = D_{k_{i,1}}(c_i)$.
4. $w = D_k(c)$. Split w into m and h.
5. check if h can be recovered from $KH_k(m)$ and r_i recovered from $KH_{k_{i,2}}(w)$.

R_i accepts m as a valid message originated from Alice only if both $h = KH_k(m)$ and $r_i = KH_{k_{i,2}}(w)$ hold.

Table 7. SCS1M — A Signcryption Scheme for Multiple Recipients

and SCS2M are far more efficient than the signature-then-encryption based on Schnorr signature and ElGamal encryption, both in terms of computational cost and communication overhead.

Comparison with RFC1421 — RFC1421 [18] relies on RSA. As the discrete logarithm and factorization problems are of equal complexity with our current knowledge, we assume that $|n_a| = |n_b| = |p|$. First, two observations on computational costs can be made:

(1) For Alice the sender — The number of modular exponentiations is $t + 1$ with RFC1421, as against t with SCS1M and SCS2M. Among the $r + 1$ exponentiations with RFC1421, one is for RSA signature generation which involves a full length exponent, and the remaining are for RSA public key encryption which generally only involves small exponents. The t exponentiations with SCS1M and

SCS2M all involve exponents from $[1, \ldots, q - 1]$. In addition, both SCS1M and SCS2M involve more hashing, modular multiplications and additions. Hence it is fair to say that from Alice the sender's point of view, neither SCS1M nor SCS2M shows an advantage in computational cost over CFR1421.

(2) For a recipient R_i — The number of modular exponentiations is two with RFC1421, and on average 1.17 with SCS1M and SCS2M. Since one of the two exponentiations with RFC1421 is invested in RSA decryption which involves a full size exponent, SCS1M and SCS2M are faster than RFC1421 from R_i's point of view.

A significant advantage of SCS1M and SCS2M over RFC1421, however, lies in its low communication overhead: RFC1421 expands a message by $|n_a| + \sum_{i=1,\ldots,t} |n_i|$ bits, which is a number of times larger than $t \cdot (|k| + |KH.(\cdot)| + |q|) + |KH.(\cdot)|$, the communication overhead of SCS1M and SCS2M. In conclusion, the following can be said: SCS1M and SCS2M share a similar computational cost with the scheme in RFC1421, but they have a significantly lower communication overhead than RFC1421.

A final note follows: comparisons between the new schemes and RSA or discrete logarithm based schemes in other aspects, including key management, forward secrecy, past recovery, repudiation settlement and users' group or world orientation, are similar to the case of a single recipient, and hence are ommitted here.

7 Applications of Signcryption

The proposed signcryption schemes are compact and particularly suitable for smart card based applications. We envisage that they will find innovative applications in many areas including digital cash payment systems, EDI and personal heath cards. Currently, we are working on signcryption based efficient solutions to the following problems: (1) secure and authenticated key establishment in a single small data packet [32], (2) secure multicasting over the Internet [20], (3) authenticated key recovery [24], (4) secure ATM networks [12], and (5) secure and light weight electronic transaction protocols.

Acknowledgment

Part of this work was completed while I was on sabbatical leave at the University of Tokyo. I would like to take this opportunity to thank Professor Hideki Imai for his hospitality.

The very idea of combining signature with encryption can be partially traced many years back when I was still Professor Imai's PhD student and learnt the beauty of Imai-Hirakawa scheme, a revolutionary invention that combines modulation with error-correcting codes with an aim to achieve more reliable and efficient communcations.

Thanks also go to Dr Minghua Qu who pointed out the potential risk of double-payment by Alice to a pair of collusive friends Bob and Cathy, to Dr Burt

Kaliski who first noticed a lack of forward secrecy with the signryption schemes, and to Drs Markus Michels and Holger Petersen who pointed out the problem with using Chaum's 4-move zero-knowledge protocol in repudiation settlement by a dishonest judge.

References

1. Bellare, M., Canetti, R., Krawczyk, H.: Keying hash functions for message authentication. In Advances in Cryptology - CRYPTO'96 (Berlin, New York, Tokyo, 1996) vol. 1109 of Lecture Notes in Computer Science Springer-Verlag pp. 1–15.
2. Bellare, M., Jakobsson, M., Yung, M.: Round-optimal zero-knowledge arguments based on any one-way function. In Advances in Cryptology - EUROCRYPT'97 (Berlin, Tokyo, 1997) vol. 1233 of Lecture Notes in Computer Science Springer-Verlag pp. 280–305.
3. Bellare, M., Rogaway, P.: Random oracles are practical: A paradigm for designing efficient protocols. In Proceedings of the First ACM Conference on Computer and Communications Security (New York, November 1993) The Association for Computing Machinery pp. 62–73.
4. Brickell, E., McCurley, K.: Interactive identification and digital signatures. AT&T Technical Journal (1991) 73–86.
5. Chaum, D.: Zero-knowledge undeniable signatures. In Advances in Cryptology - EUROCRYPT'90 (Berlin, New York, Tokyo, 1990) vol. 473 of Lecture Notes in Computer Science Springer-Verlag pp. 458–464.
6. Chen, M., Hughes, E.: Protocol failures related to order of encryption and signature: Computation of discrete logarithms in RSA groups April 1997. (Draft).
7. Coppersmith, D.: Finding a small root of a univariate modular equation. In Advances in Cryptology - EUROCRYPT'96 (Berlin, Tokyo, 1996) vol. 1070 of Lecture Notes in Computer Science Springer-Verlag pp. 153–165.
8. Coppersmith, D., Franklin, M., Patarin, J., Reiter, M.: Low-exponent RSA with related messages. In Advances in Cryptology - EUROCRYPT'96 (Berlin, Tokyo, 1996) vol. 1070 of Lecture Notes in Computer Science Springer-Verlag pp. 1–9.
9. Diffie, W., Hellman, M.: New directions in cryptography. IEEE Transactions on Information Theory IT-22 (1976) 472–492.
10. Diffie, W., van Oorschot, P., Wiener, M.: Authentication and authenticated key exchange. Designs, Codes and Cryptography 2 (1992) 107–125.
11. ElGamal, T.: A public key cryptosystem and a signature scheme based on discrete logarithms. IEEE Transactions on Information Theory IT-31 (1985) 469–472.
12. Gamage, C., Zheng, Y.: Secure high speed networking with ABT and signcryption 1997. (submitted for publication).
13. Harkins, D., Carrel, D.: The resolution of ISAKMP with Oakley February 1997. Internet-draft (draft-ietf-ipsec-isakmp-oakley-03.txt).
14. Horster, P., Michels, M., Petersen, H.: Meta-ElGamal signature schemes. In Proceedings of the second ACM Conference on Computer and Communications Security (New York, November 1994) ACM pp. 96–107.
15. Kilian, J., Petrank, E.: An efficient non-interactive zero-knowledge proof system for NP with general assumption. Electronic Colloquium on Computational Complexity **Reports Series** (1995).
16. Koblitz, N.: Elliptic curve cryptosystems. Mathematics of Computation 48 (1987) 203–209.

17. Lenstra, A.: Using cyclotomic polynomials to construct efficient discrete logarithm cryptosystems over finite fields. In Information Security and Privacy – Proceedings of ACISP'97 (Berlin, New York, Tokyo, 1997) vol. 1270 of Lecture Notes in Computer Science Springer-Verlag pp. 127–138.

18. Linn, J.: Privacy enhancement for internet electronic mail: Part I: Message encryption and authentication procedures. RFC 1421 IETF 1993.

19. Matsumoto, T., Imai, H.: On the key predistribution systems: A practical solution to the key distribution problem. In Advances in Cryptology - CRYPTO'87 (Berlin, New York, Tokyo, 1987) vol. 239 of Lecture Notes in Computer Science Springer-Verlag pp. 185–193.

20. Matsuura, K., Zheng, Y., Imai, H.: Analysis of and improvements on CBT multicast key-distribution 1997. (submitted for publication).

21. Menezes, A., van Oorschot, P., Vanstone, S.: Handbook of Applied Cryptography. CRC Press 1996.

22. National Bureau of Standards:. Data encryption standard. Federal Information Processing Standards Publication FIPS PUB 46 U.S. Department of Commerce January 1977.

23. National Institute of Standards and Technology:. Digital signature standard (DSS). Federal Information Processing Standards Publication FIPS PUB 186 U.S. Department of Commerce May 1994.

24. Nishioka, T., Matsuura, K., Zheng, Y., Imai, H.: A proposal for authenticated key recovery system. In Proceedings of 1997 Joint Workshop on Information Security and Cryptography (JW-ISC'97) (Seoul, 1997) KIISC (Korea) pp. 189–196.

25. Nyberg, K., Rueppel, R.: Message recovery for signature schemes based on the discrete logarithm problem. Designs, Codes and Cryptography 7 (1996) 61–81.

26. Schnorr, C. P.: Efficient identification and signatures for smart cards. In Advances in Cryptology - CRYPTO'89 (Berlin, New York, Tokyo, 1990) vol. 435 of Lecture Notes in Computer Science Springer-Verlag pp. 239–251.

27. Shamir, A.: How to share a secret. Communications of the ACM 22 (1979) 612–613.

28. Shamir, A.: RSA for paranoids. CryptoBytes 1 (1995) 1–4.

29. Zheng, Y.: Improved public key cryptosystems secure against chosen ciphertext attacks. Technical Report 94-1 University of Wollongong Australia January 1994.

30. Zheng, Y.: Digital signcryption or how to achieve cost(signature & encryption) $\ll$ cost(signature) + cost(encryption). In Advances in Cryptology - CRYPTO'97 (Berlin, New York, Tokyo, 1997) vol. 1294 of Lecture Notes in Computer Science Springer-Verlag pp. 165–179.

31. Zheng, Y.: The SPEED cipher. In Proceedings of Financial Cryptography'97 (Berlin, New York, Tokyo, 1997) vol. 1318 of Lecture Notes in Computer Science Springer-Verlag.

32. Zheng, Y., Imai, H.: Compact and unforgeable session key establishment over an ATM network. In Proceedings of IEEE Infocom'98 IEEE.

33. Zheng, Y., Seberry, J.: Immunizing public key cryptosystems against chosen ciphertext attacks. IEEE Journal on Selected Areas in Communications 11 (1993) 715–724.

A New Digital Cash Scheme
Based on Blind Nyberg-Rueppel Digital Signature

Khanh Quoc Nguyen, Yi Mu and Vijay Varadharajan

School of Computing & IT, University of Western Sydney, Nepean,
PO Box 10, Kingswood, NSW 2747, Australia
Email: {qnguyen,yimu,vijay}@st.nepean.uws.edu.au

Abstract. We propose a new untraceable digital cash scheme using blind Nyberg-Rueppel digital signature. The scheme provides security features such as client anonymity, coin forgery prevention and double spending detection. The proposed scheme is also more efficient than previously proposed schemes by Chaum and Brands.

1 Introduction

An untraceable digital cash scheme allows a client to obtain a valid coin from the bank and to anonymously spend the coin to a vendor. The vendor later deposits the coin to the bank. When the bank sees the coin, it can validate the coin but should not be able to link the coin to the information supplied on the coin issuing process. Consequently, the bank and the vendor cannot trace any transaction made by the customer; in other words, client's privacy is protected against both the vendor and the bank.

The concept of untraceable digital cash scheme was introduced by Chaum et al. [4]. The transaction untraceability proposed by Chaum is based on the use of zero-knowledge proof, which is computationally expensive and not efficient enough for practical use. Recent studies [1,6–8] have resulted in various improvements on Chaum's scheme. In particular, protocols proposed by Brands [1] and Ferguson [6] achieve transaction untraceability without requiring zero-knowledge proof.

This paper presents a new untraceable digital cash scheme based on the blind Nyberg-Rueppel signature scheme. Our scheme does not involve expensive zero knowledge proof and seems to be practical for use in application such as electronic commerce. The rest of the paper is organized as follows. Section 2 reviews the blind Nyberg-Rueppel digital signature scheme. Section 3 introduces our new digital cash scheme and describes the protocols for withdrawal, payment and deposit phases. Section 4 considers security characteristics of the proposed scheme.

2 Blind Nyberg-Rueppel digital signature

In this section, we describe the Nyberg-Rueppel digital signature and its blind signature version proposed in [2].

2.1 Basic Nyberg-Rueppel digital signature

Assume that x is the secret key of the signer. $y = g^x \bmod p$ is then the public key of the signer, where $g \in \mathcal{Z}_p$ and p is a prime. We also need another prime q such that $g^q = 1$. g, q, p are public information.

To sign a message $m \in \mathcal{Z}_p$, the signer selects a random number $k \in \mathcal{Z}_q$ and computes r and s as follows:

$$r = mg^k \bmod p,$$
$$s = xr + k \bmod q.$$

The pair (r, s) is the signature of the message m. To verify the validity of a signature, one checks:

$$m = g^{-s} y^r r \bmod p. \tag{1}$$

This scheme provides message recovery, hence the signature need not be accompanied by the message m.

2.2 Blinding the Nyberg-Rueppel digital signature

To obtain a blind Nyberg-Rueppel digital signature on a message m from the signer, the verifier needs to get a pair (r, s) in the form:

$$r = mg^k \bmod p,$$
$$s = xr + k \bmod q,$$

in such a way that the signer does not learn anything about either r or s. This can be achieved using the following process:

1. The signer selects $\tilde{k} \in \mathcal{Z}_q$, computes $\tilde{r} = g^{\tilde{k}} (\bmod p)$, and sends $\tilde{r}$ to the verifier.
2. The verifier selects $\alpha, \beta \in \mathcal{Z}_q$, computes $r = mg^\alpha \tilde{r}^\beta (\bmod p)$, $\tilde{m} = r\beta^{-1}$ and sends $\tilde{m}$ to the signer.
3. The signer computes $\tilde{s} = \tilde{m}x + \tilde{k}$ and then forwards $\tilde{s}$ to the verifier.
4. The verifier computes $s = \tilde{s}\beta + \alpha (\bmod q)$.

The pair (r, s) is then a blind signature of the signer on message m. The validity of the signature (r, s) for message m is done by verifying

$$g^{-s} y^r r = mg^{-\tilde{s}\beta + xr + \tilde{k}\beta + \alpha} = mg^{-\tilde{m}x\beta - \tilde{k}\beta + xr + \tilde{k}\beta} = m (\bmod p). \tag{2}$$

Furthermore, as α and β are randomly chosen, the signer does not learn anything about (r, s). For a given signature (r, s), there exists an unique pair of α and β. Thus for each signature from the signer, the verifier can generate only one blind signature. Detailed discussion on the security of this scheme can be found in [2].

3 A New Digital Cash Scheme

We use $\mathcal{B}$ to denote the bank, $\mathcal{C}$ to denote a client and $\mathcal{V}$ to denote a vendor.

(p, q, g) are public information and they satisfy $g^q = 1 \bmod p$. $\mathcal{B}$ has a secret key (x). $\mathcal{B}$ also chooses two random numbers w_1 and w_2, computes $g_1 = g^{w_1}$, $g_2 = g^{w_2}$ as well as $h_1 = g_1^x$ and $h_2 = g_2^x$. g_1, g_2, h_1 and h_2 are then made public. Each client in the system has a pair of secret and public keys (u, v) such that $v = g_1 g_2^u \bmod p$. The public key v is registered with the bank as the client's identity. $\mathcal{C}$ is given $w = v^x$ as the bank certificate of the client identity. It might also be necessary for the bank to prove to $\mathcal{C}$ that $log_v(w) = log_g(g^x)$, where g^x is the bank public key. This can be done using Chaum-Pedersen interactive signature algorithm [5].

Let us now consider three phases in the scheme, namely withdrawal, payment, and deposit. $\mathcal{C}$ first withdraws some electronic coins from the bank using the withdrawal protocol, then spends those electronic coins with $\mathcal{V}$ using the payment protocol, and finally deposits the received coins at $\mathcal{B}$ using the deposit protocol. This is an off-line cash scheme and the bank is not involved in the payment phase.

3.1 Withdrawal protocol

When $\mathcal{C}$ wishes to withdraw some coins, $\mathcal{C}$ and $\mathcal{B}$ must go through some authentication process. For each coin, the following protocol is run:

$\mathcal{C}$ $\mathcal{B}$

$$k \in \mathcal{Z}_q$$
$$\delta \leftarrow v^k \bmod p$$

$$\xleftarrow{\hspace{1cm} \delta \hspace{1cm}}$$

$$y, x_1, x_2 \in \mathcal{Z}_q^*$$
$$\alpha \leftarrow w^y \bmod p$$
$$\beta \leftarrow v^y \bmod p$$
$$\lambda \leftarrow h_1^{x_1} h_2^{x_2} \bmod p$$
$$m \leftarrow \mathcal{H}(\alpha, \beta, \lambda)$$
$$a, b \in \mathcal{Z}_q^*$$
$$r \leftarrow m\beta^a \delta^{bw} \bmod p$$
$$m' \leftarrow r/b \bmod q$$

$$\xrightarrow{\hspace{1cm} m' \hspace{1cm}}$$

$$s' \leftarrow m'x + k \bmod q$$

$$\xleftarrow{\hspace{1cm} s' \hspace{1cm}}$$

$$s \leftarrow s'b + a \bmod q$$

1: $\mathcal{B}$ chooses a random number $k \in \mathcal{Z}_q$, computes $\delta = v^k \bmod p$ and forwards δ to $\mathcal{C}$.

2: $\mathcal{C}$ generates three random numbers (y, x_1, x_2), computes $\alpha = w^y$, $\beta = v^y$ and $\lambda = h_1^{x_1} h_2^{x_2}$.

3: C forms the message $m = \mathcal{H}(\alpha, \beta, \lambda)$, generates a random number a and a Nyberg-Rueppel blind factor b, calculates $r = m\beta^a \delta^{bw}$ and sends $m' = c/b$ to $\mathcal{B}$.

4: $\mathcal{B}$ computes its Nyberg-Rueppel signature on the blind message m' by forming $s' = m'x + k$ to C and sends it to C.

5: C removes the blind factor b and obtains $s = s'b + a = rx + kb + a$.

At the end of the withdrawal protocol, $[\alpha, \beta, \lambda, r, s]$ represents a valid coin. It can be verified using the following equation:

$$\mathcal{H}(\alpha, \beta, \lambda) = \beta^{-s}\alpha^r r \bmod p. \tag{3}$$

Proposition 1. (Completeness) *If C and $\mathcal{B}$ both perform the computations correctly, then (3) is true.*

Proof

We have $s = s'b + a$, $s' = m'x + k$ and $m' = r/b$ so $s = ((r/b)x + k)b + a = rx + kb + a \bmod p$. On the other hands, $r = m\beta^a\delta^{yb}$ which is equivalent to mv^{ay+kby}.

Thus we have:

$$
\begin{aligned}
\beta^{-s}\alpha^r r &= (v^y)^{-s}(w^y)^r r \\
&= (v^y)^{-rx-kb-a}(v^{xy})^r r \\
&= v^{(-rxy-kby-ay)}v^{rxy}r \\
&= v^{(-kby-ay)}r \\
&= v^{(-kby-ay)}mv^{(ay+kby)} \\
&= m \\
&= \mathcal{H}(\alpha, \beta, \lambda)(\bmod p).
\end{aligned}
$$

$\square$

Proposition 2. (Soundness)
Assuming that the security of blind Nyberg-Rueppel signature holds, the client cannot generate more than one coin that satisfies (3).

Proof

Assume that it is possible to create more than one valid coin from one withdrawal. As $\mathcal{H}$ is a strong one-way hash function, in order to create more than one valid coin from one withdrawal, the client must find a method to form a valid blind Nyberg-Rueppel signature on the message $\tilde{m} = \mathcal{H}(\tilde{\alpha}, \tilde{\beta}, \tilde{\lambda})$ from a blind Nyberg-Rueppel signature on another message $m = \mathcal{H}(\alpha, \beta, \lambda)$.

Because hash functions do not have any relational property, so creating a valid signature on $\tilde{m}$ from the signature on the message m is equivalent to creating a valid signature on a random message from valid signatures on some other messages. This is not feasible if we assume that the blind Nyberg-Rueppel signature is secure[2]. $\square$

Proposition 3. (Blindness)
After the withdrawal transaction, the bank will not have any specific information about each coin. The coin that was withdrawn is anonymous.

Proof
It is straightforward to see that, in the computation of each term in the coin $[\alpha, \beta, \lambda, r, s]$, there is at least one random number which is secretly chosen by the client and unknown to all the others. So after the withdrawal, the bank (and the vendors) would not have any information on the coin other than the fact that the coin is valid, i.e. the coin satisfies (3) □

3.2 Payment protocol

When C wishes to pay the coin $[\alpha, \beta, \lambda, r, s]$ to V, the following protocol is used:

C $\hspace{8cm}$ V

$\hspace{6cm} c \leftarrow \mathcal{H}(V\|Date\|Time\|\ldots)$

$\xleftarrow{\hspace{3cm} c \hspace{3cm}}$

$r_1 = x_1 + cy \bmod q$
$r_2 = x_2 + ucy \bmod q$

$\xrightarrow{\hspace{1.5cm} r_1, r_2, [\alpha, \beta, \lambda, r, s] \hspace{1.5cm}}$

$\hspace{6cm} \mathcal{H}(\alpha, \beta, \lambda) = \beta^{-s}\alpha^r.r$
$\hspace{6cm} h_1^{r_1} h_2^{r_2} = \alpha^c \lambda$

1: V generates a random challenge c and sends it to C. This challenge should be unique for each transaction. For example, it can be computed as $c = \mathcal{H}(V\|Date\|Time\|\ldots)$
2: Upon receiving c, C computes a response (r_1, r_2), where $r_1 = x_1 + cy \bmod q$ and $r_2 = x_2 + ucy \bmod q$, and sends it to V.
3: V checks Nyberg-Rueppel signature on the message $\mathcal{H}(\alpha, \beta, \lambda)$ and verifies that (r_1, r_2) are indeed consistent with the challenge c. If the checks are successful, then the coin is valid

V accepts the coin if $\mathcal{H}(\alpha, \beta, \lambda) = \beta^{-s}\alpha^r r$ and $h_1^{r_1} h_2^{r_2} = \alpha^c \lambda$. V then delivers the requested service to C and stores $(c, r_1, r_2, [\alpha, \beta, \lambda, r, s])$.

Proposition 4. (Completeness)
If the client and the vendor follow the correct procedures given above, then $\mathcal{H}(\alpha, \beta, \lambda) = \beta^{-s}\alpha^r r$ and $h_1^{r_1} h_2^{r_2} = \alpha^c \lambda$ must hold.

Proof
If the client sends the correct coin $[\alpha, \beta, \lambda, r, s]$, from Propositions 1 and 2, $\mathcal{H}(\alpha, \beta, \lambda) = \beta^{-s}\alpha^r r$.
Now consider $\alpha^c \lambda$:

$$\alpha^c \lambda = w^{yc} h_1^{x_1} h_2^{x_2}$$
$$= v^{xyc} h_1^{x_1} h_2^{x_2}$$

$$= (g_1 g_2^u)^{xyc} h_1^{x_1} h_2^{x_2}$$
$$= (h_1 h_2^u)^{yc} h_1^{x_1} h_2^{x_2}$$
$$= h_1^{x_1+cy} h_2^{x_2+cyu}$$
$$= h_1^{r_1} h_2^{r_2} (\bmod\ p).$$

$\square$

Proposition 5. (Soundness 1)
$\mathcal{V}$ will accept the coin iff $\mathcal{H}(\alpha, \beta, \lambda) = \beta^{-s} \alpha^r r$ is true.

Proof
From Propositions 1 and 2, $\mathcal{H}(\alpha, \beta, \lambda) = \beta^{-s} \alpha^r r$, iff the coin $[\alpha, \beta, \lambda, r, s]$ was withdrawn correctly or the coin is valid. Therefore if the equation $\mathcal{H}(\alpha, \beta, \lambda) = \beta^{-s} \alpha^r r$ is true, then $\mathcal{V}$ must accept the coin.

$\square$

Proposition 6. (Soundness 2)
Assuming that the coin is valid, for a random challenge r, the client must send $r_1 = x_1 + cy$ and $r_2 = x_2 + ucy$; otherwise $h_1^{r_1} h_2^{r_2} = \alpha^c \lambda$ will not hold .

Proof
Every coin withdrawn by $\mathcal{C}$ contains a blind Nyberg-Rueppel digital signature with the base being the public key v of the client. As the coin is valid, $m = \beta^{-s} \alpha^r r$ is satisfied, then α and β must be some power of base v^x and v respectively. This means that $\alpha = v^{xy}$ for some random number y.

Hence

$$\alpha^c \lambda = v^{xcy} \lambda$$
$$= (g_1 g_2^u)^{xcy}$$
$$= h_1^{cy} h_2^{cuy}$$

On an other hand, if the coin is accepted, $h_1^{r_1} h_2^{r_2} = \alpha^c \lambda$ must be true. It means $h_1^{r_1} h_2^{r_2} = h_1^{cy} h_2^{cuy} \lambda$ or $\lambda = h_1^{r_1-cy} h_2^{r_2-cuy}$.

Let $x_1' = r_1 - cy$ and $x_2' = r_2 - cuy$. Then we have $\lambda = h_1^{x_1'} h_2^{x_2'}$. The pair (x_1', x_2') must be known by the client before the transaction. Moreover, this pair is unique from the client's perspective as s/he does not know $log_{h_1}(h_2)$.

As in the case of the withdrawal phase, $\mathcal{C}$ generates $\lambda = h_1^{x_1} h_2^{x_2}$. Hence $x_1 \equiv x_1'$; $x_2 \equiv x_2'$ and $r_1 = x_1 + cy$; $r_2 = x_2 + cyu$.

$\square$

3.3 Deposit

$\mathcal{V}$ can deposit at the bank the coins s/he has received at any suitable time. For each received coin, $\mathcal{V}$ sends $(c, r_1, r_2, [\alpha, \beta, \lambda, r, s])$ to $\mathcal{B}$. $\mathcal{B}$ also checks

$$\mathcal{H}(\alpha, \beta, \lambda) = \beta^{-s} \alpha^r r$$
$$\text{and } h_1^{r_1} h_2^{r_2} = \alpha^c \lambda.$$

If both are satisfied, then $\mathcal{B}$ accepts the coin.

4 Security Issues

Let us now consider the following security aspects: client anonymity, transaction untraceability, double-spending detection and coin forgery.

Client Anonymity: Client anonymity is protected unconditionally in our scheme. Each coin is blindly signed by the bank. When the client pays a coin to a vendor, it is not feasible for the vendor and the bank to link the coin and the client. During the payment protocol, apart from the coin, the client needs to show the response: $r_1 = x_1 + cy$ and $r_2 = x_2 + cuy$. With x_1 and x_2 secretly chosen by the client, it is impossible to compute u, v or w from the response. So client's anonymity is unconditionally protected.

Transaction Untraceability: Our scheme treats each coin independently and there is no connection between any two coins. Hence when two coins are withdrawn by the same user and are spent in two different transactions, it is impossible to find any link between the two transactions from these coins. This leads to untraceability of transactions.

Double Spending Detection: Detection of double spending is major concern for any untraceable digital cash scheme. If C has double-spent a coin $[\alpha, \beta, \lambda, r, s]$, the bank can obtain two the different responses (r_1, r_2) and (r'_1, r'_2) for two different challenges c and c', where $r_1 = x_1 + cy$, $r_2 = x_2 + cyu$, $r'_1 = x_1 + c'y$ and $r'_2 = x_2 + c'yu$. B now can compute

$$\frac{r_1 - r'_1}{c - c'} = \frac{x_1 + cy - x_1 - c'y}{c - c'} = y,$$

$$\frac{r_2 - r'_2}{c - c'} = \frac{x_2 + cyu - x_2 - c'yu}{c - c'} = yu.$$

From y and yu, the bank can easily obtain u. After obtaining u, B computes $v = g_1 g_2^u$ and finds the match between this value and the ones in the bank's client list. With such a match, B can charge the client with double-spending. The evidence is *undeniable* as d is the client's secret information, which is not possible to determine unless the client has double-spent.

Coin Forgery: It is computationally impossible to forge our coins. To forge a coin, the client needs to create a blind Nyberg-Rueppel signature on $m = \mathcal{H}(\alpha, \beta, \lambda)$, which is not possible according to [2]. Combining several old coins to get a new coin is also infeasible, as each coin contains $m = \mathcal{H}(\alpha, \beta, \lambda)$ and $\mathcal{H}$ is a strong one-way hashing function.

5 Comparison to Related Work

The most notable schemes for electronic cash are proposed by Chaum *et al.*[4], Ferguson[6] and Brands[1].

Chaum's proposal uses zero-knowledge proof to achieve double-spending detection. Zero-knowledge requires more than one challenge from the vendor for each coin. In fact, the minimal number of challenges for each coin is twenty, which makes the proposal inefficient compared to our scheme.

Ferguson's scheme [6] uses a polynomial secret-sharing mechanism to realise double-spending detection. However, the withdrawal protocol of this scheme is inefficient.

Brands's scheme uses a method that is similar to the blind Schnorr's one-time digital signature and is fairly efficient. However our scheme is more efficient than Brands's scheme: Each coin in Brands' scheme contains six terms; while it contains five in ours. Verifying each Brands's coin requires seven discrete exponentiations; while verifying our coin needs only five.

References

1. S.Brands, " Untraceable off-line cash in wallet with observers", *Advances of Cryptology - CRYPTO '93 Proceedings*, Springer-Verlag,1994, pp.302-318.
2. J. Camenisch and J.Piveteau, M. Stadler, "Blind Signatures Based on the Discrete Logarithm Problem", *Advances of Cryptology- Eurocrypt'94 Proceedings*, Springer-Verlag, 1994, pp.428-432.
3. D.Chaum, " Security without Identification: Transaction systems to make Big Brother obsolete," *Communications of ACM, vol.28, no.10, pp.1030-1044, Oct.85.*
4. D.Chaum, A.Fiat and M.Naor, "Untraceable electronic cash", in *Advances in Cryptology - CRYPTO '88 Proceedings*, pp.319-327,1990.
5. D.Chaum and T.Pedersen, "Wallet Databases with Observers", *Advances in Cryptology - CRYPTO'92 Proceedings*, Springer-Verlag, 1993.
6. N.T.Ferguson, " Single Term Off-Line Coins",*Advances in Cryptology - EUROCRYPT '93 Proceedings*, Springer-Verlag, 1994, pp.318-328
7. T.Okamoto, K.Ohta, " Universal Electronic Cash", *Advances of Cryptology - CRYPTO '91 Proceedings*, Springer Verlag, 1991.
8. L.A.M.Schoenmakers, "An efficient electronic payment system withstanding parallel attacks", *CWI Technical Report CS-R9522*, 1995.

An Incremental Payment Method for Internet Based Streaming Real-Time Media

Andreas Fuchsberger*

Information Security Group, Department of Computer Science, Royal Holloway, University of London, Egham, Surrey, TW20 0EX, UK

Abstract. Described is a method for linking payment to delivery of streaming data for real-time delivery of audio and/or video data using Internet technologies.

1 Introduction

The Internet is rapidly evolving into a mass audience broadcast medium. A direct result of the phenomenal growth of the World Wide Web (WWW) is also the number of people who connect to the Internet for leisure in order to "browse the Web". Most content on the WWW is still static, i.e. once downloaded and viewed does not change. As such its delivery mechanism, the Hypertext Transfer Protocol (http) [2], has been optimized for *fast*, and *complete* delivery. This delivery mechanism does not lend itself well to audio and video data, in general all data has to be downloaded before it can be played. Additionally video on the Internet has remained in formats originally designed for CD-ROM delivery such as Apple's QuickTime [7] and Microsoft's AVI [4]. These formats were not designed for Internet bandwidths, frequently the download times were 10 – 20 times the length of the video clip and clips are short, often not more than 20 – 30 seconds.

Streaming the data provides a solution by continually emitting the audio and video data at the maximum rate the recipient can receive the data. The semantics of audio and video data can be considered to be different from that of a static text or images. In static text and images any missing data can severely impact the semantics of the whole. This is not necessarily true for dynamic data such as video and audio. By their very nature, any loss of data is only temporal and will be replaced later. This is even more so when the technologies used for encoding of video and audio take losses into account and reduce impact by "spreading" the information encoded.

As the Internet is a "anyone-to-many" network which contrasts to more traditional broadcast networks of television or radio, which are "someone-to-many" this allows anyone, who has the appropriate hardware to become an instant world wide broadcaster. The increased number of "multi-media PCs" [1] in the

---

* A.Fuchsberger@rhbnc.ac.uk

[1] A "multi-media PC" is term used by the computer trade industry to describe an above average PC with, at a minimum an audio capability, CD-ROM reader and high resolution graphics capability

homes used for leisure provides a substantial potential audience able to receive these broadcasts. Together this allows for the creation of niche broadcasters, in way that hasn't been possible before. However it is fair to assume that any commercial channels intending to broadcast this way will be unable to fund their operation solely through the means open to current day broadcasters, advertising or mandatory license fees. More probably they will be required to fund themselves through subscription or "pay-per-view".

Using the Internet as the broadcast medium also enables the related application of a virtual tape/video vault. Broadcaster can archive their programs using standard hardware and make them available at request to their audience. This audio or audio/video "on-demand" service offers an additional revenue channel.

Currently the quality of the video leaves a lot to be desired, the image has been described as "postage stamp" size and jerky, with only a 7 – 10 frames per second (fps) in contrast 25 fps on standard broadcast television. No doubt the quality will increase as compression technology improves and more bandwidth to the home becomes more readily available.

Streaming of data for real-time delivery of audio/video is a relatively new technology for the Internet. However there are already a number of products that allow users to watch and listen to these broadcasts, examples of such technologies, whereby this is not a complete list, are:

- Xing Technologies' Streamworks [18]
- Progressive Networks', RealAudio and RealVideo [13].
- VDOnet's VDOLive [9],
- Microsoft's Netshow [5]
- Netscape's LiveMedia [6]
- Vxtreme's Web Theatre [21]
- Vivo [19]
- Macromedia [11]
- Vocaltec's Internet Wave [20]
- DSP Group's TrueSpeech [8]

Since the first version of this paper, Microsoft have announced a major investment in Progressive Networks and a convergence in streaming technologies of RealAudio/Video and Netshow. The newest release of RealAudio/Video already supports Microsoft's native streaming format.

2 Linking Payment to quality of service

Current technology for streaming data usually relies on user datagram protocol (UDP) [15] which has a lower network latency than the transmission control protocol (TCP) [16]. Whilst TCP is connection oriented and supplies a reliable channel, UDP is connectionless and unreliable, and as such has a lower overhead resulting in its lower network latency. Other less used technologies for streaming are Multicast [1] and the real time protocol (RTP) [17]. Until other delivery mechanism are available RTP also uses UDP as its underlying mechanism.

Since UDP is unreliable, packets can be dropped due to network congestion or other disruptions, this also reduces the quality of the audio/video stream. By linking payment to the actual successful delivery of the streamed data, the user only has to pay for data received and therefore links payment to quality of the service.

In theory any payment scheme could be used to link successful receipt of streamed data to payment. Most electronic schemes are based on public-key cryptography and digital signatures. During payment at least one and often more than one digital signature must be created and verified. This has the disadvantage that the efficiency of the payment scheme depends on the efficiency of the digital signature scheme. However streaming data is a time sensitive operation. In addition the total amount to be paid is composed of many individual payments of small amounts and each payment must be paid in real time upon successful receipt of the streamed data. Depending on the charging structure imposed by the content provider, payments need to be made at very short intervals. Furthermore such an application of payment schemes would require a lot of storage at the recipient side increasing linearly with the number of payments required.

Clearly this is undesirable. A useful payment scheme must therefore have the following properties.

- Efficient and suitable for streaming data
- Reduce storage requirements for completed payments

The following method is an application on the idea of a "tick-payment" put forward by [14], for encoding amounts in messages. which itself is an application the password scheme devised by Lamport [10]. An earlier application of repeated computations of one-way functions is described in [12] and attributed to Winternitz (1979). In relation to payment systems a similar idea is used in [3] to encode amounts.

Tick payments have the above properties. A tick payment initialy requires the same computation as a normal payment based on digital signatures. Then the payment of the ith tick requires at most $T - i$ computations of an easily computable function. Verification of each tick only requires one computation of this function. After the required number of ticks have been paid only a few hundred bits more than a simple digital signature payment are required.

Tick payments have the property of requiring monotone decreasing payments. Linking a tick payment to audio/video data stream based on UDP using the same delivery mechanism as for the data stream, does not provide the required reliable service. The scheme therefore has to be modified by either:

- using a different transport mechanism for the tick payment data.
- modify the tick payment mechanism not to require monotone ticks.

3 Payment Mechanisms

The perceived quality of audio and video streaming services is defined by the *codec* (from coder/decoder). The encoder codec is responsible for the compression of the raw binary data from A/D converter thereby reducing the transmission bandwidth required. At this stage trade-offs are made, higher quality requires more bandwidth. As an illustration, Uncompressed broadcast television has a basic data of roughly 100 Megabits per second. The popular 28.8 modems give only 20 Kilobits per second data rate.

In newer on-demand streaming technologies such as RealAudio/Video and Netshow the server can in advance to the actual transmission negotiate a number parameters including bandwidth values and delivery methods.

During the transmission the client can influence the server by e.g. requesting retransmissions of lost data, the client may also send statistics back to the server allowing the server to make adjustments to the transmission.

3.1 Review of tick payments

The following section reviews the underlying idea of tick payments. It is heavily based on an paper by Torben P. Pedersen.

In [14] Pedersen describes an electronic payment scheme as a triple $(v, m, \sigma(m))$. Where m is a message which includes the amount to be paid, $\sigma(m)$ is a digital signature and v denotes all other messages exchanged during payment.

Verifying a payment involves checking that m contains the expected information and $\sigma(m)$ verifies as a signature for m and v.

For the idea of tick payments a length preserving function f is used. f^i denotes i evaluations of f for $i \in N$. f^0 is the identity and $f^i = f \circ f^{i-i}$ for $i = 1, 2, \ldots$.

Tick payments are added to the previously described electronic payment system by providing a new way of encoding amounts in the message m. The message m is computed as before except it encodes the amount 0. Then a new message m' is computed as $m' = m \parallel T \parallel \alpha_0$, where $\parallel$ denotes concatenation, T is a fixed parameter and $\alpha_0 \in \{0,1\}^n$ is computed by the payer as $\alpha_0 = f^T(\alpha)$, where α is chosen at random in $\{0,1\}^n$. T is used to "count-down" the number of ticks and is set previously before the start of the tick payments. The payer then computes $\sigma(m')$ and sends $(m', \sigma(m'))$. This pair is verified as in a normal payment as previously described. Until now the payee has not received payment of any ticks. In order to get payment the i'th tick ($i \geq 1$) the following takes place:

1. The payer sends $\alpha_i = f^{T-i}(\alpha)$ to the recipient.
2. The recipient verifies that $f(\alpha_i) = \alpha_{i-1}$ (α_{i-1} was received in the previous round, α_0 was received in m').

This process can continue for payment of at least T ticks. An amount corresponding to t ticks is encoded as $\alpha_t \in \{0,1\}^n$ satisfying $f^t(\alpha_t) = \alpha_0$. Only α_0 (which is part of m) and the last received value, α_t, need be remembered.

In section 4.1 of [14] choices for f are discussed. By restricting the input of f to n-bit strings a one-way *permutation* can be used. This leads to the possibility of choosing f as a *trapdoor permutation*. If the only the payer knows how to invert f the payer can avoid the need for T and have $\alpha_0 = \alpha$. If α_{i-1} has been used to pay for tick $(i - 1)$, then $\alpha_i = f^{-1}(\alpha_{i-1})$ can be used to pay for the i'th tick. The advantage is that no value for T has to be set in advance. The RSA function is an obvious candidate for f. Although requiring more computation than a hash function, this would still be feasible for tick lengths in the range of seconds.

Pedersen shows that such a system is *secure*.

3.2 Linking payment and delivery

Using tick payments it is possible to build or extend current streaming architectures to "pay-as-you-play" semantics.

The messages exchanged would resemble the following:

1. The client requests an audio/video stream from the server.
2. The server acknowledges the request and includes parameters for delivery, e.g. delivery mechanism and price.
3. Client and Server negotiate bit rate, codec and tick interval.
4. The client sends initial payment message $(m', \sigma(m'))$
5. The server begins streaming.
6. After the specified time the client sends a tick payment message.
7. The server receives the tick payment verifies it and continues streaming.

The last two steps are repeated until either the audio/video stream has finished, or the client breaks the connection. The server would also cease streaming if the required ticks are not received in the required time frame, ensuring the client doesn't receive data it did not pay for. After the delivery phase the server can present α_0 which was part of m and the last received tick α_i to its bank for reimbursmant.

4 Implementation Architectures

The streaming audio/video technology products that are available today are undergoing high speed development and change. Most products are only available as beta releases and subject to modification.

This section describes possible implementation architectures for linking payment to quality of service.

There tend to be two places where it is most sensible to put security services, to which payment can be classified:

- at lowest level possible in a network stack
- at the highest level possible in the application itself

The first has the advantage that as a security service it can be used by any application, but requires the the service is as generic as possible to provide the flexibility required. This is a non trivial task. It has the disadvantage that the service is not easily linked to the semantics of the data. This disadvantage is best overcome by implementing the service in the latter approach. This section describes an implementation approach for the latter method. For streaming audio/video this is the codec.

So far producers of codecs have concentrated on the quality of the reproduction taken as function against the total bandwidth requirement. It is at this level that it would make the most sense to introduce a charging mechanism. The codec has the necessary information regarding the quality of the channel, current bit rate and other operational parameters, it is also able to pass messages to the streaming server allowing for the necessary feedback required for a payment protocol.

As an aside this give a method of controlling the distribution of any captured audio/video stream.

Netscape, Progressive Networks and Microsoft all offer codec independence for their streaming products. Using any of these frameworks should make it possible to implement a codec which supplies a payment service.

Implementing a new codec however does not facilitate a wide distribution of a payment streaming service. It would therefore make more sense to "wrap" an encryption/payment codec around an existing codec. This encryption/payment codec would use a "real" codec for the decoding of the encoder bit stream, the encryption/payment wrap would generate the ticks and encryption keys according parameters specified.

5 Discussion

The described method shows a way of linking payment to delivery of the audio and video on the Internet. Tick payments are used as the underlying technology for linking. These are reviewed and described in Section 3.1 based on previously published work by Pedersen. Section 3.2 shows how the tick payments can be linked to streaming services to provide "pay-as-you-play" semantics. Section 4 gives an overview of how to provide "pay-as-you-play" semantics using current streaming services. Section 1 discusses the business case for providing these services.

For content providers "pay-as-you-play" semantics have the advantage that they do not require users to enter subscription contracts and therefore user are much more lucky to succumb to impulse purchases. For consumers "pay-as-you-play" allows them to sample as many content providers as they wish without having to make ongoing financial commitments.

Many micro payment systems have been devised and claim to solve the problems associated with electronic commerce. This example however links a solution to a real problem.

6 Acknowledgments

The author gratefully acknowledges the support given by the Hewlett-Packard Company, HP Labs Bristol, UK, as well as Dieter Gollmann of Royal Holloway, University of London and the anonymous reviewers for their helpful comments.

References

1. S. Armstrong, A. Freier, and K. Marzullo. RFC 1301: Multicast Transport Protocol, February 1992.
2. T. Berners-Lee, R. Fielding, and H. Nielsen. RFC 1945: Hypertext transfer protocol — HTTP/1.0, May 1996.
3. J. Bos and David Chaum. Smartcash: A practical electronic payment system. Technical Report CS-R9035, CWI, August 1990.
4. Microsoft Corp. Activemovie. http://www.microsoft.com/actvieplatform/default.asp.
5. Microsoft Corp. Netshow. http://www.microsoft.com/netshow.
6. Netscape Corp. Livemedia. http://home.netscape.com/livemedia.
7. Apple Computer Inc. Quicktime. http://quicktime.apple.com/.
8. DSP Group Inc. Truespeech. http://www.dspg.com/.
9. VDOnet Inc. Vdolive. http://www.vdo.net/.
10. Leslie Lamport. Password authentication with insecure communicatation. *Communications of the ACM*, 11(24):770–772, 1981.
11. Macromedia. Video. http://www.macromedia.com/.
12. R. C. Merkle. A certified digital signature. In *Advances in Cryptography – proceedings of CRYPTO 89*, volume 435 of *Lecture Notes in Computer Science*, pages 218–238. Springer-Verlag, 1990.
13. Progressive Networks. Realmedia. http://www.prognet.com/.
14. Torben P. Pedersen. Electronic payments of small amounts. DAIMI PB-495, Computer Science Department, Aarhus University, http://www.daimi.aau.dk/BRICS/DAIMI/PB/495, 1995.
15. J. Postel. RFC 768: User Datagram Protocol, August 1980.
16. J. Postel. RFC 793: Transmission Control Protocol, September 1981.
17. H. Schulzrinne, S. Casner, R. Frederick, and V. Jacobson. RFC 1889: RTP: A Transport Protocol for real-time applications, January 1996.
18. Xing Technologies. Streamworks. http://www.xingtech.com/streamworks.
19. Vivo. Vivo. http://www.vivo.com/.
20. Vocaltec. Internet wave. http://www.vocaltec.com/.
21. Vxtreme. Web theatre. http://www.vxtreme.com/.

A New Identity-Based Key Exchange Protocol Minimizing Computation and Communication

Shahrokh Saeednia[1] and Rei Safavi-Naini[2]

[1] Université Libre de Bruxelles
Département d'Informatique
CP 212, Boulevard du Triomphe
1050 Bruxelles, Belgium
saeednia@ulb.ac.be

[2] University of Wollongong
Department of Computer Science
Northfields Ave., Wollongong 2522, Australia
rei@uow.edu.au

Abstract. We propose a new identity-based key exchange protocol that minimizes the computation and communication required by participants in the protocol, and show that its security is closely related to some well-known difficult problems. More specifically, we will argue that forging a key linked to a given identity is related to the difficulty of RSA inversion while finding the key established by the protocol is equivalent to breaking the Diffie-Hellman problem with composite modulus.

1 Introduction

Since the introduction of identity-based public keys by Shamir [8] many identification schemes and key distribution systems applying this elegant idea have been proposed. In identity-based schemes either the user's identity is served as his public key, or the public key is closely related to the identity. In both cases the corresponding secret key is computed by a trusted third party (TTP) in such a way that it is computationally infeasible for an adversary to create a faked identity. The use of identity-based public key systems is very important in the case of key exchange protocols designed for large networks. In the absence of such systems, users' public keys must be bound to their identities using a TTP signature. This information must be either stored in a large public file or given to the users. In both cases additional computation and communication is required and at least, insuring the authenticity of the public keys requires verification of the TTP's signature.

This paper proposes a new identity-based key exchange protocol that is a modification of Saeednia's protocols [7] and minimizes the cost of computation and communication. Saeednia proposed an identity-based protocol that provided an important property: even if an adversary accidentally discovers the secret keys of two users, all previously exchanged keys between them will remain unknown to him. However the communication complexity of this protocol is not minimum, as each party must send his public key (that is not the same as his identity) to the other party, before the start of the protocol. This shortcoming is removed in a second protocol proposed in the same paper, but at the cost of loosing the above mentioned property.

We propose a protocol that combines the advantages of both of these protocols and has also other interesting features such as the public key of each user is his identity and so even less computation is required. Our proposal has some similarity with Okamoto's protocol [6], but is immune to an attack which is successful on Okamoto's protocol. Our basic protocol may be modified to provide the key confirmation during the main protocol. Note that the key confirmation is generally achieved by extra handshake messages between the parties, after computing the keys.

2 Description of the protocol

Set-up:

In this phase the TTP chooses

- an integer n as the product of two large distinct random primes p and q of almost the same size, such that $p - 1 = 2p'$ and $q - 1 = 2q'$, where p' and q' are also prime integers,
- two distinct bases α and $\beta \neq 1$ of order $r = p'q'$,
- a large integer (e.g., 150 bits) $u < r$, and
- a one-way hash function f that outputs integers of moderately small size (e.g., 50 bits).

The TTP makes β, u, f and n public, keeps r secret and discards p and q afterward.

Note that α is not published since users do not need to know it during the protocol but, as shown below, it may be computed from a valid pair of public and secret keys.

Key Generation:

The key generation phase is as follows. A user visits the TTP and upon successful identification, receives a pair of private and public key. TTP does the following:

- prepares the user's public key, ID, by hashing the string I corresponding to his identity. That is, $ID = f(I)$,
- computes the user's secret key as the pair (x, y) where $x = \alpha^{ID^{-1}}$ (mod n), $y = \beta^{-ID^{-1}}$ (mod n) and ID^{-1} is computed modulo r.

Key Establishment:

The protocol is executed in two steps and has only one transfer of data by each party. It is as follows:

$$A \qquad\qquad\qquad\qquad B$$

Step 1:

$t \in_R Z_u$

$v = y \cdot x^t \pmod{n}$

$\qquad\qquad\qquad\qquad\qquad\qquad\qquad t' \in_R Z_u$

$\qquad\qquad\qquad\qquad\qquad\qquad\qquad v' = y' \cdot x'^{t'} \pmod{n}$

$$\xrightarrow{\quad v \quad}$$

$$\xleftarrow{\quad v' \quad}$$

Step 2:

$ID' = f(I')$

$K = (v'^{ID'} \cdot \beta)^t \pmod{n}$

$\qquad\qquad\qquad\qquad\qquad\qquad\qquad ID = f(I)$

$\qquad\qquad\qquad\qquad\qquad K = (v^{ID} \cdot \beta)^{t'} \pmod{n}$

The key computed by the two communicants is $\alpha^{tt'}$.

3   Observations on the security of the protocol

3.1   Security from the TTP's point of view

It follows from the way the secret key has been chosen that

$$\alpha = x^{ID} \pmod{n} \qquad \text{and} \qquad \beta^{-1} = y^{ID} \pmod{n}$$

This shows that computing a secret pair (x, y) corresponding to a given ID is equivalent to RSA inversion, which is known to be intractable. The use of the one-way function f is required because otherwise if I (and not ID) is used for computing x and y, then for a given valid triple, (I, x, y), it is easy to construct many triples $(I/j, x^j, y^j)$, for any $j \neq 1$ dividing I. If I/j corresponds to an acceptable identity then the attack is successful.

Clearly, if I is a prime integer or an integer with hard factorization, even without f it would be hard to forge key pairs. However, I reflects the user's identity and in general does not have neither of these properties.

3.2 Security from the users' point of view with respect to passive adversaries

The common key computed by the honest parties is equal to $\alpha^{tt'}$ (mod n), which is the same as the key calculated in the Diffie-Hellman protocol [2]. An adversary tapping the line between A and B has exactly the same information as in the Diffie-Hellman protocol with composite modulus [9,5]. Indeed, once the messages v and v' are transmitted, the adversary could only compute α^t and $\alpha^{t'}$ (as the parties do), but does not know t and t'. So, in order to determine the common key established by the protocol, the adversary should solve a Diffie-Hellman problem with composite modulus which is as hard as both factoring and computing discrete logarithms as proven by McCurely [5].

3.3 Security from the users' point of view with respect to active adversaries

In order to impersonate a user, say A, without knowing his secret key, an adversary C has to choose the message v such that $v^{ID} \cdot \beta = \alpha^z$, where z is known to C[1]. Indeed, if C sends this message to B, the key value evaluated by B will be $\alpha^{zt'}$, which could also be computed by C as $(v'^{ID'} \cdot \beta)^z$. Conversely, if the value of $v^{ID} \cdot \beta$ is of the form $\alpha^z \cdot \gamma$, even if γ is known to C, he still is unable to compute the same key as computed by B, because, the latter computes $K = \alpha^{zt'} \cdot \gamma^{t'}$, which cannot be computed by C, since $\gamma^{t'}$ is unknown to him. Clearly, a good v should be of the form $\beta^{-ID^{-1}} \cdot \alpha^w$, for any known w. However, if C knows ID^{-1}, he can easily compute x and y, as the TTP does.

This informal discussion shows that the knowledge of y is sufficient for impersonating a user. However, the fact that x is secret provides additional security that we discuss further in this section.

3.4 Security from each user's point of view with respect to all others

Our protocol is not zero-knowledge in the sense of [4] or [3], because no simulator can construct a key in polynomial-time. Still, it may formally be proved that messages sent by a party leak no useful knowledge that enables the other party (or an eavesdropper) to gain any knowledge about x or y. Here, we only give an informal proof.

When receiving v from A, B can compute α^t which he knows is equal to $(x^t)^{ID}$. Now, if he can derive x^t from this relation, he can easily determine y which is sufficient for impersonating A as shown above. However, this would mean to break an instance of the RSA scheme with ID as the public key. Now if B can break the RSA scheme, he does not need to receive v, since he can already compute x and y from α, β and ID.

---

[1] Note that v may be formed by a combination of previous messages sent by A, but in this case the related z is not known to C.

3.5 Additional security

We conclude this section by comparing our protocol with the one proposed by Okamoto. In both protocols, if an adversary knows the random number t corresponding to a given message v sent by A to B, then he may successfully impersonate A in the future by replaying that session. In fact, the adversary can always send v to B and, knowing the related t, compute the common key, exactly as A does.

The difference between the two protocols, however, is that in Okamoto's protocol the secret key can easily be compromised from the knowledge of a pair (v, t) (messages are of the form $s \cdot \alpha^t$, where s is the secret key and α is a prescribed base). This is not possible in our protocol since x is part of the secret key. This feature allows us to prevent this attack by slightly changing the messages of the protocol. It suffices that each pair of users shares a counter (that may be known to everybody) that keeps track of the number of previous sessions. The counter is started at 1 and is increased by 1 with the start of every new session. Let $count$ denote the current value of the counter shared between A and B. Now, the messages that A sends to B are of the form $y.x^{ct}$, where $c = f(I, I', count)$ is the image of the counter linked to their identities. In this case, the common key value computed by both parties is $\alpha^{ctt'}$. It is easy to see that, with this modification, even with the knowledge of c and t only one session key may be computed by adversaries, but it is no longer possible to replay that session later.

Note that, the use of f, I and I' is mandatory because if $count$ is directly used for computing v, an adversary (who accidentally discovered the random t corresponding to a given session) may still replay once that session under the name of A with another user B'.

4 How to reach assurance about the origin of messages

A common problem in key exchange protocols is tampering with the communicated messages by an opponent. This could result in two different keys to be computed by the two parties without them being aware of this fact. To ensure the sameness of the key and to detect this fraud, an encrypted message using the established key is sent by each party to the other, and its successful decryption by the latter is regarded as providing the required assurance. This however, implies additional message transfer by each party, which is not desirable.

By introducing a counter in our protocol, the assurance about the sameness of the key may be achieved during the protocol and not as a separate challenge/response transfer after the keys are computed. For this purpose, it suffices that each party send a witness for v together with the message v, proving that the secret key of the user is actually used to form v.

In the revised protocol α will be made public by the TTP.

$$A \qquad\qquad\qquad\qquad B$$

Step 1:

$$c = f(I, I', count)$$
$$t \in_R Z_u$$
$$v = y \cdot x^{ct} \pmod{n}$$
$$w = \alpha^t \pmod{n}$$

$$c = f(I, I', count)$$
$$t' \in_R Z_u$$
$$v' = y' \cdot x'^{ct'} \pmod{n}$$
$$w' = \alpha^{t'} \pmod{n}$$

$$\xrightarrow{\quad v, w \quad}$$

$$\xleftarrow{\quad v', w' \quad}$$

Step 2:

$$ID' = f(I')$$
$$z_1 = v'^{ID'} \cdot \beta \pmod{n}$$
$$z_2 = w'^c \pmod{n}$$
$$\text{if } z_1 = z_2 \text{ then}$$
$$K = z_1^t \pmod{n}$$

$$ID = f(I)$$
$$z_1' = v^{ID} \cdot \beta \pmod{n}$$
$$z_2' = w^c \pmod{n}$$
$$\text{if } z_1' = z_2' \text{ then}$$
$$K = z_1'^{t'} \pmod{n}$$

It is straightforward to see that if RSA inversion is hard it is computationally infeasible for an adversary to create a valid pair (v, w). Indeed, we have

$$v^{ID} \cdot \beta = w^c \pmod{n}.$$

Therefore, since ID, c and β are fixed values, by assigning any value[2] to v or w, the adversary has to break an instance of the RSA scheme to compute the other.

5 Work in progress

In Eurocrypt '94 Burmester and Desmedt proposed [1] an efficient conference key distribution system. The problem with that protocol is, however, the authentication of the messages exchanged between the users. The solution that they proposed consists of combining the protocol with an authentication scheme, which in itself requires additional communication between parties. In another paper, we show how to generalize our protocol to design an identity-based conference key distribution system similar to that of Burmester and Desmedt, offering both privacy and authentication.

---

[2] For $v = w = 0$ the test would always be successful. However, this may be detected and rejected by the users before performing the test.

References

1. M. Burmester and Y. Desmedt, "A secure and efficient conference key distribution system", *Advances in Cryptology* (Proceedings of *Eurocrypt* '94), Lecture Notes in Computer Science, vol. 950, Springer-Verlag, 1994, pp. 275-286
2. W. Diffie and M. Hellman, "New directions in cryptography", *IEEE Trans. Inform. Theory*, vol. 22, 1976, pp. 644-654
3. U. Feige, A. Fiat and A.Shamir, "Zero-knowledge proofs of identity", *Journal of Cryptology*, vol. 1, no. 2, 1988, pp. 77-94
4. S. Goldwasser, S. Micali and C. Rackoff, "The knowledge complexity of interactive proof systems", *SIAM J. Comp.*, vol. 18, 1989, pp. 186-208
5. K. McCurley, "A key distribution system equivalent to factoring", *Journal of Cryptology*, vol. 1, no. 2, 1988, pp. 95-105
6. E. Okamoto, "Key distribution systems based on identification information", *Advances in Cryptology* (Proceedings of *Crypto* '87), Lecture Notes in Computer Science, vol. 293, Springer-Verlag, 1988, pp. 194-202
7. S. Saeednia, "Identity-based and self-certified key-exchange protocols", *Information Security and Privacy* (Proceedings of *ACISP* '97), Lecture Notes in Computer Science, vol. 1270, Springer-Verlag, 1997, pp. 303-313
8. A. Shamir, "Identity-based cryptosystems and signature schemes", *Advances in Cryptology* (Proceedings of *Crypto* '84), Lecture Notes in Computer Science, vol. 196, Springer-Verlag, 1985, pp. 47-53
9. Z. Shmuley, "Composite Diffie-Hellman public-key generating systems are hard to break", Technical Report 356, Computer Science Department, Technion, Feb. 1985

The Application of ID-Based Key Distribution Systems to an Elliptic Curve

Hisao Sakazaki,[1] Eiji Okamoto[1] and Masahiro Mambo[1,2]

[1] School of Information Science, Japan Advanced Institute of Science and Technology
1-1 Asahidai, Tatsunokuchi, Nomi, Ishikawa, 923-1292, Japan
e-mail: sakazaki@jaist.ac.jp , okamoto@jaist.ac.jp
[2] Present affiliation: Education Center for Information Processing, Tohoku University
Kawauchi, Aoba, Sendai, 980-8576, Japan
e-mail: mambo@ecip.tohoku.ac.jp

Abstract. A key distribution system is a system in which users securely generate a common key. One kind of identity-based key distribution system was proposed by E. Okamoto[1]. Its security depends on the difficulty of factoring a composite number of two large primes like RSA public-key cryptosystem. Another kind of identity-based key distribution system was proposed by K. Nyberg, R.A. Rueppel[7]. Its security depends on the difficulty of the discrete logarithm problem.

On the other hand, Koblitz and Miller described how a group of points on an elliptic curve over a finite field can be used to construct a public key cryptosystem.

In 1997, we proposed an ID-based key distribution system over an elliptic curve[14], as well as over a ring Z/nZ. Its security depends on the difficulty of factoring a composite number of two large primes. We showed that the system is more suitable for the implementation on an elliptic curve than on a ring Z/nZ[14].

In this paper, we apply the Nyberg-Rueppel ID-based key distribution system[7] to an elliptic curve. It provides relatively small block size and high security. This public key scheme can be efficiently implemented. However the scheme[7] requires relatively large data transmission. As a solution to this problem, we improve the scheme. The improved scheme is very efficient since the data transferred for generation of a common key is reduced to half of the previous one.

1 Introduction

A key distribution system is a system in which users securely generate a common key. The ID-based key distribution system called ID-KDS, is a key distribution system such that public keys used for key distribution are generated from ID information. It is a promising key distribution system, since ID-KDS can be used not only for key distribution but also for authentication. There are a lot of reports about ID-KDS constructed on the ring Z/nZ.

In 1986, E. Okamoto proposed an ID-based key distribution system whose security depends on the difficulty of factoring a composite number of two large primes like RSA public-key cryptosystem.

On the other hand, Koblitz and Miller described how a group of points on an elliptic curve over a finite field could be used to construct public key cryptosystems. Compared with ID-KDS constructed on the ring Z/nZ, not much is known on ID-KDS constructed on the elliptic curve.

In 1997, we studied whether the ID-KDS proposed by E. Okamoto can be constructed on elliptic curves or not[14]. The original ID-KDS cannot be constructed on an elliptic curve in a straightforward way. This is because the point corresponding to the user's identity ID cannot be defined on the elliptic curve. As a solution to this problem, we proposed a new ID-KDS on an elliptic curve[14].

The new scheme can be also constructed on a ring Z/nZ. We compared the new scheme on the elliptic curve with one on the ring Z/nZ[14]. The order of the optimal basepoint in the former scheme is 4 times greater than that in the latter scheme. Thus, the proposed scheme is more suitable for implementation on an elliptic curve than on a ring Z/nZ.

However, since security of the new scheme[14] depends on the difficulty of factoring a composite number of two large primes, we must construct elliptic curves over enough large underlying finite fields for adequate security. As a result, it appears that the cost of generating a common key on the elliptic curve is higher than the cost of generating a common key on the ring Z/nZ.

In this paper, our motivation is to study another scheme whose security depends on the difficulty of the discrete logarithm problem. Therefore we apply Nyberg-Rueppel scheme[7] to an elliptic curve. It provides relatively small block size and high security. It can be efficiently implemented. However the scheme[7] requires relatively large transferred data. As a solution to this problem, we propose an improvement on the scheme. The improved scheme is very efficient since the data transferred for generation of a common key is reduced to half of the previous one.

This paper is organized as follows. Section 2 summarizes an ID-KDS over a finite field, which is based on the difficulty of the discrete logarithm problem[7]. Section 3 discusses an ID-KDS over an elliptic curve, which is based on the difficulty of the elliptic curve discrete logarithm problem. In section 4, we propose an improvement on the scheme. Section 5 summarizes message recovery signatures and forgeries against it[13]. And we study the relation between message recovery signatures and the improved scheme. Finally, we propose an improvement on the scheme over an elliptic curve.

2 An ID-KDS over a Finite Field based on the Difficulty of the Discrete Logarithm Problem

This section summarizes an ID-KDS over a finite field, which is based on the difficulty of the discrete logarithm problem[7].

This system consists of three phases.

Generation phase of information

Let p be a large prime. Let $g \in F_p^*$ be a basepoint, whose order is q. Let $a_C \in F_p^*$ be a secret key of the center, and $b_C \equiv g^{a_C} \ mod \ p$ be a public key of the center.

Participation phase

Let ID_A be the identity of user Alice.

(1) Alice chooses a secret number $a_A \in F_p^*$, and sends $g^{a_A} \pmod{p}$ to the center. The key center checks whether Alice knows a_A, which is the discrete logarithm of g^{a_A}.

(2) The key center chooses a random number $k_A \in F_p^*$, and computes $r_A \equiv g^{a_A} \cdot ID_A^{-1} \cdot g^{-k_A} \bmod p$. Next, the center computes s_A satisfying $k_A \equiv s_A + r_A \cdot a_C \bmod q$, and sends (r_A, s_A) to Alice.

To sum up, the key center sends a message recovery signature (r_A, s_A) on a message $g^{a_A} \cdot ID_A^{-1}$ to Alice.

(3) Alice checks $g^{s_A} \cdot b_C^{r_A} \cdot r_A \equiv g^{a_A} \cdot ID_A^{-1} \bmod p$.

Generation phase of a common key

We assume here that both Alice and Bob wish to obtain their common key. First, Alice sends (r_A, s_A) to Bob. Similarly Bob sends (r_B, s_B) to Alice. Next, she computes

$$K_{AB} \equiv ((g^{s_B} \cdot b_C^{r_B} \cdot r_B)ID_B)^{a_A} \quad \bmod\ p.$$

Similarly he computes

$$K_{BA} \equiv ((g^{s_A} \cdot b_C^{r_A} \cdot r_A)ID_A)^{a_B} \quad \bmod\ p.$$

Then $K_{AB} = K_{BA}$, since

$$
\begin{aligned}
K_{AB} &\equiv ((g^{s_B} \cdot b_C^{r_B} \cdot r_B)ID_B)^{a_A} \\
&\equiv ((g^{a_B} \cdot ID_B^{-1})ID_B)^{a_A} \\
&\equiv g^{a_A \cdot a_B} \\
&\equiv K_{BA} \qquad \qquad (\bmod\ p).
\end{aligned}
$$

This scheme has advantage that even the key center could not know the user's secret key.

3 An ID-KDS over an Elliptic Curve based on the Difficulty of the Elliptic Curve Discrete Logarithm Problem

In this section, we apply the ID-KDS[7] to an elliptic curve.

Here, $x(P)$ denotes the $x-$coordinate of P.

Generation phase of information

Let p be a large prime. Let $a, b \in F_p$ be two parameters satisfying $4a^3 + 27b^2 \neq 0 \pmod{p}$. An elliptic curve over F_p with parameters a and b is defined as the set of point (x, y) with $x, y \in F_p$ satisfying $y^2 \equiv x^3 + ax + b \bmod p$ together with a special element, called the point at infinity. Such a curve is denoted $E_p(a, b)$ or E_p. Let $G \in E_p(a, b)$ be a basepoint, whose order is q.

Let $a_C \in F_p^*$ be a secret key of the center, and $\mathbf{B}_C = a_C \cdot \mathbf{G}$ over E_p be a public key of the center.

Participation phase

Let ID_A be the identity of user Alice.

(1) Alice chooses a secret number $a_A \in F_p^*$, and sends x_A, where $a_A\mathbf{G} = (x_A, y_A)$, to the center. The key center checks whether Alice knows a_A, which is the elliptic curve discrete logarithm of $a_A\mathbf{G}$.

(2) The key center chooses a random number $k_A \in F_p^*$, and computes $r_A \equiv x_A \cdot ID_A^{-1} \cdot \mathrm{x}(k_A\mathbf{G})^{-1} \bmod p$. Next, the key center computes s_A satisfying $k_A \equiv s_A + r_A \cdot a_C \bmod q$, and sends (r_A, s_A) to Alice.

To sum up, the key center sends a message recovery signature constructed on an elliptic curve (r_A, s_A) on a message $x_A \cdot ID_A^{-1}$ to Alice.

(3) Alice checks $\mathrm{x}(s_A\mathbf{G} + r_A\mathbf{B}_C)r_A = x_A \cdot ID_A^{-1}$.

Generation phase of a common key

We assume here that both Alice and Bob wish to obtain their common key.

First, Alice sends (r_A, s_A) and β_A, where β_A is 1-bit auxiliary information for reconstructing the y−coordinate uniquely, to Bob. Similarly Bob sends (r_B, s_B) and β_B to Alice.

Next, she computes

$$x_B \equiv (\mathrm{x}(s_B\mathbf{G} + r_B\mathbf{B}_C)r_B)ID_B \quad \bmod p,$$

and reconstructs $a_B\mathbf{G} = (x_B, y_B)$ by β_B. Then she computes

$$\mathbf{K}_{AB} = a_A(x_B, y_B) \quad over\ E_p.$$

Similarly he computes

$$x_A \equiv (\mathrm{x}(s_A\mathbf{G} + r_A\mathbf{B}_C)r_A)ID_A \quad \bmod p,$$

and reconstructs $a_A\mathbf{G} = (x_A, y_A)$ by β_A. Then he computes

$$\mathbf{K}_{BA} = a_B(x_A, y_A) \quad over\ E_p.$$

Then $\mathbf{K}_{AB} = \mathbf{K}_{BA}$, since

$$\begin{aligned}
\mathbf{K}_{AB} &= a_A(x_B, y_B) \\
&= a_A \cdot a_B \ \mathbf{G} \\
&= \mathbf{K}_{BA} \qquad over\ E_p.
\end{aligned}$$

4　An Improvement on the ID-KDS based on the Difficulty of the Discrete Logarithm Problem

The Nyberg-Rueppel scheme[7] requires relatively large data transmission. As a solution to this problem, we improve the scheme. The improved scheme is very efficient, since the data transferred for generation of a common key is reduced to half of the previous one. In section 6, we propose an improvement on the scheme over an elliptic curve.

4.1 An improvement on the ID-KDS over a field based on the difficulty of the discrete logarithm problem

We propose an improvement on the previous one. It is very efficient since the data transferred for generation of a common key is short.

Generation phase of information

Let p be a large prime. Let $g \in F_p^*$ be a basepoint, whose order is q. Let $a_C \in F_p^*$ be a secret key of the center, and $b_C \equiv g^{a_C} \bmod p$ be a public key of the center.

Participation phase

Let ID_A be the identity of user Alice.

(1) Alice chooses a secret number $a_A \in F_p^*$, and sends g^{a_A} $(\bmod\ p)$ to the center. The key center checks whether Alice knows a_A, which is the discrete logarithm of g^{a_A}.

(2) The key center chooses a random number $k_A \in F_p^*$, and computes $r_A \equiv g^{a_A} \cdot ID_A^{-1} \cdot g^{k_A} \bmod p$. Next, the key center computes s_A satisfying $s_A \equiv k_A + r_A \cdot a_C \bmod q$ and computes $EN_{g^{a_A}}((r_A, s_A))$, where $EN_{g^{a_A}}((r_A, s_A))$ denotes encryption of (r_A, s_A) using key g^{a_A}. After that the key center sends $EN_{g^{a_A}}((r_A, s_A))$ to Alice.

(3) Alice computes $(r_A, s_A) = DE_{a_A}(EN_{g^{a_A}}((r_A, s_A)))$, where $DE_{a_A}(y)$ denotes decryption of y using key a_A. She checks $g^{-s_A} \cdot b_C^{r_A} \cdot r_A \equiv g^{a_A} \cdot ID_A^{-1}$ and treats s_A as another secret key.

Generation phase of a common key

We assume here that both Alice and Bob wish to obtain their common key. First, Alice sends r_A to Bob. Similarly Bob sends r_B to Alice.

Next, she computes

$$T_B \equiv b_C^{r_B} \cdot r_B \cdot ID_B \quad \bmod p.$$

Then $T_B \equiv g^{a_B + s_B}$, since

$$g^{-s_B} \cdot b_C^{r_B} \cdot r_B \equiv g^{a_B} \cdot ID_B^{-1}$$
$$b_C^{r_B} \cdot r_B \equiv g^{s_B} \cdot g^{a_B} \cdot ID_B^{-1}$$
$$b_C^{r_B} \cdot r_B \cdot ID_B \equiv g^{a_B + s_B}$$
$$T_B \equiv g^{a_B + s_B}$$

Alice computes

$$K_{AB} \equiv T_B^{a_A + s_A} \quad \bmod p.$$

Similarly Bob computes

$$K_{BA} \equiv (b_C^{r_A} \cdot r_A \cdot ID_A)^{a_B + s_B} \quad \bmod p.$$

Then $K_{AB} = K_{BA}$, since

$$K_{AB} \equiv T_B^{a_A + s_A}$$
$$\equiv (g^{a_B + s_B})^{a_A + s_A}$$
$$\equiv g^{(a_A + s_A) \cdot (a_B + s_B)}$$
$$\equiv K_{BA} \qquad (\bmod\ p).$$

This scheme has advantage that the date transferred for generation of a common key is shorter than the previous one.

4.2 Equivalent classes

In this section, we study the relation between the security of this improvement and the previous one.

Proposition

We assume that a forger pretend to be Alice.

If in the improvement, the forger can obtain a common key of Alice and Bob, by a function f in time polynomial without knowledge of the secret keys of Alice, then in the previous one, the forger can obtain a common key of Alice and Bob, by the function f in time polynomial without knowledge of the secret key of Alice.

Proof

For input ID_A, output $(e, r) := f(ID_A)$, where $g^e \equiv b_C^r \cdot r \cdot ID_A \bmod p$. Then $\forall s \in F_p$, $g^{e+s} \equiv g^s \cdot b_C^r \cdot r \cdot ID_A \bmod p$. Therefore the forger can obtain a common key in the previous one.

5 Message Recovery Signatures and Forgeries against Message Recovery Signatures

5.1 Message recovery signatures

Message recovery signature has six variants[13]. We quickly talk about it. To sign a message $m \in F_p^*$, the center chooses a random number $k \in F_p^*$, and computes

$$
\begin{aligned}
r &\equiv m \cdot g^{-k} &&\bmod p \\
r' &\equiv r &&\bmod q \\
\alpha k &\equiv \beta + \gamma \cdot a_C \bmod q, &&\quad (1)
\end{aligned}
$$

where (α, β, γ) is a permutation of $(\pm 1, \pm r', \pm s)$. Then the signature is given by (r, s). The message can be recovered by computing the following equation

$$
m \equiv g^{\frac{\beta}{\alpha}} \cdot b_C^{\frac{\gamma}{\alpha}} \cdot r \quad \bmod p.
$$

The signature equation (1) leads to the following six equations if we neglect the $\pm$ signs.

Scheme 1	$s \cdot k \equiv 1 + r' \cdot a_C$
Scheme 2	$r' \cdot k \equiv 1 + s \cdot a_C$
Scheme 3	$k \equiv s + r' \cdot a_C$
Scheme 4	$s \cdot k \equiv r' + a_C$
Scheme 5	$r' \cdot k \equiv s + a_C$
Scheme 6	$k \equiv r' + s \cdot a_C$

5.2 Forgeries against message recovery signatures

Two forgeries against some schemes of message recovery signatures have been presented in [11, 12], which are called the recovery equation attack using the basepoint g and the signature equation attack using the basepoint g. And further three forgeries have been presented in [13], which are called the recovery equation attack using b_C, the signature equation attack using b_C and the homomorphism attack. The last attack is the same as the signature equation attack using g and b_C in one chosen message scenario. The following table summarizes the relation between MR signature and the attack[13]. It shows strongness of each signature against each forgery, where "O" denotes strongness, "X" denotes vulnerability.

	MR signatures						MR signatures constructed on an elliptic curve					
	$S1$	$S2$	$S3$	$S4$	$S5$	$S6$	$S1$	$S2$	$S3$	$S4$	$S5$	$S6$
Recovery EQ attack(using g)	X	X	O	X	O	X	O	O	O	O	O	O
Recovery EQ attack(using b_C)	X	O	X	X	X	O	O	O	O	O	O	O
Signature EQ attack(using g)	O	O	X	X	X	X	O	O	X	X	X	X
Signature EQ attack(using b_C)	X	X	X	O	O	X	X	X	X	O	O	X
Homomorphism attack	O	X	X	O	X	X	O	O	O	O	O	O

5.3 Security of an ID-KDS based on the difficulty of the discrete logarithm problem

The recovery equation attack using b_C, the signature equation attack using g and b_C, and the homomorphism attack can forge a message of worthless form only, like $m \cdot b_C^e$. Therefore such forgeries do not present a real threat on the ID-KDS based on the difficulty of the discrete logarithm problem.

However since the recovery equation attack using the basepoint g can forge a message of special form like $m \cdot g^e$, the forgery presents a real threat on it.

Therefore as the countermeasure, we have to adopt the scheme 3 (or 5).

6 An Improvement on the Scheme over an Elliptic Curve

The previous table shows that message recovery signature constructed on an elliptic curve is strong to all recovery equation attack and homomorphism attack. In other words, the x-coordinate function of an elliptic curve dose not have a property, like homomorphism. Therefore all message recovery signatures constructed on an elliptic curve, are strong against the recovery equation attack and homomorphism attack[13]. However for the construction of improvement on an elliptic curve, it is cumbersome. To sum up, $T_B := x(r_B \mathbf{B}_C) \cdot r_B \cdot ID_B \neq x((a_B + s_B)\mathbf{G})$, since

$$x(-s_B \mathbf{G} + r_B \mathbf{B}_C) \cdot r_B = x(a_B \mathbf{G}) \cdot ID_B^{-1}$$
$$x(-s_B \mathbf{G} + r_B \mathbf{B}_C) \cdot r_B \cdot ID_B = x(a_B \mathbf{G})$$
$$x(r_B \mathbf{B}_C) \cdot r_B \cdot ID_B \neq x((a_B + s_B)\mathbf{G})$$
$$T_B \neq x((a_B + s_B)\mathbf{G})$$

It is difficult to construct the improvement scheme over an elliptic curve in a straightforward way. Therefore we propose the following improvement on an elliptic curve.

Generation phase of information

Let $G \in E_p(a, b)$ be a basepoint, whose order is q. Let $a_C \in F_p^*$ be a secret key of the center, and $\mathbf{B}_C = a_C \mathbf{G}$ *over* E_p be a public key of the center.

Participation phase

Let ID_A be the identity of user Alice.

(1) Alice chooses a secret number $a_A \in F_p^*$, and sends $a_A \mathbf{G} = (x_A, y_A)$ to the key center. The key center checks whether Alice knows a_A, which is the elliptic curve discrete logarithm of $a_A \mathbf{G}$.

(2) The key center chooses a random number $k_A \in F_p^*$, and computes $\mathbf{R}_A = a_A \mathbf{G} + k_A \mathbf{G}$ *over* E_p, $r_A \equiv x(\mathbf{R}_A) \cdot ID_A^{-1}$ *mod* p. After that, the key center computes s_A satisfying $s_A \equiv k_A + r_A \cdot a_C$ *mod* q. Next, the key center computes $EN_{a_A \mathbf{G}}((r_A, s_A))$, and sends it to Alice.

(3) Alice computes $(r_A, s_A) = DE_{a_A}(EN_{a_A \mathbf{G}}((r_A, s_A)))$, and checks $r_A \mathbf{B}_C + \mathbf{R}_A = (a_A + s_A)\mathbf{G}$. Then she treats s_A as another secret key.

Generation phase of a common key

We assume here that both Alice and Bob wish to obtain their common key.

First, Alice sends r_A and β_A, where β_A is 1-bit auxiliary information for reconstructing the y-coordinate uniquely, to Bob. Similarly Bob sends r_B, β_B to Alice.

Next, she computes

$$x(\mathbf{R}_B) \equiv r_B \cdot ID_B \quad mod \ p,$$

and reconstructs $\mathbf{R}_B$ by β_B. Then she computes

$$\mathbf{K}_{AB} = (a_A + s_A)(r_B \mathbf{B}_C + \mathbf{R}_B).$$

Similarly he computes

$$\mathbf{K}_{BA} = (a_B + s_B)(r_A \mathbf{B}_C + \mathbf{R}_A).$$

Then $\mathbf{K}_{AB} = \mathbf{K}_{BA}$, since

$$\begin{aligned}
\mathbf{K}_{AB} &= (a_A + s_A)(r_B \mathbf{B}_C + \mathbf{R}_B) \\
&= (a_A + s_A)((r_B \cdot a_C)\mathbf{G} + \mathbf{R}_B) \\
&= (a_A + s_A)((s_B - k_B)\mathbf{G} + (a_B + k_B)\mathbf{G}) \\
&= ((a_A + s_A) \cdot (a_B + s_B))\mathbf{G}.
\end{aligned}$$

7 Zero Element Attack

There is a minor attak against the improvement scheme on the finite field. We shall call it the zero element attack.

Zero element attack

A forger pretend to be Alice. The forger sends $r = 0$ to Bob. Then Bob computes $K = b_C^0 \cdot 0 \cdot ID_A = 0$. Since $K = 0$, the common key is easily obtained.

A countermeasure to this attack is to implement the protocol so that $r = 0$ is disallowed.

On the other hand, the improvement scheme on the elliptic curve is strong against the zero element attack, since $\mathbf{K} \neq \mathcal{O}$.

8   Conclusion

In this paper, we have proposed the the improvement on the scheme proposed by Nyberg and Rueppel. The improved scheme is very efficient since the data transferred for generation of a common key is reduced to half of the previous one.

Furthermore we have applied the improvement to an elliptic curve. It provides relatively small block size and high security.

References

1. E. Okamoto, "An Introduction to the Theory of Cryptography", Kyoritsu Shuppan, 1993.
2. J.H. Silverman, J. Tate, "Rational Points on Elliptic Curves", Springer-Verlag, 1994.
3. K. Koyama, U.M. Maurer, T. Okamoto and S. Vanstone, "New public-keyschemes based on elliptic curves over the ring Z_n", *Advances in Cryptology-Proceedings of CRYPT'91*, LNCS 576, pp.252-266, 1991.
4. H. Tanaka, "Identity-Based Non -Interactive Key Sharing Scheme and Its Application to Some Cryptographic Systems", *Proceedings of Symposium on Cryptography and Information Security*, SCIS'94, 1994.
5. T. Matsumoto, H. Imai, "Key Predistribution System", *The transactions of the institute of electronics information and communication engineers*, Vol.J71-A, No.11, pp2046-2053, 1988.
6. C.G. Günther, "An identity-based key-exchange protocol", *Advances in Cryptology-Proceedings of EUROCRYPT'89*, LNCS 434, pp.29-37, 1990.
7. K. Nyberg, R.A. Rueppel, "A New Signature Scheme Based on the DSA Giving Message Recovery", *Proceedings of 1st ACM Conference on Computer and Communications Security*, 1993.
8. A. Miyaji, "A message recovery signature scheme equivalent to DSA over elliptic curves", *Advances in Cryptology-Proceedings of ASIACRYPT'96*, LNCS 1163, pp.1-14, 1996.
9. A. Menezes, T. Okamoto and S. Vanstone, "Reducing elliptic curve logarithms to logarithms in a finite field", *Proceedings of 22st Annual ACM Symposium on the Theory of Computing*, pp.80-89, 1991.
10. N. Koblitz, "A Course in number theory and cryptocraphy", Springer-Verlag, 1987.
11. K. Nyberg, R.A. Rueppel, "Message recovery for signature schemes based on the discrete logarithm problem", *Advances in Cryptology-Proceedings of EUROCRYPT'94*, LNCS 950, pp.182-193, 1995.

12. K. Nyberg, R.A. Rueppel, "Message recovery for signature schemes based on the discrete logarithm problem", *Designs Codes and Cryptography* pp.61-81, 1996.

13. A. Miyaji, "Strengthened Message Recovery Signature Scheme", *Proceedings of Symposium on Cryptography and Information Security,* SCIS'96, 1996.

14. H. Sakazaki, E. Okamoto and M. Mambo, "ID-based Key Distribution System over Elliptic Curves", *Proceedings of Symposium on Cryptography and Information Security,* SCIS'97, 1997.

On Reconciliation of Discrepant Sequences Shared Through Quantum Mechanical Channels

†e-mail : yamazaki@eng.tamagawa.ac.jp

†6-1-1, Tmagawagakuen, Machida, Tokyo, 194, Japan
Department of Information and Communication Eng.,
Faculty of Eng., Tamagawa University.

‡6-1-1, Tmagawagakuen, Machida, Tokyo, 194, Japan
Tamagawa University Research Institute.

Abstract

In the practical quantum key distribution system, discrepancies may occur on the secret random sequences shared through a quantum mechanical channel even in the absence of an eavesdropper because of an imperfect system configuration and noises. The discrepancies may be spread and expanded through a following privacy amplification. Therefore all the discrepancies must be removed at this point. The reconciliation protocol was proposed by Bennett et al. As long as the authors know, however, detailed investigation on the protocol has not been reported.

In this report, we investigate the reconciliation protocol proposed by Bennett et al. and consider to optimize it.

1 INTRODUCTION

The quantum cryptography was proposed to realize a secure key distribution. The security of quantum key distribution (QKD) system depends on some constraints based on physical principles (e.g. uncertainty principle, quantum correlation, etc.). So far, several types of quantum cryptosystems have been proposed, and several experiments have succeeded[1, 2, 3, 4, 5, 6]. One of the most significant features of the QKD system is that the system uses both a private (secret) quantum channel and a public classical one. The former is used to transmit a random sequence for making a secret key, and the latter is used to perform several procedures to make the sequences secret enough. If there exists someone eavesdropping on the legitimate users' private channel, that effects on the measurement results

at the receiver side. It can be ascertained by the users whether someone has eavesdropped or not by publicly exchanging a part of the shared
sequences and checking them whether their transmitter version and the
receiver version agree to each other or not.

In the practical QKD system, however, even if there exists no eavesdropper, some discrepancies may occur between the transmitter and the
receiver versions of shared sequences due to the imperfect system configuration and noises[4, 5, 6]. Even small amount of discrepancies may be
spread and expanded by the following privacy amplification[7, 8]. Therefore, it is very important to reconcile the two versions of the sequences
at this point. Bennett et al. proposed a reconciliation protocol and used
it in their experiment[4, 7] (call 'BBBSS protocol' hereafter). During the
protocol, the sequence must be shortened to reduce the information that
the eavesdropper have got on it by listening to the legitimate users' public
discussion. Then, the longer the reconciled sequences are, the more efficient we consider the protocol to be. The efficiency[1] depends largely on
one of parameters of the protocol. In the experiment, however, they used
the parameter as they think good empirically instead of the optimum.

In this paper, we investigate BBBSS protocol and consider to optimize
it. The protocol consists of several passes. First, we optimize the parameter for each pass. After that we consider to apply the optimum parameter
adaptively to the protocol and show its efficiency from the numerical results. Finally, we compare the BBBSS protocol using the optimum parameter with respect to the efficiency to the protocol called "Cascade" which
was proposed by Brassard and Salvail, and which is almost optimum[9].

2 PRELIMINARIES

2.1 Discrepant Sequences to be Reconciled

In the QKD systems, the transmitter first transmits a random sequence
through the private channel, a part of which will be used to make a secret
key. For this purpose, any QKD system uses quantum signals which no one
can discriminate without error, in order to prevent someone from eavesdropping on the channel without being detected. For example, in the BB84
QKD protocol[1], a transmitter and a receiver have two sources and two detectors, respectively. One source transmits a particle with one of two kinds
of rectilinear polarizations (i.e. horizontal and vertical polarizations), and
the other does a particle with one of two kinds of circular polarizations
(i.e. right circular and left circular polarizations). On the other hand, the
receiver has two detectors one of which can discriminate the two rectilinear

---

[1]The term 'efficiency' used here is different from that used in [9].

polarized particles in perfect but can not discriminate circular polarized ones at all, and the other of which does vise versa. Then, if the receiver uses the detector corresponding to the source which the transmitter has used, they can get the same information "0" or "1" without revealing the information itself. Since the transmitter and the receiver independently select one of two sources and detectors, respectively, almost half of the transmitted bits should be abandoned. Therefore, after transmitting appropriate amount of random bits, they publicly announce which source and detector were used in each bit transmission, and discard bit positions where they selected their devices incorrectly.

In an ideal QKD system, if there exists no eavesdropper on the private channel, the transmitter and the receiver versions of resultant sequences should agree to each other. In the practical systems, however, there may happen some discrepancies on these two versions of the sequences due to the imperfect system configuration and noises[2] even in the absence of the eavesdropper. It is necessary for these sequences to agree with each other for making a crypt key. Furthermore, even if the discrepancy is not many, the following privacy amplification may spread and expand the discrepancies. Therefore, the discrepancies should be reconciled at this stage of the QKD protocol.

One of the most general methods to detect and correct errors occurring during the communication is to apply error control codes before sending it. In the QKD system, however, this may not be appropriate for the following reasons:

1. Almost half of the transmitted bits are discarded.

2. The eavesdropper can also use the regularity imposed on the sequences for error correction.

Thus, in the QKD systems, the purely random sequence without any regularity should be transmitted first through the private channel, and then the discrepant sequences should be reconciled by public discussion afterward.

In this paper, we restrict ourselves to consider a private channel being binary symmetric (BSC) with error probability of ϵ, for simplicity. We will denote the length of the discrepant sequences to be reconciled, namely, the initial sequence length by N_s.

2.2 Theoretical Limit

The QKD system uses both a private quantum channel and a public classical channel. Usually, the private channel costs much higher than the

---

[2] In the experimental cryptosystem reported so far, probability of bit error is from 3% to 7%.

public channel. So, for given initial sequence length N_s, the longer the final length N_f^R of the accordant sequences after reconciliation is, the more efficient we consider the protocol R to be. Thus, the purpose of this study is to find the efficient reconciliation protocol. First of all, let us consider the theoretical limit of the protocol efficiency in order to give the optimum condition of the protocol.

Let X and Y be sequences of the transmitter and the receiver, respectively. Their initial length is N_s. Since, Y is the sequence transmitted through the BSC with error probability ε, the amount of ambiguity to the sequence of the others are

$$H(X|Y) = H(Y|X) = N_s \mathcal{H}(\varepsilon), \quad \text{[bits]} \tag{1}$$

where $\mathcal{H}(\cdot)$ is an entropy function, and $H(\cdot|\cdot)$ is the conditional entropy. Therefore it requires the legitimate users to exchange at least $N_s \mathcal{H}(\varepsilon)$[bits] of information publicly on the average to reconcile these discrepant sequences. Listening to this discussion, an eavesdropper may get at most $N_s \mathcal{H}(\varepsilon)$[bits] of information on the sequences. Then, the legitimate users must discard at least $N_s \mathcal{H}(\varepsilon)$ of bits to make the information leaked to the eavesdropper useless. As the result, we have the maximum of the average length of the resultant sequences, which have no discordant bits and almost no information about which the eavesdropper know, as follows:

$$N_f^{\max} = N_s \left(1 - \mathcal{H}(\varepsilon)\right). \tag{2}$$

Here, we define the efficiency ζ^R of a protocol R as the ratio of the average length N_f^R of the resultant sequences to the initial length N_s.

$$\zeta^R = \frac{N_f^R}{N_s}. \tag{3}$$

Then, the efficiency of the protocol R satisfies the following condition.

$$\frac{\zeta^R}{\zeta^{\max}} \leq 1. \tag{4}$$

Finally, we define the optimality of the reconciliation protocol as follows:

Definition [Optimum Reconciliation Protocol]

The reconciliation protocol is optimum if it satisfies the equality of eq.(4)[3].

---

[3]The optimum condition defined here is equivalent to that in [9].

3 RECONCILIATION

3.1 The BBBSS Protocol

The algorithm of the BBBSS reconciliation protocol proposed by Bennett et al. is given in the following[4].

[The BBBSS PROTOCOL]

1. Permute bit positions of shared sequences at random.

2. Divide the resultant sequences into some blocks of size l_B. The following steps are carried out for each block.

    (a) Compare parities of corresponding blocks .

    (b) If the parities agree to each other, accept the corresponding blocks as no discrepancy tentatively. If they disagree, remove the discrepancy by bisective search.

    (c) Discard the last bit of block or subblock whose parity has been exposed.

3. Repeat[4] the steps 1 and 2 until exposed parities of all corresponding blocks agree to one another, and it can be believed that no discrepancy remains in the sequences[5].

4. Consider the resultant sequences as secret random ones and use them as keys.

In the above algorithm, parities of blocks and subblocks are publicly shown to find and to remove discrepancies in the steps 2-(a) and (b). Since the disclosed parities may help an eavesdropper to identify the legitimate users' sequences, the last bits of blocks and subblocks of which parities are disclosed, are discarded in the step 2-(c) to make them being of no use to her.

3.2 Optimization of the Protocol

As shown previously, we have to decide the block size l_B to perform the BBBSS protocol. It seems that the efficiency of the BBBSS protocol largely depends on the block size. For example, if the block size is too small so that most of the block does not contain any discrepancies, large number of parities compared to the total number of discrepant bits have to be exposed, so that the sequences are to be shortened more than necessity.

---

[4] We call this unit consisting of steps 1 and 2 "pass". So, the protocol may repeat the pass several times.

[5] The legitimate users can know that their sequences have no more discrepancies only in a probabilistic manner.

On the other hand, if the block size is too big so that most of blocks have many discrepancies, the sequences are divided into a fewer blocks. Though fewer parities of blocks are disclosed in each pass, once a discrepancy is detected, almost $\log(l_B - 1)$ parities have to be disclosed to remove it and then the same number of bits are to be abandoned. Furthermore, some of blocks containing discrepancies would not be detected because the number of discrepancies in the block is even. Therefore, the bits of sequences would be abandoned more than necessity, too, for a big block size case. It seems that there is a suitable block size for given error rate of the sequences.

In order to make a pair of sequences to be concordant, one execution of the BBBSS protocol repeats passes several times. Since the length of the sequences and the number of discrepant bits change pass by pass, and so does the error rate of the sequences, the block size should be optimized not for throughout the protocol but for each pass.

First, we define the reconciliation rate η as the inverse of the required number of discarded bits to remove one discrepancy. Assuming the length, the block size and the error rate of the sequences of ith pass to be N^i, l_B^i and e^i, respectably, and assuming the probability that an discrepancy is detected in a block to be $P_{det.}^i$, the expected number of disclosed parities during the pass is

$$\frac{N^i}{l_B^i} + P_{det.}^i \cdot \frac{N^i}{l_B^i} \log(l_B^i - 1). \tag{5}$$

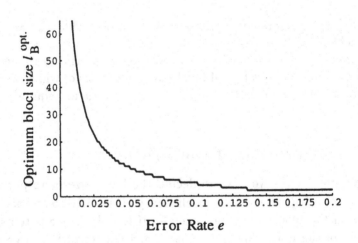

Figure 1: The optimum block size fot the BBBSS protocol.

An expected number of the removed discrepant bits in the pass is $P_{det.}^i N^i / l_B^i$. Then the reconciliation rate η^i is given as follows:

$$\eta^i = \frac{P_{det.}^i}{1 + P_{det.}^i \log(l_B^i - 1)}, \tag{6}$$

where $P_{det.}^i$ is the probability that a block has an odd number of discrepancies, represented by l_B^i and e^i as follows:

$$P_{det.}^i = \sum_{k=0}^{\lfloor (l_B^i - 1)/2 \rfloor} \binom{l_B}{2k+1} e^{i \, 2k+1} (1 - e^i)^{l_B^i - (2k+1)}. \tag{7}$$

We define optimum block size $l_B^{opt.}$ as the size which maximizes the reconciliation rate η for given error rate of the sequences. The optimum block size $l_B^{opt.}$ is drawn as the function of error rate e of sequences for a certain pass in Fig.1. It is found that $l_B^{opt.}$ is a monotonously decreasing function of e as would be expected.

In order to use the optimum block size for each pass, the error rate of the sequences at the pass have to be estimated. That can be performed by using the results of removed discrepancies for previous passes. As will be shown later, we use not the results of all previous passes but that of just the previous pass.

3.3 Numerical Results

The BBBSS reconciliation protocol is investigated by a computer simulation and obtain the efficiency ζ^{BBBSS} for the sequences of several initial length N_s, and the channel error probability ϵ from 0.005 to 0.15. In this simulation, we use the optimum block size $l_B^{opt.}$ corresponding to the error rate of the sequence which is estimated from the result of just the previous pass. As the error rate of the sequences decreases, the optimum block size increases. Here, we set the maximum block size to a half of the sequence length. That is, we use the block size $\tilde{l}_B^i$ in our simulation defined as follows:

$$\tilde{l}_B^i = \min\{l_B^{opt.}(e^i), \; N^i/2\}. \tag{8}$$

In order to make the probability to fail in the reconciliation to be small, we finish the protocol after repeating passes until no discrepant parities occur during the eleven successive passes, so that the failure probability is almost 2^{-11}. For random permutation of bit positions, we use interleavers. To cope with various block size, we interleave the sequences three times with the depth of 10, 30 and 175 in each pass. The numerical results are average of ten simulation results with different random numbers.

First, we show the efficiency ζ^{BBBSS} of the BBBSS protocol for the initial sequence length of 10000 in Fig.2. When the error probability ϵ of the private channel is 0.01, the protocol generates the accordant sequences of the length of 90% of the initial one. The length of the resultant sequences become a half of the initial length at ϵ of 0.085.

Fig.3 shows the ratio of the efficiency of the BBBSS protocol to that of the theoretical limit. It is seen that by use of the proposed optimization the BBBSS protocol can generate the accordant sequences of the length more than 90% of the theoretical limit if the channel error probability ϵ is less than 0.06.

In the next, let us consider the error rate estimation method. As mentioned above, we estimate the error rate of the sequence in each pass by using the detected error number, block size and the sequence length of just the previous pass. However, one can think that he can estimate the error rate more precisely by using those not of just one previous pass but of all previous passes. To show whether it is the case or not, we compare the efficiency of the BBBSS protocol using the error rate estimated the above method to that using that calculated with actually existing errors (cunning method). Fig.4 shows the comparison for the initial sequence length of 10000. The solid line is for the estimation and the dashed line is for the cunning method. There is no significant difference between them. And it can be said that the estimation used here is sufficient for this purpose.

Finally, we show the dependence of the initial sequence length N_s on the protocol efficiency ζ^{BBBSS}. When the number of samples is small, the statistical error becomes large. Then, in order to make error rate estimation to be precise enough, the number of blocks contained in the sequences must be larger than a certain amount. That is, there is a lower limit of the initial sequence length for the protocol to be efficient. Fig. 5 shows the dependence of the initial sequence length on the efficiency of the BBBSS protocol for the channel error probability ϵ of 0.01, 0.05, 0.1 and 0.15. It is found from these curbs that the efficiency increases as the initial length becomes long, and that the efficiency is almost constant for l_B over 10000. As a result, we can say that for efficient reconciliation by the BBBSS protocol, the initial length of the sequences should be longer than 10000.

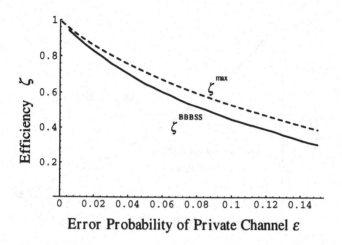

Figure 2: The efficiency of the BBBSS protocol. ($N_s = 10000$)

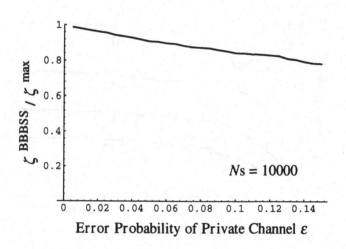

Figure 3: The ratio of the efficiency of the BBBSS protocol to the theoretical limit.($N_s = 10000$.)

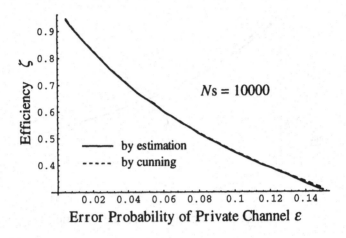

Figure 4: On the estimation of error rate of the sequence. ($N_s = 10000$.)

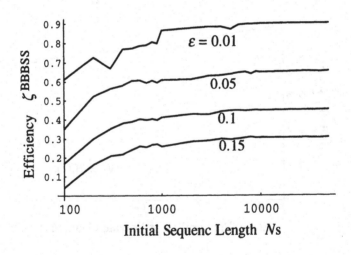

Figure 5: Dependence of the initial sequence length on the efficiency of the BBBSS protocol. ε is an error probability of a private channel.

Table 1: Comparison of the BBBSS protocol to another protocol '*Cascade*'.

ϵ	ζ^{BBBSS}	$\zeta^{Cascade}$	$\dfrac{\zeta^{BBBSS}}{\zeta^{Cascade}}$ [%]
0.01	0.8999	0.9114	98.7
0.05	0.6490	0.6714	96.7
0.10	0.4477	0.4557	98.2
0.15	0.3058	0.2400	127.4

3.4 Comparison to Another Protocol

Brassard and Salvail proposed a practical and almost optimum reconciliation protocol called "Cascade"[9]. They said that the protocol is close to the theoretical bound for ϵ up to 0.15. In this section, we compare the BBBSS protocol using the proposed optimization to the protocol "Cascade" without explaining it in detail.

Tab.1 shows the efficiency ζ^{BBBSS} and $\zeta^{Cascade}$ of the two protocol for ϵ of 0.01, 0.05, 0.1 and 0.15. The results[6] are for the initial sequence length of 10000. From Tab.1 it is found that the BBBSS protocol is comparable to the protocol "Cascade", and then it seems that the BBBSS protocol using the proposed optimization is almost optimum.

4 CONCLUSIONS

In this report, we investigated the protocol, especially the BBBSS protocol, to reconcile the discrepant sequences transmitted through the private channel. We proposed the optimization method for the BBBSS protocol and showed that the protocol performs close to the theoretical limit with the proposed optimization. Finally, we compared the BBBSS protocol by using the optimization to another reconciliation protocol called "Cascade" which seems to be the best practical protocol so far. As the result, the BBBSS protocol using the optimization is comparable to the "Cascade'.

ACKNOWLEDGEMENT

The authors would like to acknowledge Drs. M. Ban (Advanced Research Laboratory of Hitachi) and M. Sasaki (Communication Research Laboratory, Ministry of Posts and Telecommunications) for their valuable comments and stimulating discussion. They also wish to thank Dr. R. Peralta (University of Wisconsin), Dr. K. Matsuura (University of Tokyo) and the reviewers of this paper for their helpful comments.

---

[6] We cited these data of the Cascade from [9].

References

[1] C. II. Bennett and G. Brassard, in *Proc. of the IEEE Int. Conf. on Computers, Systems, and Signal Processing, Bangalore, India* (IEEE, New York, 1984), p.175.

[2] A. K. Ekert, *Phys. Rev. Lett.*, vol. 67, p.661, 1991.

[3] C. H. Bennett, *Phys. Rev. Lett.* vol.68, p.3121, 1992.

[4] C. H. Bennett, F. Bessette, G. Brassard, L. Salvail and J. Smolin, *J. Cryptol.* vol.5, p.3, 1992.

[5] P. D. Townsend, *Elec. Lett.* vol.30, p.809, 1994.

[6] A. Muller, II. Zbinden and N. Gisin, *Europhys. Lett.* vol.33, p.335, 1996.

[7] C. II. Bennett, F. Bessette, G. Brassard and J.-M. Robert, *SIAM J. COMPUT.*, vol. 17, p.210, 1988.

[8] C. II. Bennett , G. Brassard, C. Crépeau and U. M. Maurer, *IEEE Trans. Inform. Thoery* , vol. 41, p.1915, 1995.

[9] G. Brassard and L. Salvail, *Advances in Cryptology-Proc. Eurocrypt '93*, p.410, 1994.

Author Index

Lecture Notes in Computer Science

For information about Vols. 1–1315

please contact your bookseller or Springer-Verlag

Vol. 1316: M. Li, A. Maruoka (Eds.), Algorithmic Learning Theory. Proceedings, 1997. XI, 461 pages. 1997. (Subseries LNAI).

Vol. 1317: M. Leman (Ed.), Music, Gestalt, and Computing. IX, 524 pages. 1997. (Subseries LNAI).

Vol. 1318: R. Hirschfeld (Ed.), Financial Cryptography. Proceedings, 1997. XI, 409 pages. 1997.

Vol. 1319: E. Plaza, R. Benjamins (Eds.), Knowledge Acquisition, Modeling and Management. Proceedings, 1997. XI, 389 pages. 1997. (Subseries LNAI).

Vol. 1320: M. Mavronicolas, P. Tsigas (Eds.), Distributed Algorithms. Proceedings, 1997. X, 333 pages. 1997.

Vol. 1321: M. Lenzerini (Ed.), AI*IA 97: Advances in Artificial Intelligence. Proceedings, 1997. XII, 459 pages. 1997. (Subseries LNAI).

Vol. 1322: H. Hußmann, Formal Foundations for Software Engineering Methods. X, 286 pages. 1997.

Vol. 1323: E. Costa, A. Cardoso (Eds.), Progress in Artificial Intelligence. Proceedings, 1997. XIV, 393 pages. 1997. (Subseries LNAI).

Vol. 1324: C. Peters, C. Thanos (Eds.), Research and Advanced Technology for Digital Libraries. Proceedings, 1997. X, 423 pages. 1997.

Vol. 1325: Z.W. Raś, A. Skowron (Eds.), Foundations of Intelligent Systems. Proceedings, 1997. XI, 630 pages. 1997. (Subseries LNAI).

Vol. 1326: C. Nicholas, J. Mayfield (Eds.), Intelligent Hypertext. XIV, 182 pages. 1997.

Vol. 1327: W. Gerstner, A. Germond, M. Hasler, J.-D. Nicoud (Eds.), Artificial Neural Networks – ICANN '97. Proceedings, 1997. XIX, 1274 pages. 1997.

Vol. 1328: C. Retoré (Ed.), Logical Aspects of Computational Linguistics. Proceedings, 1996. VIII, 435 pages. 1997. (Subseries LNAI).

Vol. 1329: S.C. Hirtle, A.U. Frank (Eds.), Spatial Information Theory. Proceedings, 1997. XIV, 511 pages. 1997.

Vol. 1330: G. Smolka (Ed.), Principles and Practice of Constraint Programming – CP 97. Proceedings, 1997. XII, 563 pages. 1997.

Vol. 1331: D. W. Embley, R. C. Goldstein (Eds.), Conceptual Modeling – ER '97. Proceedings, 1997. XV, 479 pages. 1997.

Vol. 1332: M. Bubak, J. Dongarra, J. Waśniewski (Eds.), Recent Advances in Parallel Virtual Machine and Message Passing Interface. Proceedings, 1997. XV, 518 pages. 1997.

Vol. 1333: F. Pichler. R.Moreno-Díaz (Eds.), Computer Aided Systems Theory – EUROCAST'97. Proceedings, 1997. XII, 626 pages. 1997.

Vol. 1334: Y. Han, T. Okamoto, S. Qing (Eds.), Information and Communications Security. Proceedings, 1997. X, 484 pages. 1997.

Vol. 1335: R.H. Möhring (Ed.), Graph-Theoretic Concepts in Computer Science. Proceedings, 1997. X, 376 pages. 1997.

Vol. 1336: C. Polychronopoulos, K. Joe, K. Araki, M. Amamiya (Eds.), High Performance Computing. Proceedings, 1997. XII, 416 pages. 1997.

Vol. 1337: C. Freksa, M. Jantzen, R. Valk (Eds.), Foundations of Computer Science. XII, 515 pages. 1997.

Vol. 1338: F. Plášil, K.G. Jeffery (Eds.), SOFSEM'97: Theory and Practice of Informatics. Proceedings, 1997. XIV, 571 pages. 1997.

Vol. 1339: N.A. Murshed, F. Bortolozzi (Eds.), Advances in Document Image Analysis. Proceedings, 1997. IX, 345 pages. 1997.

Vol. 1340: M. van Kreveld, J. Nievergelt, T. Roos, P. Widmayer (Eds.), Algorithmic Foundations of Geographic Information Systems. XIV, 287 pages. 1997.

Vol. 1341: F. Bry, R. Ramakrishnan, K. Ramamohanarao (Eds.), Deductive and Object-Oriented Databases. Proceedings, 1997. XIV, 430 pages. 1997.

Vol. 1342: A. Sattar (Ed.), Advanced Topics in Artificial Intelligence. Proceedings, 1997. XVII, 516 pages. 1997. (Subseries LNAI).

Vol. 1343: Y. Ishikawa, R.R. Oldehoeft, J.V.W. Reynders, M. Tholburn (Eds.), Scientific Computing in Object-Oriented Parallel Environments. Proceedings, 1997. XI, 295 pages. 1997.

Vol. 1344: C. Ausnit-Hood, K.A. Johnson, R.G. Pettit, IV, S.B. Opdahl (Eds.), Ada 95 – Quality and Style. XV, 292 pages. 1997.

Vol. 1345: R.K. Shyamasundar, K. Ueda (Eds.), Advances in Computing Science - ASIAN'97. Proceedings, 1997. XIII, 387 pages. 1997.

Vol. 1346: S. Ramesh, G. Sivakumar (Eds.), Foundations of Software Technology and Theoretical Computer Science. Proceedings, 1997. XI, 343 pages. 1997.

Vol. 1347: E. Ahronovitz, C. Fiorio (Eds.), Discrete Geometry for Computer Imagery. Proceedings, 1997. X, 255 pages. 1997.

Vol. 1348: S. Steel, R. Alami (Eds.), Recent Advances in AI Planning. Proceedings, 1997. IX, 454 pages. 1997. (Subseries LNAI).

Vol. 1349: M. Johnson (Ed.), Algebraic Methodology and Software Technology. Proceedings, 1997. X, 594 pages. 1997.

Vol. 1350: H.W. Leong, H. Imai, S. Jain (Eds.), Algorithms and Computation. Proceedings, 1997. XV, 426 pages. 1997.